BERNARD SHAW (1856-1950)

❧ Although born in Dublin of a middle-class, Protestant family, Shaw took no part in the Irish Literary Revival but went to London and is consequently identified with British social and literary movements. His activities as a London critic of music and drama produced his best-known non-dramatic works, *The Quintessence of Ibsenism* (1891) and *The Perfect Wagnerite* (1898). His interest in Henry George, Karl Marx, and other social theorists led to his affiliation with the Fabian Socialists, for whom he wrote numerous tracts. He was also much influenced by Butler and Ibsen.

❧ Ingenious and witty, Shaw's comedies present a fearless intellectual criticism of his age. Aware of the discrepancy between the accepted conventions of life and what really lies underneath, Shaw rebelled against muddled thinking and smug prudishness. He hoped to puncture hollow pretentions and restore intellectual courage.

PAUL KOZELKA, Ph.D., author of the Introductions to each play, is Professor of Theatre, Teachers College, Columbia University. Author of a *Glossary to the Plays of Bernard Shaw,* he is a member of the Executive Committee of the American National Theatre and Academy (ANTA), and has been responsible for nearly sixty dramatic productions.

This edition includes Shaw's original Prefaces and Notes.

FOUR PLAYS
BY
Bernard
Shaw

FOREWORD AND INTRODUCTIONS
BY PAUL KOZELKA

PUBLISHED BY POCKET BOOKS NEW YORK

POCKET BOOKS, a Simon & Schuster division of
GULF & WESTERN CORPORATION
1230 Avenue of the Americas, New York, N.Y. 10020

ISBN: 0-671-49109-1

First Pocket Books printing December, 1965

10   9   8   7   6

Table of Contents

FOUR PLAYS
BY
Bernard
Shaw

Foreword

THE DEVIL'S DISCIPLE, CANDIDA, CAESAR AND CLEOPATRA AND MAN AND SUPERMAN

The Devil's Disciple, Candida, Caesar and Cleopatra and *Man and Superman* constitute an excellent introduction to one of the greatest minds of this century. Shaw did for the English stage what Ibsen did for the Continental theatre and O'Neill for the American. These men of dramatic genius opened new doors, explored new territories and forced people to reconsider conventional habits of thought.

Shaw wrote over fifty plays and almost every one of them is a dramatized sermon or exhortation on the desperate need to reform society before it is too late. All his life he fought against poverty, exploitation of people and land, vivisection, vaccination, censorship, out-moded divorce laws, monogamy, blinding patriotism, pessimism and democracy for its own sake.

If he opposed so many institutions and conventions, what did he advocate? He believed in the sanctity of the human will (primarily his own), and a special kind of Christian Socialism; he promoted a new phonetic alphabet, supported plans for a national theatre. He also admired the ruthlessness of tycoons and dictators. He knew the persuasive power of wit in making people accept his ideas and turned the theatre into an entertaining and intellectual experience. At the time of his death in 1950 at the age of ninety-four, Shaw had become a world figure and he was universally mourned, even by those who thought him an irresponsible gadfly and clown; the theatre districts of New York and London dimmed their lights in tribute to him.

Bernard Shaw spent the first twenty years of his life in Dublin where he was born in 1856. From his father, an amiable, unsuccessful business man and secret drinker, Shaw inherited his wit, along with a hatred of smoking and drinking. From his mother, a loveless woman who neglected her children, he inherited his love for music and an independent spirit. He attended various schools but concluded his formal education at sixteen. His natural curiosity and intellectual zest set him on the path to discover things for himself, a path he never left for the rest of his life.

When he was twenty, Shaw moved to London where he worked for the Edison Telephone Company. He persuaded landlords to allow the company to install telephone poles on their property. He spent his free time in the British Museum educating himself on Shakespeare and other great writers, going to concerts and writing novels that no one would publish. When he was twenty-six, he heard Henry George, the American, lecture on his single-tax plan by which a government would raise all the money it needed with a single tax on land. The lecture affected Shaw so deeply that he gave up everything to study Marxism. With Beatrice and Sydney Webb, Shaw founded the Fabian Society in 1884. The society, from which the present Labor Party developed, promoted social reform through the parliamentary process. Shaw knew the results of poverty from bitter experience and threw himself behind the Fabian cause with all his energy. He lectured, debated and wrote essays and pamphlets.

In addition to his efforts for socialist reform, Shaw became in turn an art critic, a music critic and a drama critic. He attacked romanticism in the arts and fought for Ibsen, Wagner, Degas and Manet when they were being introduced to a scornful public. As a drama critic, Shaw demanded a new drama, a drama of reality, of ideas, of purpose, the kind of play, in fact, which he began to write in 1892 but which was not successfully received until 1898, when his ninth play, *Caesar and Cleopatra*, was produced.

Shaw turned from his work as critic and pamphleteer to the theatre so that he could reach a larger and more powerful audience. Through the magic of the theatre he could present an absorbing plot, colorful characters, witty dialogue, tense climaxes and when the emotions of the spectators were aroused and the barriers down, he could stun them with an idea or action they would not normally accept.

Shaw wrote fifty-four plays from 1892 until 1950 and all but a few are teaching plays, full of revolutionary ideas and

striking theatrical effects. Shaw often published his plays before the first performance. For each play he wrote a Preface,
sometimes related to the play, sometimes not. The Prefaces
provide further insight into his mind and give him a chance to
develop his ideas with brilliant and persuasive clarity. Because
he knew the theatre so well as audience, critic, actor and
director, Shaw's stage directions and remarks in parentheses
are unusually vivid. They make play reading almost as effective
as play going.

Spiritually and morally he had the strength of a giant—
hence his iron self-discipline, his passion for justice and his
appetite for hard work. Outwardly he was tall, brash and prepossessing, but inwardly he was shy, sensitive and withdrawn
—hence his admiration for prize-fighters and dictators like
Hitler, Mussolini and Stalin. When he was forty-two, he married Charlotte Payne-Townshend, a wealthy woman of forty-
one. Theirs was a purely platonic, affectionate marriage in
spite of the commotion Shaw raised with his apparently passionate letters to Ellen Terry and Mrs. Patrick Campbell.

In 1905 he bought a home in Ayot St. Lawrence, a hamlet
twenty-five miles north of London, for a weekend retreat but
maintained a London apartment which included an office
where he could write out his plays and essays in Pitman shorthand. Because Mrs. Shaw liked to travel, the Shaws took many
trips, sometimes around the world, even though Shaw often
became seasick.

He made only one trip to the United States, stopping in
California as a guest of William Randolph Hearst and in New
York to give a lecture at the Metropolitan Opera House. Although he did not know this country at first hand, he knew
a great deal about our institutions, policies and national characteristics. Whenever possible, he made fun of our bungling
democracy, our materialistic goals and our noisy behavior.
Nevertheless, he was enthusiastic about American vigor, Pro-
hibition and certain experiments in communal living. Shaw's
wide interests are revealed by the Americans he admired:
Gene Tunney, Helen Wills, Upton Sinclair, Henry Wallace,
Pola Negri, Charlie Chaplin and Mark Twain.

Shaw knew other countries and national traits besides
America and Americans, of course. A passionate reader, observer and thinker, Shaw—with his knowledge of science, religion, education, government, morals, social welfare, history,

music, art and politics—commanded an international audience.
A tireless teacher and inveterate preacher, Shaw was the
eternal scold, but a delightful scold, and a wonderfully witty
one.

The Devil's Disciple, Candida, Caesar and Cleopatra and
Man and Superman provide superlative examples of Shaw's
timelessness, his universal appeal, and his disarming ability
to combine serious ideas with sparkling dialogue. The reader
will enjoy comparing and contrasting the ideological, moral
and spiritual conflicts developed in these four plays. In *The
Devil's Disciple* and *Candida* the arguments are presented by
three leading characters but in *Caesar and Cleopatra* and *Man
and Superman*, the debate is divided between only two chief
characters. Whether the argument is carried by two, three, six
or a dozen distinctive characters, we may be sure that Shaw,
the reformer, speaks loudly and clearly through them all.

The bibliography, which follows, includes some of the best
writing on Shaw. The reader is encouraged to start with the
plays of Shaw, then move to the Prefaces and then to the books
about Shaw. Each step will be a stimulating, enriching experience.

> —Paul Kozelka
> Teachers College, Columbia University
> New York, N.Y.
> 1965

Suggested Readings

BENTLEY, ERIC. *Bernard Shaw*. New York, 1957.

An excellent, compact, closely reasoned and highly literate analysis of Shaw's thinking on politics, economics, religion and the theatre.

CHESTERTON, G. K. *George Bernard Shaw*. London, 1909.

Still one of the best books on Shaw, this early volume is an interesting analysis from the Roman Catholic point of view.

ERVINE, ST. JOHN. *Bernard Shaw: His Life, Work and Friends*. New York, 1956.

A highly detailed history of Shaw's life with accounts of his ancestors, early life and his full career. Ervine frequently amplifies Shaw's ideas with his own thoughts.

HENDERSON, ARCHIBALD. *George Bernard Shaw: Man of the Century*. New York, 1956.

Detailed, chronological, fully documented history of Shaw, his experiences, ideas and accomplishments. Professor Henderson, recently retired from the faculty of the University of North Carolina, has been Shaw's official biographer since the early years of this century.

KOZELKA, PAUL. *A Glossary to the Plays of Bernard Shaw*. New York, 1959.

Definitions and pronunciations of unusual terms and proper names found in Shaw's plays.

KRONENBERGER, LOUIS. *George Bernard Shaw: A Critical Survey*. Cleveland and New York, 1953.

Twenty-one essays written between 1901 and 1951 by great critics of England and America covering Shaw's main ideas. Although varying in quality and length, the essays are significant clues to Shaw's reputation.

MANDER, RAYMOND AND MITCHENSON, JOE. *The Theatrical Companion to Shaw: A Pictorial Record of the First Performances of the Plays of George Bernard Shaw*. London, 1954.

A valuable and interesting collection of statistics, articles and pictures.

PATCH, BLANCHE. *Thirty Years with G. B. S.* New York, 1951.

Miss Patch served as Shaw's secretary from 1920 to 1950. Her anecdotes about Shaw's personal life, his friends and his habits make fascinating reading.

Pearson, Hesketh. *G. B. S.: A Full-Length Portrait*. New York, 1942.

A chatty and informative account with many direct quotations from conversations and letters of Shaw.

SHENFIELD, MARGARET. *Bernard Shaw: A Pictorial Biography*. New York, 1962.

With a photograph on almost every page, this book captures the atmosphere of the eras in Shaw's life, and the writing, which is concise and picturesque, presents facts and opinions in an arresting manner.

The Devil's Disciple

A Melodrama

The Devil's Disciple

INTRODUCTORY NOTE TO *THE DEVIL'S DISCIPLE*

The Devil's Disciple, written in 1896-97, is an exciting play to read. The action of the play occurs in the town of Webster-bridge, New Hampshire, in 1777, during The American Revolution. It is like modern horse operas and suspense shows written for television: Each act ends in a "cliff-hanging" episode. The characters include a poor little orphan girl; a fiercely puritanical mother; a sentimental heroine; several clumsy soldiers; a handsome, noble hero and someone who looks and acts suspiciously like a villain. But *The Devil's Disciple* is a melodrama with a difference. The hero acts out of unselfish idealism and not for love of a beautiful blonde; the mother, who should be sweet and loving, is a hypocritical tyrant who turns her warped sense of morality into awful vindictiveness; the minister, who should protect his wife, changes coats with the hero both literally and symbolically and discovers his true vocation in action rather than preaching.

The court-martial scene is probably the funniest scene of its kind in dramatic literature. It revolves around General Burgoyne whose witty sarcasm is adapted from authentic military and political records of the colonial period. The only liberty that Shaw took was to make him aware, a little before it happened in history, that General Howe would not meet him at Albany with reinforcements, a failure that forced Burgoyne to surrender at Saratoga.

Visually, *The Devil's Disciple* progresses in a highly theatrical way from the gloominess of Act I, through the warm comfort of Act II, to the pseudo-romantic prison scene, the colorful court-martial scene and the noisy, exciting execution scene, all in Act III. Characterizations, too, develop satisfyingly, if good actors play the roles of Dick Dudgeon, who takes the part of the devil's advocate to rebel against senseless customs; Judith, who longs for a Lochinvar; Reverend Anderson, who finally discovers what a life of service means and

3

General Burgoyne, who remains a gentleman even though he despises the futility and waste of warfare. After all, eleven major wars were fought during Shaw's lifetime. Shaw never lost an opportunity to attack the needless destruction of war and to make fun of military pomp and circumstance.

ACT I

At the most wretched hour between a black night and a wintry morning in the year 1777, Mrs. Dudgeon, of New Hampshire, is sitting up in the kitchen and general dwelling room of her farm house on the outskirts of the town of Websterbridge. She is not a prepossessing woman. No woman looks her best after sitting up all night; and Mrs. Dudgeon's face, even at its best, is grimly trenched by the channels into which the barren forms and observances of a dead Puritanism can pen a bitter temper and a fierce pride. She is an elderly matron who has worked hard and got nothing by it except dominion and detestation in her sordid home, and an unquestioned reputation for piety and respectability among her neighbors, to whom drink and debauchery are still so much more tempting than religion and rectitude, that they conceive goodness simply as self-denial. This conception is easily extended to others-denial, and finally generalized as covering anything disagreeable. So Mrs. Dudgeon, being exceedingly disagreeable, is held to be exceedingly good. Short of flat felony, she enjoys complete license except for amiable weaknesses of any sort, and is consequently, without knowing it, the most licentious woman in the parish on the strength of never having broken the seventh commandment or missed a Sunday at the Presbyterian church.

The year 1777 is the one in which the passions roused by the breaking-off of the American colonies from England, more by their own weight than their own will, boiled up to shooting point, the shooting being idealized to the English mind as suppression of rebellion and maintenance of British dominion, and to the American as defence of liberty, resistance to tyranny, and self-sacrifice on the altar of the Rights of Man. Into the merits of these idealizations it is not here necessary to inquire: suffice it to say, without prejudice, that they have convinced both Americans and English that the most high minded course for them to pursue is to kill as many of one another as possible,

5

and that military operations to that end are in full swing, morally supported by confident requests from the clergy of both sides for the blessing of God on their arms.

Under such circumstances many other women besides this disagreeable Mrs. Dudgeon find themselves sitting up all night waiting for news. Like her, too, they fall asleep towards morning at the risk of nodding themselves into the kitchen fire. Mrs. Dudgeon sleeps with a shawl over her head, and her feet on a broad fender of iron laths, the step of the domestic altar of the fireplace, with its huge hobs and boiler, and its hinged arm above the smoky mantel-shelf for roasting. The plain kitchen table is opposite the fire, at her elbow, with a candle on it in a tin sconce. Her chair, like all the others in the room, is uncushioned and unpainted; but as it has a round railed back and a seat conventionally molded to the sitter's curves, it is comparatively a chair of state. The room has three doors, one on the same side as the fireplace, near the corner, leading to the best bedroom; one, at the opposite end of the opposite wall, leading to the scullery and washhouse; and the housedoor, with its latch, heavy lock, and clumsy wooden bar, in the front wall, between the window in its middle and the corner next the bedroom door. Between the door and the window a rack of pegs suggests to the deductive observer that the men of the house are all away, as there are no hats or coats on them. On the other side of the window the clock hangs on a nail, with its white wooden dial, black iron weights, and brass pendulum. Between the clock and the corner, a big cupboard, locked, stands on a dwarf dresser full of common crockery.

On the side opposite the fireplace, between the door and the corner, a shamelessly ugly black horsehair sofa stands against the wall. An inspection of its stridulous surface shews that Mrs. Dudgeon is not alone. A girl of sixteen or seventeen has fallen asleep on it. She is a wild, timid looking creature with black hair and tanned skin. Her frock, a scanty garment, is rent, weatherstained, berrystained, and by no means scrupulously clean. It hangs on her with a freedom which, taken with her brown legs and bare feet, suggests no great stock of underclothing.

Suddenly there comes a tapping at the door, not loud enough to wake the sleepers. Then knocking, which disturbs Mrs. Dudgeon a little. Finally the latch is tried, whereupon she springs up at once.

MRS. DUDGEON (*threateningly*). Well, why don't you open the door? (*She sees that the girl is asleep, and immediately raises a clamor of heartfelt vexation.*) Well, dear, dear me! Now this is—(*shaking her*) wake up, wake up: do you hear?

THE GIRL (*sitting up*). What is it?

MRS. DUDGEON. Wake up; and be ashamed of yourself, you unfeeling sinful girl, falling asleep like that, and your father hardly cold in his grave.

THE GIRL (*half asleep still*). I didn't mean to. I dropped off——

MRS. DUDGEON (*cutting her short*). Oh yes, you've plenty of excuses, I daresay. Dropped off! (*Fiercely, as the knocking recommences.*) Why don't you get up and let your uncle in? after me waiting up all night for him! (*She pushes her rudely off the sofa.*) There: I'll open the door: much good you are to wait up. Go and mend that fire a bit.

The girl, cowed and wretched, goes to the fire and puts a log on. Mrs. Dudgeon unbars the door and opens it, letting into the stuffy kitchen a little of the freshness and a great deal of the chill of the dawn, also her second son Christy, a fattish, stupid, fairhaired, roundfaced man of about twenty-two, muffled in a plaid shawl and grey overcoat. He hurries, shivering, to the fire, leaving Mrs. Dudgeon to shut the door.

CHRISTY (*at the fire*). F—f—f! but it is cold. (*Seeing the girl, and staring lumpishly at her.*) Why, who are you?

THE GIRL (*shyly*). Essie.

MRS. DUDGEON. Oh, you may well ask. (*To Essie.*) Go to your room, child, and lie down, since you haven't feeling enough to keep you awake. Your history isn't fit for your own ears to hear.

ESSIE. I——

MRS. DUDGEON (*peremptorily*). Don't answer me, Miss; but shew your obedience by doing what I tell you. (*Essie, almost in tears, crosses the room to the door near the sofa.*) And don't forget your prayers. (*Essie goes out.*) She'd have gone to bed last night just as if nothing had happened if I'd let her.

CHRISTY (*phlegmatically*). Well, she can't be expected to feel Uncle Peter's death like one of the family.

MRS. DUDGEON. What are you talking about, child? Isn't she his daughter—the punishment of his wickedness and shame? (*She assaults her chair by sitting down.*)

CHRISTY (*staring*). Uncle Peter's daughter!

MRS. DUDGEON. Why else should she be here? D'ye think I've not had enough trouble and care put upon me bringing up my own girls, let alone you and your good-for-nothing brother, without having your uncle's bastards——

CHRISTY (*interrupting her with an apprehensive glance at the door by which Essie went out*). Sh! She may hear you.

MRS. DUDGEON (*raising her voice*). Let her hear me. People who fear God don't fear to give the devil's work its right name. (*Christy, soullessly indifferent to the strife of Good and Evil, stares at the fire, warming himself.*) Well, how long are you going to stare there like a stuck pig? What news have you for me?

CHRISTY (*taking off his hat and shawl and going to the rack to hang them up*). The minister is to break the news to you. He'll be here presently.

MRS. DUDGEON. Break what news?

CHRISTY (*standing on tiptoe, from boyish habit, to hang his hat up, though he is quite tall enough to reach the peg, and speaking with callous placidity, considering the nature of the announcement*). Father's dead too.

MRS. DUDGEON (*stupent*). Your father!

CHRISTY (*sulkily, coming back to the fire and warming himself again, attending much more to the fire than to his mother*). Well, it's not my fault. When we got to Nevinstown we found him ill in bed. He didn't know us at first. The minister sat up with him and sent me away. He died in the night.

MRS. DUDGEON (*bursting into dry angry tears*). Well, I do think this is hard on me—very hard on me. His brother, that was a disgrace to us all his life, gets hanged on the public gallows as a rebel; and your father, instead of staying at home where his duty was, with his own family, goes after him and dies, leaving everything on my shoulders. After sending this girl to me to take care of, too! (*She plucks her shawl vexedly over her ears.*) It's sinful, so it is; downright sinful.

CHRISTY (*with a slow, bovine cheerfulness, after a pause*). I think it's going to be a fine morning, after all.

MRS. DUDGEON (*railing at him*). A fine morning! And your father newly dead! Where's your feelings, child?

CHRISTY (*obstinately*). Well, I didn't mean any harm. I suppose a man may make a remark about the weather even if his father's dead.

MRS. DUDGEON (*bitterly*). A nice comfort my children are to me! One son a fool, and the other a lost sinner that's left his home to live with smugglers and gypsies and villains, the scum of the earth!

Someone knocks.

CHRISTY (*without moving*). That's the minister.

MRS. DUDGEON (*sharply*). Well, aren't you going to let Mr. Anderson in?

Christy goes sheepishly to the door. Mrs. Dudgeon buries her face in her hands, as it is her duty as a widow to be over-come with grief. Christy opens the door, and admits the minister, Anthony Anderson, a shrewd, genial, ready Presbyterian divine of about 50, with something of the authority of his pro-fession in his bearing. But it is an altogether secular authority, sweetened by a conciliatory, sensible manner not at all sug-gestive of a quite thoroughgoing other-worldliness. He is a strong, healthy man, too, with a thick, sanguine neck; and his keen, cheerful mouth cuts into somewhat fleshy corners. No doubt an excellent parson, but still a man capable of making the most of this world, and perhaps a little apologetically conscious of getting on better with it than a sound Presby-terian ought.

ANDERSON (*to Christy, at the door, looking at Mrs. Dudgeon whilst he takes off his cloak*). Have you told her?

CHRISTY. She made me. (*He shuts the door; yawns; and loafs across to the sofa, where he sits down and presently drops off to sleep.*)

Anderson looks compassionately at Mrs. Dudgeon. Then he hangs his cloak and hat on the rack. Mrs. Dudgeon dries her eyes and looks up at him.

ANDERSON. Sister: the Lord has laid his hand very heavily upon you.

MRS. DUDGEON (*with intensely recalcitrant resignation*). It's His will, I suppose; and I must bow to it. But I do think it hard. What call had Timothy to go to Springtown, and remind everybody that he belonged to a man that was being hanged?—and (*spitefully*) that deserved it, if ever a man did.

ANDERSON (*gently*). They were brothers, Mrs. Dudgeon.

MRS. DUDGEON. Timothy never acknowledged him as his brother after we were married: he had too much respect for me to insult me with such a brother. Would such a selfish

wretch as Peter have come thirty miles to see Timothy hanged,
do you think? Not thirty yards, not he. However, I must bear
my cross as best I may: least said is soonest mended.

ANDERSON (*very grave, coming down to the fire to stand
with his back to it*). Your eldest son was present at the execution, Mrs. Dudgeon.

MRS. DUDGEON (*disagreeably surprised*). Richard?

ANDERSON (*nodding*). Yes.

MRS. DUDGEON (*vindictively*). Let it be a warning to him.
He may end that way himself, the wicked, dissolute, godless—
(*She suddenly stops; her voice fails; and she asks, with evident
dread.*) Did Timothy see him?

ANDERSON. Yes.

MRS. DUDGEON (*holding her breath*). Well?

ANDERSON. He only saw him in the crowd: they did not
speak. (*Mrs. Dudgeon, greatly relieved, exhales the pent up
breath and sits at her ease again.*) Your husband was greatly
touched and impressed by his brother's awful death. (*Mrs.
Dudgeon sneers. Anderson breaks off to demand with some
indignation.*) Well, wasn't it only natural, Mrs. Dudgeon? He
softened towards his prodigal son in that moment. He sent
for him to come to see him.

MRS. DUDGEON (*her alarm renewed*). Sent for Richard!

ANDERSON. Yes; but Richard would not come. He sent his
father a message; but I'm sorry to say it was a wicked message—an awful message.

MRS. DUDGEON. What was it?

ANDERSON. That he would stand by his wicked uncle, and
stand against his good parents, in this world and the next.

MRS. DUDGEON (*implacably*). He will be punished for it.
He will be punished for it—in both worlds.

ANDERSON. That is not in our hands, Mrs. Dudgeon.

MRS. DUDGEON. Did I say it was, Mr. Anderson? We are
told that the wicked shall be punished. Why should we do our
duty and keep God's law if there is to be no difference made
between us and those who follow their own likings and dis-
likings, and make a jest of us and of their Maker's word?

ANDERSON. Well, Richard's earthly father has been merciful to him; and his heavenly judge is the father of us all.

MRS. DUDGEON (*forgetting herself*). Richard's earthly father
was a softheaded——

ANDERSON (*shocked*). Oh!

MRS. DUDGEON (*with a touch of shame*). Well, I am Richard's mother. If I am against him who has any right to be for him? (*Trying to conciliate him.*) Won't you sit down, Mr. Anderson? I should have asked you before; but I'm so troubled.

ANDERSON. Thank you. (*He takes a chair from beside the fireplace, and turns it so that he can sit comfortably at the fire. When he is seated he adds, in the tone of a man who knows that he is opening a difficult subject.*) Has Christy told you about the new will?

MRS. DUDGEON (*all her fears returning*). The new will! Did Timothy—? (*She breaks off, gasping, unable to complete the question.*)

ANDERSON. Yes. In his last hours he changed his mind.

MRS. DUDGEON (*white with intense rage*). And you let him rob me?

ANDERSON. I had no power to prevent him giving what was his to his own son.

MRS. DUDGEON. He had nothing of his own. His money was the money I brought him as my marriage portion. It was for me to deal with my own money and my own son. He dare not have done it if I had been with him; and well he knew it. That was why he stole away like a thief to take advantage of the law to rob me by making a new will behind my back. The more shame on you, Mr. Anderson,—you, a minister of the gospel—to act as his accomplice in such a crime.

ANDERSON (*rising*). I will take no offence at what you say in the first bitterness of your grief.

MRS. DUDGEON (*contemptuously*). Grief!

ANDERSON. Well, of your disappointment, if you can find it in your heart to think that the better word.

MRS. DUDGEON. My heart! My heart! And since when, pray, have you begun to hold up our hearts as trustworthy guides for us?

ANDERSON (*rather guiltily*). I—er——

MRS. DUDGEON (*vehemently*). Don't lie, Mr. Anderson. We are told that the heart of man is deceitful above all things, and desperately wicked. My heart belonged, not to Timothy, but to that poor wretched brother of his that has just ended his days with a rope round his neck—aye, to Peter Dudgeon. You know it: old Eli Hawkins, the man to whose pulpit you suc-

ceeded, though you are not worthy to loose his shoe latchet,
told it you when he gave over our souls into your charge. He
warned me and strengthened me against my heart, and made
me marry a Godfearing man—as he thought. What else but
that discipline has made me the woman I am? And you, you
who followed your heart in your marriage, you talk to me of
what I find in my heart. Go home to your pretty wife, man;
and leave me to my prayers. (*She turns from him and leans
with her elbows on the table, brooding over her wrongs and
taking no further notice of him.*)

ANDERSON (*willing enough to escape*). The Lord forbid
that I should come between you and the source of all comfort!
(*He goes to the rack for his coat and hat.*)

MRS. DUDGEON (*without looking at him*). The Lord will
know what to forbid and what to allow without your help.

ANDERSON. And whom to forgive, I hope—Eli Hawkins
and myself, if we have ever set up our preaching against His
law. (*He fastens his cloak, and is now ready to go.*) Just one
word—on necessary business, Mrs. Dudgeon. There is the
reading of the will to be gone through; and Richard has a
right to be present. He is in the town; but he has the grace to
say that he does not want to force himself in here.

MRS. DUDGEON. He shall come here. Does he expect us to
leave his father's house for his convenience? Let them all come,
and come quickly, and go quickly. They shall not make the
will an excuse to shirk half their day's work. I shall be ready,
never fear.

ANDERSON (*coming back a step or two*). Mrs. Dudgeon:
I used to have some little influence with you. When did I lose
it?

MRS. DUDGEON (*still without turning to him*). When you
married for love. Now you're answered.

ANDERSON. Yes: I am answered. (*He goes out, musing.*)

MRS. DUDGEON (*to herself, thinking of her husband*). Thief!
Thief! (*She shakes herself angrily out of the chair; throws
back the shawl from her head; and sets to work to prepare the
room for the reading of the will, beginning by replacing Anderson's chair against the wall, and pushing back her own to the
window. Then she calls, in her hard, driving, wrathful way.*)
Christy. (*No answer: he is fast asleep.*) Christy. (*She shakes
him roughly.*) Get up out of that; and be ashamed of yourself
—sleeping, and your father dead! (*She returns to the table;*

puts the candle on the mantelshelf; and takes from the table drawer a red table cloth which she spreads.)

CHRISTY (*rising reluctantly*). Well, do you suppose we are never going to sleep until we are out of mourning?

MRS. DUDGEON. I want none of your sulks. Here: help me to set this table. (*They place the table in the middle of the room, with Christy's end towards the fireplace and Mrs. Dudgeon's towards the sofa. Christy drops the table as soon as possible, and goes to the fire, leaving his mother to make the final adjustments of its position.*) We shall have the minister back here with the lawyer and all the family to read the will before you have done toasting yourself. Go and wake that girl; and then light the stove in the shed: you can't have your breakfast here. And mind you wash yourself, and make yourself fit to receive the company. (*She punctuates these orders by going to the cupboard; unlocking it; and producing a decanter of wine, which has no doubt stood there untouched since the last state occasion in the family, and some glasses, which she sets on the table. Also two green ware plates, on one of which she puts a barmbrack with a knife beside it. On the other she shakes some biscuits out of a tin, putting back one or two, and counting the rest.*) Now mind: there are ten biscuits there: let there be ten there when I come back after dressing myself. And keep your fingers off the raisins in that cake. And tell Essie the same. I suppose I can trust you to bring in the case of stuffed birds without breaking the glass? (*She replaces the tin in the cupboard, which she locks, pocketing the key carefully.*)

CHRISTY (*lingering at the fire*). You'd better put the inkstand instead, for the lawyer.

MRS. DUDGEON. That's no answer to make to me, sir. Go and do as you're told. (*Christy turns sullenly to obey.*) Stop: take down that shutter before you go, and let the daylight in: you can't expect me to do all the heavy work of the house with a great heavy lout like you idling about.

Christy takes the window bar out of its clamps, and puts it aside; then opens the shutter, shewing the grey morning. Mrs. Dudgeon takes the sconce from the mantelshelf; blows out the candle; extinguishes the snuff by pinching it with her fingers, first licking them for the purpose; and replaces the sconce on the shelf.

CHRISTY (*looking through the window*). Here's the minister's wife.

MRS. DUDGEON (*displeased*). What! Is she coming here?

CHRISTY. Yes.

MRS. DUDGEON. What does she want troubling me at this hour, before I'm properly dressed to receive people?

CHRISTY. You'd better ask her.

MRS. DUDGEON (*threateningly*). You'd better keep a civil tongue in your head. (*He goes sulkily towards the door. She comes after him, plying him with instructions.*) Tell that girl to come to me as soon as she's had her breakfast. And tell her to make herself fit to be seen before the people. (*Christy goes out and slams the door in her face.*) Nice manners, that! (*Someone knocks at the house door: she turns and cries inhospitably.*) Come in. (*Judith Anderson, the minister's wife, comes in. Judith is more than twenty years younger than her husband, though she will never be as young as he in vitality. She is pretty and proper and ladylike, and has been admired and petted into an opinion of herself sufficiently favorable to give her a self-assurance which serves her instead of strength. She has a pretty taste in dress, and in her face the pretty lines of a sentimental character formed by dreams. Even her little self-complacency is pretty, like a child's vanity. Rather a pathetic creature to any sympathetic observer who knows how rough a place the world is. One feels, on the whole, that Anderson might have chosen worse, and that she, needing protection, could not have chosen better.*) Oh, it's you, is it, Mrs. Anderson?

JUDITH (*very politely—almost patronizingly*). Yes. Can I do anything for you, Mrs. Dudgeon? Can I help to get the place ready before they come to read the will?

MRS. DUDGEON (*stiffly*). Thank you, Mrs. Anderson, my house is always ready for anyone to come into.

MRS. ANDERSON (*with complacent amiability*). Yes, indeed it is. Perhaps you had rather I did not intrude on you just now.

MRS. DUDGEON. Oh, one more or less will make no difference this morning, Mrs. Anderson. Now that you're here, you'd better stay. If you wouldn't mind shutting the door! (*Judith smiles, implying "How stupid of me!" and shuts it with an exasperating air of doing something pretty and becoming.*) That's better. I must go and tidy myself a bit. I suppose you don't mind stopping here to receive anyone that comes until I'm ready.

JUDITH (*graciously giving her leave*). Oh yes, certainly. Leave them to me, Mrs. Dudgeon; and take your time. (*She hangs her cloak and bonnet on the rack.*)

MRS. DUDGEON (*half sneering*). I thought that would be more in your way than getting the house ready. (*Essie comes back.*) Oh, here you are! (*Severely.*) Come here: let me see you. (*Essie timidly goes to her. Mrs. Dudgeon takes her roughly by the arm and pulls her round to inspect the results of her attempt to clean and tidy herself—results which shew little practice and less conviction.*) Mm! That's what you call doing your hair properly, I suppose. It's easy to see what you are, and how you were brought up. (*She throws her arms away, and goes on, peremptorily.*) Now you listen to me and do as you're told. You sit down there in the corner by the fire; and when the company comes don't dare to speak until you're spoken to. (*Essie creeps away to the fireplace.*) Your father's people had better see you and know you're there: they're as much bound to keep you from starvation as I am. At any rate they might help. But let me have no chattering and making free with them, as if you were their equal. Do you hear?

ESSIE. Yes.

MRS. DUDGEON. Well, then go and do as you're told. (*Essie sits down miserably on the corner of the fender farthest from the door.*) Never mind her, Mrs. Anderson: you know who she is and what she is. If she gives you any trouble, just tell me; and I'll settle accounts with her. (*Mrs. Dudgeon goes into the bedroom, shutting the door sharply behind her as if even it had to be made to do its duty with a ruthless hand.*)

JUDITH (*patronizing Essie, and arranging the cake and wine on the table more becomingly.*) You must not mind if your aunt is strict with you. She is a very good woman, and desires your good too.

ESSIE (*in listless misery*). Yes.

JUDITH (*annoyed with Essie for her failure to be consoled and edified, and to appreciate the kindly condescension of the remark*). You are not going to be sullen, I hope, Essie.

ESSIE. No.

JUDITH. That's a good girl! (*She places a couple of chairs at the table with their backs to the window, with a pleasant sense of being a more thoughtful housekeeper than Mrs. Dudgeon.*) Do you know any of your father's relatives?

ESSIE. No. They wouldn't have anything to do with him: they were too religious. Father used to talk about Dick Dudgeon; but I never saw him.

JUDITH (*ostentatiously shocked*). Dick Dudgeon! Essie: do you wish to be a really respectable and grateful girl, and to make a place for yourself here by steady good conduct?

ESSIE (*very half-heartedly*). Yes.

JUDITH. Then you must never mention the name of Richard Dudgeon—never even think about him. He is a bad man.

ESSIE. What has he done?

JUDITH. You must not ask questions about him, Essie. You are too young to know what it is to be a bad man. But he is a smuggler; and he lives with gypsies; and he has no love for his mother and his family; and he wrestles and plays games on Sunday instead of going to church. Never let him into your presence, if you can help it, Essie; and try to keep yourself and all womanhood unspotted by contact with such men.

ESSIE. Yes.

JUDITH (*again displeased*). I am afraid you say Yes and No without thinking very deeply.

ESSIE. Yes. At least I mean——

JUDITH (*severely*). What do you mean?

ESSIE (*almost crying*). Only—my father was a smuggler; and— (*Someone knocks.*)

JUDITH. They are beginning to come. Now remember your aunt's directions, Essie; and be a good girl. (*Christy comes back with the stand of stuffed birds under a glass case, and an inkstand, which he places on the table.*) Good morning, Mr. Dudgeon. Will you open the door, please: the people have come.

CHRISTY. Good morning. (*He opens the house door.*)

The morning is now fairly bright and warm; and Anderson, who is the first to enter, has left his cloak at home. He is accompanied by Lawyer Hawkins, a brisk, middleaged man in brown riding gaiters and yellow breeches, looking as much squire as solicitor. He and Anderson are allowed precedence as representing the learned professions. After them comes the family, headed by the senior uncle, William Dudgeon, a large, shapeless man, bottle-nosed and evidently no ascetic at table. His clothes are not the clothes, nor his anxious wife the wife,

*of a prosperous man. The junior uncle, Titus Dudgeon, is a
wiry little terrier of a man, with an immense and visibly purse-
proud wife, both free from the cares of the William household.*

*Hawkins at once goes briskly to the table and takes the chair
nearest the sofa, Christy having left the inkstand there. He
puts his hat on the floor beside him, and produces the will.
Uncle William comes to the fire and stands on the hearth
warming his coat tails, leaving Mrs. William derelict near the
door. Uncle Titus, who is the lady's man of the family, rescues
her by giving her his disengaged arm and bringing her to the
sofa, where he sits down warmly between his own lady and his
brother's. Anderson hangs up his hat and waits for a word
with Judith.*

JUDITH. She will be here in a moment. Ask them to wait.
(*She taps at the bedroom door. Receiving an answer from
within, she opens it and passes through.*)

ANDERSON (*taking his place at the table at the opposite end
to Hawkins*). Our poor afflicted sister will be with us in a
moment. Are we all here?

CHRISTY (*at the house door, which he has just shut*). All
except Dick.

*The callousness with which Christy names the reprobate jars
on the moral sense of the family. Uncle William shakes his
head slowly and repeatedly. Mrs. Titus catches her breath
convulsively through her nose. Her husband speaks.*

UNCLE TITUS. Well, I hope he will have the grace not to
come. I hope so.

*The Dudgeons all murmur assent, except Christy, who goes
to the window and posts himself there, looking out. Hawkins
smiles secretively as if he knew something that would change
their tune if they knew it. Anderson is uneasy: the love of
solemn family councils, especially funereal ones, is not in his
nature. Judith appears at the bedroom door.*

JUDITH (*with gentle impressiveness*). Friends, Mrs. Dudgeon. (*She takes the chair from beside the fireplace; and
places it for Mrs. Dudgeon, who comes from the bedroom in
black, with a clean handkerchief to her eyes. All rise, except
Essie. Mrs. Titus and Mrs. William produce equally clean
handkerchiefs and weep. It is an affecting moment.*)

UNCLE WILLIAM. Would it comfort you, sister, if we were
to offer up a prayer?

UNCLE TITUS. Or sing a hymn?

ANDERSON (*rather hastily*). I have been with our sister this morning already, friends. In our hearts we ask a blessing.

ALL (*except Essie*). Amen.

They all sit down, except Judith, who stands behind Mrs. Dudgeon's chair.

JUDITH (*to Essie*). Essie: did you say Amen?

ESSIE (*scaredly*). No.

JUDITH. Then say it, like a good girl.

ESSIE. Amen.

UNCLE WILLIAM (*encouragingly*). That's right: that's right. We know how you are; but we are willing to be kind to you if you are a good girl and deserve it. We are all equal before the Throne.

This republican sentiment does not please the women, who are convinced that the Throne is precisely the place where their superiority, often questioned in this world, will be recognized and rewarded.

CHRISTY (*at the window*). Here's Dick.

Anderson and Hawkins look round sociably. Essie, with a gleam of interest breaking through her misery, looks up. Christy grins and gapes expectantly at the door. The rest are petrified with the intensity of their sense of Virtue menaced with outrage by the approach of flaunting Vice. The reprobate appears in the doorway, graced beyond his alleged merits by the morning sunlight. He is certainly the best looking member of the family; but his expression is reckless and sardonic, his manner defiant and satirical, his dress picturesquely careless. Only, his forehead and mouth betray an extraordinary steadfastness; and his eyes are the eyes of a fanatic.

RICHARD (*on the threshold, taking off his hat*). Ladies and gentlemen: your servant, your very humble servant. (*With this comprehensive insult, he throws his hat to Christy with a suddenness that makes him jump like a negligent wicket keeper, and comes into the middle of the room, where he turns and deliberately surveys the company.*) How happy you all look! how glad to see me! (*He turns towards Mrs. Dudgeon's chair; and his lip rolls up horribly from his dog tooth as he meets her look of undisguised hatred.*) Well, mother: keeping up appearances as usual? that's right, that's right. (*Judith pointedly moves away from his neighborhood to the other side of the kitchen, holding her skirt instinctively as if to save it from contamination. Uncle Titus promptly marks his approval of her action by rising from the sofa, and placing a chair for her to sit down upon.*) What! Uncle William! I haven't seen you since you gave up drinking. (*Poor Uncle William, shamed, would protest; but Richard claps him heartily on his shoulder, adding*) you have given it up, haven't you? (*releasing him with a playful push*) of course you have: quite right too: you overdid it. (*He turns away from Uncle William and makes for the sofa.*) And now, where is that upright horsedealer Uncle Titus? Uncle Titus: come forth. (*He comes upon him holding the chair as Judith sits down.*) As usual, looking after the ladies.

UNCLE TITUS (*indignantly*). Be ashamed of yourself, sir——

RICHARD (*interrupting him and shaking his hand in spite of him*). I am: I am; but I am proud of my uncle—proud of all my relatives—(*again surveying them*) who could look at them and not be proud and joyful? (*Uncle Titus, overborne, resumes his seat on the sofa. Richard turns to the table.*) Ah, Mr. Anderson, still at the good work, still shepherding them. Keep them up to the mark, minister, keep them up to the mark. Come! (*with a spring he seats himself on the table and takes up the decanter*) clink a glass with me, Pastor, for the sake of old times.

ANDERSON. You know, I think, Mr. Dudgeon, that I do not drink before dinner.

RICHARD. You will, some day, Pastor: Uncle William used to drink before breakfast. Come: it will give your sermons unction. (*He smells the wine and makes a wry face.*) But do not begin on my mother's company sherry. I stole some when I was six years old; and I have been a temperate man ever since. (*He puts the decanter down and changes the subject.*) So I hear you are married, Pastor, and that your wife has a most ungodly allowance of good looks.

ANDERSON (*quietly indicating Judith*). Sir: you are in the presence of my wife. (*Judith rises and stands with stony propriety.*)

RICHARD (*quickly slipping down from the table with instinctive good manners*). Your servant, madam: no offence. (*He looks at her earnestly.*) You deserve your reputation; but I'm sorry to see by your expression that you're a good woman. (*She looks shocked, and sits down amid a murmur of indignant sympathy from his relatives. Anderson, sensible enough to*

*know that these demonstrations can only gratify and encourage
a man who is deliberately trying to provoke them, remains perfectly goodhumored.*) All the same, Pastor, I respect you more
than I did before. By the way, did I hear, or did I not, that our
late lamented Uncle Peter, though unmarried, was a father?

UNCLE TITUS. He had only one irregular child, sir.

RICHARD. Only one! He thinks one a mere trifle! I blush
for you, Uncle Titus.

ANDERSON. Mr. Dudgeon, you are in the presence of your
mother and her grief.

RICHARD. It touches me profoundly, Pastor. By the way,
what has become of the irregular child?

ANDERSON (*pointing to Essie*). There, sir, listening to you.

RICHARD (*shocked into sincerity*). What! Why the devil
didn't you tell me that before? Children suffer enough in
this house without— (*He hurries remorsefully to Essie.*)
Come, little cousin! never mind me: it was not meant to hurt
you. (*She looks up gratefully at him. Her tearstained face
affects him violently, and he bursts out, in a transport of
wrath.*) Who has been making her cry? Who has been ill-
treating her? By God——

MRS. DUDGEON (*rising and confronting him*). Silence your
blasphemous tongue. I will bear no more of this. Leave my
house.

RICHARD. How do you know it's your house until the will
is read? (*They look at one another for a moment with intense
hatred; and then she sinks, checkmated, into her chair. Richard goes boldly up past Anderson to the window, where he
takes the railed chair in his hand.*) Ladies and gentlemen: as
the eldest son of my late father, and the unworthy head of this
household, I bid you welcome. By your leave, Minister Anderson: by your leave, Lawyer Hawkins. The head of the
table for the head of the family. (*He places the chair at the
table between the minister and the attorney; sits down between
them; and addresses the assembly with a presidential air.*) We
meet on a melancholy occasion: a father dead! an uncle actually hanged, and probably damned. (*He shakes his head de-
ploringly. The relatives freeze with horror.*) That's right:
pull your longest faces (*his voice suddenly sweetens gravely
as his glance lights on Essie*) provided only there is hope in the
eyes of the child. (*Briskly.*) Now then, Lawyer Hawkins:
business, business. Get on with the will, man.

TITUS. Do not let yourself be ordered or hurried, Mr. Hawkins.

HAWKINS (*very politely and willingly*). Mr. Dudgeon means no offence, I feel sure. I will not keep you one second, Mr. Dudgeon. Just while I get my glasses—(*He fumbles for them. The Dudgeons look at one another with misgiving.*)

RICHARD. Aha! They notice your civility, Mr. Hawkins. They are prepared for the worst. A glass of wine to clear your voice before you begin. (*He pours out one for him and hands it; then pours one for himself.*)

HAWKINS. Thank you, Mr. Dudgeon. Your good health, sir.

RICHARD. Yours, sir. (*With the glass half way to his lips, he checks himself, giving a dubious glance at the wine, and adds, with quaint intensity.*) Will anyone oblige me with a glass of water?

Essie, who has been hanging on his every word and movement, rises stealthily and slips out behind Mrs. Dudgeon through the bedroom door, returning presently with a jug and going out of the house as quietly as possible.

HAWKINS. The will is not exactly in proper legal phraseology.

RICHARD. No: my father died without the consolations of the law.

HAWKINS. Good again, Mr. Dudgeon, good again. (*Preparing to read.*) Are you ready, sir?

RICHARD. Ready, aye ready. For what we are about to receive, may the Lord make us truly thankful. Go ahead.

HAWKINS (*reading*). "This is the last will and testament of me Timothy Dudgeon on my deathbed at Nevinstown on the road from Springtown to Websterbridge on this twenty-fourth day of September, one thousand seven hundred and seventy seven. I hereby revoke all former wills made by me and declare that I am of sound mind and know well what I am doing and that this is my real will according to my own wish and affections."

RICHARD (*glancing at his mother*). Aha!

HAWKINS (*shaking his head*). Bad phraseology, sir, wrong phraseology. "I give and bequeath a hundred pounds to my younger son Christopher Dudgeon, fifty pounds to be paid to him on the day of his marriage to Sarah Wilkins if she will have him, and ten pounds on the birth of each of his children up to the number of five."

RICHARD. How if she won't have him?

CHRISTY. She will if I have fifty pounds.

RICHARD. Good, my brother. Proceed.

HAWKINS. "I give and bequeath to my wife Annie Dudgeon, born Annie Primrose"—you see he did not know the law, Mr. Dudgeon: your mother was not born Annie: she was christened so—"an annuity of fifty-two pounds a year for life (*Mrs. Dudgeon, with all eyes on her, holds herself convulsively rigid*) to be paid out of the interest on her own money"—there's a way to put it, Mr. Dudgeon! Her own money!

MRS. DUDGEON. A very good way to put God's truth. It was every penny my own. Fifty-two pounds a year!

HAWKINS. "And I recommend her for her goodness and piety to the forgiving care of her children, having stood between them and her as far as I could to the best of my ability."

MRS. DUDGEON. And this is my reward! (*Raging inwardly.*) You know what I think, Mr. Anderson: you know the word I gave to it.

ANDERSON. It cannot be helped, Mrs. Dudgeon. We must take what comes to us. (*To Hawkins.*) Go on, sir.

HAWKINS. "I give and bequeath my house at Webster-bridge with the land belonging to it and all the rest of my property soever to my eldest son and heir, Richard Dudgeon."

RICHARD. Oho! The fatted calf, Minister, the fatted calf.

HAWKINS. "On these conditions——"

RICHARD. The devil! Are there conditions?

HAWKINS. "To wit: first, that he shall not let my brother Peter's natural child starve or be driven by want to an evil life."

RICHARD (*emphatically, striking his fist on the table*). Agreed.

Mrs. Dudgeon, turning to look malignantly at Essie, misses her and looks quickly round to see where she has moved to; then, seeing that she has left the room without leave, closes her lips vengefully.

HAWKINS. "Second, that he shall be a good friend to my old horse Jim"—(*again shaking his head*) he should have written James, sir.

RICHARD. James shall live in clover. Go on.

HAWKINS. —"and keep my deaf farm laborer Prodger Feston in his service."

RICHARD. Prodger Feston shall get drunk every Saturday.

HAWKINS. "Third, that he make Christy a present on his marriage out of the ornaments in the best room."

RICHARD (*holding up the stuffed birds*). Here you are, Christy.

CHRISTY (*disappointed*). I'd rather have the China peacocks.

RICHARD. You shall have both. (*Christy is greatly pleased.*) Go on.

HAWKINS. "Fourthly and lastly, that he try to live at peace with his mother as far as she will consent to it."

RICHARD (*dubiously*). Hm! Anything more, Mr. Hawkins?

HAWKINS (*solemnly*). "Finally I give and bequeath my soul into my Maker's hands, humbly asking forgiveness for all my sins and mistakes, and hoping that he will so guide my son that it may not be said that I have done wrong in trusting to him rather than to others in the perplexity of my last hour in this strange place."

ANDERSON. Amen.

THE UNCLES AND AUNTS. Amen.

RICHARD. My mother does not say Amen.

MRS. DUDGEON (*rising, unable to give up her property without a struggle*). Mr. Hawkins: is that a proper will? Remember, I have his rightful, legal will, drawn up by yourself, leaving all to me.

HAWKINS. This is a very wrongly and irregularly worded will, Mrs. Dudgeon; though (*turning politely to Richard*) it contains in my judgment an excellent disposal of his property.

ANDERSON (*interposing before Mrs. Dudgeon can retort*). That is not what you are asked, Mr. Hawkins. Is it a legal will?

HAWKINS. The courts will sustain it against the other.

ANDERSON. But why, if the other is more lawfully worded?

HAWKINS. Because, sir, the courts will sustain the claim of a man—and that man the eldest son—against any woman, if they can. I warned you, Mrs. Dudgeon, when you got me to draw that other will, that it was not a wise will, and that though you might make him sign it, he would never be easy until he revoked it. But you wouldn't take advice; and now

Mr. Richard is cock of the walk. (*He takes his hat from the floor; rises; and begins pocketing his papers and spectacles.*)

This is the signal for the breaking-up of the party. Anderson takes his hat from the rack and joins Uncle William at the fire. Uncle Titus fetches Judith her things from the rack. The three on the sofa rise and chat with Hawkins. Mrs. Dudgeon, now an intruder in her own house, stands erect, crushed by the weight of the law on women, accepting it, as she has been trained to accept all monstrous calamities, as proofs of the greatness of the power that inflicts them, and of her own wormlike insignificance. For at this time, remember, Mary Wollstonecraft is as yet only a girl of eighteen, and her Vindication of the Rights of Women is still fourteen years off. Mrs. Dudgeon is rescued from her apathy by Essie, who comes back with the jug full of water. She is taking it to Richard when Mrs. Dudgeon stops her.

MRS. DUDGEON (*threatening her*). Where have you been? (*Essie, appalled, tries to answer, but cannot.*) How dare you go out by yourself after the orders I gave you?

ESSIE. He asked for a drink—(*She stops, her tongue cleaving to her palate with terror.*)

JUDITH (*with gentler severity*). Who asked for a drink? (*Essie, speechless, points to Richard.*)

RICHARD. What! I!

JUDITH (*shocked*). Oh Essie, Essie!

RICHARD. I believe I did. (*He takes a glass and holds it to Essie to be filled. Her hand shakes.*) What! afraid of me?

ESSIE (*quickly*). No. I— (*She pours out the water.*)

RICHARD (*tasting it*). Ah, you've been up the street to the market gate spring to get that. (*He takes a draught.*) Delicious! Thank you. (*Unfortunately, at this moment he chances to catch sight of Judith's face, which expresses the most prudish disapproval of his evident attraction for Essie, who is devouring him with her grateful eyes. His mocking expression returns instantly. He puts down the glass; deliberately winds his arm round Essie's shoulders; and brings her into the middle of the company. Mrs. Dudgeon being in Essie's way as they come past the table, he says.*) By your leave, mother (*and compels her to make way for them*). What do they call you? Bessie?

ESSIE. Essie.

RICHARD. Essie, to be sure. Are you a good girl, Essie?

ESSIE (*greatly disappointed that he, of all people, should begin at her in this way*). Yes. (*She looks doubtfully at Judith.*) I think so. I mean I—I hope so.

RICHARD. Essie: did you ever hear of a person called the devil?

ANDERSON (*revolted*). Shame on you, sir, with a mere child——

RICHARD. By your leave, Minister: I do not interfere with your sermons: do not you interrupt mine. (*To Essie.*) Do you know what they call me, Essie?

ESSIE. Dick.

RICHARD (*amused: patting her on the shoulder*). Yes, Dick; but something else too. They call me the Devil's Disciple.

ESSIE. Why do you let them?

RICHARD (*seriously*). But it's true. I was brought up in the other service; but I knew from the first that the Devil was my natural master and captain and friend. I saw that he was in the right, and that the world cringed to his conqueror only through fear. I prayed secretly to him; and he comforted me, and saved me from having my spirit broken in this house of children's tears. I promised him my soul, and swore an oath that I would stand up for him in this world and stand by him in the next. (*Solemnly.*) That promise and that oath made a man of me. From this day this house is his home; and no child shall cry in it: this hearth is his altar; and no soul shall ever cower over it in the dark evenings and be afraid. Now (*turning forcibly on the rest*) which of you good men will take this child and rescue her from the house of the devil?

JUDITH (*coming to Essie and throwing a protecting arm about her*). I will. You should be burnt alive.

ESSIE. But I don't want to. (*She shrinks back, leaving Richard and Judith face to face.*)

RICHARD (*to Judith*). Actually doesn't want to, most virtuous lady!

UNCLE TITUS. Have a care, Richard Dudgeon. The law——

RICHARD (*turning threateningly on him*). Have a care, you. In an hour from this there will be no law here but martial law. I passed the soldiers within six miles on my way here: before noon Major Swindon's gallows for rebels will be up in the market place.

ANDERSON (*calmly*). What have we to fear from that, sir?

RICHARD. More than you think. He hanged the wrong man

at Springtown: he thought Uncle Peter was respectable, because the Dudgeons had a good name. But his next example will be the best man in the town to whom he can bring home a rebellious word. Well, we're all rebels; and you know it.

ALL THE MEN (*except Anderson*). No, no, no!

RICHARD. Yes, you are. You haven't damned King George up hill and down dale as I have; but you've prayed for his defeat; and you, Anthony Anderson, have conducted the service, and sold your family bible to buy a pair of pistols. They mayn't hang me, perhaps; because the moral effect of the Devil's Disciple dancing on nothing wouldn't help them. But a Minister! (*Judith, dismayed, clings to Anderson*) or a lawyer! (*Hawkins smiles like a man able to take care of himself*) or an upright horsedealer! (*Uncle Titus snarls at him in rage and terror*) or a reformed drunkard (*Uncle William, utterly unnerved, moans and wobbles with fear*) eh? Would that shew that King George meant business—ha?

ANDERSON (*perfectly self-possessed*). Come, my dear: he is only trying to frighten you. There is no danger. (*He takes her out of the house. The rest crowd to the door to follow him, except Essie, who remains near Richard.*)

RICHARD (*boisterously derisive*). Now then: how many of you will stay with me; run up the American flag on the devil's house; and make a fight for freedom? (*They scramble out, Christy among them, hustling one another in their haste.*) Ha ha! Long live the devil! (*To Mrs. Dudgeon, who is following them.*) What, mother! are you off too?

MRS. DUDGEON (*deadly pale, with her hand on her heart as if she had received a deathblow*). My curse on you! My dying curse! (*She goes out.*)

RICHARD (*calling after her*). It will bring me luck. Ha ha ha!

ESSIE (*anxiously*). Mayn't I stay?

RICHARD (*turning to her*). What! Have they forgotten to save your soul in their anxiety about their own bodies? Oh yes: you may stay. (*He turns excitedly away again and shakes his fist after them. His left fist, also clenched, hangs down. Essie seizes it and kisses it, her tears falling on it. He starts and looks at it.*) Tears! The devil's baptism! (*She falls on her knees, sobbing. He stoops goodnaturedly to raise her, saying.*) Oh yes, you may cry that way, Essie, if you like.

ACT II

Minister Anderson's house is in the main street of Webster-bridge, not far from the town hall. To the eye of the eighteenth century New Englander, it is much grander than the plain farmhouse of the Dudgeons; but it is so plain itself that a modern house agent would let both at about the same rent. The chief dwelling room has the same sort of kitchen fireplace, with boiler, toaster hanging on the bars, movable iron griddle socketed to the hob, hook above for roasting, and broad fender, on which stand a kettle and a plate of buttered toast. The door, between the fireplace and the corner, has neither panels, fingerplates nor handles: it is made of plain boards, and fastens with a latch. The table is a kitchen table, with a treacle colored cover of American cloth, chapped at the corners by draping. The tea service on it consists of two thick cups and saucers of the plainest ware, with milk jug and bowl to match, each large enough to contain nearly a quart, on a black japanned tray, and, in the middle of the table, a wooden trencher with a big loaf upon it, and a square half pound block of butter in a crock. The big oak press facing the fire from the opposite side of the room is for use and storage, not for ornament; and the minister's house coat hangs on a peg from its door, shewing that he is out; for when he is in, it is his best coat that hangs there. His big riding boots stand beside the press, evidently in their usual place, and rather proud of themselves. In fact, the evolution of the minister's kitchen, dining room and drawing room into three separate apartments has not yet taken place; and so, from the point of view of our pampered period, he is no better off than the Dudgeons.

But there is a difference, for all that. To begin with, Mrs. Anderson is a pleasanter person to live with than Mrs. Dudgeon. To which Mrs. Dudgeon would at once reply, with reason, that Mrs. Anderson has no children to look after; no poultry, pigs nor cattle; a steady and sufficient income not directly dependent on harvests and prices at fairs; an

27

*affectionate husband who is a tower of strength to her: in short,
that life is as easy at the minister's house as it is hard at the
farm. This is true; but to explain a fact is not to alter it; and
however little credit Mrs. Anderson may deserve for making
her home happier, she has certainly succeeded in doing it. The
outward and visible signs of her superior social pretensions
are, a drugget on the floor, a plaster ceiling between the tim-
bers, and chairs which, though not upholstered, are stained
and polished. The fine arts are represented by a mezzotint
portrait of some Presbyterian divine, a copperplate of
Raphael's St. Paul preaching at Athens, a rococo presentation
clock on the mantelshelf, flanked by a couple of miniatures,
a pair of crockery dogs with baskets in their mouths, and, at
the corners, two large cowrie shells. A pretty feature of the
room is the low wide latticed window, nearly its whole width,
with little red curtains running on a rod half way up it to serve
as a blind. There is no sofa; but one of the seats, standing near
the press, has a railed back and is long enough to accommodate
two people easily. On the whole, it is rather the sort of room
that the nineteenth century has ended in struggling to get back
to under the leadership of Mr. Philip Webb and his disciples in
domestic architecture, though no genteel clergyman would
have tolerated it fifty years ago.*

*The evening has closed in; and the room is dark except for
the cosy firelight and the dim oil lamps seen through the window in the wet street, where there is a quiet, steady, warm,
windless downpour of rain. As the town clock strikes the
quarter, Judith comes in with a couple of candles in earthenware candlesticks, and sets them on the table. Her self-conscious airs of the morning are gone: she is anxious and frightened. She goes to the window and peers into the street. The
first thing she sees there is her husband, hurrying home
through the rain. She gives a little gasp of relief, not very far
removed from a sob, and turns to the door. Anderson comes in,
wrapped in a very wet cloak.*

JUDITH (*running to him*). Oh, here you are at last, at last!
(*She attempts to embrace him.*)

ANDERSON (*keeping her off*). Take care, my love: I'm wet.
Wait till I get my cloak off. (*He places a chair with its back
to the fire; hangs his cloak on it to dry; shakes the rain from his
hat and puts it on the fender; and at last turns with his hands
outstretched to Judith.*) Now! (*She flies into his arms.*) I

am not late, am I? The town clock struck the quarter as I came in at the front door. And the town clock is always fast.

JUDITH. I'm sure it's slow this evening. I'm so glad you're back.

ANDERSON (*taking her more closely in his arms*). Anxious, my dear.

JUDITH. A little.

ANDERSON. Why, you've been crying.

JUDITH. Only a little. Never mind: it's all over now. (*A bugle call is heard in the distance. She starts in terror and retreats to the long seat, listening.*) What's that?

ANDERSON (*following her tenderly to the seat and making her sit down with him*). Only King George, my dear. He's returning to barracks, or having his roll called, or getting ready for tea, or booting or saddling or something. Soldiers don't ring the bell or call over the banisters when they want anything: they send a boy out with a bugle to disturb the whole town.

JUDITH. Do you think there is really any danger?

ANDERSON. Not the least in the world.

JUDITH. You say that to comfort me, not because you believe it.

ANDERSON. My dear: in this world there is always danger for those who are afraid of it. There's a danger that the house will catch fire in the night; but we shan't sleep any the less soundly for that.

JUDITH. Yes, I know what you always say; and you're quite right. Oh, quite right: I know it. But—I suppose I'm not brave: that's all. My heart shrinks every time I think of the soldiers.

ANDERSON. Never mind that, dear: bravery is none the worse for costing a little pain.

JUDITH. Yes, I suppose so. (*Embracing him again.*) Oh how brave you are, my dear! (*With tears in her eyes.*) Well, I'll be brave too: you shan't be ashamed of your wife.

ANDERSON. That's right. Now you make me happy. Well, well! (*He rises and goes cheerily to the fire to dry his shoes.*) I called on Richard Dudgeon on my way back; but he wasn't in.

JUDITH (*rising in consternation*). You called on that man!

ANDERSON (*reassuring her*). Oh, nothing happened, dearie. He was out.

JUDITH (*almost in tears, as if the visit were a personal humiliation to her*). But why did you go there?

ANDERSON (*gravely*). Well, it is all the talk that Major Swindon is going to do what he did in Springtown—make an example of some notorious rebel, as he calls us. He pounced on Peter Dudgeon as the worst character there; and it is the general belief that he will pounce on Richard as the worst here.

JUDITH. But Richard said——

ANDERSON (*goodhumoredly cutting her short*). Pooh! Richard said! He said what he thought would frighten you and frighten me, my dear. He said what perhaps (God forgive him!) he would like to believe. It's a terrible thing to think of what death must mean for a man like that. I felt that I must warn him. I left a message for him.

JUDITH (*querulously*). What message?

ANDERSON. Only that I should be glad to see him for a moment on a matter of importance to himself; and that if he would look in here when he was passing he would be welcome.

JUDITH (*aghast*). You asked that man to come here!

ANDERSON. I did.

JUDITH (*sinking on the seat and clasping her hands*). I hope he won't come! Oh, I pray that he may not come!

ANDERSON. Why? Don't you want him to be warned?

JUDITH. He must know his danger. Oh, Tony, is it wrong to hate a blasphemer and a villain? I do hate him. I can't get him out of my mind: I know he will bring harm with him. He insulted you: he insulted me: he insulted his mother.

ANDERSON (*quaintly*). Well, dear, let's forgive him; and then it won't matter.

JUDITH. Oh, I know it's wrong to hate anybody; but——

ANDERSON (*going over to her with humorous tenderness*). Come, dear, you're not so wicked as you think. The worst sin towards our fellow creatures is not to hate them, but to be indifferent to them: that's the essence of inhumanity. After all, my dear, if you watch people carefully, you'll be surprised to find how like hate is to love. (*She starts, strangely touched— even appalled. He is amused at her.*) Yes: I'm quite in earnest. Think of how some of our married friends worry one another, tax one another, are jealous of one another, can't bear to let one another out of sight for a day, are more like jailers and slave-owners than lovers. Think of those very same people with their enemies, scrupulous, lofty, self-respecting, determined to be independent of one another, careful of how they speak of one another—pooh! haven't you often thought that if they only knew it, they were better friends to their enemies than to their own husbands and wives? Come: depend on it, my dear, you are really fonder of Richard than you are of me, if you only knew it. Eh?

JUDITH. Oh, don't say that: don't say that, Tony, even in jest. You don't know what a horrible feeling it gives me.

ANDERSON (*laughing*). Well, well: never mind, pet. He's a bad man; and you hate him as he deserves. And you're going to make the tea, aren't you?

JUDITH (*remorsefully*). Oh yes, I forgot. I've been keeping you waiting all this time. (*She goes to the fire and puts on the kettle.*)

ANDERSON (*going to the press and taking his coat off*). Have you stitched up the shoulder of my old coat?

JUDITH. Yes, dear. (*She goes to the table, and sets about putting the tea into the teapot from the caddy.*)

ANDERSON (*as he changes his coat for the older one hanging on the press, and replaces it by the one he has just taken off*). Did anyone call when I was out?

JUDITH. No, only—(*Someone knocks at the door. With a start which betrays her intense nervousness, she retreats to the farther end of the table with the tea caddy and spoon in her hands, exclaiming.*) Who's that?

ANDERSON (*going to her and patting her encouragingly on the shoulder*). All right, pet, all right. He won't eat you, whoever he is. (*She tries to smile, and nearly makes herself cry. He goes to the door and opens it. Richard is there, without overcoat or cloak.*) You might have raised the latch and come in, Mr. Dudgeon. Nobody stands on much ceremony with us. (*Hospitably.*) Come in. (*Richard comes in carelessly and stands at the table, looking round the room with a slight pucker of his nose at the mezzotinted divine on the wall. Judith keeps her eyes on the tea caddy.*) Is it still raining? (*He shuts the door.*)

RICHARD. Raining like the very (*his eye catches Judith's as she looks quickly and haughtily up . . .*)—I beg your pardon; but (*shewing that his coat is wet*) you see——!

ANDERSON. Take it off, sir; and let it hang before the fire a while; my wife will excuse your shirtsleeves. Judith: put in another spoonful of tea for Mr. Dudgeon.

RICHARD (*eyeing him cynically*). The magic of property, Pastor! Are even you civil to me now that I have succeeded to my father's estate?

Judith throws down the spoon indignantly.

ANDERSON (*quite unruffled, and helping Richard off with his coat*). I think, sir, that since you accept my hospitality, you cannot have so bad an opinion of it. Sit down. (*With the coat in his hand, he points to the railed seat. Richard, in his shirtsleeves, looks at him half quarrelsomely for a moment; then, with a nod, acknowledges that the minister has got the better of him, and sits down on the seat. Anderson pushes his cloak into a heap on the seat of the chair at the fire, and hangs Richard's coat on the back in its place.*)

RICHARD. I come, sir, on your own invitation. You left word you had something important to tell me.

ANDERSON. I have a warning which it is my duty to give you.

RICHARD (*quickly rising*). You want to preach to me. Excuse me: I prefer a walk in the rain. (*He makes for his coat.*)

ANDERSON (*stopping him*). Don't be alarmed, sir; I am no great preacher. You are quite safe. (*Richard smiles in spite of himself. His glance softens: he even makes a gesture of excuse. Anderson, seeing that he has tamed him, now addresses him earnestly.*) Mr. Dudgeon: you are in danger in this town.

RICHARD. What danger?

ANDERSON. Your uncle's danger. Major Swindon's gallows.

RICHARD. It is you who are in danger. I warned you——

ANDERSON (*interrupting him goodhumoredly but authoritatively*). Yes, yes, Mr. Dudgeon; but they do not think so in the town. And even if I were in danger, I have duties here which I must not forsake. But you are a free man. Why should you run any risk?

RICHARD. Do you think I should be any great loss, Minister?

ANDERSON. I think that a man's life is worth saving, whoever it belongs to. (*Richard makes him an ironical bow. Anderson returns the bow humorously.*) Come: you'll have a cup of tea, to prevent you catching cold?

RICHARD. I observe that Mrs. Anderson is not quite so pressing as you are, Pastor.

JUDITH (*almost stifled with resentment, which she has been expecting her husband to share and express for her at every insult of Richard's*). You are welcome for my husband's sake. (*She brings the teapot to the fireplace and sets it on the hob.*)

RICHARD. I know I am not welcome for my own, madam. (*He rises.*) But I think I will not break bread here, Minister.

ANDERSON (*cheerily*). Give me a good reason for that.

RICHARD. Because there is something in you that I respect, and that makes me desire to have you for my enemy.

ANDERSON. That's well said. On those terms, sir, I will accept your enmity or any man's. Judith: Mr. Dudgeon will stay to tea. Sit down: it will take a few minutes to draw by the fire. (*Richard glances at him with a troubled face; then sits down with his head bent, to hide a convulsive swelling of his throat.*) I was just saying to my wife, Mr. Dudgeon, that enmity—(*She grasps his hand and looks imploringly at him, doing both with an intensity that checks him at once.*) Well, well, I mustn't tell you, I see; but it was nothing that need leave us worse friends—enemies, I mean. Judith is a great enemy of yours.

RICHARD. If all my enemies were like Mrs. Anderson, I should be the best Christian in America.

ANDERSON (*gratified, patting her hand*). You hear that, Judith? Mr. Dudgeon knows how to turn a compliment.

The latch is lifted from without.

JUDITH (*starting*). Who is that?

Christy comes in.

CHRISTY (*stopping and staring at Richard*). Oh, are you here?

RICHARD. Yes. Begone, you fool: Mrs. Anderson doesn't want the whole family to tea at once.

CHRISTY (*coming further in*). Mother's very ill.

RICHARD. Well, does she want to see me?

CHRISTY. No.

RICHARD. I thought not.

CHRISTY. She wants to see the minister—at once.

JUDITH (*to Anderson*). Oh, not before you've had some tea.

ANDERSON. I shall enjoy it more when I come back, dear. (*He is about to take up his cloak.*)

CHRISTY. The rain's over.

ANDERSON (*dropping the cloak and picking up his hat from the fender*). Where is your mother, Christy?

CHRISTY. At Uncle Titus's.

ANDERSON. Have you fetched the doctor?

CHRISTY. No: she didn't tell me to.

ANDERSON. Go on there at once: I'll overtake you on his doorstep. (*Christy turns to go.*) Wait a moment. Your brother must be anxious to know the particulars.

RICHARD. Psha! not I: he doesn't know; and I don't care. (*Violently.*) Be off, you oaf. (*Christy runs out. Richard adds, a little shamefacedly.*) We shall know soon enough.

ANDERSON. Well, perhaps you will let me bring you the news myself. Judith: will you give Mr. Dudgeon his tea, and keep him here until I return?

JUDITH (*white and trembling*). Must I——

ANDERSON (*taking her hands and interrupting her to cover her agitation*). My dear: I can depend on you?

JUDITH (*with a piteous effort to be worthy of his trust*). Yes.

ANDERSON (*pressing her hand against his cheek*). You will not mind two old people like us, Mr. Dudgeon. (*Going.*) I shall not say good evening: you will be here when I come back. (*He goes out.*)

They watch him pass the window, and then look at each other dumbly, quite disconcerted. Richard, noting the quiver of her lips, is the first to pull himself together.

RICHARD. Mrs. Anderson: I am perfectly aware of the nature of your sentiments towards me. I shall not intrude on you. Good evening. (*Again he starts for the fireplace to get his coat.*)

JUDITH (*getting between him and the coat.*) No, no. Don't go: please don't go.

RICHARD (*roughly*). Why? You don't want me here.

JUDITH. Yes, I—(*Wringing her hands in despair.*) Oh, if I tell you the truth, you will use it to torment me.

RICHARD (*indignantly*). Torment! What right have you to say that? Do you expect me to stay after that?

JUDITH. I want you to stay; but (*suddenly raging at him like an angry child*) it is not because I like you.

RICHARD. Indeed!

JUDITH. Yes: I had rather you did go than mistake me about that. I hate and dread you; and my husband knows it. If you are not here when he comes back, he will believe that I disobeyed him and drove you away.

RICHARD (*ironically*). Whereas, of course, you have really

been so kind and hospitable and charming to me that I only want to go away out of mere contrariness, eh?

Judith, unable to bear it, sinks on the chair and bursts into tears.

RICHARD. Stop, stop, stop, I tell you. Don't do that. (*Putting his hand to his breast as if to a wound.*) He wrung my heart by being a man. Need you tear it by being a woman? Has he not raised you above my insults, like himself? (*She stops crying, and recovers herself somewhat, looking at him with a scared curiosity.*) There: that's right. (*Sympathetically.*) You're better now, aren't you? (*He puts his hand encouragingly on her shoulder. She instantly rises haughtily, and stares at him defiantly. He at once drops into his usual sardonic tone.*) Ah, that's better. You are yourself again: so is Richard. Well, shall we go to tea like a quiet respectable couple, and wait for your husband's return?

JUDITH (*rather ashamed of herself*). If you please. I—I am sorry to have been so foolish. (*She stoops to take up the plate of toast from the fender.*)

RICHARD. I am sorry, for your sake, that I am—what I am. Allow me. (*He takes the plate from her and goes with it to the table.*)

JUDITH (*following with the teapot*). Will you sit down? (*He sits down at the end of the table nearest the press. There is a plate and knife laid there. The other plate is laid near it; but Judith stays at the opposite end of the table, next to the fire, and takes her place there, drawing the tray towards her.*) Do you take sugar?

RICHARD. No; but plenty of milk. Let me give you some toast. (*He puts some on the second plate, and hands it to her, with the knife. The action shews quietly how well he knows that she has avoided her usual place so as to be as far from him as possible.*)

JUDITH (*consciously*). Thanks. (*She gives him his tea.*) Won't you help yourself?

RICHARD. Thanks. (*He puts a piece of toast on his own plate; and she pours out tea for herself.*)

JUDITH (*observing that he tastes nothing*). Don't you like it? You are not eating anything.

RICHARD. Neither are you.

JUDITH (*nervously*). I never care much for my tea. Please don't mind me.

RICHARD (*looking dreamily round*). I am thinking. It is all so strange to me. I can see the beauty and peace of this home: I think I have never been more at rest in my life than at this moment; and yet I know quite well I could never live here. It's not in my nature, I suppose, to be domesticated. But it's very beautiful: it's almost holy. (*He muses a moment, and then laughs softly.*)

JUDITH (*quickly*). Why do you laugh?

RICHARD. I was thinking that if any stranger came in here now, he would take us for man and wife.

JUDITH (*taking offence*). You mean, I suppose, that you are more my age than he is.

RICHARD (*staring at this unexpected turn*). I never thought of such a thing. (*Sardonic again.*) I see there is another side to domestic joy.

JUDITH (*angrily*). I would rather have a husband whom everybody respects than——than——

RICHARD. Than the devil's disciple. You are right; but I daresay your love helps him to be a good man, just as your hate helps me to be a bad one.

JUDITH. My husband has been very good to you. He has forgiven you for insulting him, and is trying to save you. Can you not forgive him for being so much better than you are? How dare you belittle him by putting yourself in his place?

RICHARD. Did I?

JUDITH. Yes, you did. You said that if anybody came in they would take us for man and——(*She stops, terror-stricken, as a squad of soldiers tramps past the window.*) The English soldiers! Oh, what do they——

RICHARD (*listening*). Sh!

A VOICE (*outside*). Halt! Four outside: two in with me.

Judith half rises, listening and looking with dilated eyes at Richard, who takes up his cup prosaically, and is drinking his tea when the latch goes up with a sharp click, and an English sergeant walks into the room with two privates, who post themselves at the door. He comes promptly to the table between them.

THE SERGEANT. Sorry to disturb you, mum! duty! Anthony Anderson: I arrest you in King George's name as a rebel.

JUDITH (*pointing at Richard*). But that is not—— (*He looks up quickly at her, with a face of iron. She stops her mouth hastily with the hand she has raised to indicate him, and stands staring affrightedly.*)

THE SERGEANT. Come, Parson; put your coat on and come along.

RICHARD. Yes: I'll come. (*He rises and takes a step towards his own coat; then recollects himself, and, with his back to the sergeant, moves his gaze slowly round the room without turning his head until he sees Anderson's black coat hanging up on the press. He goes composedly to it; takes it down; and puts it on. The idea of himself as a parson tickles him: he looks down at the black sleeve on his arm, and then smiles slyly at Judith, whose white face shews him that what she is painfully struggling to grasp is not the humor of the situation but its horror. He turns to the sergeant, who is approaching him with a pair of handcuffs hidden behind him, and says lightly.*) Did you ever arrest a man of my cloth before, Sergeant?

THE SERGEANT (*instinctively respectful, half to the black coat, half to Richard's good breeding*). Well, no, sir. At least, only an army chaplain. (*Shewing the handcuffs.*) I'm sorry, sir; but duty——

RICHARD. Just so, Sergeant. Well, I'm not ashamed of them: thank you kindly for the apology. (*He holds out his hands.*)

SERGEANT (*not availing himself of the offer*). One gentleman to another, sir. Wouldn't you like to say a word to your missis, sir, before you go?

RICHARD (*smiling*). Oh, we shall meet again before—eh? (*Meaning "before you hang me."*)

SERGEANT (*loudly, with ostentatious cheerfulness*). Oh, of course, of course. No call for the lady to distress herself. Still—(*in a lower voice, intended for Richard alone*) your last chance, sir.

They look at one another significantly for a moment. Then Richard exhales a deep breath and turns towards Judith.

RICHARD (*very distinctly*). My love. (*She looks at him, pitiably pale, and tries to answer, but cannot—tries also to come to him, but cannot trust herself to stand without the support of the table.*) This gallant gentleman is good enough to allow us a moment of leavetaking. (*The sergeant retires delicately and joins his men near the door.*) He is trying to spare you the truth; but you had better know it. Are you listening to me? (*She signifies assent.*) Do you understand that

I am going to my death? (*She signifies that she understands.*)
Remember, you must find our friend who was with us just
now. Do you understand? (*She signifies yes.*) See that you get
him safely out of harm's way. Don't for your life let him
know of my danger; but if he finds it out, tell him that he
cannot save me: they would hang him; and they would not
spare me. And tell him that I am steadfast in my religion as
he is in his, and that he may depend on me to the death. (*He
turns to go, and meets the eye of the sergeant, who looks a
little suspicious. He considers a moment, and then, turning
roguishly to Judith with something of a smile breaking
through his earnestness, says.*) And now, my dear, I am afraid
the sergeant will not believe that you love me like a wife
unless you give one kiss before I go.

*He approaches her and holds out his arms. She quits the
table and almost falls into them.*

JUDITH (*the words choking her*). I ought to—it's murder——

RICHARD. No: only a kiss (*softly to her*) for his sake.

JUDITH. I can't. You must——

RICHARD (*folding her in his arms with an impulse of compassion for her distress*). My poor girl!

*Judith, with a sudden effort, throws her arms round him;
kisses him; and swoons away, dropping from his arms to the
ground as if the kiss had killed her.*

RICHARD (*going quickly to the sergeant*). Now, Sergeant:
quick, before she comes to. The handcuffs. (*He puts out his
hands.*)

SERGEANT (*pocketing them*). Never mind, sir: I'll trust you.
You're a game one. You ought to a bin a soldier, sir. Between
them two, please. (*The soldiers place themselves one before
Richard and one behind him. The sergeant opens the door.*)

RICHARD (*taking a last look around him*). Goodbye, wife:
goodbye, home. Muffle the drums, and quick march!

*The sergeant signs to the leading soldier to march. They
file out quickly.* ° ° ° ° ° ° ° ° ° ° ° °
° *When Anderson returns from Mrs. Dudgeon's he is astonished to find the room apparently empty and almost in darkness except for the glow from the fire; for one of the candles
has burnt out, and the other is at its last flicker.*

ANDERSON. Why, what on earth——? (*Calling.*) Judith,
Judith! (*He listens: there is no answer.*) Hm! (*He goes to the
cupboard; takes a candle from the drawer; lights it at the*

JUDITH. No: this is how I break it. I cannot keep my promises to him: why should I keep my promises to you?

ANDERSON. Don't speak so strangely, my love. It sounds insincere to me. (*She looks unutterable reproach at him.*) Yes, dear, nonsense is always insincere; and my dearest is talking nonsense. Just nonsense. (*Her face darkens into dumb obstinacy. She stares straight before her, and does not look at him again, absorbed in Richard's fate. He scans her face; sees that his rallying has produced no effect; and gives it up, making no further effort to conceal his anxiety.*) I wish I knew what has frightened you so. Was there a struggle? Did he fight?

JUDITH. No. He smiled.

ANDERSON. Did he realise his danger, do you think?

JUDITH. He realised yours.

ANDERSON. Mine!

JUDITH (*monotonously*). He said, "See that you get him safely out of harm's way." I promised: I can't keep my promise. He said, "Don't for your life let him know of my danger." I've told you of it. He said that if you found it out, you could not save him—that they will hang him and not spare you.

ANDERSON (*rising in generous indignation*). And you think that I will let a man with that much good in him die like a dog, when a few words might make him die like a Christian? I'm ashamed of you, Judith.

JUDITH. He will be steadfast in his religion as you are in yours; and you may depend on him to the death. He said so.

ANDERSON. God forgive him! What else did he say?

JUDITH. He said goodbye.

ANDERSON (*fidgeting nervously to and fro in great concern*). Poor fellow, poor fellow! You said goodbye to him in all kindness and charity, Judith, I hope.

JUDITH. I kissed him.

ANDERSON. What! Judith!

JUDITH. Are you angry?

ANDERSON. No, no. You were right: you were right. Poor fellow, poor fellow! (*Greatly distressed.*) To be hanged like that at his age! And then did they take him away?

JUDITH (*wearily*). Then you were here: that's the next thing I remember. I suppose I fainted. Now bid me goodbye, Tony. Perhaps I shall faint again. I wish I could die.

ANDERSON. No, no, my dear: you must pull yourself together and be sensible. I am in no danger—not the least in the world.

JUDITH (*solemnly*). You are going to your death, Tony— your sure death, if God will let innocent men be murdered. They will not let you see him: they will arrest you the moment you give your name. It was for you the soldiers came.

ANDERSON (*thunderstruck*). For me!!! (*His fists clinch; his neck thickens; his face reddens; the fleshy purses under his eyes become injected with hot blood; the man of peace vanishes, transfigured into a choleric and formidable man of war. Still, she does not come out of her absorption to look at him: her eyes are steadfast with a mechanical reflection of Richard's steadfastness.*)

JUDITH. He took your place: he is dying to save you. That is why he went in your coat. That is why I kissed him.

ANDERSON (*exploding*). Blood an' owns! (*His voice is rough and dominant, his gesture full of brute energy.*) Here! Essie, Essie!

ESSIE (*running in*). Yes.

ANDERSON (*impetuously*). Off with you as hard as you can run, to the inn. Tell them to saddle the fastest and strongest horse they have (*Judith rises breathless, and stares at him incredulously*)—the chestnut mare, if she's fresh—without a moment's delay. Go into the stable yard and tell the black man there that I'll give him a silver dollar if the horse is waiting for me when I come, and that I am close on your heels. Away with you. (*His energy sends Essie flying from the room. He pounces on his riding boots; rushes with them to the chair at the fire; and begins pulling them on.*)

JUDITH (*unable to believe such a thing of him*). You are not going to him!

ANDERSON (*busy with the boots*). Going to him! What good would that do? (*Growling to himself as he gets the first boot on with a wrench.*) I'll go to them, so I will. (*To Judith peremptorily.*) Get me the pistols: I want them. And money, money: I want money—all the money in the house. (*He stoops over the other boot, grumbling.*) A great satisfaction it would be to him to have my company on the gallows. (*He pulls on the boot.*)

JUDITH. You are deserting him, then?

ANDERSON. Hold your tongue, woman; and get me the pistols. (*She goes to the press and takes from it a leather belt*

*with two pistols, a powder horn, and a bag of bullets attached
to it. She throws it on the table. Then she unlocks a drawer in
the press and takes out a purse. Anderson grabs the belt and
buckles it on, saying.*) If they took him for me in my coat, perhaps they'll take me for him in his. (*Hitching the belt into its
place.*) Do I look like him?

JUDITH (*turning with the purse in her hand*). Horribly unlike him.

ANDERSON (*snatching the purse from her and emptying it on
the table*). Hm! We shall see.

JUDITH (*sitting down helplessly*). Is it of any use to pray,
do you think, Tony?

ANDERSON (*counting the money*). Pray! Can we pray Swindon's rope off Richard's neck?

JUDITH. God may soften Major Swindon's heart.

ANDERSON (*contemptuously—pocketing a handful of
money*). Let him, then. I am not God; and I must go to work
another way. (*Judith gasps at the blasphemy. He throws the
purse on the table.*) Keep that. I've taken 25 dollars.

JUDITH. Have you forgotten even that you are a minister?

ANDERSON. Minister be—faugh! My hat: where's my hat?
(*He snatches up hat and cloak, and puts both on in hot haste.*)
Now listen, you. If you can get a word with him by pretending
you're his wife, tell him to hold his tongue until morning:
that will give me all the start I need.

JUDITH (*solemnly*). You may depend on him to the death.

ANDERSON. You're a fool, a fool, Judith (*for a moment
checking the torrent of his haste, and speaking with something
of his old quiet and impressive conviction*). You don't know
the man you're married to. (*Essie returns. He swoops at her at
once.*) Well: is the horse ready?

ESSIE (*breathless*). It will be ready when you come.

ANDERSON. Good. (*He makes for the door.*)

JUDITH (*rising and stretching out her arms after him involuntarily*). Won't you say goodbye?

ANDERSON. And waste another half minute! Psha! (*He
rushes out like an avalanche.*)

ESSIE (*hurrying to Judith*). He has gone to save Richard,
hasn't he?

JUDITH. To save Richard! No: Richard has saved him. He
has gone to save himself. Richard must die.

Essie screams with terror and falls on her knees, hiding her face. Judith, without heeding her, looks rigidly straight in front of her, at the vision of Richard, dying.

ACT III

*Early next morning the sergeant, at the British headquarters
in the Town Hall, unlocks the door of a little empty panelled
waiting room, and invites Judith to enter. She has had a bad
night, probably a rather delirious one; for even in the reality
of the raw morning, her fixed gaze comes back at moments
when her attention is not strongly held.*

*The sergeant considers that her feelings do her credit, and is
sympathetic in an encouraging military way. Being a fine
figure of a man, vain of his uniform and of his work, he feels
specially qualified, in a respectful way, to console her.*

SERGEANT. You can have a quiet word with him here, mum.

JUDITH. Shall I have long to wait?

SERGEANT. No, mum, not a minute. We kep him in the
Bridewell for the night; and he's just been brought over here
for the court-martial. Don't fret, mum: he slept like a child,
and has made a rare good breakfast.

JUDITH (*incredulously*). He is in good spirits!

SERGEANT. Tip top, mum. The chaplain looked in to see
him last night; and he won seventeen shillings off him at
spoil five. He spent it among us like the gentleman he is.
Duty's duty, mum, of course; but you're among friends here.
(*The tramp of a couple of soldiers is heard approaching.*)
There: I think he's coming. (*Richard comes in, without a sign
of care or captivity in his bearing. The sergeant nods to the
two soldiers, and shews them the key of the room in his hand.
They withdraw.*) Your good lady, sir.

RICHARD (*going to her*). What! My wife. My adored one.
(*He takes her hand and kisses it with a perverse, raffish
gallantry.*) How long do you allow a brokenhearted husband
for leave-taking, Sergeant?

SERGEANT. As long as we can, sir. We shall not disturb
you till the court sits.

RICHARD. But it has struck the hour.

47

SERGEANT. So it has, sir; but there's a delay. General Burgoyne's just arrived—Gentlemanly Johnny we call him, sir—and he won't have done finding fault with everything this side of half past. I know him, sir: I served with him in Portugal. You may count on twenty minutes, sir; and by your leave I won't waste any more of them. (*He goes out, locking the door. Richard immediately drops his raffish manner and turns to Judith with considerate sincerity.*)

RICHARD. Mrs. Anderson: this visit is very kind of you. And how are you after last night? I had to leave you before you recovered; but I sent word to Essie to go and look after you. Did she understand the message?

JUDITH (*breathless and urgent*). Oh, don't think of me: I haven't come here to talk about myself. Are they going to—to—(*meaning "to hang you"*)?

RICHARD (*whimsically*). At noon, punctually. At least, that was when they disposed of Uncle Peter. (*She shudders.*) Is your husband safe? Is he on the wing?

JUDITH. He is no longer my husband.

RICHARD (*opening his eyes wide*). Eh!

JUDITH. I disobeyed you. I told him everything. I expected him to come here and save you. I wanted him to come here and save you. He ran away instead.

RICHARD. Well, that's what I meant him to do. What good would his staying have done? They'd only have hanged us both.

JUDITH (*with reproachful earnestness*). Richard Dudgeon: on your honor, what would you have done in his place?

RICHARD. Exactly what he has done, of course.

JUDITH. Oh, why will you not be simple with me—honest and straightforward? If you are so selfish as that, why did you let them take you last night?

RICHARD (*gaily*). Upon my life, Mrs. Anderson, I don't know. I've been asking myself that question ever since; and I can find no manner of reason for acting as I did.

JUDITH. You know you did it for his sake, believing he was a more worthy man than yourself.

RICHARD (*laughing*). Oho! No: that's a very pretty reason, I must say; but I'm not so modest as that. No: it wasn't for his sake.

JUDITH (*after a pause, during which she looks shamefacedly at him, blushing painfully*). Was it for my sake?

RICHARD (*gallantly*). Well, you had a hand in it. It must have been a little for your sake. You let them take me, at all events.

JUDITH. Oh, do you think I have not been telling myself that all night? Your death will be at my door. (*Impulsively, she gives him her hand, and adds, with intense earnestness.*) If I could save you as you saved him, I would do it, no matter how cruel the death was.

RICHARD (*holding her hand and smiling, but keeping her almost at arm's length*). I am very sure I shouldn't let you.

JUDITH. Don't you see that I can save you?

RICHARD. How? By changing clothes with me, eh?

JUDITH (*disengaging her hand to touch his lips with it*). Don't (*meaning "Don't jest"*). No: by telling the Court who you really are.

RICHARD (*frowning*). No use: they wouldn't spare me; and it would spoil half his chance of escaping. They are determined to cow us by making an example of somebody on that gallows to-day. Well, let us cow them by showing that we can stand by one another to the death. That is the only force that can send Burgoyne back across the Atlantic and make America a nation.

JUDITH (*impatiently*). Oh, what does all that matter?

RICHARD (*laughing*). True: what does it matter? what does anything matter? You see, men have these strange notions, Mrs. Anderson; and women see the folly of them.

JUDITH. Women have to lose those they love through them.

RICHARD. They can easily get fresh lovers.

JUDITH (*revolted*). Oh! (*Vehemently.*) Do you realise that you are going to kill yourself?

RICHARD. The only man I have any right to kill, Mrs. Anderson. Don't be concerned: no woman will lose her lover through my death. (*Smiling.*) Bless you, nobody cares for me. Have you heard that my mother is dead?

JUDITH. Dead!

RICHARD. Of heart disease—in the night. Her last word to me was her curse: I don't think I could have borne her blessing. My other relatives will not grieve much on my account. Essie will cry for a day or two; but I have provided for her: I made my own will last night.

JUDITH (*stonily, after a moment's silence*). And I!

RICHARD (*surprised*). You?

JUDITH. Yes, I. Am I not to care at all?

RICHARD (*gaily and bluntly*). Not a scrap. Oh, you expressed your feelings towards me very frankly yesterday. What happened may have softened you for the moment; but believe me, Mrs. Anderson, you don't like a bone in my skin or a hair on my head. I shall be as good a riddance at 12 to-day as I should have been at 12 yesterday.

JUDITH (*her voice trembling*). What can I do to shew you that you are mistaken?

RICHARD. Don't trouble. I'll give you credit for liking me a little better than you did. All I say is that my death will not break your heart.

JUDITH (*almost in a whisper*). How do you know? (*She puts her hands on his shoulders and looks intently at him.*)

RICHARD (*amazed—divining the truth*). Mrs. Anderson!!! (*The bell of the town clock strikes the quarter. He collects himself, and removes her hands, saying rather coldly.*) Excuse me: they will be here for me presently. It is too late.

JUDITH. It is not too late. Call me as witness: they will never kill you when they know how heroically you have acted.

RICHARD (*with some scorn*). Indeed! But if I don't go through with it, where will the heroism be? I shall simply have tricked them; and they'll hang me for that like a dog. Serve me right too!

JUDITH (*wildly*). Oh, I believe you want to die.

RICHARD (*obstinately*). No I don't.

JUDITH. Then why not try to save yourself? I implore you —listen. You said just now that you saved him for my sake— yes (*clutching him as he recoils with a gesture of denial*) a little for my sake. Well, save yourself for my sake. And I will go with you to the end of the world.

RICHARD (*taking her by the wrists and holding her a little way from him, looking steadily at her*). Judith.

JUDITH (*breathless—delighted at the name*). Yes.

RICHARD. If I said—to please you—that I did what I did ever so little for your sake, I lied as men always lie to women. You know how much I have lived with worthless men—aye, and worthless women too. Well, they could all rise to some sort of goodness and kindness when they were in love. (*The word love comes from him with true Puritan scorn.*) That has taught me to set little store by the goodness that only comes out red hot. What I did last night, I did in cold blood, caring not half so much for your husband, or (*ruthlessly*) for you (*she droops, stricken*) as I do for myself. I had no motive and no interest: all I can tell you is that when it came to the point whether I would take my neck out of the noose and put another man's into it, I could not do it. I don't know why not: I see myself as a fool for my pains; but I could not and I cannot. I have been brought up standing by the law of my own nature; and I may not go against it, gallows or no gallows. (*She has slowly raised her head and is now looking full at him.*) I should have done the same for any other man in the town, or any other man's wife. (*Releasing her.*) Do you understand that?

JUDITH. Yes: you mean that you do not love me.

RICHARD. (*revolted—with fierce contempt*). Is that all it means to you?

JUDITH. What more—what worse—can it mean to me? (*The sergeant knocks. The blow on the door jars on her heart.*) Oh, one moment more. (*She throws herself on her knees.*) I pray to you——

RICHARD. Hush! (*Calling.*) Come in. (*The sergeant unlocks the door and opens it. The guard is with him.*)

SERGEANT (*coming in*). Time's up, sir.

RICHARD. Quite ready, Sergeant. Now, my dear. (*He attempts to raise her.*)

JUDITH (*clinging to him*). Only one thing more—I entreat, I implore you. Let me be present in the court. I have seen Major Swindon: he said I should be allowed if you asked it. You will ask it. It is my last request: I shall never ask you anything again. (*She clasps his knee.*) I beg and pray it of you.

RICHARD. If I do, will you be silent?

JUDITH. Yes.

RICHARD. You will keep faith?

JUDITH. I will keep—— (*She breaks down, sobbing.*)

RICHARD (*taking her arm to lift her*). Just—her other arm, Sergeant.

They go out, she sobbing convulsively, supported by the two men.

Meanwhile, the Council Chamber is ready for the court martial. It is a large, lofty room, with a chair of state in the middle under a tall canopy with a gilt crown, and maroon cur-

*tains with the royal monogram G. R. In front of the chair is
a table, also draped in maroon, with a bell, a heavy inkstand,
and writing materials on it. Several chairs are set at the table.
The door is at the right hand of the occupant of the chair of
state when it has an occupant: at present it is empty. Major
Swindon, a pale, sandy haired, very conscientious looking man
of about forty-five, sits at the end of the table with his back to
the door, writing. He is alone until the sergeant announces the
General in a subdued manner which suggests that Gentlemanly
Johnny has been making his presence felt rather heavily.*

SERGEANT. The General, sir.

*Swindon rises hastily. The General comes in, the sergeant
goes out. General Burgoyne is fifty-five, and very well preserved. He is a man of fashion, gallant enough to have made a
distinguished marriage by an elopement, witty enough to write
successful comedies, aristocratically connected enough to have
had opportunities of high military distinction. His eyes, large,
brilliant, apprehensive, and intelligent, are his most remarkable feature: without them his fine nose and small mouth would
suggest rather more fastidiousness and less force than go to
the making of a first-rate general. Just now the eyes are angry
and tragic, and the mouth and nostrils tense.*

BURGOYNE. Major Swindon, I presume.

SWINDON. Yes. General Burgoyne, if I mistake not. (*They
bow to one another ceremoniously.*) I am glad to have the
support of your presence this morning. It is not particularly
lively business, hanging this poor devil of a minister.

BURGOYNE (*throwing himself into Swindon's chair*). No,
sir, it is not. It is making too much of the fellow to execute
him: what more could you have done if he had been a member
of the Church of England? Martyrdom, sir, is what these
people like: it is the only way in which a man can become
famous without ability. However, you have committed us to
hanging him: and the sooner he is hanged the better.

SWINDON. We have arranged it for 12 o'clock. Nothing
remains to be done except to try him.

BURGOYNE (*looking at him with suppressed anger*). Nothing—except to save our own necks, perhaps. Have you heard
the news from Springtown?

SWINDON. Nothing special. The latest reports are satisfactory.

BURGOYNE (*rising in amazement*). Satisfactory, sir! Satisfactory!! (*He stares at him for a moment, and then adds, with grim intensity.*) I am glad you take that view of them.

SWINDON (*puzzled*). Do I understand that in your opinion——

BURGOYNE. I do not express my opinion. I never stoop to that habit of profane language which unfortunately coarsens our profession. If I did, sir, perhaps I should be able to express my opinion of the news from Springtown—the news which you (*severely*) have apparently not heard. How soon do you get news from your supports here?—in the course of a month, eh?

SWINDON (*turning sulky*). I suppose the reports have been taken to you, sir, instead of to me. Is there anything serious?

BURGOYNE (*taking a report from his pocket and holding it up*). Springtown's in the hands of the rebels. (*He throws the report on the table.*)

SWINDON (*aghast*). Since yesterday!

BURGOYNE. Since two o'clock this morning. Perhaps we shall be in their hands before two o'clock to-morrow morning. Have you thought of that?

SWINDON (*confidently*). As to that, General, the British soldier will give a good account of himself.

BURGOYNE (*bitterly*). And therefore, I suppose, sir, the British officer need not know his business: the British soldier will get him out of all his blunders with the bayonet. In future, sir, I must ask you to be a little less generous with the blood of your men, and a little more generous with your own brains.

SWINDON. I am sorry I cannot pretend to your intellectual eminence, sir. I can only do my best, and rely on the devotion of my countrymen.

BURGOYNE (*suddenly becoming suavely sarcastic*). May I ask are you writing a melodrama, Major Swindon?

SWINDON (*flushing*). No, sir.

BURGOYNE. What a pity! What a pity! (*Dropping his sarcastic tone and facing him suddenly and seriously.*) Do you at all realize, sir, that we have nothing standing between us and destruction but our own bluff and the sheepishness of these colonists? They are men of the same English stock as ourselves: six to one of us (*repeating it emphatically*), six to one, sir; and nearly half our troops are Hessians, Brunswickers, German dragoons, and Indians with scalping knives. These are the countrymen on whose devotion you rely! Suppose the colonists find a leader! Suppose the news from Springtown should turn out to mean that they have already found a leader! What shall we do then? Eh?

SWINDON (*sullenly*). Our duty, sir, I presume.

BURGOYNE (*again sarcastic—giving him up as a fool*). Quite so, quite so. Thank you, Major Swindon, thank you. Now you've settled the question, sir—thrown a flood of light on the situation. What a comfort to me to feel that I have at my side so devoted and able an officer to support me in this emergency! I think, sir, it will probably relieve both our feelings if we proceed to hang this dissenter without further delay (*he strikes the bell*), especially as I am debarred by my principles from the customary military vent for my feelings. (*The sergeant appears.*) Bring your man in.

SERGEANT. Yes, sir.

BURGOYNE. And mention to any officer you may meet that the court cannot wait any longer for him.

SWINDON (*keeping his temper with difficulty*). The staff is perfectly ready, sir. They have been waiting your convenience for fully half an hour. Perfectly ready, sir.

BURGOYNE (*blandly*). So am I. (*Several officers come in and take their seats. One of them sits at the end of the table furthest from the door, and acts throughout as clerk to the court, making notes of the proceedings. The uniforms are those of the 9th, 20th, 21st, 24th, 47th, 53rd, and 62nd British Infantry. One officer is a Major General of the Royal Artillery. There are also German officers of the Hessian Rifles, and of German dragoon and Brunswicker regiments.*) Oh, good morning, gentlemen. Sorry to disturb you, I am sure. Very good of you to spare us a few moments.

SWINDON. Will you preside, sir?

BURGOYNE (*becoming additionally polished, lofty, sarcastic and urbane now that he is in public*). No, sir: I feel my own deficiencies too keenly to presume so far. If you will kindly allow me, I will sit at the feet of Gamaliel. (*He takes the chair at the end of the table next the door, and motions Swindon to the chair of state, waiting for him to be seated before sitting down himself.*)

SWINDON (*greatly annoyed*). As you please, sir. I am only trying to do my duty under excessively trying circumstances. (*He takes his place in the chair of state.*)

Burgoyne, relaxing his studied demeanor for the moment, sits down and begins to read the report with knitted brows and careworn looks, reflecting on his desperate situation and Swindon's uselessness. Richard is brought in. Judith walks beside him. Two soldiers precede and two follow him, with the sergeant in command. They cross the room to the wall opposite the door; but when Richard has just passed before the chair of state the sergeant stops him with a touch on the arm, and posts himself behind him, at his elbow. Judith stands timidly at the wall. The four soldiers place themselves in a squad near her.

BURGOYNE (*looking up and seeing Judith*). Who is that woman?

SERGEANT. Prisoner's wife, sir.

SWINDON (*nervously*). She begged me to allow her to be present; and I thought——

BURGOYNE (*completing the sentence for him ironically*). You thought it would be a pleasure for her. Quite so, quite so. (*Blandly.*) Give the lady a chair; and make her thoroughly comfortable.

The sergeant fetches a chair and places it near Richard.

JUDITH. Thank you, sir. (*She sits down after an awestricken curtsy to Burgoyne, which he acknowledges by a dignified bend of his head.*)

SWINDON (*to Richard, sharply*). Your name, sir?

RICHARD (*affable, but obstinate*). Come: you don't mean to say that you've brought me here without knowing who I am?

SWINDON. As a matter of form, sir, give your name.

RICHARD. As a matter of form then, my name is Anthony Anderson, Presbyterian minister in this town.

BURGOYNE (*interested*). Indeed! Pray, Mr. Anderson, what do you gentlemen believe?

RICHARD. I shall be happy to explain if time is allowed me. I cannot undertake to complete your conversion in less than a fortnight.

SWINDON (*snubbing him*). We are not here to discuss your views.

BURGOYNE (*with an elaborate bow to the unfortunate Swindon*). I stand rebuked.

SWINDON (*embarrassed*). Oh, not you, I as——

BURGOYNE. Don't mention it. (*To Richard, very politely.*) Any political views, Mr. Anderson?

RICHARD. I understand that that is just what we are here to find out.

SWINDON (*severely*). Do you mean to deny that you are a rebel?

RICHARD. I am an American, sir.

SWINDON. What do you expect me to think of that speech, Mr. Anderson?

RICHARD. I never expect a soldier to think, sir.

Burgoyne is boundlessly delighted by this retort, which almost reconciles him to the loss of America.

SWINDON (*whitening with anger*). I advise you not to be insolent, prisoner.

RICHARD. You can't help yourself, General. When you make up your mind to hang a man, you put yourself at a disadvantage with him. Why should I be civil to you? I may as well be hanged for a sheep as a lamb.

SWINDON. You have no right to assume that the court has made up its mind without a fair trial. And you will please not address me as General. I am Major Swindon.

RICHARD. A thousand pardons. I thought I had the honor of addressing Gentlemanly Johnny.

Sensation among the officers. The sergeant has a narrow escape from a guffaw.

BURGOYNE (*with extreme suavity*). I believe I am Gentlemanly Johnny, sir, at your service. My more intimate friends call me General Burgoyne. (*Richard bows with perfect politeness.*) You will understand, sir, I hope, since you seem to be a gentleman and a man of some spirit in spite of your calling, that if we should have the misfortune to hang you, we shall do so as a mere matter of political necessity and military duty, without any personal ill-feeling.

RICHARD. Oh, quite so. That makes all the difference in the world, of course.

They all smile in spite of themselves; and some of the younger officers burst out laughing.

JUDITH (*her dread and horror deepening at every one of these jests and compliments*). How can you?

RICHARD. You promised to be silent.

BURGOYNE (*to Judith, with studied courtesy*). Believe me, madam, your husband is placing us under the greatest obligation by taking this very disagreeable business so thoroughly in the spirit of a gentleman. Sergeant: give Mr. Anderson a chair. (*The sergeant does so. Richard sits down.*) Now, Major Swindon: we are waiting for you.

SWINDON. You are aware, I presume, Mr. Anderson, of your obligations as a subject of His Majesty King George the Third.

RICHARD. I am aware, sir, that His Majesty King George the Third is about to hang me because I object to Lord North's robbing me. *sycophant*

SWINDON. That is a treasonable speech, sir.

RICHARD (*briefly*). Yes. I meant it to be.

BURGOYNE (*strongly deprecating this line of defence, but still polite*). Don't you think, Mr. Anderson, that this is rather —if you will excuse the word—a vulgar line to take? Why should you cry out robbery because of a stamp duty and a tea duty and so forth? After all, it is the essence of your position as a gentleman that you pay with a good grace.

RICHARD. It is not the money, General. But to be swindled by a pig-headed lunatic like King George——

SWINDON (*scandalised*). Chut, sir—silence!

SERGEANT (*in stentorian tones, greatly shocked*). Silence!

BURGOYNE (*unruffled*). Ah, that is another point of view. My position does not allow of my going into that, except in private. But (*shrugging his shoulders*) of course, Mr. Anderson, if you are determined to be hanged (*Judith flinches*), there's nothing more to be said. An unusual taste! however (*with a final shrug*)——!

SWINDON (*to Burgoyne*). Shall we call witnesses?

RICHARD. What need is there of witnesses? If the townspeople here had listened to me, you would have found the streets barricaded, the houses loopholed, and the people in arms to hold the town against you to the last man. But you arrived, unfortunately, before we had got out of the talking stage; and then it was too late.

SWINDON (*severely*). Well, sir, we shall teach you and your townspeople a lesson they will not forget. Have you anything more to say?

RICHARD. I think you might have the decency to treat me as a prisoner of war, and shoot me like a man instead of hanging me like a dog.

BURGOYNE (*sympathetically*). Now there, Mr. Anderson,

you talk like a civilian, if you will excuse my saying so. Have you any idea of the average marksmanship of the army of His Majesty King George the Third? If we make you up a firing party, what will happen? Half of them will miss you: the rest will make a mess of the business and leave you to the provo-marshal's pistol. Whereas we can hang you in a perfectly workmanlike and agreeable way. (*Kindly.*) Let me persuade you to be hanged, Mr. Anderson?

JUDITH (*sick with horror*). My God!

RICHARD (*to Judith*). Your promise! (*To Burgoyne.*) Thank you, General: that view of the case did not occur to me before. To oblige you, I withdraw my objection to the rope. Hang me, by all means.

BURGOYNE (*smoothly*). Will 12 o'clock suit you, Mr. Anderson?

RICHARD. I shall be at your disposal then, General.

BURGOYNE (*rising*). Nothing more to be said, gentlemen. (*They all rise.*)

JUDITH (*rushing to the table*). Oh, you are not going to murder a man like that, without a proper trial—without thinking of what you are doing—without— (*She cannot find words.*)

RICHARD. Is this how you keep your promise?

JUDITH. If I am not to speak, you must. Defend yourself: save yourself: tell them the truth.

RICHARD (*worriedly*). I have told them truth enough to hang me ten times over. If you say another word you will risk other lives; but you will not save mine.

BURGOYNE. My good lady, our only desire is to save unpleasantness. What satisfaction would it give you to have a solemn fuss made, with my friend Swindon in a black cap and so forth? I am sure we are greatly indebted to the admirable tact and gentlemanly feeling shewn by your husband.

JUDITH (*throwing the words in his face*). Oh, you are mad. Is it nothing to you what wicked thing you do if only you do it like a gentleman? Is it nothing to you whether you are a murderer or not, if only you murder in a red coat? (*Desperately.*) You shall not hang him: that man is not my husband.

The officers look at one another, and whisper: some of the Germans asking their neighbors to explain what the woman has said. Burgoyne, who has been visibly shaken by Judith's reproach, recovers himself promptly at this new development. Richard meanwhile raises his voice above the buzz.

RICHARD. I appeal to you, gentlemen, to put an end to this. She will not believe that she cannot save me. Break up the court.

BURGOYNE (*in a voice so quiet and firm that it restores silence at once*). One moment, Mr. Anderson. One moment, gentlemen. (*He resumes his seat. Swindon and the officers follow his example.*) Let me understand you clearly, madam. Do you mean that this gentleman is not your husband, or merely—I wish to put this with all delicacy—that you are not his wife?

JUDITH. I don't know what you mean. I say that he is not my husband—that my husband has escaped. This man took his place to save him. Ask anyone in the town—send out into the street for the first person you find there, and bring him in as a witness. He will tell you that the prisoner is not Anthony Anderson.

BURGOYNE (*quietly, as before*). Sergeant.

SERGEANT. Yes, sir.

BURGOYNE. Go out into the street and bring in the first townsman you see there.

SERGEANT (*making for the door*). Yes, sir.

BURGOYNE (*as the sergeant passes*). The first clean, sober townsman you see.

SERGEANT. Yes, sir. (*He goes out.*)

BURGOYNE. Sit down, Mr. Anderson—if I may call you so for the present. (*Richard sits down.*) Sit down, madam, whilst we wait. Give the lady a newspaper.

RICHARD (*indignantly*). Shame!

BURGOYNE (*keenly, with a half smile*). If you are not her husband, sir, the case is not a serious one—for her. (*Richard bites his lip, silenced.*)

JUDITH (*to Richard, as she returns to her seat*). I couldn't help it. (*He shakes his head. She sits down.*)

BURGOYNE. You will understand of course, Mr. Anderson, that you must not build on this little incident. We are bound to make an example of somebody.

RICHARD. I quite understand. I suppose there's no use in my explaining.

BURGOYNE. I think we should prefer independent testimony, if you don't mind.

The sergeant, with a packet of papers in his hand, returns conducting Christy, who is much scared.

SERGEANT (*giving Burgoyne the packet*). Dispatches, sir. Delivered by a corporal of the 53rd. Dead beat with hard riding, sir.

Burgoyne opens the dispatches, and presently becomes absorbed in them. They are so serious as to take his attention completely from the court-martial.

SERGEANT (*to Christy*). Now then. Attention; and take your hat off. (*He posts himself in charge of Christy, who stands on Burgoyne's side of the court.*)

RICHARD (*in his usual bullying tone to Christy*). Don't be frightened, you fool: you're only wanted as a witness. They're not going to hang you.

SWINDON. What's your name?

CHRISTY. Christy.

RICHARD (*impatiently*). Christopher Dudgeon, you blatant idiot. Give your full name.

SWINDON. Be silent, prisoner. You must not prompt the witness.

RICHARD. Very well. But I warn you you'll get nothing out of him unless you shake it out of him. He has been too well brought up by a pious mother to have any sense or manhood left in him.

BURGOYNE (*springing up and speaking to the sergeant in a startling voice*). Where is the man who brought these?

SERGEANT. In the guard-room, sir.

Burgoyne goes out with a haste that sets the officers exchanging looks.

SWINDON (*to Christy*). Do you know Anthony Anderson, the Presbyterian minister?

CHRISTY. Of course I do. (*Implying that Swindon must be an ass not to know it.*)

SWINDON. Is he here?

CHRISTY (*staring round*). I don't know.

SWINDON. Do you see him?

CHRISTY. No.

SWINDON. You seem to know the prisoner?

CHRISTY. Do you mean Dick?

SWINDON. Which is Dick?

CHRISTY (*pointing to Richard*). Him.

SWINDON. What is his name?

CHRISTY. Dick.

RICHARD. Answer properly, you jumping jackass. What do they know about Dick?

CHRISTY. Well, you are Dick, aren't you? What am I to say?

SWINDON. Address me, sir; and do you, prisoner, be silent. Tell us who the prisoner is.

CHRISTY. He's my brother Dick—Richard—Richard Dudgeon.

SWINDON. Your brother!

CHRISTY. Yes.

SWINDON. You are sure he is not Anderson.

CHRISTY. Who?

RICHARD (*exasperatedly*). Me, me, me you——

SWINDON. Silence, sir.

SERGEANT (*shouting*). Silence.

RICHARD (*impatiently*). Yah! (*To Christy.*) He wants to know am I Minister Anderson. Tell him, and stop grinning like a zany.

CHRISTY (*grinning more than ever*). You Pastor Anderson! (*To Swindon.*) Why, Mr. Anderson's a minister—a very good man; and Dick's a bad character: the respectable people won't speak to him. He's the bad brother: I'm the good one. (*The officers laugh outright. The soldiers grin.*)

SWINDON. Who arrested this man?

SERGEANT. I did, sir. I found him in the minister's house, sitting at tea with the lady with his coat off, quite at home. If he isn't married to her, he ought to be.

SWINDON. Did he answer to the minister's name?

SERGEANT. Yes, sir, but not to a minister's nature. You ask the chaplain, sir.

SWINDON (*to Richard, threateningly*). So, sir, you have attempted to cheat us. And your name is Richard Dudgeon?

RICHARD. You've found it out at last, have you?

SWINDON. Dudgeon is a name well known to us, eh?

RICHARD. Yes: Peter Dudgeon, whom you murdered, was my uncle.

SWINDON. Hm! (*He compresses his lips, and looks at Richard with vindictive gravity.*)

CHRISTY. Are they going to hang you, Dick?

RICHARD. Yes. Get out: they've done with you.

CHRISTY. And I may keep the china peacocks?

RICHARD (*jumping up*). Get out. Get out, you blithering baboon, you. (*Christy flies, panicstricken.*)

SWINDON (*rising—all rise*). Since you have taken the minister's place, Richard Dudgeon, you shall go through with it. The execution will take place at 12 o'clock as arranged; and unless Anderson surrenders before then you shall take his place on the gallows. Sergeant: take your man out.

JUDITH (*distracted*). No, no——

SWINDON (*fiercely, dreading a renewal of her entreaties*). Take that woman away.

RICHARD (*springing across the table with a tiger-like bound, and seizing Swindon by the throat*). You infernal scoundrel——

The sergeant rushes to the rescue from one side, the soldiers from the other. They seize Richard and drag him back to his place. Swindon, who has been thrown supine on the table, rises, arranging his stock. He is about to speak, when he is anticipated by Burgoyne, who has just appeared at the door with two papers in his hand: a white letter and a blue dispatch.

BURGOYNE (*advancing to the table, elaborately cool*). What is this? What's happening? Mr. Anderson: I'm astonished at you.

RICHARD. I am sorry I disturbed you, General. I merely wanted to strangle your understrapper there. (*Breaking out violently at Swindon.*) Why do you raise the devil in me by bullying the woman like that? You oatmeal faced dog, I'd twist your cursed head off with the greatest satisfaction. (*He puts out his hands to the sergeant.*) Here: handcuff me, will you; or I'll not undertake to keep my fingers off him.

The sergeant takes out a pair of handcuffs and looks to Burgoyne for instructions.

BURGOYNE. Have you addressed profane language to the lady, Major Swindon?

SWINDON (*very angry*). No, sir, certainly not. That question should not have been put to me. I ordered the woman to be removed, as she was disorderly; and the fellow sprang at me. Put away those handcuffs. I am perfectly able to take care of myself.

RICHARD. Now you talk like a man, I have no quarrel with you.

BURGOYNE. Mr. Anderson——

SWINDON. His name is Dudgeon, sir, Richard Dudgeon. He is an impostor.

BURGOYNE (*brusquely*). Nonsense, sir; you hanged Dudgeon at Springtown.

RICHARD. It was my uncle, General.

BURGOYNE. Oh, your uncle. (*To Swindon, handsomely.*) I beg your pardon, Major Swindon. (*Swindon acknowledges the apology stiffly. Burgoyne turns to Richard.*) We are somewhat unfortunate in our relations with your family. Well, Mr. Dudgeon, what I wanted to ask you is this: Who is (*reading the name from the letter*) William Maindeck Parshotter?

RICHARD. He is the Mayor of Springtown.

BURGOYNE. Is William—Maindeck and so on—a man of his word?

RICHARD. Is he selling you anything?

BURGOYNE. No.

RICHARD. Then you may depend on him.

BURGOYNE. Thank you, Mr.—'m Dudgeon. By the way, since you are not Mr. Anderson, do we still—eh, Major Swindon? (*meaning "do we still hang him?"*)

RICHARD. The arrangements are unaltered, General.

BURGOYNE. Ah, indeed. I am sorry. Good morning, Mr. Dudgeon. Good morning, madam.

RICHARD (*interrupting Judith almost fiercely as she is about to make some wild appeal, and taking her arm resolutely*). Not one word more. Come.

She looks imploringly at him, but is overborne by his determination. They are marched out by the four soldiers: the sergeant, very sulky, walking between Swindon and Richard, whom he watches as if he were a dangerous animal.

BURGOYNE. Gentlemen: we need not detain you. Major Swindon: a word with you. (*The officers go out. Burgoyne waits with unruffled serenity until the last of them disappears. Then he becomes very grave, and addresses Swindon for the first time without his title.*) Swindon: do you know what this is (*shewing him the letter*)?

SWINDON. What?

BURGOYNE. A demand for a safe-conduct for an officer of their militia to come here and arrange terms with us.

SWINDON. Oh, they are giving in.

BURGOYNE. They add that they are sending the man who

raised Springtown last night and drove us out; so that we
may know that we are dealing with an officer of importance.

SWINDON. Pooh!

BURGOYNE. He will be fully empowered to arrange the
terms of—guess what.

SWINDON. Their surrender, I hope.

BURGOYNE. No: our evacuation of the town. They offer us
just six hours to clear out.

SWINDON. What monstrous impudence!

BURGOYNE. What shall we do, eh?

SWINDON. March on Springtown and strike a decisive blow
at once.

BURGOYNE (*quietly*). Hm! (*Turning to the door.*) Come
to the adjutant's office.

SWINDON. What for?

BURGOYNE. To write out that safe-conduct. (*He puts his
hand to the door knob to open it.*)

SWINDON (*who has not budged*). General Burgoyne.

BURGOYNE (*returning*). Sir?

SWINDON. It is my duty to tell you, sir, that I do not consider
the threats of a mob of rebellious tradesmen a sufficient reason for our giving way.

BURGOYNE (*imperturbable*). Suppose I resign my command
to you, what will you do?

SWINDON. I will undertake to do what we have marched
south from Boston to do, and what General Howe has marched
north from New York to do: effect a junction at Albany and
wipe out the rebel army with our united forces.

BURGOYNE (*enigmatically*). And will you wipe out our enemies in London, too?

SWINDON. In London! What enemies?

BURGOYNE (*forcibly*). Jobbery and snobbery, incompetence and Red Tape. (*He holds up the dispatch and adds
with despair in his face and voice.*) I have just learnt, sir, that
General Howe is still in New York.

SWINDON (*thunderstruck*). Good God! He has disobeyed
orders!

BURGOYNE (*with sardonic calm*). He has received no orders,
sir. Some gentleman in London forgot to dispatch them: he
was leaving town for his holiday, I believe. To avoid upsetting
his arrangements, England will lose her American colonies; and

in a few days you and I will be at Saratoga with 5,000 men to face 16,000 rebels in an impregnable position.

SWINDON (*appalled*). Impossible!

BURGOYNE (*coldly*). I beg your pardon!

SWINDON. I can't believe it! What will History say?

BURGOYNE. History, sir, will tell lies, as usual. Come: we must send the safe-conduct. (*He goes out.*)

SWINDON (*following distractedly*). My God, my God! We shall be wiped out.

As noon approaches there is excitement in the market place. The gallows which hangs there permanently for the terror of evildoers, with such minor advertizers and examples of crime as the pillory, the whipping post, and the stocks, has a new rope attached, with the noose hitched up to one of the uprights, out of reach of the boys. Its ladder, too, has been brought out and placed in position by the town beadle, who stands by to guard it from unauthorized climbing. The Websterbridge townsfolk are present in force, and in high spirits; for the news has spread that it is the devil's disciple and not the minister that the Continentals (so they call Burgoyne's forces) are about to hang: consequently the execution can be enjoyed without any misgiving as to its righteousness, or to the cowardice of allowing it to take place without a struggle. There is even some fear of a disappointment as midday approaches and the arrival of the beadle with the ladder remains the only sign of preparation. But at last reassuring shouts of Here they come: Here they are, are heard; and a company of soldiers with fixed bayonets, half British infantry, half Hessians, tramp quickly into the middle of the market place, driving the crowd to the sides.

SERGEANT. Halt. Front. Dress. (*The soldiers change their column into a square enclosing the gallows, their petty officers, energetically led by the sergeant, hustling the persons who find themselves inside the square out at the corners.*) Now then! Out of it with you: out of it. Some o' you'll get strung up yourselves presently. Form that square there, will you, you damned Hoosians. No use talkin' German to them: talk to their toes with the butt ends of your muskets: they'll understand that. Get out of it, will you? (*He comes upon Judith, standing near the gallows.*) Now then: you've no call here.

JUDITH. May I not stay? What harm am I doing?

SERGEANT. I want none of your argufying. You ought to be ashamed of yourself, running to see a man hanged that's not your husband. And he's no better than yourself. I told my major he was a gentleman; and then he goes and tries to strangle him, and calls his blessed Majesty a lunatic. So out of it with you, double quick.

JUDITH. Will you take these two silver dollars and let me stay?

The sergeant, without an instant's hesitation, looks quickly and furtively round as he shoots the money dexterously into his pocket. Then he raises his voice in virtuous indignation.

SERGEANT. Me take money in the execution of my duty! Certainly not. Now I'll tell you what I'll do, to teach you to corrupt the King's officer. I'll put you under arrest until the execution's over. You just stand there; and don't let me see you as much as move from that spot until you're let. (*With a swift wink at her he points to the corner of the square behind the gallows on his right, and turns noisily away, shouting.*) Now then dress up and keep 'em back, will you?

Cries of Hush and Silence are heard among the townsfolk; and the sound of a military band, playing the Dead March from Saul, is heard. The crowd becomes quiet at once; and the sergeant and petty officers, hurrying to the back of the square, with a few whispered orders and some stealthy hustling cause it to open and admit the funeral procession, which is protected from the crowd by a double file of soldiers. First come Burgoyne and Swindon, who, on entering the square, glance with distaste at the gallows, and avoid passing under it by wheeling a little to the right and stationing themselves on that side. Then Mr. Brudenell, the chaplain, in his surplice, with his prayer book open in his hand, walking beside Richard, who is moody and disorderly. He walks doggedly through the gallows frame-work, and posts himself a little in front of it. Behind him comes the executioner, a stalwart soldier in his shirtsleeves. Follow-ing him, two soldiers haul a light military waggon. Finally comes the band, which posts itself at the back of the square, and finishes the Dead March. Judith, watching Richard pain-fully, steals down to the gallows, and stands leaning against its right post. During the conversation which follows, the two soldiers place the cart under the gallows, and stand by the shafts, which point backwards. The executioner takes a set of steps from the cart and places it ready for the prisoner to mount. Then he climbs the tall ladder which stands against the gallows, and cuts the string by which the rope is hitched up; so that the noose drops dangling over the cart, into which he steps as he descends.

RICHARD (*with suppressed impatience, to Brudenell*). Look here, sir: this is no place for a man of your profession. Hadn't you better go away?

SWINDON. I appeal to you, prisoner, if you have any sense of decency left, to listen to the ministrations of the chaplain, and pay due heed to the solemnity of the occasion.

THE CHAPLAIN (*gently reproving Richard*). Try to control yourself, and submit to the divine will. (*He lifts his book to proceed with the service.*)

RICHARD. Answer for your own will, sir, and those of your accomplices here (*indicating Burgoyne and Swindon*): I see little divinity about them or you. You talk to me of Christianity when you are in the act of hanging your enemies. Was there ever such blasphemous nonsense! (*To Swindon, more rudely.*) You've got up the solemnity of the occasion, as you call it, to impress the people with your own dignity—Handel's music and a clergyman to make murder look like piety! Do you suppose *I* am going to help you? You've asked me to choose the rope because you don't know your own trade well enough to shoot me properly. Well, hang away and have done with it.

SWINDON (*to the chaplain*). Can you do nothing with him, Mr. Brudenell?

CHAPLAIN. I will try, sir. (*Beginning to read.*) "Man that is born of woman hath——"

RICHARD (*fixing his eyes on him*). "Thou shalt not kill." *The book drops in Brudenell's hands.*

CHAPLAIN (*confessing his embarrassment*). What am I to say, Mr. Dudgeon?

RICHARD. Let me alone, man, can't you?

BURGOYNE (*with extreme urbanity*). I think, Mr. Brudenell, that as the usual professional observations seem to strike Mr. Dudgeon as incongruous under the circumstances, you had better omit them until—er—until Mr. Dudgeon can no longer be inconvenienced by them. (*Brudenell, with a shrug, shuts his book and retires behind the gallows.*) You seem in a hurry, Mr. Dudgeon.

RICHARD (*with the horror of death upon him*). Do you think this is a pleasant sort of thing to be kept waiting for?

You've made up your mind to commit murder: well, do it and have done with it.

BURGOYNE. Mr. Dudgeon: we are only doing this——

RICHARD. Because you're paid to do it.

SWINDON. You insolent— (*He swallows his rage.*)

BURGOYNE (*with much charm of manner*). Ah, I am really sorry that you should think that, Mr. Dudgeon. If you knew what my commission cost me, and what my pay is, you would think better of me. I should be glad to part from you on friendly terms.

RICHARD. Hark ye, General Burgoyne. If you think that I like being hanged, you're mistaken. I don't like it; and I don't mean to pretend that I do. And if you think I'm obliged to you for hanging me in a gentlemanly way, you're wrong there too. I take the whole business in devilish bad part; and the only satisfaction I have in it is that you'll feel a good deal meaner than I'll look when it's over. (*He turns away, and is striding to the cart when Judith advances and interposes with her arms stretched out to him. Richard, feeling that a very little will upset his self-possession, shrinks from her, crying.*) What are you doing here? This is no place for you. (*She makes a gesture as if to touch him. He recoils impatiently.*) No: go away, go away; you'll unnerve me. Take her away, will you?

JUDITH. Won't you bid me good-bye?

RICHARD (*allowing her to take his hand*). Oh good-bye, good-bye. Now go—go—quickly. (*She clings to his hand—will not be put off with so cold a last farewell—at last, as he tries to disengage himself, throws herself on his breast in agony.*)

SWINDON (*angrily to the sergeant, who, alarmed at Judith's movement, has come from the back of the square to pull her back, and stopped irresolutely on finding that he is too late*). How is this? Why is she inside the lines?

SERGEANT (*guiltily*). I dunno, sir. She's that artful—can't keep her away.

BURGOYNE. You were bribed.

SERGEANT (*protesting*). No, sir——

SWINDON (*severely*). Fall back. (*He obeys.*)

RICHARD (*imploringly to those around him, and finally to Burgoyne, as the least stolid of them*). Take her away. Do you think I want a woman near me now?

BURGOYNE (*going to Judith and taking her hand*). Here, madam: you had better keep inside the lines; but stand here behind us; and don't look.

Richard, with a great sobbing sigh of relief as she releases him and turns to Burgoyne, flies for refuge to the cart and mounts into it. The executioner takes off his coat and pinions him.

JUDITH (*resisting Burgoyne quietly and drawing her hand away*). No: I must stay. I won't look. (*She goes to the right of the gallows. She tries to look at Richard, but turns away with a frightful shudder, and falls on her knees in prayer. Brudenell comes towards her from the back of the square.*)

BURGOYNE (*nodding approvingly as she kneels*). Ah, quite so. Do not disturb her, Mr. Brudenell: that will do very nicely. (*Brudenell nods also, and withdraws a little, watching her sympathetically. Burgoyne resumes his former position, and takes out a handsome gold chronometer.*) Now then, are those preparations made? We must not detain Mr. Dudgeon.

By this time Richard's hands are bound behind him; and the noose is round his neck. The two soldiers take the shaft of the waggon, ready to pull it away. The executioner, standing in the cart behind Richard, makes a sign to the sergeant.

SERGEANT (*to Burgoyne*). Ready, sir.

BURGOYNE. Have you anything more to say, Mr. Dudgeon? It wants two minutes of twelve still.

RICHARD (*in the strong voice of a man who has conquered the bitterness of death*). Your watch is two minutes slow by the town clock, which I can see from here, General. (*The town clock strikes the first stroke of twelve. Involuntarily the people flinch at the sound, and a subdued groan breaks from them.*) Amen! my life for the world's future!

ANDERSON (*shouting as he rushes into the market place*). Amen; and stop the execution. (*He bursts through the line of soldiers opposite Burgoyne, and rushes, panting, to the gallows.*) I am Anthony Anderson, the man you want.

The crowd, intensely excited, listens with all its ears. Judith, half rising, stares at him; then lifts her hands like one whose dearest prayer has been granted.

SWINDON. Indeed. Then you are just in time to take your place on the gallows. Arrest him.

At a sign from the sergeant, two soldiers come forward to seize Anderson.

ANDERSON (*thrusting a paper under Swindon's nose*).
There's my safe-conduct, sir.

SWINDON (*taken aback*). Safe-conduct! Are you——!

ANDERSON (*emphatically*). I am. (*The two soldiers take
him by the elbows.*) Tell these men to take their hands off me.

SWINDON (*to the men*). Let him go.

SERGEANT. Fall back.

*The two men return to their places. The townsfolk raise a
cheer; and begin to exchange exultant looks, with a presenti-
ment of triumph as they see their Pastor speaking with their
enemies in the gate.*

ANDERSON (*exhaling a deep breath of relief, and dabbing
his perspiring brow with his handkerchief*). Thank God, I
was in time!

BURGOYNE (*calm as ever, and still watch in hand*). Ample
time, sir. Plenty of time. I should never dream of hanging
any gentleman by an American clock. (*He puts up his watch.*)

ANDERSON. Yes: we are some minutes ahead of you already,
General. Now tell them to take the rope from the neck of that
American citizen.

BURGOYNE (*to the executioner in the cart—very politely*).
Kindly undo Mr. Dudgeon.

*The executioner takes the rope from Richard's neck, unties
his hands, and helps him on with his coat.*

JUDITH (*stealing timidly to Anderson*). Tony.

ANDERSON (*putting his arm round her shoulders and bantering her affectionately*). Well, what do you think of your husband, now, eh?—eh??—eh???

JUDITH. I am ashamed— (*She hides her face against his
breast.*)

BURGOYNE (*to Swindon*). You look disappointed, Major
Swindon.

SWINDON. You look defeated, General Burgoyne.

BURGOYNE. I am, sir; and I am humane enough to be glad
of it. (*Richard jumps down from the car, Brudenell offering
his hand to help him, and runs to Anderson, whose left hand he
shakes heartily, the right being occupied by Judith.*) By the
way, Mr. Anderson, I do not quite understand. The safe-
conduct was for a commander of the militia. I understand
you are a—(*he looks as pointedly as his good manners permit
at the riding boots, the pistols, and Richard's coat, and adds*)
a clergyman.

ANDERSON (*between Judith and Richard*). Sir: it is in the hour of trial that a man finds his true profession. This foolish young man (*placing his hand on Richard's shoulder*) boasted himself the Devil's Disciple; but when the hour of trial came to him, he found that it was his destiny to suffer and be faithful to the death. I thought myself a decent minister of the gospel of peace; but when the hour of trial came to me, I found that it was my destiny to be a man of action and that my place was amid the thunder of the captains and the shouting. So I am starting life at fifty as Captain Anthony Anderson of the Springtown militia; and the Devil's Disciple here will start presently as the Reverend Richard Dudgeon, and wag his pow in my old pulpit, and give good advice to this silly sentimental little wife of mine. (*Putting his other hand on her shoulder. She steals a glance at Richard to see how the prospect pleases him*). Your mother told me, Richard, that I should never have chosen Judith if I'd been born for the ministry. I am afraid she was right; so, by your leave, you may keep my coat and I'll keep yours.

RICHARD. Minister—I should say Captain. I have behaved like a fool.

JUDITH. Like a hero.

RICHARD. Much the same thing, perhaps. (*With some bitterness toward himself.*) But no: If I had been any good, I should have done for you what you did for me, instead of making a vain sacrifice.

ANDERSON. Not vain, my boy. It takes all sorts to make a world—saints as well as soldiers. (*Turning to Burgoyne.*) And now, General, time presses; and America is in a hurry. Have you realized that though you may occupy towns and win battles, you cannot conquer a nation?

BURGOYNE. My good sir, without a Conquest you cannot have an aristocracy. Come and settle the matter at my quarters.

ANDERSON. At your service, sir. (*To Richard.*) See Judith home for me, will you, my boy? (*He hands her over to him.*) Now, General. (*He goes busily up the market place towards the Town Hall, leaving Judith and Richard together. Burgoyne follows him a step or two; then checks himself and turns to Richard.*)

BURGOYNE. Oh, by the way, Mr. Dudgeon, I shall be glad to see you at lunch at half-past one. (*He pauses a moment, and adds, with politely veiled slyness.*) Bring Mrs. Anderson, if she will be so good. (*To Swindon, who is fuming.*) Take it quietly, Major Swindon: your friend the British soldier can stand up to anything except the British War Office. (*He follows Anderson.*)

SERGEANT (*to Swindon*). What orders, sir?

SWINDON (*savagely*). Orders! What use are orders now? There's no army. Back to quarters; and be d— (*He turns on his heel and goes.*)

SERGEANT (*pugnacious and patriotic, repudiating the idea of defeat*). 'Tention. Now then: cock up your chins, and shew 'em you don't care a damn for 'em. Slope arms! Fours! Wheel! Quick march!

The drum marks time with a tremendous bang; the band strikes up British Grenadiers; and the sergeant, Brudenell, and the English troops march off defiantly to their quarters. The townsfolk press in behind, and follow them up the market, jeering at them; and the town band, a very primitive affair, brings up the rear, playing Yankee Doodle. Essie, who comes in with them, runs to Richard.

ESSIE. Oh, Dick!

RICHARD (*good-humoredly, but wilfully*). Now, now: come, come! I don't mind being hanged; but I will not be cried over.

ESSIE. No, I promise. I'll be good. (*She tries to restrain her tears, but cannot.*) I—I want to see where the soldiers are going to. (*She goes a little way up the market, pretending to look after the crowd.*)

JUDITH. Promise me you will never tell him.

RICHARD. Don't be afraid.

They shake hands on it.

ESSIE (*calling to them*). They're coming back. They want you.

Jubilation in the market. The townsfolk surge back again in wild enthusiasm with their band, and hoist Richard on their shoulders, cheering him.

NOTES TO THE DEVIL'S DISCIPLE

BURGOYNE

General John Burgoyne, who is presented in this play for the first time (as far as I am aware) on the English stage, is not a conventional stage soldier, but as faithful a portrait as it is in the nature of stage portraits to be. His objection to profane swearing is not borrowed from Mr. Gilbert's H. M. S. Pinafore: it is taken from the Code of Instructions drawn up by himself for his officers when he introduced Light Horse into the English army. His opinion that English soldiers should be treated as thinking beings was no doubt as unwelcome to the military authorities of his time, when nothing was thought of ordering a soldier a thousand lashes, as it will be to those modern victims of the flagellation neurosis who are so anxious to revive that discredited sport. His military reports are very clever as criticisms, and are humane and enlightened within certain aristocratic limits, best illustrated perhaps by his declaration, which now sounds so curious, that he should blush to ask for promotion on any other ground than that of family influence. As a parliamentary candidate, Burgoyne took our common expression "fighting an election" so very literally that he led his supporters to the poll at Preston in 1768 with a loaded pistol in each hand, and won the seat, though he was fined £1,000, and denounced by Junius, for the pistols.

It is only within quite recent years that any general recognition has become possible for the feeling that led Burgoyne, a professed enemy of oppression in India and elsewhere, to accept his American command when so many other officers threw up their commissions rather than serve in a civil war against the Colonies. His biographer De Fonblanque, writing in 1876, evidently regarded his position as indefensible. Nowadays, it is sufficient to say that Burgoyne was an Imperialist. He sympathized with the colonists; but when they proposed as a remedy the disruption of the Empire, he regarded that as a step backward in civilization. As he put it to the House of Commons, "while we remember that we are contending against brothers and fellow subjects, we must also remember that we are contending in this crisis for the fate of the British Empire." Eighty-four years after his defeat, his republican conquerors themselves engaged in a civil war for the integrity of their Union. In 1885 the Whigs, who represented the anti-Burgoyne tradition of American Independence in English politics, abandoned Gladstone and made common cause with their political opponents in defence of the Union between England and Ireland. Only the other day England sent 200,000 men into the field south of the equator to fight out the question whether South Africa should develop as a Federation of British Colonies or as an indepedent Afrikander United States. In all these cases the Unionists who were detached from their parties were called renegades, as Burgoyne was. That, of course, is only one of the unfortunate consequences of the fact that mankind, being for the most part incapable of politics, accepts vituperation as an easy and congenial substitute. Whether Burgoyne or Washington, Lincoln or Davis, Gladstone or Bright, Mr. Chamberlain or Mr. Leonard Courtney was in the right will never be settled, because it will never be possible to prove that the government of the victor has been better for mankind than the government of the vanquished would have been. It is true that the victors have no doubt on the point; but to the dramatist, that certainty of theirs is only part of the human comedy. The American Unionist is often a Separatist as to Ireland; the English Unionist often sympathizes with the Polish Home Ruler; and both English and American Unionists are apt to be Disruptionists as regards that Imperial Ancient of Days, the Empire of China. Both are Unionists concerning Canada, but with a difference as to the precise application to it of the Monroe doctrine. As for me, the dramatist, I smile, and lead the conversation back to Burgoyne.

Burgoyne's surrender at Saratoga made him that occasionally necessary part of our British system, a scapegoat. The explanation of his defeat given in the play is founded on a passage quoted by De Fonblanque from Fitzmaurice's Life of Lord Shelburne, as follows: "Lord George Germain, having among other peculiarities a particular dislike to be put out of his way on any occasion, had arranged to call at his office on his way to the country to sign the dispatches; but as those addressed to Howe had not been faircopied, and he was not disposed to be balked of his projected visit to Kent, they were not signed then and were forgotten on his return home." These were the dispatches instructing Sir William Howe, who was in New York, to effect a junction at Albany with Burgoyne, who had marched from Boston for that purpose. Burgoyne got as far as Saratoga, where, failing the expected reinforcement, he was hopelessly outnumbered, and his officers picked off, Boer fashion, by the American farmer-sharpshooters. His own collar was pierced by a bullet. The publicity of his defeat, however, was more than compensated at home by the fact that Lord George's trip to Kent had not been interfered with, and that nobody knew about the oversight of the dispatch. The policy of the English Government and Court for the next two years was simply concealment of Germain's neglect. Burgoyne's demand for an inquiry was defeated in the House of Commons by the court party; and when he at last obtained a committee, the king got rid of it by a prorogation. When Burgoyne realized what had happened about the instructions to Howe (the scene in which I have represented him as learning it before Saratoga is not historical: the truth did not dawn on him until many months afterwards) the king actually took advantage of his being a prisoner of war in England on parole, and ordered him to return to America into captivity. Burgoyne immediately resigned all his appointments; and this practically closed his military career, though he was afterwards made Commander of the Forces in Ireland for the purpose of banishing him from parliament.

The episode illustrates the curious perversion of the English sense of honor when the privileges and prestige of the aristocracy are at stake. Mr. Frank Harris said, after the disastrous battle of Modder River, that the English, having lost America a century ago because they preferred George III, were quite prepared to lose South Africa to-day because they preferred aristocratic commanders to successful ones. Horace Walpole, when the parliamentary recess came at a critical period of the War of Independence, said that the Lords could not be expected to lose their pheasant shooting for the sake of America. In the working class, which, like all classes, has its own official aristocracy, there is the same reluctance to discredit an institution or to "do a man out of his job." At bottom, of course, this apparently shameless sacrifice of great public interests to petty personal ones is simply the preference of the ordinary man for the things he can feel and understand to the things that are beyond his capacity. It is stupidity, not dishonesty.

Burgoyne fell a victim to this stupidity in two ways. Not only was he thrown over, in spite of his high character and distinguished services, to screen a court favorite who had actually been cashiered for cowardice and misconduct in the field fifteen years before; but his peculiar critical temperament and talent, artistic, satirical, rather histrionic, and his fastidious delicacy of sentiment, his fine spirit and humanity, were just the qualities to make him disliked by stupid people because of their dread of ironic criticism. Long after his death, Thackeray, who had an intense sense of human character, but was typically stupid in valuing and interpreting it, instinctively sneered at him and exulted in his defeat. That sneer represents the common English attitude towards the Burgoyne type. Every instance in which the critical genius is defeated, and the stupid genius (for both temperaments have their genius) "muddles through all right," is popular in England. But Burgoyne's failure was not the work of his own temperament, but of the stupid temperament. What man could do under the circumstances he did, and did handsomely and loftily. He fell, and his ideal empire was dismembered, not through his own misconduct, but because Sir George Germain overestimated the importance of his Kentish holiday, and underestimated the difficulty of conquering those remote and inferior creatures, the colonists. And King George and the rest of the nation agreed, on the whole, with Germain. It is a significant point that in America, where Burgoyne was an enemy and an invader, he was admired and praised. The climate there is no doubt more favorable to intellectual vivacity.

I have described Burgoyne's temperament as rather histrionic; and the reader will have observed that the Burgoyne of the Devil's Disciple is a man who plays his part in life, and makes all its points, in the manner of a born high comedian. If he had been killed at Saratoga, with all his comedies unwritten, and his plan for turning As You Like It into a Beggar's Opera unconceived, I should still have painted the same picture of him on the strength of his reply to the articles of capitulation proposed to him by his American conqueror General Gates. Here they are:

PROPOSITION.	ANSWER.
1. General Burgoyne's army being reduced by repeated defeats, by desertion, sickness, etc., their provisions exhausted, their military horses, tents and baggage taken or destroyed, their retreat cut off, and their camp invested, they can only be allowed to surrender as prisoners of war.	Lieut.-General Burgoyne's army, however reduced, will never admit that their retreat is cut off while they have arms in their hands.
2. The officers and soldiers may keep the baggage belonging to them. The Generals of the United States never permit individuals to be pillaged.	Noted.
3. The troops under his Excellency General Burgoyne will be conducted by the most convenient route to New England, marching by easy marches, and sufficiently provided for by the way.	Agreed.
4. The officers will be admitted on parole and will be treated with the liberality customary in such cases, so long as they, by proper behavior, continue to deserve it; but those who are apprehended having broke their parole, as some British officers have done, must expect to be close confined.	There being no officer in this army under, or capable of being under, the description of breaking parole, this article needs no answer.
5. All public stores, artillery, arms, ammunition, carriages, horses, etc., etc., must be delivered to commissaries appointed to receive them.	All public stores may be delivered, arms excepted.
6. These terms being agreed to and signed, the troops under his Excellency's, General Burgoyne's command, may be drawn up in their encampments, where they will be ordered to ground their arms, and may thereupon be marched to the river-side on their way to Bennington.	This article is inadmissible in any extremity. Sooner than this army will consent to ground their arms in their encampments, they will rush on the enemy determined to take no quarter.

And, later on, "If General Gates does not mean to recede from the 6th article, the treaty ends at once: the army will to a man proceed to any act of desperation sooner than submit to that article."

Here you have the man at his Burgoynest. Need I add that he had his own way; and that when the actual ceremony of surrender came, he would have played poor General Gates off the stage, had not that commander risen to the occasion by handing him back his sword.

In connection with the reference to Indians with scalping knives, who, with the troops hired from Germany, made up about half Burgoyne's force, I may mention that Burgoyne offered two of them a reward to guide a Miss McCrea, betrothed to one of the English officers, into the English lines. The two braves quarrelled about the reward; and the more sensitive of them, as a protest against the unfairness of the other, tomahawked the young lady. The usual retaliations were proposed under the popular titles of justice and so forth; but as the tribe of the slayer would certainly have followed suit by a massacre of whites on the Canadian frontier, Burgoyne was compelled to forgive the crime, to the intense disgust of indignant Christendom.

BRUDENELL

Brudenell is also a real person. At least an artillery chaplain of that name distinguished himself at Saratoga by reading the burial service over Major Fraser under fire, and by a quite readable adventure, chronicled by Burgoyne, with Lady Harriet Ackland. Lady Harriet's husband achieved the remarkable feat of killing himself, instead of his adversary, in a duel. He overbalanced himself in the heat of his swordsmanship, and fell with his head against a pebble. Lady Harriet then married the warrior chaplain, who, like Anthony Anderson in the play, seems to have mistaken his natural profession.

The rest of the Devil's Disciple may have actually occurred, like most stories invented by dramatists; but I cannot produce any documents. Major Swindon's name is invented; but the man, of course, is real. There are dozens of him extant to this day.

Candida

〰〰〰〰〰〰

INTRODUCTORY NOTE TO *CANDIDA*

If *The Devil's Disciple* follows the style of melodrama, *Candida*, written in 1895-96, follows outwardly the style of Ibsen. *Candida*, in fact, is Shaw's reply to Ibsen's Nora in *Doll's House:* "in the real typical doll's house it is the man who is the doll." Candida is one of Shaw's new women who is wife, mother, mistress, organizer and independent thinker all in one. James Barrie in *What Every Woman Knows* treats this same theme sentimentally and Thornton Wilder in *The Skin of Our Teeth* treats it with more nobility and timelessness, but *Candida* is more important in the history of drama because of the fresh air and honesty the heroine introduced to the Victorian theatre.

Shaw, ever the teacher, presents his ideas on Christian Socialism through Candida's husband, Reverend Morell, who was modelled in part on some of Shaw's clergymen friends. Some people see the young Shaw in the character of Marchbanks but Shaw said that the poet grew out of De Quincey's adolescence as described in *Confessions*. Another theatrically effective character is Candida's father, whose speeches are written in a peculiar Cockney dialect, and whose purpose in the play, like that of the stenographer, is to introduce humor and to dramatize the minister's modern religious attitudes.

Theoretically, *Candida* should be harder to perform although easier to read than *The Devil's Disciple* because it is less colorful and there are many long "discussion" scenes with no opportunity for physical action. But with good actors in every role and a talented director, *Candida* can still move, shock and delight audiences.

ACT I

A fine October morning in the northeast suburbs of London,
a vast district many miles away from the London of Mayfair
and St. James's, much less known there than the Paris of the
Rue de Rivoli and the Champs Elysées, and much less narrow,
squalid, fetid and airless in its slums; strong in comfortable,
prosperous middle class life; wide streeted; myriad-populated;
well-served with ugly iron urinals, Radical clubs, tram lines,
and a perpetual stream of yellow cars; enjoying in its main
thoroughfares the luxury of grass-grown "front gardens," un-
trodden by the foot of man save as to the path from the gate
to the hall door; but blighted by an intolerable monotony of
miles and miles of graceless, characterless brick houses, black
iron railings, stony pavements, slated roofs, and respectably ill
dressed or disreputably poorly dressed people, quite accustomed to the place, and mostly plodding about somebody
else's work, which they would not do if they themselves could
help it. The little energy and eagerness that crop up shew
themselves in cockney cupidity and business "push." Even the
policemen and the chapels are not infrequent enough to break
the monotony. The sun is shining cheerfully; there is no fog;
and though the smoke effectually prevents anything, whether
faces and hands or bricks and mortar, from looking fresh and
clean, it is not hanging heavily enough to trouble a Londoner.

This desert of unattractiveness has its oasis. Near the outer
end of the Hackney Road is a park of 217 acres, fenced in,
not by railings, but by a wooden paling, and containing plenty
of greensward, trees, a lake for bathers, flower beds with the
flowers arranged carefully in patterns by the admired cockney
art of carpet gardening and a sandpit, imported from the
seaside for the delight of the children, but speedily deserted on
its becoming a natural vermin preserve for all the petty fauna
of Kingsland, Hackney and Hoxton. A bandstand, an unfin-
ished forum for religious, anti-religious and political orators,

83

cricket pitches, a gymnasium, and an old fashioned stone kiosk are among its attractions. Whenever the prospect is bounded by trees or rising green grounds, it is a pleasant place. Where the ground stretches flat to the grey palings, with bricks and mortar, sky signs, crowded chimneys and smoke beyond, the prospect makes it desolate and sordid.

The best view of Victoria Park is from the front window of St. Dominic's Parsonage, from which not a single chimney is visible. The parsonage is a semi-detached villa with a front garden and a porch. Visitors go up the flight of steps to the porch: tradespeople and members of the family go down by a door under the steps to the basement, with a breakfast room, used for all meals, in front, and the kitchen at the back. Upstairs, on the level of the hall door, is the drawing-room, with its large plate glass window looking on the park. In this room, the only sitting-room that can be spared from the children and the family meals, the parson, the Reverend James Mavor Morell does his work. He is sitting in a strong round-backed revolving chair at the right hand end of a long table, which stands across the window, so that he can cheer himself with the view of the park at his elbow. At the opposite end of the table, adjoining it, is a little table only half the width of the other, with a typewriter on it. His typist is sitting at this machine, with her back to the window. The large table is littered with pamphlets, journals, letters, nests of drawers, an office diary, postage scales and the like. A spare chair for visitors having business with the parson is in the middle, turned to his end. Within reach of his hand is a stationery case, and a cabinet photograph in a frame. Behind him the right hand wall, recessed above the fireplace, is fitted with bookshelves, on which an adept eye can measure the parson's divinity and casuistry by a complete set of Browning's poems and Maurice's Theological Essays, and guess at his politics from a yellow backed Progress and Poverty, Fabian Essays, a Dream of John Ball, Marx's Capital, and half a dozen other literary landmarks in Socialism. Opposite him on the left, near the typewriter, is the door. Farther down the room, opposite the fireplace, a bookcase stands on a cellaret, with a sofa near it. There is a generous fire burning; and the hearth, with a comfortable armchair and a japanned flower-painted coal scuttle at one side, a miniature chair for a boy or girl on the other, a nicely varnished wooden mantelpiece, with neatly molded shelves, tiny bits of mirror let into the panels, and a travelling clock in a leather case (the inevitable wedding present), and on the wall above a large autotype of the chief figure in Titian's Virgin of the Assumption, is very inviting. Altogether the room is the room of a good housekeeper, vanquished, as far as the table is concerned, by an untidy man, but elsewhere mistress of the situation. The furniture, in its ornamental aspect, betrays the style of the advertised "drawing-room suite" of the pushing suburban furniture dealer; but there is nothing useless or pretentious in the room. The paper and panelling are dark, throwing the big cheery window and the park outside into strong relief.

The Reverend James Mavor Morell is a Christian Socialist clergyman of the Church of England, and an active member of the Guild of St. Matthew and the Christian Social Union. A vigorous, genial, popular man of forty, robust and good-looking, full of energy, with pleasant, hearty, considerate manners, and a sound, unaffected voice, which he uses with the clean, athletic articulation of a practised orator, and with a wide range and perfect command of expression. He is a first-rate clergyman, able to say what he likes to whom he likes, to lecture people without setting himself up against them, to impose his authority on them without humiliating them, and to interfere in their business without impertinence. His wellspring of spiritual enthusiasm and sympathetic emotion has never run dry for a moment: he still eats and sleeps heartily enough to win the daily battle between exhaustion and recuperation triumphantly. Withal, a great baby, pardonably vain of his powers and unconsciously pleased with himself. He has a healthy complexion, a good forehead, with the brows somewhat blunt, and the eyes bright and eager, a mouth resolute, but not particularly well cut, and a substantial nose, with the mobile, spreading nostrils of the dramatic orator, but, like all his features, void of subtlety.

The typist, Miss Proserpine Garnett, is a brisk little woman of about 30, of the lower middle class, neatly but cheaply dressed in a black merino skirt and a blouse, rather pert and quick of speech, and not very civil in her manner, but sensitive and affectionate. She is clattering away busily at her machine whilst Morell opens the last of his morning's letters. He realizes its contents with a comic groan of despair.

PROSERPINE. Another lecture?

MORELL. Yes. The Hoxton Freedom Group want me to
address them on Sunday morning (*great emphasis on "Sunday," this being the unreasonable part of the business*). What
are they?

PROSERPINE. Communist Anarchists, I think.

MORELL. Just like Anarchists not to know that they can't
have a parson on Sunday! Tell them to come to church if
they want to hear me: it will do them good. Say I can only
come on Mondays and Thursdays. Have you the diary there?

PROSERPINE (*taking up the diary*). Yes.

MORELL. Have I any lecture on for next Monday?

PROSERPINE (*referring to diary*). Tower Hamlets Radical
Club.

MORELL. Well, Thursday then?

PROSERPINE. English Land Restoration League.

MORELL. What next?

PROSERPINE. Guild of St. Matthew on Monday. Independent Labor Party, Greenwich Branch, on Thursday.
Monday, Social-Democratic Federation, Mile End Branch.
Thursday, first Confirmation class— (*Impatiently.*) Oh, I'd
better tell them you can't come. They're only half a dozen
ignorant and conceited costermongers without five shillings
between them.

MORELL (*amused*). Ah; but you see they're near relatives
of mine, Miss Garnett.

PROSERPINE (*staring at him*). Relatives of yours!

MORELL. Yes: we have the same father—in Heaven.

PROSERPINE (*relieved*). Oh, is that all?

MORELL (*with a sadness which is a luxury to a man whose
voice expresses it so finely*). Ah, you don't believe it. Everybody says it: nobody believes it—nobody. (*Briskly, getting
back to business.*) Well, well! Come, Miss Proserpine, can't
you find a date for the costers? What about the 25th?: that
was vacant the day before yesterday.

PROSERPINE (*referring to diary*). Engaged—the Fabian
Society.

MORELL. Bother the Fabian Society! Is the 28th gone, too?

PROSERPINE. City dinner. You're invited to dine with the
Founder's Company.

MORELL. That'll do; I'll go to the Hoxton Group of Freedom instead. (*She enters the engagement in silence, with*

implacable disparagement of the Hoxton Anarchists in every line of her face. Morell bursts open the cover of a copy of The Church Reformer, *which has come by post, and glances through Mr. Stewart Hendlam's leader and the Guild of St. Matthew news. These proceedings are presently enlivened by the appearance of Morell's curate, the Reverend Alexander Mill, a young gentleman gathered by Morell from the nearest University settlement, whither he had come from Oxford to give the east end of London the benefit of his university training. He is a conceitedly well intentioned, enthusiastic, immature person, with nothing positively unbearable about him except a habit of speaking with his lips carefully closed for half an inch from each corner, a finicking articulation, and a set of horribly corrupt vowels, notably ow for o, this being his chief means of bringing Oxford refinement to bear on Hackney vulgarity. Morell, whom he has won over by a doglike devotion, looks up indulgently from* The Church Reformer *as he enters, and remarks.*) Well, Lexy! Late again, as usual.

LEXY. I'm afraid so. I wish I could get up in the morning.

MORELL (*exulting in his own energy*). Ha! ha! (*Whimsically.*) Watch and pray, Lexy: watch and pray.

LEXY. I know. (*Rising wittily to the occasion.*) But how can I watch and pray when I am asleep? Isn't that so, Miss Prossy?

PROSERPINE (*sharply*). Miss Garnett, if you please.

LEXY. I beg your pardon—Miss Garnett.

PROSERPINE. You've got to do all the work to-day.

LEXY. Why?

PROSERPINE. Never mind why. It will do you good to earn your supper before you eat it, for once in a way, as I do. Come: don't dawdle. You should have been off on your rounds half an hour ago.

LEXY (*perplexed*). Is she in earnest, Morell?

MORELL (*in the highest spirits—his eyes dancing*). Yes. I am going to dawdle to-day.

LEXY. You! You don't know how.

MORELL (*heartily*). Ha! ha! Don't I? I'm going to have this day all to myself—or at least the afternoon. My wife's coming back: she's due here at 11:45.

LEXY (*surprised*). Coming back already—with the children? I thought they were to stay to the end of the month.

MORELL. So they are: she's only coming up for two days, to get some flannel things for Jimmy, and to see how we're getting on without her.

LEXY (*anxiously*). But, my dear Morell, if what Jimmy and Fluffy had was scarlatina, do you think it wise—

MORELL. Scarlatina!—rubbish, German measles. I brought it into the house myself from the Pycroft Street School. A parson is like a doctor, my boy: he must face infection as a soldier must face bullets. (*He rises and claps Lexy on the shoulder.*) Catch the measles if you can, Lexy: she'll nurse you; and what a piece of luck that will be for you!—eh?

LEXY (*smiling uneasily*). It's so hard to understand you about Mrs. Morell—

MORELL (*tenderly*). Ah, my boy, get married—get married to a good woman; and then you'll understand. That's a foretaste of what will be best in the Kingdom of Heaven we are trying to establish on earth. That will cure you of dawdling. An honest man feels that he must pay Heaven for every hour of happiness with a good spell of hard, unselfish work to make others happy. We have no more right to consume happiness without producing it than to consume wealth without producing it. Get a wife like my Candida; and you'll always be in arrear with your repayment.

He pats Lexy affectionately on the back, and is leaving the room when Lexy calls to him.

LEXY. Oh, wait a bit: I forgot. (*Morell halts and turns with the door knob in his hand.*) Your father-in-law is coming round to see you. (*Morell shuts the door again, with a complete change of manner.*)

MORELL (*surprised and not pleased*). Mr. Burgess?

LEXY. Yes. I passed him in the park, arguing with somebody. He gave me good day and asked me to let you know that he was coming.

MORELL (*half incredulous*). But he hasn't called here for— I may almost say for years. Are you sure, Lexy? You're not joking, are you?

LEXY (*earnestly*). No, sir, really.

MORELL (*thoughtfully*). Hm! Time for him to take another look at Candida before she grows out of his knowledge. (*He resigns himself to the inevitable, and goes out. Lexy looks after him with beaming, foolish worship.*)

LEXY. What a good man! What a thorough, loving soul he is!

He takes Morell's place at the table, making himself very comfortable as he takes out a cigaret.

PROSERPINE (*impatiently, pulling the letter she has been working at off the typewriter and folding it*). Oh, a man ought to be able to be fond of his wife without making a fool of himself about her.

LEXY (*shocked*). Oh, Miss Prossy!

PROSERPINE (*rising busily and coming to the stationery case to get an envelope, in which she encloses the letter as she speaks*). Candida here, and Candida there, and Candida everywhere! (*She licks the envelope.*) It's enough to drive anyone out of their senses (*thumping the envelope to make it stick*) to hear a perfectly commonplace woman raved about in that absurd manner merely because she's got good hair, and a tolerable figure.

LEXY (*with reproachful gravity*). I think her extremely beautiful, Miss Garnett. (*He takes the photograph up; looks at it; and adds, with even greater impressiveness.*) Extremely beautiful. How fine her eyes are!

PROSERPINE. Her eyes are not a bit better than mine—now! (*He puts down the photograph and stares austerely at her.*) And you know very well that you think me dowdy and second rate enough.

LEXY (*rising majestically*). Heaven forbid that I should think of any of God's creatures in such a way! (*He moves stiffly away from her across the room to the neighborhood of the bookcase.*)

PROSERPINE. Thank you. That's very nice and comforting.

LEXY (*saddened by her depravity*). I had no idea you had any feeling against Mrs. Morell.

PROSERPINE (*indignantly*). I have no feeling against her. She's very nice, very good-hearted: I'm very fond of her and can appreciate her real qualities far better than any man can. (*He shakes his head sadly and turns to the bookcase, looking along the shelves for a volume. She follows him with intense pepperiness.*) You don't believe me? (*He turns and faces her. She pounces at him with spitfire energy.*) You think I'm jealous. Oh, what a profound knowledge of the human heart you have, Mr. Lexy Mill! How well you know the weaknesses of Woman, don't you? It must be so nice to be a man and have a fine penetrating intellect instead of mere emotions like us, and to know that the reason we don't share your amorous delusions is that we're all jealous of one another! (*She abandons him with a toss of her shoulders, and crosses to the fire to warm her hands.*)

LEXY. Ah, if you women only had the same clue to Man's strength that you have to his weakness, Miss Prossy, there would be no Woman Question.

PROSERPINE (*over her shoulder, as she stoops, holding her hands to the blaze*). Where did you hear Morell say that? You didn't invent it yourself: you're not clever enough.

LEXY. That's quite true. I am not ashamed of owing him that, as I owe him so many other spiritual truths. He said it at the annual conference of the Women's Liberal Federation. Allow me to add that though they didn't appreciate it, I, a mere man, did. (*He turns to the bookcase again, hoping that this may leave her crushed.*)

PROSERPINE (*putting her hair straight at the little panel of mirror in the mantelpiece*). Well, when you talk to me, give me your own ideas, such as they are, and not his. You never cut a poorer figure than when you are trying to imitate him.

LEXY (*stung*). I try to follow his example, not to imitate him.

PROSERPINE (*coming at him again on her way back to her work*). Yes, you do: you imitate him. Why do you tuck your umbrella under your left arm instead of carrying it in your hand like anyone else? Why do you walk with your chin stuck out before you, hurrying along with that eager look in your eyes—you, who never get up before half past nine in the morning? Why do you say "knoaledge" in church, though you always say "knolledge" in private conversation! Bah! do you think I don't know? (*She goes back to the typewriter.*) Here, come and set about your work: we've wasted enough time for one morning. Here's a copy of the diary for to-day. (*She hands him a memorandum.*)

LEXY (*deeply offended*). Thank you. (*He takes it and stands at the table with his back to her, reading it. She begins to transcribe her shorthand notes on the typewriter without troubling herself about his feelings. Mr. Burgess enters unannounced. He is a man of sixty, made coarse and sordid by the compulsory selfishness of petty commerce, and later on softened into sluggish bumptiousness by overfeeding and com-*

*mercial success. A vulgar, ignorant, guzzling man, offensive
and contemptuous to people whose labor is cheap, respectful
to wealth and rank, and quite sincere and without rancor or
envy in both attitudes. Finding him without talent, the world
has offered him no decently paid work except ignoble work,
and he has become in consequence, somewhat hoggish. But he
has no suspicion of this himself, and honestly regards his commercial prosperity as the inevitable and socially wholesome
triumph of the ability, industry, shrewdness and experience
in business of a man who in private is easygoing, affectionate
and humorously convivial to a fault. Corporeally, he is a podgy
man, with a square, clean shaven face and a square beard
under his chin; dust colored, with a patch of grey in the
centre, and small watery blue eyes with a plaintively sentimental expression, which he transfers easily to his voice by
his habit of pompously intoning his sentences.)*

BURGESS (*stopping on the threshold, and looking round*).
They told me Mr. Morell was here.

PROSERPINE (*rising*). He's upstairs. I'll fetch him for you.

BURGESS (*staring boorishly at her*). You're not the same
young lady as hused to typewrite for him?

PROSERPINE. No.

BURGESS (*assenting*). No: she was young-er. (*Miss Garnett stolidly stares at him; then goes out with great dignity.
He receives this quite obtusely, and crosses to the hearth-rug,
where he turns and spreads himself with his back to the fire.*)
Startin' on your rounds, Mr. Mill?

LEXY (*folding his paper and pocketing it*). Yes: I must be
off presently.

BURGESS (*momentously*). Don't let me detain you, Mr. Mill.
What I come about is private between me and Mr. Morell.

LEXY (*huffily*). I have no intention of intruding, I am
sure, Mr. Burgess. Good morning.

BURGESS (*patronizingly*). Oh, good morning to you. (*Morell
returns as Lexy is making for the door.*)

MORELL (*to Lexy*). Off to work?

LEXY. Yes, sir.

MORELL (*patting him affectionately on the shoulder*). Take
my silk handkerchief and wrap your throat up. There's a
cold wind. Away with you.

Lexy brightens up, and goes out.

BURGESS. Spoilin' your curates, as usu'l, James. Good

mornin'. When I pay a man, an' 'is livin' depen's on me, I keep him in his place.

MORELL (*rather shortly*). I always keep my curates in their places as my helpers and comrades. If you get as much work out of your clerks and warehousemen as I do out of my curates, you must be getting rich pretty fast. Will you take your old chair?

He points with curt authority to the arm chair beside the fireplace; then takes the spare chair from the table and sits down in front of Burgess.

BURGESS (*without moving*). Just the same as hever, James!

MORELL. When you last called—it was about three years ago, I think—you said the same thing a little more frankly. Your exact words then were: "Just as big a fool as ever, James?"

BURGESS (*soothingly*). Well, perhaps I did; but (*with conciliatory cheerfulness*) I meant no offence by it. A clorgyman is privileged to be a bit of a fool, you know; it's on'y becomin' in his profession that he should. Anyhow, I come here, not to rake up hold differences, but to let bygones be bygones. (*Suddenly becoming very solemn, and approaching Morell.*) James: three year ago, you done me a hill turn. You done me hout of a contrac'; an' when I gev you 'arsh words in my nat'ral disappointment, you turned my daughrter again me. Well, I've come to act the part of a Cherischin. (*Offering his hand.*) I forgive you, James.

MORELL (*starting up*). Confound your impudence!

BURGESS (*retreating, with almost lachrymose deprecation of this treatment*). Is that becomin' language for a clorgyman, James?—and you so partic'lar, too?

MORELL (*hotly*). No, sir, it is not becoming language for a clergyman. I used the wrong word. I should have said damn your impudence: that's what St. Paul, or any honest priest would have said to you. Do you think I have forgotten that tender of yours for the contract to supply clothing to the workhouse?

BURGESS (*in a paroxysm of public spirit*). I acted in the interest of the ratepayers, James. It was the lowest tender: you can't deny that.

MORELL. Yes, the lowest, because you paid worse wages than any other employer—starvation wages—aye, worse than starvation wages—to the women who made the clothing. Your wages would have driven them to the streets to keep body and soul together. (*Getting angrier and angrier.*) Those women were my parishioners. I shamed the Guardians out of accepting your tender: I shamed the ratepayers out of letting them do it: I shamed everybody but you. (*Boiling over.*) How dare you, sir, come here and offer to forgive me, and talk about your daughter, and—

BURGESS. Easy, James, easy, easy. Don't git hinto a fluster about nothink. I've howned I was wrong.

MORELL (*fuming about*). Have you? I didn't hear you.

BURGESS. Of course I did. I hown it now. Come: I harsk your pardon for the letter I wrote you. Is that enough?

MORELL (*snapping his fingers*). That's nothing. Have you raised the wages?

BURGESS (*triumphantly*). Yes.

MORELL (*stopping dead*). What!

BURGESS (*unctuously*). I've turned a moddle hemployer. I don't hemploy no women now: they're all sacked; and the work is done by machinery. Not a man 'as less than sixpence a *hour*; and the skilled 'ands gits the Trade Union rate. (*Proudly.*) What 'ave you to say to me now?

MORELL (*overwhelmed*). Is it possible! Well, there's more joy in heaven over one sinner that repenteth— (*Going to Burgess with an explosion of apologetic cordiality.*) My dear Burgess, I most heartily beg your pardon for my hard thoughts of you. (*Grasps his hand.*) And now, don't you feel the better for the change? Come, confess, you're happier. You look happier.

BURGESS (*ruefully*). Well, p'raps I do. I s'pose I must, since you notice it. At all events, I git my contrax asseppit (accepted) by the County Council. (*Savagely.*) They dussent 'ave nothink to do with me unless I paid fair wages—curse 'em for a parcel o' meddlin' fools!

MORELL (*dropping his hand, utterly discouraged*). So that was why you raised the wages! (*He sits down moodily.*)

BURGESS (*severely, in spreading, mounting tones*). Why else should I do it? What does it lead to but drink and huppishness in workin' men? (*He seats himself magisterially in the easy chair.*) It's hall very well for you, James: it gits you hinto the papers and makes a great man of you; but you never think of the 'arm you do, puttin' money into the pockets of workin' men that they don't know 'ow to spend,

and takin' it from people that might be makin' a good huse
on it.

MORELL (*with a heavy sigh, speaking with cold politeness*).
What is your business with me this morning? I shall not
pretend to believe that you are here merely out of family
sentiment.

BURGESS (*obstinately*). Yes, I ham—just family sentiment
and nothink else.

MORELL (*with weary calm*). I don't believe you!

BURGESS (*rising threateningly*). Don't say that to me again,
James Mavor Morell.

MORELL (*unmoved*). I'll say it just as often as may be
necessary to convince you that it's true. I don't believe you.

BURGESS (*collapsing into an abyss of wounded feeling*). Oh,
well, if you're determined to be unfriendly, I s'pose I'd better
go. (*He moves reluctantly towards the door. Morell makes
no sign. He lingers.*) I didn't hexpect to find a hun-forgivin'
spirit in you, James. (*Morell still not responding, he takes a
few more reluctant steps doorwards. Then he comes back
whining.*) We huseter git on well enough, spite of our different
opinions. Why are you so changed to me? I give you my word
I come here in pyorr (*pure*) frenliness, not wishin' to be on
bad terms with my hown daughrter's 'usban'. Come, James:
be a Cherischin and shake 'ands. (*He puts his hand sentimentally on Morell's shoulder.*)

MORELL (*looking up at him thoughtfully*). Look here, Burgess. Do you want to be as welcome here as you were before
you lost that contract?

BURGESS. I do, James. I do—honest.

MORELL. Then why don't you behave as you did then?

BURGESS (*cautiously removing his hand*). 'Ow d'y'mean?

MORELL. I'll tell you. You thought me a young fool then.

BURGESS (*coaxingly*). No, I didn't, James. I—

MORELL (*cutting him short*). Yes, you did. And I thought
you an old scoundrel.

BURGESS (*most vehemently deprecating this gross self-
accusation on Morell's part*). No, you didn't, James. Now you
do yourself a hinjustice.

MORELL. Yes, I did. Well, that did not prevent our getting
on very well together. God made you what I call a scoundrel
as he made me what you call a fool. (*The effect of his observa-
tion on Burgess is to remove the keystone of his moral arch.*

He becomes bodily weak, and, with his eyes fixed on Morell in a helpless stare, puts out his hand apprehensively to balance himself, as if the floor had suddenly sloped under him. Morell proceeds in the same tone of quiet conviction.) It was not for me to quarrel with his handiwork in the one case more than in the other. So long as you come here honestly as a self-respecting, thorough, convinced scoundrel, justifying your scoundrelism, and proud of it, you are welcome. But (*and now Morell's tone becomes formidable; and he rises and strikes the back of the chair for greater emphasis*) I won't have you here snivelling about being a model employer and a converted man when you're only an apostate with your coat turned for the sake of a County Council contract. (*He nods at him to enforce the point; then goes to the hearth-rug, where he takes up a comfortably commanding position with his back to the fire, and continues.*) No: I like a man to be true to himself, even in wickedness. Come now: either take your hat and go; or else sit down and give me a good scoundrelly reason for wanting to be friends with me. (*Burgess, whose emotions have subsided sufficiently to be expressed by a dazed grin, is relieved by this concrete proposition. He ponders it for a moment, and then, slowly and very modestly, sits down in the chair Morell has just left.*) That's right. Now, out with it.

BURGESS (*chuckling in spite of himself*). Well, you are a queer bird, James, and no mistake. But (*almost enthusiastically*) one carnt 'elp likin' you; besides, as I said afore, of course one don't take all a clorgyman says seriously, or the world couldn't go on. Could it now? (*He composes himself for graver discourse, and turning his eyes on Morell proceeds with dull seriousness.*) Well, I don't mind tellin' you, since it's your wish we should be free with one another, that I did think you a bit of a fool once; but I'm beginnin' to think that p'r'aps I was be'ind the times a bit.

MORELL (*delighted*). Aha! You're finding that out at last, are you?

BURGESS (*portentously*). Yes, times 'as changed mor'n I could a believed. Five yorr (year) ago, no sensible man would a thought o' takin' up with your ideas. I hused to wonder you was let preach at all. Why, I know a clorgyman that 'as bin kep' hout of his job for yorrs by the Bishop of London, although the pore feller's not a bit more religious than you are. But to-day, if henyone was to offer to bet me a thousan' poun' that you'll end by bein' a bishop yourself, I shouldn't venture to take the bet. You and yore crew are gettin' hinfluential: I can see that. They'll 'ave to give you something someday, if it's only to stop yore mouth. You 'ad the right instinc' arter all, James: the line you took is the payin' line in the long run fur a man o' your sort.

MORELL (*decisively—offering his hand*). Shake hands, Burgess. Now you're talking honestly. I don't think they'll make me a bishop; but if they do, I'll introduce you to the biggest jobbers I can get to come to my dinner parties.

BURGESS (*who has risen with a sheepish grin and accepted the bond of friendship*). You will 'ave your joke, James. Our quarrel's made up now, isn't it?

A WOMAN'S VOICE. Say yes, James.

Startled, they turn quickly and find that Candida has just come in, and is looking at them with an amused maternal indulgence which is her characteristic expression. She is a woman of 33, well built, well nourished, likely, one guesses, to become matronly later on, but now quite at her best, with the double charm of youth and motherhood. Her ways are those of a woman who has found that she can always manage people by engaging their affection, and who does so frankly and instinctively without the smallest scruple. So far, she is like any other pretty woman who is just clever enough to make the most of her sexual attractions for trivially selfish ends; but Candida's serene brow, courageous eyes, and well-set mouth and chin signify largeness of mind and dignity of character to ennoble her cunning in the affections. A wisehearted observer, looking at her, would at once guess that whoever had placed the Virgin of the Assumption over her hearth did so because he fancied some spiritual resemblance between them, and yet would not suspect either her husband or herself of any such idea, or indeed of any concern with the art of Titian.

Just now she is in bonnet and mantle, laden with a strapped rug with her umbrella stuck through it, a handbag, and a supply of illustrated papers.

MORELL (*shocked at his remissness*). Candida! Why— (*Looks at his watch, and is horrified to find it so late.*) My darling! (*Hurrying to her and seizing the rug strap, pouring forth his remorseful regrets all the time.*) I intended to meet you at the train. I let the time slip. (*Flinging the rug on the sofa.*) I was so engrossed by—(*returning to her*)—I forgot—oh! (*He embraces her with penitent emotion.*)

BURGESS (*a little shamefaced and doubtful of his reception*). How orr you, Candy? (*She, still in Morell's arms, offers him her cheek, which he kisses.*) James and me is come to a unnerstandin'—a honorable unnerstandin'. Ain' we, James?

MORELL (*impetuously*). Oh, bother your understanding! You've kept me late for Candida. (*With compassionate fervor.*) My poor love: how did you manage about the luggage?—how—

CANDIDA (*stopping him and disengaging herself*). There, there, there. I wasn't alone. Eugene came down yesterday; and we traveled up together.

MORELL (*pleased*). Eugene!

CANDIDA. Yes: he's struggling with my luggage, poor boy. Go out, dear, at once; or he will pay for the cab; and I don't want that. (*Morell hurries out. Candida puts down her handbag; then takes off her mantle and bonnet and puts them on the sofa with the rug, chatting meanwhile.*) Well, papa, how are you getting on at home?

BURGESS. The 'ouse ain't worth livin' in since you left it, Candy. I wish you'd come round and give the gurl a talkin' to. Who's this Eugene that's come with you?

CANDIDA. Oh, Eugene's one of James's discoveries. He found him sleeping on the Embankment last June. Haven't you noticed our new picture (*pointing to the Virgin*)? He gave us that.

BURGESS (*incredulously*). Garn! D'you mean to tell me—your hown father!—that cab touts or such like, orf the Embankment, buys pictur's like that? (*Severely.*) Don't deceive me, Candy: it's a 'Igh Church pictur; and James chose it hisself.

CANDIDA. Guess again. Eugene isn't a cab tout.

BURGESS. Then wot is he? (*Sarcastically.*) A nobleman, I 'spose.

CANDIDA (*delighted—nodding*). Yes. His uncle's a peer—a real live earl.

BURGESS (*not daring to believe such good news*). No!

CANDIDA. Yes. He had a seven day bill for £55 in his pocket when James found him on the Embankment. He thought he couldn't get any money for it until the seven days were up; and he was too shy to ask for credit. Oh, he's a dear boy! We are very fond of him.

BURGESS (*pretending to belittle the aristocracy, but with his eyes gleaming*). Hm, I thort you wouldn't git a piorr's (peer's) nevvy visitin' in Victoria Park unless he were a bit of a flat. (*Looking again at the picture.*) Of course I don't 'old with that pictur, Candy; but still it's a 'igh class, fust-rate work of art: I can see that. Be sure you hintroduce me to him, Candy. (*He looks at his watch anxiously.*) I can only stay about two minutes.

Morell comes back with Eugene, whom Burgess contemplates moist-eyed with enthusiasm. He is a strange, shy youth of eighteen, slight, effeminate, with a delicate childish voice, and a hunted, tormented expression and shrinking manner that shew the painful sensitiveness that very swift and acute apprehensiveness produces in youth, before the character has grown to its full strength. Yet everything that his timidity and frailty suggests is contradicted by his face. He is miserably irresolute, does not know where to stand or what to do with his hands and feet, is afraid of Burgess, and would run away into solitude if he dared; but the very intensity with which he feels a perfectly commonplace position shews great nervous force, and his nostrils and mouth shew a fiercely petulant wilfulness, as to the quality of which his great imaginative eyes and fine brow are reassuring. He is so entirely uncommon as to be almost unearthly; and to prosaic people there is something noxious in this unearthliness, just as to poetic people there is something angelic in it. His dress is anarchic. He wears an old blue serge jacket, unbuttoned over a woollen lawn tennis shirt, with a silk handkerchief for a cravat, trousers matching the jacket, and brown canvas shoes. In these garments he has apparently lain in the heather and waded through the waters; but there is no evidence of his having ever brushed them.

As he catches sight of a stranger on entering, he stops, and edges along the wall on the opposite side of the room.

MORELL (*as he enters*). Come along: you can spare us quarter of an hour, at all events. This is my father-in-law, Mr. Burgess—Mr. Marchbanks.

MARCHBANKS (*nervously backing against the bookcase*). Glad to meet you, sir.

BURGESS (*crossing to him with great heartiness, whilst Morell joins Candida at the fire*). Glad to meet you, I'm

shore, Mr. Morchbanks. (*Forcing him to shake hands.*)
'Ow do you find yoreself this weather? 'Ope you ain't lettin'
James put no foolish ideas into your 'ed?

MARCHBANKS. Foolish ideas! Oh, you mean Socialism. No.

BURGESS. That's right. (*Again looking at his watch.*) Well,
I must go now: there's no 'elp for it. Yo're not comin' my way,
are you, Mr. Morchbanks?

MARCHBANKS. Which way is that?

BURGESS. Victawriar Pork Station. There's a city train at
12:25.

MORELL. Nonsense. Eugene will stay to lunch with us, I
expect.

MARCHBANKS (*anxiously excusing himself*). No—I—I—

BURGESS. Well, well, I shan't press you: I bet you'd rather
lunch with Candy. Some night, I 'ope, you'll come and dine
with me at my club, the Freeman Founders in Nortn Folgit.
Come, say you will.

MARCHBANKS. Thank you, Mr. Burgess. Where is Norton
Folgate—down in Surrey, isn't it? (*Burgess, inexpressibly
tickled, begins to splutter with laughter.*)

CANDIDA (*coming to the rescue*). You'll lose your train,
papa, if you don't go at once. Come back in the afternoon
and tell Mr. Marchbanks where to find the club.

BURGESS (*roaring with glee*). Down in Surrey—har, har!
that's not a bad one. Well, I never met a man as didn't know
Nortn Folgit before. (*Abashed at his own noisiness.*) Good-
bye, Mr. Morchbanks: I know yo're too 'ighbred to take my
pleasantry in bad part. (*He again offers his hand.*)

MARCHBANKS (*taking it with a nervous jerk*). Not at all.

BURGESS. Bye, bye, Candy. I'll look in again later on. So
long, James.

MORELL. Must you go?

BURGESS. Don't stir. (*He goes out with unabated heartiness.*)

MORELL. Oh, I'll see you out. (*He follows him out. Eugene
stares after them apprehensively, holding his breath until
Burgess disappears.*)

CANDIDA (*laughing*). Well, Eugene. (*He turns with a start
and comes eagerly towards her, but stops irresolutely as he
meets her amused look.*) What do you think of my father?

MARCHBANKS. I—I hardly know him yet. He seems to be a
very nice old gentleman.

CANDIDA (*with gentle irony*). And you'll go to the Freeman Founders to dine with him, won't you?

MARCHBANKS (*miserably, taking it quite seriously*). Yes, if it will please you.

CANDIDA (*touched*). Do you know, you are a very nice boy, Eugene, with all your queerness. If you had laughed at my father I shouldn't have minded; but I like you ever so much better for being nice to him.

MARCHBANKS. Ought I to have laughed? I noticed that he said something funny; but I am so ill at ease with strangers; and I never can see a joke! I'm very sorry. (*He sits down on the sofa, his elbows on his knees and his temples between his fists, with an expression of hopeless suffering.*)

CANDIDA (*bustling him goodnaturedly*). Oh, come! You great baby, you! You are worse than usual this morning. Why were you so melancholy as we came along in the cab?

MARCHBANKS. Oh, that was nothing. I was wondering how much I ought to give the cabman. I know it's utterly silly; but you don't know how dreadful such things are to me— how I shrink from having to deal with strange people. (*Quickly and reassuringly.*) But it's all right. He beamed all over and touched his hat when Morell gave him two shillings. I was on the point of offering him ten. (*Candida laughs heartily. Morell comes back with a few letters and newspapers which have come by the midday post.*)

CANDIDA. Oh, James, dear, he was going to give the cabman ten shillings—ten shillings for a three minutes' drive—oh, dear!

MORELL (*at the table, glancing through the letters*). Never mind her, Marchbanks. The overpaying instinct is a generous one: better than the underpaying instinct, and not so common.

MARCHBANKS (*relapsing into dejection*). No: cowardice, incompetence. Mrs. Morell's quite right.

CANDIDA. Of course she is. (*She takes up her handbag.*) And now I must leave you to James for the present. I suppose you are too much of a poet to know the state a woman finds her house in when she's been away for three weeks. Give me my rug. (*Eugene takes the strapped rug from the couch, and gives it to her. She takes it in her left hand, having the bag in her right.*) Now hang my cloak across my arm. (*He obeys.*) Now my hat. (*He puts it into the hand which has the bag.*) Now open the door for me. (*He hurries up before her and opens the door.*) Thanks. (*She goes out; and Marchbanks shuts the door.*)

MORELL (*still busy at the table*). You'll stay to lunch, Marchbanks, of course.

MARCHBANKS (*scared*). I mustn't. (*He glances quickly at Morell, but at once avoids his frank look, and adds, with obvious disingenuousness.*) I can't.

MORELL (*over his shoulder*). You mean you won't.

MARCHBANKS (*earnestly*). No: I should like to, indeed. Thank you very much. But—but——

MORELL (*breezily, finishing with the letters and coming close to him*). But—but—but—but—bosh! If you'd like to stay, stay. You don't mean to persuade me you have anything else to do. If you're shy, go and take a turn in the park and write poetry until half past one; and then come in and have a good feed.

MARCHBANKS. Thank you, I should like that very much. But I really mustn't. The truth is, Mrs. Morell told me not to. She said she didn't think you'd ask me to stay to lunch, but that I was to remember, if you did, that you didn't really want me to. (*Plaintively.*) She said I'd understand; but I don't. Please don't tell her I told you.

MORELL (*drolly*). Oh, is that all? Won't my suggestion that you should take a turn in the park meet the difficulty?

MARCHBANKS. How?

MORELL (*exploding good-humoredly*). Why, you duffer—— (*But this boisterousness jars himself as well as Eugene. He checks himself, and resumes, with affectionate seriousness.*) No: I won't put it in that way. My dear lad: in a happy marriage like ours, there is something very sacred in the return of the wife to her home. (*Marchbanks looks quickly at him, half anticipating his meaning.*) An old friend or a truly noble and sympathetic soul is not in the way on such occasions; but a chance visitor is. (*The hunted, horror-stricken expression comes out with sudden vividness in Eugene's face as he understands. Morell, occupied with his own thought, goes on without noticing it*). Candida thought I would rather not have you here; but she was wrong. I'm very fond of you, my boy, and I should like you to see for yourself what a happy thing it is to be married as I am.

MARCHBANKS. Happy!—your marriage! You think that! You believe that!

MORELL (*buoyantly*). I know it, my lad. La Rochefoucauld said that there are convenient marriages, but no delightful ones. You don't know the comfort of seeing through and through a thundering liar and rotten cynic like that fellow. Ha, ha! Now off with you to the park, and write your poem. Half past one, sharp, mind: we never wait for anybody.

MARCHBANKS (*wildly*). No: stop: you shan't. I'll force it into the light.

MORELL (*puzzled*). Eh? Force what?

MARCHBANKS. I must speak to you. There is something that must be settled between us.

MORELL (*with a whimsical glance at the clock*). Now?

MARCHBANKS (*passionately*). Now. Before you leave this room. (*He retreats a few steps, and stands as if to bar Morell's way to the door.*)

MORELL (*without moving, and gravely, perceiving now that there is something serious the matter*). I'm not going to leave it, my dear boy: I thought you were. (*Eugene, baffled by his firm tone, turns his back on him, writhing with anger. Morell goes to him and puts his hand on his shoulder strongly and kindly, disregarding his attempt to shake it off.*) Come: sit down quietly; and tell me what it is. And remember: we are friends, and need not fear that either of us will be anything but patient and kind to the other, whatever we may have to say.

MARCHBANKS (*twisting himself round on him*). Oh, I am not forgetting myself: I am only (*covering his face desperately with his hands*) full of horror. (*Then, dropping his hands, and thrusting his face forward fiercely at Morell, he goes on threateningly.*) You shall see whether this is a time for patience and kindness. (*Morell, firm as a rock, looks indulgently at him.*) Don't look at me in that self-complacent way. You think yourself stronger than I am; but I shall stagger you if you have a heart in your breast.

MORELL (*powerfully confident*). Stagger me, my boy. Out with it.

MARCHBANKS. First—

MORELL. First?

MARCHBANKS. I love your wife.

Morell recoils, and, after staring at him for a moment in utter amazement, bursts into uncontrollable laughter. Eugene is taken aback, but not disconcerted; and he soon becomes in-dignant and contemptuous.

MORELL (*sitting down to have his laugh out*). Why, my dear child, of course you do. Everybody loves her: they can't help it. I like it. But (*looking up whimsically at him*) I say, Eugene: do you think yours is a case to be talked about? You're under twenty: she's over thirty. Doesn't it look rather too like a case of calf love?

MARCHBANKS (*vehemently*). You dare say that of her! You think that way of the love she inspires! It is an insult to her!

MORELL (*rising quickly, in an altered tone*). To her! Eugene: take care. I have been patient. I hope to remain patient. But there are some things I won't allow. Don't force me to shew you the indulgence I should shew to a child. Be a man.

MARCHBANKS (*with a gesture as if sweeping something be-hind him*). Oh, let us put aside all that cant. It horrifies me when I think of the doses of it she has had to endure in all the weary years during which you have selfishly and blindly sacrificed her to minister to your self-sufficiency—you (*turning on him*) who have not one thought—one sense—in common with her.

MORELL (*philosophically*). She seems to bear it pretty well. (*Looking him straight in the face.*) Eugene, my boy: you are making a fool of yourself—a very great fool of yourself. There's a piece of wholesome plain speaking for you.

MARCHBANKS. Oh, do you think I don't know all that? Do you think that the things people make fools of themselves about are any less real and true than the things they behave sensibly about? (*Morell's gaze wavers for the first time. He instinctively averts his face and stands listening, startled and thoughtful.*) They are more true: they are the only things that are true. You are very calm and sensible and moderate with me because you can see that I am a fool about your wife; just as no doubt that old man who was here just now is very wise over your socialism, because he sees that you are a fool about it. (*Morell's perplexity deepens markedly. Eugene follows up his advantage, plying him fiercely with questions.*) Does that prove you wrong? Does your complacent superiority to me prove that I am wrong?

MORELL (*turning on Eugene, who stands his ground*). Marchbanks: some devil is putting these words into your mouth. It is easy—terribly easy—to shake a man's faith in himself. To take advantage of that to break a man's spirit is devil's work. Take care of what you are doing. Take care.

MARCHBANKS (*ruthlessly*). I know. I'm doing it on purpose. I told you I should stagger you.

They confront one another threateningly for a moment. Then Morell recovers his dignity.

MORELL (*with noble tenderness*). Eugene: listen to me. Some day, I hope and trust, you will be a happy man like me. (*Eugene chafes intolerantly, repudiating the worth of his happiness. Morell, deeply insulted, controls himself with fine forbearance, and continues steadily, with great artistic beauty of delivery.*) You will be married; and you will be working with all your might and valor to make every spot on earth as happy as your own home. You will be one of the makers of the Kingdom of Heaven on earth; and—who knows?—you may be a pioneer and master builder where I am only a humble journeyman; for don't think, my boy, that I cannot see in you, young as you are, promise of higher powers than I can ever pretend to. I well know that it is in the poet that the holy spirit of man—the god within him—is most godlike. It should make you tremble to think of that—to think that the heavy burthen and great gift of a poet may be laid upon you.

MARCHBANKS (*unimpressed and remorseless, his boyish crudity of assertion telling sharply against Morell's oratory*). It does not make me tremble. It is the want of it in others that makes me tremble.

MORELL (*redoubling his force of style under the stimulus of his genuine feeling and Eugene's obduracy*). Then help to kindle it in them—in me—not to extinguish it. In the future—when you are as happy as I am—I will be your true brother in the faith. I will help you to believe that God has given us a world that nothing but our own folly keeps from being a paradise. I will help you to believe that every stroke of your work is sowing happiness for the great harvest that all —even the humblest—shall one day reap. And last, but trust me, not least, I will help you to believe that your wife loves you and is happy in her home. We need such help, Marchbanks: we need it greatly and always. There are so many things to make us doubt, if once we let our understanding be troubled. Even at home, we sit as if in camp, encompassed

by a hostile army of doubts. Will you play the traitor and
let them in on me?

MARCHBANKS (*looking round him*). Is it like this for her
here always? A woman, with a great soul, craving for reality,
truth, freedom, and being fed on metaphors, sermons, stale
perorations, mere rhetoric. Do you think a woman's soul can
live on your talent for preaching?

MORELL (*stung*). Marchbanks: you make it hard for me to
control myself. My talent is like yours insofar as it has any
real worth at all. It is the gift of finding words for divine truth.

MARCHBANKS (*impetuously*). It's the gift of the gab, nothing more and nothing less. What has your knack of fine talking
to do with the truth, any more than playing the organ has?
I've never been in your church; but I've been to your political
meetings; and I've seen you do what's called rousing the meeting to enthusiasm: that is, you excited them until they behaved
exactly as if they were drunk. And their wives looked on and
saw clearly enough what fools they were. Oh, it's an old story:
you'll find it in the Bible. I imagine King David, in his fits of
enthusiasm, was very like you. (*Stabbing him with the words.*)
"But his wife despised him in her heart."

MORELL (*wrathfully*). Leave my house. Do you hear? (*He
advances on him threateningly.*)

MARCHBANKS (*shrinking back against the couch*). Let me
alone. Don't touch me. (*Morell grasps him powerfully by the
lapel of his coat: he cowers down on the sofa and screams
passionately.*) Stop, Morell, if you strike me, I'll kill myself:
I won't bear it. (*Almost in hysterics.*) Let me go. Take your
hand away.

MORELL (*with slow, emphatic scorn*). You little snivelling,
cowardly whelp. (*Releasing him.*) Go, before you frighten
yourself into a fit.

MARCHBANKS (*on the sofa, gasping, but relieved by the
withdrawal of Morell's hand*). I'm not afraid of you: it's you
who are afraid of me.

MORELL (*quietly, as he stands over him*). It looks like it,
doesn't it?

MARCHBANKS (*with petulant vehemence*). Yes, it does.
(*Morell turns away contemptuously. Eugene scrambles to his
feet and follows him.*) You think because I shrink from being
brutally handled—because (*with tears in his voice*) I can do
nothing but cry with rage when I am met with violence—

because I can't lift a heavy trunk down from the top of a cab like you—because I can't fight you for your wife as a navvy would: all that makes you think that I'm afraid of you. But you're wrong. If I haven't got what you call British pluck, I haven't British cowardice either: I'm not afraid of a clergyman's ideas. I'll fight your ideas. I'll rescue her from her slavery to them: I'll pit my own ideas against them. You are driving me out of the house because you daren't let her choose between your ideas and mine. You are afraid to let me see her again. (*Morell, angered, turns suddenly on him. He flies to the door in involuntary dread.*) Let me alone, I say. I'm going.

MORELL (*with cold scorn*). Wait a moment: I am not going to touch you: don't be afraid. When my wife comes back she will want to know why you have gone. And when she finds that you are never going to cross our threshold again, she will want to have that explained, too. Now I don't wish to distress her by telling her that you have behaved like a blackguard.

MARCHBANKS (*coming back with renewed vehemence*). You shall—you must. If you give any explanation but the true one, you are a liar and a coward. Tell her what I said; and how you were strong and manly, and shook me as a terrier shakes a rat; and how I shrank and was terrified; and how you called me a snivelling little whelp and put me out of the house. If you don't tell her, I will: I'll write it to her.

MORELL (*taken aback*). Why do you want her to know this?

MARCHBANKS (*with lyric rapture*). Because she will understand me, and know that I understand her. If you keep back one word of it from her—if you are not ready to lay the truth at her feet as I am—then you will know to the end of your days that she really belongs to me and not to you. Good-bye. (*Going.*)

MORELL (*terribly disquieted*). Stop: I will not tell her.

MARCHBANKS (*turning near the door*). Either the truth or a lie you must tell her, if I go.

MORELL (*temporizing*). Marchbanks: it is sometimes justifiable.

MARCHBANKS (*cutting him short*). I know—to lie. It will be useless. Good-bye, Mr. Clergyman.

As he turns finally to the door, it opens and Candida enters in housekeeping attire.

CANDIDA. Are you going, Eugene? (*Looking more observantly at him.*) Well, dear me, just look at you, going out into the street in that state! You are a poet, certainly. Look at him, James! (*She takes him by the coat, and brings him forward to show him to Morell.*) Look at his collar! look at his tie! look at his hair! One would think somebody had been throttling you. (*The two men guard themselves against betraying their consciousness.*) Here! Stand still. (*She buttons his collar; ties his neckerchief in a bow; and arranges his hair.*) There! Now you look so nice that I think you'd better stay to lunch after all, though I told you you mustn't. It will be ready in half an hour. (*She puts a final touch to the bow. He kisses her hand.*) Don't be silly.

MARCHBANKS. I want to stay, of course—unless the reverend gentleman, your husband, has anything to advance to the contrary.

CANDIDA. Shall he stay, James, if he promises to be a good boy and to help me to lay the table? (*Marchbanks turns his head and looks steadfastly at Morell over his shoulder, challenging his answer.*)

MORELL (*shortly*). Oh, yes, certainly: he had better. (*He goes to the table and pretends to busy himself with his papers there.*)

MARCHBANKS (*offering his arm to Candida*). Come and lay the table. (*She takes it and they go to the door together. As they go out he adds.*) I am the happiest of men.

MORELL. So was I—an hour ago.

ACT II

The same day. The same room. Late in the afternoon. The spare chair for visitors has been replaced at the table, which is, if possible, more untidy than before. Marchbanks, alone and idle, is trying to find out how the typewriter works. Hearing someone at the door, he steals guiltily away to the window and pretends to be absorbed in the view. Miss Garnett, carrying the notebook in which she takes down Morell's letters in shorthand from his dictation, sits down at the typewriter and sets to work transcribing them, much too busy to notice Eugene. Unfortunately the first key she strikes sticks.

PROSERPINE. Bother! You've been meddling with my typewriter, Mr. Marchbanks; and there's not the least use in your trying to look as if you hadn't.

MARCHBANKS (*timidly*). I'm very sorry, Miss Garnett. I only tried to make it write.

PROSERPINE. Well, you've made this key stick.

MARCHBANKS (*earnestly*). I assure you I didn't touch the keys. I didn't, indeed. I only turned a little wheel. (*He points irresolutely at the tension wheel.*)

PROSERPINE. Oh, now I understand. (*She sets the machine to rights, talking volubly all the time.*) I suppose you thought it was a sort of barrel-organ. Nothing to do but turn the handle, and it would write a beautiful love letter for you straight off, eh?

MARCHBANKS (*seriously*). I suppose a machine could be made to write love letters. They're all the same, aren't they?

PROSERPINE (*somewhat indignantly: any such discussion, except by way of pleasantry, being outside her code of manners*). How do I know? Why do you ask me?

MARCHBANKS. I beg your pardon. I thought clever people —people who can do business and write letters, and that sort of thing—always had love affairs.

PROSERPINE (*rising, outraged*). Mr. Marchbanks! (*She*

108

looks severely at him, and marches with much dignity to the bookcase.)

MARCHBANKS (*approaching her humbly*). I hope I haven't offended you. Perhaps I shouldn't have alluded to your love affairs.

PROSERPINE (*plucking a blue book from the shelf and turning sharply on him*). I haven't any love affairs. How dare you say such a thing?

MARCHBANKS (*simply*). Really! Oh, then you are shy, like me. Isn't that so?

PROSERPINE. Certainly I am not shy. What do you mean?

MARCHBANKS (*secretly*). You must be: that is the reason there are so few love affairs in the world. We all go about longing for love: it is the first need of our natures, the loudest cry of our hearts; but we dare not utter our longing: we are too shy. (*Very earnestly.*) Oh, Miss Garnett, what would you not give to be without fear, without shame—

PROSERPINE (*scandalized*). Well, upon my word!

MARCHBANKS (*with petulant impatience*). Ah, don't say those stupid things to me: they don't deceive me: what use are they? Why are you afraid to be your real self with me? I am just like you.

PROSERPINE. Like me! Pray, are you flattering me or flattering yourself? I don't feel quite sure which. (*She turns to go back to the typewriter.*)

MARCHBANKS (*stopping her mysteriously*). Hush! I go about in search of love; and I find it in unmeasured stores in the bosoms of others. But when I try to ask for it, this horrible shyness strangles me; and I stand dumb, or worse than dumb, saying meaningless things—foolish lies. And I see the affection I am longing for given to dogs and cats and pet birds, because they come and ask for it. (*Almost whispering.*) It must be asked for: it is like a ghost: it cannot speak unless it is first spoken to. (*At his normal pitch, but with deep melancholy.*) All the love in the world is longing to speak; only it dare not, because it is shy, shy, shy. That is the world's tragedy. (*With a deep sigh he sits in the spare chair and buries his face in his hands.*)

PROSERPINE (*amazed, but keeping her wits about her— her point of honor in encounters with strange young men*). Wicked people get over that shyness occasionally, don't they?

MARCHBANKS (*scrambling up almost fiercely*). Wicked peo-

ple means people who have no love: therefore they have no
shame. They have the power to ask love because they don't
need it: they have the power to offer it because they have
none to give. (*He collapses into his seat, and adds, mournfully.*) But we, who have love, and long to mingle it with the
love of others: we cannot utter a word. (*Timidly.*) You find
that, don't you?

PROSERPINE. Look here: if you don't stop talking like this,
I'll leave the room, Mr. Marchbanks: I really will. It's not
proper.

*She resumes her seat at the typewriter, opening the blue
book and preparing to copy a passage from it.*

MARCHBANKS (*hopelessly*). Nothing that's worth saying is
proper. (*He rises, and wanders about the room in his lost
way, saying.*) I can't understand you, Miss Garnett. What am
I to talk about?

PROSERPINE (*snubbing him*). Talk about indifferent things.
Talk about the weather.

MARCHBANKS. Would you stand and talk about indifferent
things if a child were by, crying bitterly with hunger?

PROSERPINE. I suppose not.

MARCHBANKS. Well: *I* can't talk about indifferent things
with my heart crying out bitterly in its hunger.

PROSERPINE. Then hold your tongue.

MARCHBANKS. Yes: that is what it always comes to. We
hold our tongues. Does that stop the cry of your heart?—
for it does cry: doesn't it? It must, if you have a heart.

PROSERPINE (*suddenly rising with her hand pressed on her
heart*). Oh, it's no use trying to work while you talk like that.
(*She leaves her little table and sits on the sofa. Her feelings
are evidently strongly worked on.*) It's no business of yours,
whether my heart cries or not; but I have a mind to tell you,
for all that.

MARCHBANKS. You needn't. I know already that it must.

PROSERPINE. But mind: if you ever say I said so, I'll deny it.

MARCHBANKS (*compassionately*). Yes, I know. And so you
haven't the courage to tell him?

PROSERPINE (*bouncing up*). Him! Who?

MARCHBANKS. Whoever he is. The man you love. It might
be anybody. The curate, Mr. Mill, perhaps.

PROSERPINE (*with disdain*). Mr. Mill !!! A fine man to break
my heart about, indeed! I'd rather have you than Mr. Mill.

MARCHBANKS (*recoiling*). No, really—I'm very sorry; but you mustn't think of that. I—

PROSERPINE (*testily, crossing to the fire and standing at it with her back to him*). Oh, don't be frightened: it's not you. It's not any one particular person.

MARCHBANKS. I know. You feel that you could love anybody that offered—

PROSERPINE (*exasperated*). Anybody that offered! No, I do not. What do you take me for?

MARCHBANKS (*discouraged*). No use. You won't make me real answers—only those things that everybody says. (*He strays to the sofa and sits down disconsolately.*)

PROSERPINE (*nettled at what she takes to be a disparagement of her manners by an aristocrat*). Oh, well, if you want original conversation, you'd better go and talk to yourself.

MARCHBANKS. That is what all poets do: they talk to themselves out loud; and the world overhears them. But it's horribly lonely not to hear someone else talk sometimes.

PROSERPINE. Wait until Mr. Morell comes. He'll talk to you. (*Marchbanks shudders.*) Oh, you needn't make wry faces over him: he can talk better than you. (*With temper.*) He'd talk your little head off. (*She is going back angrily to her place, when, suddenly enlightened, he springs up and stops her.*)

MARCHBANKS. Ah, I understand now!

PROSERPINE (*reddening*). What do you understand?

MARCHBANKS. Your secret. Tell me: is it really and truly possible for a woman to love him?

PROSERPINE (*as if this were beyond all bounds*). Well ! !

MARCHBANKS (*passionately*). No, answer me. I want to know: I must know. *I* can't understand it. I can see nothing in him but words, pious resolutions, what people call goodness. You can't love that.

PROSERPINE (*attempting to snub him by an air of cool propriety*). I simply don't know what you're talking about. I don't understand you.

MARCHBANKS (*vehemently*). You do. You lie—

PROSERPINE. Oh!

MARCHBANKS. You do understand; and you know. (*Determined to have an answer.*) Is it possible for a woman to love him?

PROSERPINE (*looking him straight in the face*). Yes. (*He

covers his face with his hands.) Whatever is the matter with you! (*He takes down his hands and looks at her. Frightened at the tragic mask presented to her, she hurries past him at the utmost possible distance, keeping her eyes on his face until he turns from her and goes to the child's chair beside the hearth, where he sits in the deepest dejection. As she approaches the door, it opens and Burgess enters. On seeing him, she ejaculates.*) Praise heaven, here's somebody! (*She sits down, reassured, at her table. She puts a fresh sheet of paper into the typewriter as Burgess crosses to Eugene.*)

BURGESS (*bent on taking care of the distinguished visitor*). Well: so this is the way they leave you to yourself, Mr. Morchbanks. I've come to keep you company. (*Marchbanks looks up at him in consternation, which is quite lost on him.*) James is receivin' a deppitation in the dinin' room; and Candy is hupstairs educatin' of a young stitcher gurl she's hinterusted in. She's settin' there learnin' her to read out of the " 'Ev'nly Twins." (*Condolingly.*) You must find it lonesome here with no one but the typist to talk to. (*He pulls round the easy chair above fire, and sits down.*)

PROSERPINE (*highly incensed*). He'll be all right now that he has the advantage of your polished conversation: that's one comfort, anyhow. (*She begins to typewrite with clattering asperity.*)

BURGESS (*amazed at her audacity*). Hi was not addressin' myself to you, young woman, that I'm awerr of.

PROSERPINE (*tartly, to Marchbanks*). Did you ever see worse manners, Mr. Marchbanks?

BURGESS (*with pompous severity*). Mr. Morchbanks is a gentleman and knows his place, which is more than some people do.

PROSERPINE (*fretfully*). It's well you and I are not ladies and gentlemen: I'd talk to you pretty straight if Mr. Marchbanks wasn't here. (*She pulls the letter out of the machine so crossly that it tears.*) There, now I've spoiled this letter —have to be done all over again. Oh, I can't contain myself— silly old fathead!

BURGESS (*rising, breathless with indignation*). Ho! I'm a silly ole fat'ead, am I? Ho, indeed (*gasping*). Hall right, my gurl! Hall right. You just wait till I tell that to your employer. You'll see. I'll teach you: see if I don't.

PROSERPINE. I——

BURGESS (*cutting her short*). No, you've done it now. No huse a-talkin' to me. I'll let you know who I am. (*Proserpine shifts her paper carriage with a defiant bang, and disdainfully goes on with her work.*) Don't you take no notice of her, Mr. Morchbanks. She's beneath it. (*He sits down again loftily.*)

MARCHBANKS (*miserably nervous and disconcerted*). Hadn't we better change the subject. I—I don't think Miss Garnett meant anything.

PROSERPINE (*with intense conviction*). Oh, didn't I though, just!

BURGESS. I wouldn't demean myself to take notice on her.

An electric bell rings twice.

PROSERPINE (*gathering up her note-book and papers*). That's for me. (*She hurries out.*)

BURGESS (*calling after her*). Oh, we can spare you. (*Somewhat relieved by the triumph of having the last word, and yet half inclined to try to improve on it, he looks after her for a moment; then subsides into his seat by Eugene, and addresses him very confidentially.*) Now we're alone, Mr. Morchbanks, let me give you a friendly 'int that I wouldn't give to everybody. 'Ow long 'ave you known my son-in-law James here?

MARCHBANKS. I don't know. I never can remember dates. A few months, perhaps.

BURGESS. Ever notice anything queer about him?

MARCHBANKS. I don't think so.

BURGESS (*impressively*). No more you wouldn't. That's the danger in it. Well, he's mad.

MARCHBANKS. Mad!

BURGESS. Mad as a Morch 'are. You take notice on him and you'll see.

MARCHBANKS (*beginning*). But surely that is only because his opinions—

BURGESS (*touching him with his forefinger on his knee, and pressing it as if to hold his attention with it*). That's wot I used ter think, Mr. Morchbanks. Hi thought long enough that it was honly 'is opinions; though, mind you, hopinions becomes vurry serious things when people takes to hactin' on 'em as 'e does. But that's not wot I go on. (*He looks round to make sure that they are alone, and bends over to Eugene's ear.*) Wot do you think he says to me this mornin' in this very room?

MARCHBANKS. What?

BURGESS. He sez to me—this is as sure as we're settin' here now—he sez: "I'm a fool," he sez; "and yore a scounderl"—as cool as possible. Me a scounderl, mind you! And then shook 'ands with me on it, as if it was to my credit! Do you mean to tell me that that man's sane?

MORELL (*outside, calling to Proserpine, holding the door open*). Get all their names and addresses, Miss Garnett.

PROSERPINE (*in the distance*). Yes, Mr. Morell.

Morell comes in, with the deputation's documents in his hands.

BURGESS (*aside to Marchbanks*). Yorr he is. Just you keep your heye on him and see. (*Rising momentously.*) I'm sorry, James, to 'ave to make a complaint to you. I don't want to do it; but I feel I oughter, as a matter o' right and dooty.

MORELL. What's the matter?

BURGESS. Mr. Morchbanks will bear me out: he was a witness. (*Very solemnly.*) Your young woman so far forgot herself as to call me a silly ole fat'ead.

MORELL (*delighted—with tremendous heartiness*). Oh, now, isn't that exactly like Prossy? She's so frank: she can't contain herself! Poor Prossy! Ha! Ha!

BURGESS (*trembling with rage*). And do you hexpec me to put up with it from the like of 'er?

MORELL. Pooh, nonsense! you can't take any notice of it. Never mind. (*He goes to the cellaret and puts the papers into one of the drawers.*)

BURGESS. Oh, I don't mind. I'm above it. But is it right? —that's what I want to know. Is it right?

MORELL. That's a question for the Church, not for the laity. Has it done you any harm, that's the question for you, eh? Of course, it hasn't. Think no more of it. (*He dismisses the subject by going to his place at the table and setting to work at his correspondence.*)

BURGESS (*aside to Marchbanks*). What did I tell you? Mad as a 'atter. (*He goes to the table and asks, with the sickly civility of a hungry man.*) When's dinner, James?

MORELL. Not for half an hour yet.

BURGESS (*with plaintive resignation*). Gimme a nice book to read over the fire, will you, James: thur's a good chap.

MORELL. What sort of book? A good one?

BURGESS (*with almost a yell of remonstrance*). Nah-oo!

Summat pleasant, just to pass the time. (*Morell takes an illustrated paper from the table and offers it. He accepts it humbly.*) Thank yer, James. (*He goes back to his easy chair at the fire, and sits there at his ease, reading.*)

MORELL (*as he writes*). Candida will come to entertain you presently. She has got rid of her pupil. She is filling the lamps.

MARCHBANKS (*starting up in the wildest consternation*). But that will soil her hands. I can't bear that, Morell: it's a shame. I'll go and fill them. (*He makes for the door.*)

MORELL. You'd better not. (*Marchbanks stops irresolutely.*) She'd only set you to clean my boots, to save me the trouble of doing it myself in the morning.

BURGESS (*with grave disapproval*). Don't you keep a servant now, James?

MORELL. Yes; but she isn't a slave; and the house looks as if I kept three. That means that everyone has to lend a hand. It's not a bad plan: Prossy and I can talk business after breakfast whilst we're washing up. Washing up's no trouble when there are two people to do it.

MARCHBANKS (*tormentedly*). Do you think every woman is as coarse-grained as Miss Garnett?

BURGESS (*emphatically*). That's quite right, Mr. Morchbanks. That's quite right. She is coarse-grained.

MORELL (*quietly and significantly*). Marchbanks!

MARCHBANKS. Yes.

MORELL. How many servants does your father keep?

MARCHBANKS. Oh, I don't know. (*He comes back uneasily to the sofa, as if to get as far as possible from Morell's questioning, and sits down in great agony of mind, thinking of the paraffin.*)

MORELL (*very gravely*). So many that you don't know. (*More aggressively.*) Anyhow, when there's anything coarse-grained to be done, you ring the bell and throw it on to somebody else, eh? That's one of the great facts in your existence, isn't it?

MARCHBANKS. Oh, don't torture me. The one great fact now is that your wife's beautiful fingers are dabbling in paraffin oil, and that you are sitting here comfortably preaching about it—everlasting preaching, preaching, words, words, words.

BURGESS (*intensely appreciating this retort*). Ha, ha! Devil a better. (*Radiantly.*) 'Ad you there, James, straight.

Candida comes in, well aproned, with a reading lamp trimmed, filled, and ready for lighting. She places it on the table near Morell, ready for use.

CANDIDA (*brushing her finger tips together with a slight twitch of her nose*). If you stay with us, Eugene, I think I will hand over the lamps to you.

MARCHBANKS. I will stay on condition that you hand over all the rough work to me.

CANDIDA. That's very gallant; but I think I should like to see how you do it first. (*Turning to Morell.*) James: you've not been looking after the house properly.

MORELL. What have I done—or not done—my love?

CANDIDA (*with serious vexation*). My own particular pet scrubbing brush has been used for blackleading. (*A heart-breaking wail bursts from Marchbanks. Burgess looks round, amazed. Candida hurries to the sofa.*) What's the matter? Are you ill, Eugene?

MARCHBANKS. No, not ill. Only horror, horror, horror! (*He bows his head on his hands.*)

BURGESS (*shocked*). What! Got the 'orrors, Mr. Morch-banks! Oh, that's bad, at your age. You must leave it off grajally.

CANDIDA (*reassured*). Nonsense, papa. It's only poetic horror, isn't it, Eugene? (*Petting him.*)

BURGESS (*abashed*). Oh, poetic 'orror, is it? I beg your pordon, I'm shore. (*He turns to the fire again, deprecating his hasty conclusion.*)

CANDIDA. What is it, Eugene—the scrubbing brush? (*He shudders.*) Well, there! never mind. (*She sits down beside him.*) Wouldn't you like to present me with a nice new one, with an ivory back inlaid with mother-of-pearl?

MARCHBANKS (*softly and musically, but sadly and long-ingly*). No, not a scrubbing brush, but a boat—a tiny shallop to sail away in, far from the world, where the marble floors are washed by the rain and dried by the sun, where the south wind dusts the beautiful green and purple carpets. Or a chariot—to carry us up into the sky, where the lamps are stars, and don't need to be filled with paraffin oil every day.

MORELL (*harshly*). And where there is nothing to do but to be idle, selfish and useless.

CANDIDA (*jarred*). Oh, James, how could you spoil it all!

MARCHBANKS (*firing up*). Yes, to be idle, selfish and useless: that is to be beautiful and free and happy: hasn't every man desired that with all his soul for the woman he loves? That's my ideal: what's yours, and that of all the dreadful people who live in these hideous rows of houses? Sermons and scrubbing brushes! With you to preach the sermon and your wife to scrub.

CANDIDA (*quaintly*). He cleans the boots, Eugene. You will have to clean them to-morrow for saying that about him.

MARCHBANKS. Oh! don't talk about boots. Your feet should be beautiful on the mountains.

CANDIDA. My feet would not be beautiful on the Hackney Road without boots.

BURGESS (*scandalized*). Come, Candy, don't be vulgar. Mr. Morchbanks ain't accustomed to it. You're givin' him the 'orrors again. I mean the poetic ones.

Morell is silent. Apparently he is busy with his letters: really he is puzzling with misgiving over his new and alarming experience that the surer he is of his moral thrusts, the more swiftly and effectively Eugene parries them. To find himself beginning to fear a man whom he does not respect afflicts him bitterly.

Miss Garnett comes in with a telegram.

PROSERPINE (*handing the telegram to Morell*). Reply paid. The boy's waiting. (*To Candida, coming back to her machine and sitting down.*) Maria is ready for you now in the kitchen, Mrs. Morell. (*Candida rises.*) The onions have come.

MARCHBANKS (*convulsively*). Onions!

CANDIDA. Yes, onions. Not even Spanish ones—nasty little red onions. You shall help me to slice them. Come along.

She catches him by the wrist and runs out, pulling him after her. Burgess rises in consternation, and stands aghast on the hearth-rug, staring after them.

BURGESS. Candy didn't oughter 'andle a peer's nevvy like that. It's goin' too fur with it. Lookee 'ere, James; do 'e often git taken queer like that?

MORELL (*shortly, writing a telegram*). I don't know.

BURGESS (*sentimentally*). He talks very pretty. I allus had a turn for a bit of poetry. Candy takes arter me that-a-way: huse ter make me tell her fairy stories when she was on'y a little kiddy not that 'igh (*indicating a stature of two feet or thereabouts*).

MORELL (*preoccupied*). Ah, indeed. (*He blots the telegram, and goes out.*)

PROSERPINE. Used you to make the fairy stories up out of your own head?

Burgess, not deigning to reply, strikes an attitude of the haughtiest disdain on the hearth-rug.

PROSERPINE (*calmly*). I should never have supposed you had it in you. By the way, I'd better warn you, since you've taken such a fancy to Mr. Marchbanks. He's mad.

BURGESS. Mad! Wot! 'Im too!!

PROSERPINE. Mad as a March hare. He did frighten me, I can tell you just before you came in that time. Haven't you noticed the queer things he says?

BURGESS. So that's wot the poetic 'orrors means. Blame me if it didn't come into my head once or twyst that he must be off his chump! (*He crosses the room to the door, lifting up his voice as he goes.*) Well, this is a pretty sort of asylum for a man to be in, with no one but you to take care of him!

PROSERPINE (*as he passes her*). Yes, what a dreadful thing it would be if anything happened to you!

BURGESS (*loftily*). Don't you address no remarks to me. Tell your hemployer that I've gone into the garden for a smoke.

PROSERPINE (*mocking*). Oh!

Before Burgess can retort, Morell comes back.

BURGESS (*sentimentally*). Goin' for a turn in the garden to smoke, James.

MORELL (*brusquely*). Oh, all right, all right. (*Burgess goes out pathetically in the character of the weary old man. Morell stands at the table, turning over his papers, and adding, across to Proserpine, half humorously, half absently.*) Well, Miss Prossy, why have you been calling my father-in-law names?

PROSERPINE (*blushing fiery red, and looking quickly up at him, half scared, half reproachful*). I— (*She bursts into tears.*)

MORELL (*with tender gaiety, leaning across the table towards her, and consoling her*). Oh, come, come, come! Never mind, Pross: he is a silly old fathead, isn't he?

With an explosive sob, she makes a dash at the door, and vanishes, banging it. Morell, shaking his head resignedly, sighs, and goes wearily to his chair, where he sits down and sets to work, looking old and careworn.

Candida comes in. She has finished her household work and taken off the apron. She at once notices his dejected appearance, and posts herself quietly at the spare chair, looking down at him attentively; but she says nothing.

MORELL (*looking up, but with his pen raised ready to resume his work*). Well? Where is Eugene?

CANDIDA. Washing his hands in the scullery—under the tap. He will make an excellent cook if he can only get over his dread of Maria.

MORELL (*shortly*). Ha! No doubt. (*He begins writing again.*)

CANDIDA (*going nearer, and putting her hand down softly on his to stop him, as she says*). Come here, dear. Let me look at you. (*He drops his pen and yields himself at her disposal. She makes him rise and brings him a little away from the table, looking at him critically all the time.*) Turn your face to the light. (*She places him facing the window.*) My boy is not looking well. Has he been overworking?

MORELL. Nothing more than usual.

CANDIDA. He looks very pale, and grey, and wrinkled, and old. (*His melancholy deepens; and she attacks it with wilful gaiety.*) Here (*pulling him towards the easy chair*) you've done enough writing for to-day. Leave Prossy to finish it and come and talk to me.

MORELL. But—

CANDIDA. Yes, I must be talked to sometimes. (*She makes him sit down, and seats herself on the carpet beside his knee.*) Now (*patting his hand*) you're beginning to look better already. Why don't you give up all this tiresome overworking—going out every night lecturing and talking? Of course what you say is all very true and very right; but it does no good: they don't mind what you say to them one little bit. Of course they agree with you; but what's the use of people agreeing with you if they go and do just the opposite of what you tell them the moment your back is turned? Look at our congregation at St. Dominic's! Why do they come to hear you talking about Christianity every Sunday? Why, just because they've been so full of business and money-making for six days that they want to forget all about it and have a rest on the seventh, so that they can go back fresh and make money harder than ever! You positively help them at it instead of hindering them.

MORELL (*with energetic seriousness*). You know very well, Candida, that I often blow them up soundly for that. But if there is nothing in their church-going but rest and diversion, why don't they try something more amusing—more self-indulgent? There must be some good in the fact that they prefer St. Dominic's to worse places on Sundays.

CANDIDA. Oh, the worst places aren't open; and even if they were, they daren't be seen going to them. Besides, James, dear, you preach so splendidly that it's as good as a play for them. Why do you think the women are so enthusiastic?

MORELL (*shocked*). Candida!

CANDIDA. Oh, *I* know. You silly boy: you think it's your Socialism and your religion; but if it was that, they'd do what you tell them instead of only coming to look at you. They all have Prossy's complaint.

MORELL. Prossy's complaint! What do you mean, Candida?

CANDIDA. Yes, Prossy, and all the other secretaries you ever had. Why does Prossy condescend to wash up the things, and to peel potatoes and abase herself in all manner of ways for six shillings a week less than she used to get in a city office? She's in love with you, James: that's the reason. They're all in love with you. And you are in love with preaching because you do it so beautifully. And you think it's all enthusiasm for the kingdom of Heaven on earth; and so do they. You dear silly!

MORELL. Candida: what dreadful, what soul-destroying cynicism! Are you jesting? Or—can it be?—are you jealous?

CANDIDA (*with curious thoughtfulness*). Yes, I feel a little jealous sometimes.

MORELL (*incredulously*). What! Of Prossy!

CANDIDA (*laughing*). No, no, no, no. Not jealous of anybody. Jealous for somebody else, who is not loved as he ought to be.

MORELL. Me!

CANDIDA. You! Why, you're spoiled with love and worship: you get far more than is good for you. No: I mean Eugene.

MORELL (*startled*). Eugene!

CANDIDA. It seems unfair that all the love should go to you, and none to him, although he needs it so much more than you do. (*A convulsive movement shakes him in spite of himself.*) What's the matter? Am I worrying you?

MORELL (*hastily*). Not at all. (*Looking at her with troubled intensity.*) You know that I have perfect confidence in you, Candida.

CANDIDA. You vain thing! Are you so sure of your irresistible attractions?

MORELL. Candida: you are shocking me. I never thought of my attractions. I thought of your goodness—your purity. That is what I confide in.

CANDIDA. What a nasty, uncomfortable thing to say to me! Oh, you are a clergyman, James—a thorough clergyman.

MORELL (*turning away from her, heart-stricken*). So Eugene says.

CANDIDA (*with lively interest, leaning over to him with her arms on his knee*). Eugene's always right. He's a wonderful boy: I have grown fonder and fonder of him all the time I was away. Do you know, James, that though he has not the least suspicion of it himself, he is ready to fall madly in love with me?

MORELL (*grimly*). Oh, he has no suspicion of it himself, hasn't he?

CANDIDA. Not a bit. (*She takes her arms from his knee, and turns thoughtfully, sinking into a more restful attitude with her hands in her lap.*) Some day he will know—when he is grown up and experienced, like you. And he will know that I must have known. I wonder what he will think of me then.

MORELL. No evil, Candida. I hope and trust, no evil.

CANDIDA (*dubiously*). That will depend.

MORELL (*bewildered*). Depend!

CANDIDA (*looking at him*). Yes: it will depend on what happens to him. (*He looks vacantly at her.*) Don't you see? It will depend on how he comes to learn what love really is. I mean on the sort of woman who will teach it to him.

MORELL (*quite at a loss*). Yes. No. I don't know what you mean.

CANDIDA (*explaining*). If he learns it from a good woman, then it will be all right: he will forgive me.

MORELL. Forgive!

CANDIDA. But suppose he learns it from a bad woman, as so many men do, especially poetic men, who imagine all women are angels! Suppose he only discovers the value of love when he has thrown it away and degraded himself in his ignorance. Will he forgive me then, do you think?

MORELL. Forgive you for what?

CANDIDA (*realizing how stupid he is, and a little disappointed, though quite tenderly so*). Don't you understand? (*He shakes his head. She turns to him again, so as to explain with the fondest intimacy.*) I mean, will he forgive me for not teaching him myself? For abandoning him to the bad women for the sake of my goodness—my purity, as you call it? Ah, James, how little you understand me, to talk of your confidence in my goodness and purity! I would give them both to poor Eugene as willingly as I would give my shawl to a beggar dying of cold, if there were nothing else to restrain me. Put your trust in my love for you, James, for if that went, I should care very little for your sermons—mere phrases that you cheat yourself and others with every day. (*She is about to rise.*)

MORELL. His words!

CANDIDA (*checking herself quickly in the act of getting up, so that she is on her knees, but upright*). Whose words?

MORELL. Eugene's.

CANDIDA (*delighted*). He is always right. He understands you; he understands me; he understands Prossy; and you, James—you understand nothing. (*She laughs, and kisses him to console him. He recoils as if stung, and springs up.*)

MORELL. How can you bear to do that when—oh, Candida (*with anguish in his voice*) I had rather you had plunged a grappling iron into my heart than given me that kiss.

CANDIDA (*rising, alarmed*). My dear: what's the matter?

MORELL (*frantically waving her off*). Don't touch me.

CANDIDA (*amazed*). James!

They are interrupted by the entrance of Marchbanks, with Burgess, who stops near the door, staring, whilst Eugene hurries forward between them.

MARCHBANKS. Is anything the matter?

MORELL (*deadly white, putting an iron constraint on himself*). Nothing but this: that either you were right this morning, or Candida is mad.

BURGESS (*in loudest protest*). Wot! Candy mad too! Oh, come, come, come! (*He crosses the room to the fireplace, protesting as he goes, and knocks the ashes out of his pipe on the bars. Morell sits down desperately, leaning forward to hide his face, and interlacing his fingers rigidly to keep them steady.*)

CANDIDA (*to Morell, relieved and laughing*). Oh, you're only shocked! Is that all? How conventional all you unconventional people are!

BURGESS. Come: be'ave yourself, Candy. What'll Mr. Morchbanks think of you?

CANDIDA. This comes of James teaching me to think for myself, and never to hold back out of fear of what other people may think of me. It works beautifully as long as I think the same things as he does. But now, because I have just thought something different!—look at him—just look! (*She points to Morell, greatly amused. Eugene looks, and instantly presses his hand on his heart, as if some deadly pain had shot through it, and sits down on the sofa like a man witnessing a tragedy.*)

BURGESS (*on the hearth-rug*). Well, James, you certainly ain't as himpressive lookin' as usu'l.

MORELL (*with a laugh which is half a sob*). I suppose not. I beg all your pardons: I was not conscious of making a fuss. (*Pulling himself together.*) Well, well, well, well, well! (*He goes back to his place at the table, setting to work at his papers again with resolute cheerfulness.*)

CANDIDA (*going to the sofa and sitting beside Marchbanks, still in a bantering humor*). Well, Eugene, why are you so sad? Did the onions make you cry?

Morell cannot prevent himself from watching them.

MARCHBANKS (*aside to her*). It is your cruelty. I hate cruelty. It is a horrible thing to see one person make another suffer.

CANDIDA (*petting him ironically*). Poor boy, have I been cruel? Did I make it slice nasty little red onions?

MARCHBANKS (*earnestly*). Oh, stop, stop: I don't mean myself. You have made him suffer frightfully. I feel his pain in my own heart. I know that it is not your fault—it is something that must happen; but don't make light of it. I shudder when you torture him and laugh.

CANDIDA (*incredulously*). *I* torture James! Nonsense, Eugene: how you exaggerate! Silly! (*She looks round at Morell, who hastily resumes his writing. She goes to him and stands behind his chair, bending over him.*) Don't work any more, dear. Come and talk to us.

MORELL (*affectionately but bitterly*). Ah no: *I* can't talk. I can only preach.

CANDIDA (*caressing him*). Well, come and preach.

BURGESS (*strongly remonstrating*). Aw, no, Candy. 'Ang it all!

Lexy Mill comes in, looking anxious and important.

LEXY (*hastening to shake hands with Candida*). How do you do, Mrs. Morell? So glad to see you back again.

CANDIDA. Thank you, Lexy. You know Eugene, don't you?

LEXY. Oh, yes. How do you do, Marchbanks?

MARCHBANKS. Quite well, thanks.

LEXY (*to Morell*). I've just come from the Guild of St. Matthew. They are in the greatest consternation about your telegram. There's nothing wrong, is there?

CANDIDA. What did you telegraph about, James?

LEXY (*to Candida*). He was to have spoken for them to-night. They've taken the large hall in Mare Street and spent a lot of money on posters. Morell's telegram was to say he couldn't come. It came on them like a thunderbolt.

CANDIDA (*surprized, and beginning to suspect something wrong*). Given up an engagement to speak!

BURGESS. First time in his life, I'll bet. Ain't it, Candy?

LEXY (*to Morell*). They decided to send an urgent telegram to you asking whether you could not change your mind. Have you received it?

MORELL (*with restrained impatience*). Yes, yes: I got it.

LEXY. It was reply paid.

MORELL. Yes, I know. I answered it. I can't go.

CANDIDA. But why, James?

MORELL (*almost fiercely*). Because I don't choose. These people forget that I am a man: they think I am a talking machine to be turned on for their pleasure every evening of my life. May I not have one night at home, with my wife, and my friends?

They are all amazed at this outburst, except Eugene. His expression remains unchanged.

CANDIDA. Oh, James, you know you'll have an attack of bad conscience to-morrow; and *I* shall have to suffer for that.

LEXY (*intimidated, but urgent*). I know, of course, that they make the most unreasonable demands on you. But they have been telegraphing all over the place for another speaker: and they can get nobody but the President of the Agnostic League.

MORELL (*promptly*). Well, an excellent man. What better do they want?

LEXY. But he always insists so powerfully on the divorce of Socialism from Christianity. He will undo all the good we have been doing. Of course you know best; but—(*He hesitates.*)

CANDIDA (*coaxingly*). Oh, do go, James. We'll all go.

BURGESS (*grumbling*). Look 'ere, Candy! I say! Let's stay at home by the fire, comfortable. He won't need to be more'n a couple-o'-hour away.

CANDIDA. You'll be just as comfortable at the meeting. We'll all sit on the platform and be great people.

EUGENE (*terrified*). Oh, please don't let us go on the platform. No—everyone will stare at us—I couldn't. I'll sit at the back of the room.

CANDIDA. Don't be afraid. They'll be too busy looking at James to notice you.

MORELL (*turning his head and looking meaningly at her over his shoulder*). Prossy's complaint, Candida! Eh?

CANDIDA (*gaily*). Yes.

BURGESS (*mystified*). Prossy's complaint. Wot are you talking about, James?

MORELL (*not heeding him, rises; goes to the door; and holds it open, shouting in a commanding voice*). Miss Garnett.

PROSERPINE (*in the distance*). Yes, Mr. Morell. Coming.

They all wait, except Burgess, who goes stealthily to Lexy and draws him aside.

BURGESS. Listen here, Mr. Mill. Wot's Prossy's complaint? Wot's wrong with 'er?

LEXY (*confidentially*). Well, I don't exactly know; but she spoke very strangely to me this morning. I'm afraid she's a little out of her mind sometimes.

BURGESS (*overwhelmed*). Why, it must be catchin'! Four in the same 'ouse! (*He goes back to the hearth, quite lost before the instability of the human intellect in a clergyman's house.*)

PROSERPINE (*appearing on the threshold*). What is it, Mr. Morell?

MORELL. Telegraph to the Guild of St. Matthew that I am coming.

PROSERPINE (*surprised*). Don't they expect you?

MORELL (*peremptorily*). Do as I tell you.

Proserpine, frightened, sits down at her typewriter, and obeys. Morell goes across to Burgess, Candida watching his movements all the time with growing wonder and misgiving.

MORELL. Burgess: you don't want to come?

BURGESS (*in deprecation*). Oh, don't put it like that, James. It's only that it ain't Sunday, you know.

MORELL. I'm sorry. I thought you might like to be introduced to the chairman. He's on the Works Committee of the County Council and has some influence in the matter of contracts. (*Burgess wakes up at once. Morell, expecting as much, waits a moment, and says.*) Will you come?

BURGESS (*with enthusiasm*). Course I'll come, James. Ain' it always a pleasure to 'ear you?

MORELL (*turning from him*). I shall want you to take some notes at the meeting, Miss Garnett, if you have no other engagement. (*She nods, afraid to speak.*) You are coming, Lexy, I suppose.

LEXY. Certainly.

CANDIDA. We are all coming, James.

MORELL. No: you are not coming; and Eugene is not coming. You will stay here and entertain him—to celebrate your return home. (*Eugene rises, breathless.*)

CANDIDA. But, James—

MORELL (*authoritatively*). I insist. You do not want to come; and he does not want to come. (*Candida is about to protest.*) Oh, don't concern yourselves: I shall have plenty of people without you: your chairs will be wanted by unconverted people who have never heard me before.

CANDIDA (*troubled*). Eugene: wouldn't you like to come?

MORELL. I should be afraid to let myself go before Eugene: he is so critical of sermons. (*Looking at him.*) He knows I am afraid of him: he told me as much this morning. Well, I shall shew him how much afraid I am by leaving him here in your custody, Candida.

MARCHBANKS (*to himself, with vivid feeling*). That's brave. That's beautiful. (*He sits down again listening with parted lips.*)

CANDIDA (*with anxious misgiving*). But—but— Is anything the matter, James? (*Greatly troubled.*) I can't understand—

MORELL. Ah, I thought it was *I* who couldn't understand, dear. (*He takes her tenderly in his arms and kisses her on the forehead; then looks round quietly at Marchbanks.*)

ACT III

Late in the evening. Past ten. The curtains are drawn, and the lamps lighted. The typewriter is in its case; the large table has been cleared and tidied; everything indicates that the day's work is done.

Candida and Marchbanks are seated at the fire. The reading lamp is on the mantelshelf above Marchbanks, who is sitting on the small chair reading aloud from a manuscript. A little pile of manuscripts and a couple of volumes of poetry are on the carpet beside him. Candida is in the easy chair with the poker, a light brass one, upright in her hand. She is leaning back and looking at the point of it curiously, with her feet stretched towards the blaze and her heels resting on the fender, profoundly unconscious of her appearance and surroundings.

MARCHBANKS (*breaking off in his recitation*). Every poet that ever lived has put that thought into a sonnet. He must: he can't help it. (*He looks to her for assent, and notices her absorption in the poker.*) Haven't you been listening? (*No response.*) Mrs. Morell!

CANDIDA (*starting*). Eh?

MARCHBANKS. Haven't you been listening?

CANDIDA (*with a guilty excess of politeness*). Oh, yes. It's very nice. Go on, Eugene. I'm longing to hear what happens to the angel.

MARCHBANKS (*crushed—the manuscript dropping from his hand to the floor*). I beg your pardon for boring you.

CANDIDA. But you are not boring me, I assure you. Please go on. Do, Eugene.

MARCHBANKS. I finished the poem about the angel quarter of an hour ago. I've read you several things since.

CANDIDA (*remorsefully*). I'm so sorry, Eugene. I think the poker must have fascinated me. (*She puts it down.*)

MARCHBANKS. It made me horribly uneasy.

128

CANDIDA. Why didn't you tell me? I'd have put it down at once.

MARCHBANKS. I was afraid of making you uneasy, too. It looked as if it were a weapon. If I were a hero of old, I should have laid my drawn sword between us. If Morell had come in he would have thought you had taken up the poker because there was no sword between us.

CANDIDA (*wondering*). What? (*With a puzzled glance at him.*) I can't quite follow that. Those sonnets of yours have perfectly addled me. Why should there be a sword between us?

MARCHBANKS (*evasively*). Oh, never mind. (*He stoops to pick up the manuscript.*)

CANDIDA. Put that down again, Eugene. There are limits to my appetite for poetry—even your poetry. You've been reading to me for more than two hours—ever since James went out. I want to talk.

MARCHBANKS (*rising, scared*). No: I mustn't talk. (*He looks round him in his lost way, and adds, suddenly.*) I think I'll go out and take a walk in the park. (*Making for the door.*)

CANDIDA. Nonsense: it's shut long ago. Come and sit down on the hearth-rug, and talk moonshine as you usually do. I want to be amused. Don't you want to?

MARCHBANKS (*in half terror, half rapture*). Yes.

CANDIDA. Then come along. (*She moves her chair back a little to make room. He hesitates; then timidly stretches himself on the hearth-rug, face upwards, and throws back his head across her knees, looking up at her.*)

MARCHBANKS. Oh, I've been so miserable all the evening, because I was doing right. Now I'm doing wrong; and I'm happy.

CANDIDA (*tenderly amused at him*). Yes: I'm sure you feel a great grown up wicked deceiver—quite proud of yourself, aren't you?

MARCHBANKS (*raising his head quickly and turning a little to look round at her*). Take care. I'm ever so much older than you, if you only knew. (*He turns quite over on his knees, with his hands clasped and his arms on her lap, and speaks with growing impulse, his blood beginning to stir.*) May I say some wicked things to you?

CANDIDA (*without the least fear or coldness, quite nobly, and with perfect respect for his passion, but with a touch of *her wise-hearted maternal humor*). No. But you may say anything you really and truly feel. Anything at all, no matter what it is. I am not afraid, so long as it is your real self that speaks, and not a mere attitude—a gallant attitude, or a wicked attitude, or even a poetic attitude. I put you on your honor and truth. Now say whatever you want to.

MARCHBANKS (*the eager expression vanishing utterly from his lips and nostrils as his eyes light up with pathetic spirituality*). Oh, now I can't say anything: all the words I know belong to some attitude or other—all except one.

CANDIDA. What one is that?

MARCHBANKS (*softly, losing himself in the music of the name*). Candida, Candida, Candida, Candida, Candida. I must say that now, because you have put me on my honor and truth; and I never think or feel Mrs. Morell: it is always Candida.

CANDIDA. Of course. And what have you to say to Candida?

MARCHBANKS. Nothing, but to repeat your name a thousand times. Don't you feel that every time is a prayer to you?

CANDIDA. Doesn't it make you happy to be able to pray?

MARCHBANKS. Yes, very happy.

CANDIDA. Well, that happiness is the answer to your prayer. Do you want anything more?

MARCHBANKS (*in beatitude*). No: I have come into heaven, where want is unknown.

Morell comes in. He halts on the threshold, and takes in the scene at a glance.

MORELL (*grave and self-contained*). I hope I don't disturb you.

Candida starts up violently, but without the smallest embarrassment, laughing at herself. Eugene, still kneeling, saves himself from falling by putting his hands on the seat of the chair, and remains there, staring open mouthed at Morell.

CANDIDA (*as she rises*). Oh, James, how you startled me! I was so taken up with Eugene that I didn't hear your latchkey. How did the meeting go off? Did you speak well?

MORELL. I have never spoken better in my life.

CANDIDA. That was first rate! How much was the collection?

MORELL. I forgot to ask.

CANDIDA (*to Eugene*). He must have spoken splendidly, or he would never have forgotten that. (*To Morell.*) Where are all the others?

MORELL. They left long before I could get away: I thought I should never escape. I believe they are having supper somewhere.

CANDIDA (*in her domestic business tone*). Oh; in that case, Maria may go to bed. I'll tell her. (*She goes out to the kitchen.*)

MORELL (*looking sternly down at Marchbanks*). Well?

MARCHBANKS (*squatting cross-legged on the hearth-rug, and actually at ease with Morell—even impishly humorous*). Well?

MORELL. Have you anything to tell me?

MARCHBANKS. Only that I have been making a fool of myself here in private whilst you have been making a fool of yourself in public.

MORELL. Hardly in the same way, I think.

MARCHBANKS (*scrambling up—eagerly*). The very, very, very same way. I have been playing the good man just like you. When you began your heroics about leaving me here with Candida—

MORELL (*involuntarily*). Candida?

MARCHBANKS. Oh, yes: I've got that far. Heroics are infectious: I caught the disease from you. I swore not to say a word in your absence that I would not have said a month ago in your presence.

MORELL. Did you keep your oath?

MARCHBANKS (*suddenly perching himself grotesquely on the easy chair*). I was ass enough to keep it until about ten minutes ago. Up to that moment I went on desperately reading to her—reading my own poems—anybody's poems—to stave off a conversation. It was standing outside the gate of Heaven, and refusing to go in. Oh, you can't think how heroic it was, and how uncomfortable! Then—

MORELL (*steadily controlling his suspense*). Then?—

MARCHBANKS (*prosaically slipping down into a quite ordinary attitude in the chair*). Then she couldn't bear being read to any longer.

MORELL. And you approached the gate of Heaven at last?

MARCHBANKS. Yes.

MORELL. Well? (*Fiercely.*) Speak, man: have you no feeling for me?

MARCHBANKS (*softly and musically*). Then she became an angel; and there was a flaming sword that turned every way, so that I couldn't go in; for I saw that that gate was really the gate of Hell.

MORELL (*triumphantly*). She repulsed you!

MARCHBANKS (*rising in wild scorn*). No, you fool: if she had done that I should never have seen that I was in Heaven already. Repulsed me! You think that would have saved me—virtuous indignation! Oh, you are not worthy to live in the same world with her. (*He turns away contemptuously to the other side of the room.*)

MORELL (*who has watched him quietly without changing his place*). Do you think you make yourself more worthy by reviling me, Eugene?

MARCHBANKS. Here endeth the thousand and first lesson. Morell: I don't think much of your preaching after all: I believe I could do it better myself. The man I want to meet is the man that Candida married.

MORELL. The man that—? Do you mean me?

MARCHBANKS. I don't mean the Reverend James Mavor Morell, moralist and windbag. I mean the real man that the Reverend James must have hidden somewhere inside his black coat—the man that Candida loved. You can't make a woman like Candida love you by merely buttoning your collar at the back instead of in front.

MORELL (*boldly and steadily*). When Candida promised to marry me, I was the same moralist and windbag that you now see. I wore my black coat; and my collar was buttoned behind instead of in front. Do you think she would have loved me any better for being insincere in my profession?

MARCHBANKS (*on the sofa hugging his ankles*). Oh, she forgave you, just as she forgives me for being a coward, and a weakling, and what you call a snivelling little whelp and all the rest of it. (*Dreamily.*) A woman like that has divine insight: she loves our souls, and not our follies and vanities and illusions, or our collars and coats, or any other of the rags and tatters we are rolled up in. (*He reflects on this for an instant; then turns intently to question Morell.*) What I want to know is how you got past the flaming sword that stopped me.

MORELL (*meaningly*). Perhaps because I was not interrupted at the end of ten minutes.

MARCHBANKS (*taken aback*). What!

MORELL. Man can climb to the highest summits; but he cannot dwell there long.

MARCHBANKS. It's false: there can he dwell for ever and there only. It's in the other moments that he can find no rest, no sense of the silent glory of life. Where would you have me spend my moments, if not on the summits?

MORELL. In the scullery, slicing onions and filling lamps.

MARCHBANKS. Or in the pulpit, scrubbing cheap earthenware souls?

MORELL. Yes, that, too. It was there that I earned my golden moment, and the right, in that moment, to ask her to love me. *I* did not take the moment on credit; nor did I use it to steal another man's happiness.

MARCHBANKS (*rather disgustedly, trotting back towards the fireplace*). I have no doubt you conducted the transaction as honestly as if you were buying a pound of cheese. (*He stops on the brink of the hearth-rug and adds, thoughtfully, to himself, with his back turned to Morell.*) I could only go to her as a beggar.

MORELL (*starting*). A beggar dying of cold—asking for her shawl?

MARCHBANKS (*turning, surprised*). Thank you for touching up my poetry. Yes, if you like, a beggar dying of cold asking for her shawl.

MORELL (*excitedly*). And she refused. Shall I tell you why she refused? I can tell you, on her own authority. It was because of—

MARCHBANKS. She didn't refuse.

MORELL. No!

MARCHBANKS. She offered me all I chose to ask for, her shawl, her wings, the wreath of stars on her head, the lilies in her hand, the crescent moon beneath her feet—

MORELL (*seizing him*). Out with the truth, man: my wife is my wife: I want no more of your poetic fripperies. I know well that if I have lost her love and you have gained it, no law will bind her.

MARCHBANKS (*quaintly, without fear or resistance*). Catch me by the shirt collar, Morell: she will arrange it for me afterwards as she did this morning. (*With quiet rapture.*) I shall feel her hands touch me.

MORELL. You young imp, do you know how dangerous

it is to say that to me? Or (*with a sudden misgiving*) has something made you brave?

MARCHBANKS. I'm not afraid now. I disliked you before: that was why I shrank from your touch. But I saw to-day—when she tortured you—that you love her. Since then I have been your friend: you may strangle me if you like.

MORELL (*releasing him*). Eugene: if that is not a heartless lie—if you have a spark of human feeling left in you—will you tell me what has happened during my absence?

MARCHBANKS. What happened! Why, the flaming sword—(*Morell stamps with impatience.*) Well, in plain prose, I loved her so exquisitely that I wanted nothing more than the happiness of being in such love. And before I had time to come down from the highest summits, you came in.

MORELL (*suffering deeply*). So it is still unsettled—still the misery of doubt.

MARCHBANKS. Misery! I am the happiest of men. I desire nothing now but her happiness. (*With dreamy enthusiasm.*) Oh, Morell, let us both give her up. Why should she have to choose between a wretched little nervous disease like me, and a pig-headed parson like you? Let us go on a pilgrimage, you to the east and I to the west, in search of a worthy lover for her—some beautiful archangel with purple wings—

MORELL. Some fiddlestick. Oh, if she is mad enough to leave me for you, who will protect her? Who will help her? who will work for her? who will be a father to her children? (*He sits down distractedly on the sofa, with his elbows on his knees and his head propped on his clenched fists.*)

MARCHBANKS (*snapping his fingers wildly*). She does not ask those silly questions. It is she who wants somebody to protect, to help, to work for—somebody to give her children to protect, to help and to work for. Some grown up man who has become as a little child again. Oh, you fool, you fool, you triple fool! I am the man, Morell: I am the man. (*He dances about excitedly, crying.*) You don't understand what a woman is. Send for her, Morell: send for her and let her choose between— (*The door opens and Candida enters. He stops as if petrified.*)

CANDIDA (*amazed, on the threshold*). What on earth are you at, Eugene?

MARCHBANKS (*oddly*). James and I are having a preaching match; and he is getting the worst of it. (*Candida looks quickly round at Morell. Seeing that he is distressed, she hurries down to him, greatly vexed, speaking with vigorous reproach to Marchbanks.)*

CANDIDA. You have been annoying him. Now I won't have it, Eugene: do you hear? (*Putting her hand on Morell's shoulder, and quite forgetting her wifely tact in her annoyance.*) My boy shall not be worried: I will protect him.

MORELL (*rising proudly*). Protect!

CANDIDA (*not heeding him—to Eugene*). What have you been saying?

MARCHBANKS (*appalled*). Nothing—I—

CANDIDA. Eugene! Nothing?

MARCHBANKS (*piteously*). I mean—I—I'm very sorry. I won't do it again: indeed I won't. I'll let him alone.

MORELL (*indignantly, with an aggressive movement towards Eugene*). Let me alone! You young—

CANDIDA (*stopping him*). Sh—no, let me deal with him, James.

MARCHBANKS. Oh, you're not angry with me, are you?

CANDIDA (*severely*). Yes, I am—very angry. I have a great mind to pack you out of the house.

MORELL (*taken aback by Candida's vigor, and by no means relishing the sense of being rescued by her from another man*). Gently, Candida, gently. I am able to take care of myself.

CANDIDA (*petting him*). Yes, dear: of course you are. But you mustn't be annoyed and made miserable.

MARCHBANKS (*almost in tears, turning to the door*). I'll go.

CANDIDA. Oh, you needn't go: I can't turn you out at this time of night. (*Vehemently.*) Shame on you! For shame!

MARCHBANKS (*desperately*). But what have I done?

CANDIDA. I know what you have done—as well as if I had been here all the time. Oh, it was unworthy! You are like a child: you cannot hold your tongue.

MARCHBANKS. I would die ten times over sooner than give you a moment's pain.

CANDIDA (*with infinite contempt for this puerility*). Much good your dying would do me!

MORELL. Candida, my dear: this altercation is hardly quite seemly. It is a matter between two men; and I am the right person to settle it.

CANDIDA. Two men! Do you call that a man? (*To Eugene.*) You bad boy!

MARCHBANKS (*gathering a whimsically affectionate courage from the scolding*). If I am to be scolded like this, I must make a boy's excuse. He began it. And he's bigger than I am.

CANDIDA (*losing confidence a little as her concern for Morell's dignity takes the alarm*). That can't be true. (*To Morell.*) You didn't begin it, James, did you?

MORELL (*contemptuously*). No.

MARCHBANKS (*indignant*). Oh!

MORELL (*to Eugene*). You began it—this morning. (*Candida, instantly connecting this with his mysterious allusion in the afternoon to something told him by Eugene in the morning, looks quickly at him, wrestling with the enigma. Morell proceeds with the emphasis of offended superiority.*) But your other point is true. I am certainly the bigger of the two, and, I hope, the stronger, Candida. So you had better leave the matter in my hands.

CANDIDA (*again soothing him*). Yes, dear; but— (*Troubled.*) I don't understand about this morning.

MORELL (*gently snubbing her*). You need not understand, my dear.

CANDIDA. But, James, I— (*The street bell rings.*) Oh, bother! Here they all come. (*She goes out to let them in.*)

MARCHBANKS (*running to Morell*). Oh, Morell, isn't it dreadful? She's angry with us: she hates me. What shall I do?

MORELL (*with quaint desperation, clutching himself by the hair*). Eugene: my head is spinning round. I shall begin to laugh presently. (*He walks up and down the middle of the room.*)

MARCHBANKS (*following him anxiously*). No, no: she'll think I've thrown you into hysterics. Don't laugh.

Boisterous voices and laughter are heard approaching. Lexy Mill, his eyes sparkling, and his bearing denoting unwonted elevation of spirit, enters with Burgess, who is greasy and self-complacent, but has his wits about him. Miss Garnett, with her smartest hat and jacket on, follows them; but though her eyes are brighter than before, she is evidently a prey to misgiving. She places herself with her back to her typewriting table, with one hand on it to rest herself, passes the other across her forehead as if she were a little tired and giddy.

Marchbanks relapses into shyness and edges away into the corner near the window, where Morell's books are.

MILL (*exhilaratedly*). Morell: I must congratulate you. (*Grasping his hand.*) What a noble, splendid, inspired address you gave us! You surpassed yourself.

BURGESS. So you did, James. It fair kep' me awake to the last word. Didn't it, Miss Gornett?

PROSERPINE (*worriedly*). Oh, I wasn't minding you: I was trying to make notes. (*She takes out her notebook, and looks at her stenography, which nearly makes her cry.*)

MORELL. Did I go too fast, Pross?

PROSERPINE. Much too fast. You know I can't do more than a hundred words a minute. (*She relieves her feelings by throwing her notebook angrily beside her machine, ready for use next morning.*)

MORELL (*soothingly*). Oh, well, well, never mind, never mind, never mind. Have you all had supper?

LEXY. Mr. Burgess has been kind enough to give us a really splendid supper at the Belgrave.

BURGESS (*with effusive magnanimity*). Don't mention it, Mr. Mill. (*Modestly.*) You're 'arty welcome to my little treat.

PROSERPINE. We had champagne! I never tasted it before. I feel quite giddy.

MORELL (*surprised*). A champagne supper! That was very handsome. Was it my eloquence that produced all this extravagance?

MILL (*rhetorically*). Your eloquence, and Mr. Burgess's goodness of heart. (*With a fresh burst of exhilaration.*) And what a very fine fellow the chairman is, Morell! He came to supper with us.

MORELL (*with long drawn significance, looking at Burgess*). O-o-o-h, the chairman. Now I understand.

Burgess, covering a lively satisfaction in his diplomatic cunning with a deprecatory cough, retires to the hearth. Lexy folds his arms and leans against the cellaret in a high-spirited attitude. Candida comes in with glasses, lemons, and a jug of hot water on a tray.

CANDIDA. Who will have some lemonade? You know our rules: total abstinence. (*She puts the tray on the table, and takes up the lemon squeezers, looking enquiringly round at them.*)

MORELL. No use, dear. They've all had champagne. Pross has broken her pledge.

CANDIDA (*to Proserpine*). You don't mean to say you've been drinking champagne!

PROSERPINE (*stubbornly*). Yes, I do. I'm only a beer teetotaller, not a champagne teetotaller. I don't like beer. Are there any letters for me to answer, Mr. Morell?

MORELL. No more to-night.

PROSERPINE. Very well. Good-night, everybody.

LEXY (*gallantly*). Had I not better see you home, Miss Garnett?

PROSERPINE. No, thank you. I shan't trust myself with anybody to-night. I wish I hadn't taken any of that stuff. (*She walks straight out.*)

BURGESS (*indignantly*). Stuff, indeed! That gurl dunno wot champagne is! Pommery and Greeno at twelve and six a bottle. She took two glasses a'most straight hoff.

MORELL (*a little anxious about her*). Go and look after her, Lexy.

LEXY (*alarmed*). But if she should really be— Suppose she began to sing in the street, or anything of that sort.

MORELL. Just so: she may. That's why you'd better see her safely home.

CANDIDA. Do, Lexy: there's a good fellow. (*She shakes his hand and pushes him gently to the door.*)

LEXY. It's evidently my duty to go. I hope it may not be necessary. Good-night, Mrs. Morell. (*To the rest.*) Good-night. (*He goes. Candida shuts the door.*)

BURGESS. He was gushin' with hextra piety hisself arter two sips. People carn't drink like they huseter. (*Dismissing the subject and bustling away from the hearth.*) Well, James: it's time to lock up. Mr. Morchbanks: shall I 'ave the pleasure of your company for a bit of the way home?

MARCHBANKS (*affrightedly*). Yes: I'd better go. (*He hurries across to the door; but Candida places herself before it, barring his way.*)

CANDIDA (*with quiet authority*). You sit down. You're not going yet.

MARCHBANKS (*quailing*). No: I—I didn't mean to. (*He comes back into the room and sits down abjectly on the sofa.*)

CANDIDA. Mr. Marchbanks will stay the night with us, papa.

BURGESS. Oh, well, I'll say good-night. So long, James. (*He shakes hands with Morell and goes on to Eugene.*) Make 'em give you a night light by your bed, Mr. Morchbanks: it'll comfort you if you wake up in the night with a touch of that complaint of yores. Good-night.

MARCHBANKS. Thank you: I will. Good-night, Mr. Burgess. (*They shake hands and Burgess goes to the door.*)

CANDIDA (*intercepting Morell, who is following Burgess*). Stay here, dear: I'll put on papa's coat for him. (*She goes out with Burgess.*)

MARCHBANKS. Morell: there's going to be a terrible scene. Aren't you afraid?

MORELL. Not in the least.

MARCHBANKS. I never envied you your courage before. (*He rises timidly and puts his hand appealingly on Morell's forearm.*) Stand by me, won't you?

MORELL (*casting him off gently, but resolutely*). Each for himself, Eugene. She must choose between us now. (*He goes to the other side of the room as Candida returns. Eugene sits down again on the sofa like a guilty schoolboy on his best behavior.*)

CANDIDA (*between them, addressing Eugene*). Are you sorry?

MARCHBANKS (*earnestly*). Yes, heartbroken.

CANDIDA. Well, then, you are forgiven. Now go off to bed like a good little boy: I want to talk to James about you.

MARCHBANKS (*rising in great consternation*). Oh, I can't do that, Morell. I must be here. I'll not go away. Tell her.

CANDIDA (*with quick suspicion*). Tell me what? (*His eyes avoid hers furtively. She turns and mutely transfers the question to Morell.*)

MORELL (*bracing himself for the catastrophe*). I have nothing to tell her, except (*here his voice deepens to a measured and mournful tenderness*) that she is my greatest treasure on earth—if she is really mine.

CANDIDA (*coldly, offended by his yielding to his orator's instinct and treating her as if she were the audience at the Guild of St. Matthew*). I am sure Eugene can say no less, if that is all.

MARCHBANKS (*discouraged*). Morell: she's laughing at us.

MORELL (*with a quick touch of temper*). There is nothing to laugh at. Are you laughing at us, Candida?

CANDIDA (*with quiet anger*). Eugene is very quick-witted, James. I hope I am going to laugh; but I am not sure that I am not going to be very angry. (*She goes to the fireplace, and stands there leaning with her arm on the mantelpiece, and her foot on the fender, whilst Eugene steals to Morell and plucks him by the sleeve.*)

MARCHBANKS (*whispering*). Stop, Morell. Don't let us say anything.

MORELL (*pushing Eugene away without deigning to look at him*). I hope you don't mean that as a threat, Candida.

CANDIDA (*with emphatic warning*). Take care, James. Eugene: I asked you to go. Are you going?

MORELL (*putting his foot down*). He shall not go. I wish him to remain.

MARCHBANKS. I'll go. I'll do whatever you want. (*He turns to the door.*)

CANDIDA. Stop! (*He obeys.*) Didn't you hear James say he wished you to stay? James is master here. Don't you know that?

MARCHBANKS (*flushing with a young poet's rage against tyranny*). By what right is he master?

CANDIDA (*quietly*). Tell him, James.

MORELL (*taken aback*). My dear: I don't know of any right that makes me master. I assert no such right.

CANDIDA (*with infinite reproach*). You don't know! Oh, James, James! (*To Eugene, musingly.*) I wonder do you understand, Eugene! No: you're too young. Well, I give you leave to stay—to stay and learn. (*She comes away from the hearth and places herself between them.*) Now, James: what's the matter? Come: tell me.

MARCHBANKS (*whispering tremulously across to him*). Don't.

CANDIDA. Come. Out with it!

MORELL (*slowly*). I meant to prepare your mind carefully, Candida, so as to prevent misunderstanding.

CANDIDA. Yes, dear: I am sure you did. But never mind: I shan't misunderstand.

MORELL. Well—er—(*He hesitates, unable to find the long explanation which he supposed to be available.*)

CANDIDA. Well?

MORELL (*baldly*). Eugene declares that you are in love with him.

MARCHBANKS (*frantically*). No, no, no, no, never. I did not, Mrs. Morell: it's not true. I said I loved you, and that he didn't. I said that I understood you, and that he couldn't. And it was not after what passed there before the fire that I spoke: it was not, on my word. It was this morning.

CANDIDA (*enlightened*). This morning!

MARCHBANKS. Yes. (*He looks at her, pleading for credence, and then adds, simply.*) That was what was the matter with my collar.

CANDIDA (*after a pause; for she does not take in his meaning at once*). His collar! (*She turns to Morell, shocked.*) Oh, James: did you—? (*She stops.*)

MORELL (*ashamed*). You know, Candida, that I have a temper to struggle with. And he said (*shuddering*) that you despised me in your heart.

CANDIDA (*turning quickly on Eugene*). Did you say that?

MARCHBANKS (*terrified*). No!

CANDIDA (*severely*). Then James has just told me a falsehood. Is that what you mean?

MARCHBANKS. No, no: I—I—(*blurting out the explanation desperately*) —it was David's wife. And it wasn't at home: it was when she saw him dancing before all the people.

MORELL (*taking the cue with a debater's adroitness*). Dancing before all the people, Candida; and thinking he was moving their hearts by his mission when they were only suffering from—Prossy's complaint. (*She is about to protest: he raises his hand to silence her, exclaiming.*) Don't try to look indignant, Candida:—

CANDIDA (*interjecting*). Try!

MORELL (*continuing*). Eugene was right. As you told me a few hours after, he is always right. He said nothing that you did not say far better yourself. He is the poet, who sees everything; and I am the poor parson, who understands nothing.

CANDIDA (*remorsefully*). Do you mind what is said by a foolish boy, because I said something like it again in jest?

MORELL. That foolish boy can speak with the inspiration of a child and the cunning of a serpent. He has claimed that you belong to him and not to me; and, rightly or wrongly, I have come to fear that it may be true. I will not go about tortured with doubts and suspicions. I will not live with you and keep a secret from you. I will not suffer the intolerable degradation of jealousy. We have agreed—he and I—that you shall choose between us now. I await your decision.

CANDIDA (*slowly recoiling a step, her heart hardened by his rhetoric in spite of the sincere feeling behind it*). Oh! I am to choose, am I? I suppose it is quite settled that I must belong to one or the other.

MORELL (*firmly*). Quite. You must choose definitely.

MARCHBANKS (*anxiously*). Morell: you don't understand. She means that she belongs to herself.

CANDIDA (*turning on him*). I mean that and a good deal more, Master Eugene, as you will both find out presently. And pray, my lords and masters, what have you to offer for my choice? I am up for auction, it seems. What do you bid, James?

MORELL (*reproachfully*). Cand— (*He breaks down: his eyes and throat fill with tears: the orator becomes the wounded animal.*) I can't speak—

CANDIDA (*impulsively going to him*). Ah, dearest—

MARCHBANKS (*in wild alarm*). Stop: it's not fair. You mustn't show her that you suffer, Morell. I am on the rack, too; but I am not crying.

MORELL (*rallying all his forces*). Yes: you are right. It is not for pity that I am bidding. (*He disengages himself from Candida.*)

CANDIDA (*retreating, chilled*). I beg your pardon, James; I did not mean to touch you. I am waiting to hear your bid.

MORELL (*with proud humility*). I have nothing to offer you but my strength for your defence, my honesty of purpose for your surety, my ability and industry for your livelihood, and my authority and position for your dignity. That is all it becomes a man to offer to a woman.

CANDIDA (*quite quietly*). And you, Eugene? What do you offer?

MARCHBANKS. My weakness! my desolation! my heart's need!

CANDIDA (*impressed*). That's a good bid, Eugene. Now I know how to make my choice.

She pauses and looks curiously from one to the other, as if weighing them. Morell, whose lofty confidence has changed into heartbreaking dread at Eugene's bid, loses all power of concealing his anxiety. Eugene, strung to the highest tension, does not move a muscle.

MORELL (*in a suffocated voice—the appeal bursting from the depths of his anguish*). Candida!

MARCHBANKS (*aside, in a flash of contempt*). Coward!

CANDIDA (*significantly*). I give myself to the weaker of the two.

Eugene divines her meaning at once: his face whitens like steel in a furnace that cannot melt it.

MORELL (*bowing his head with the calm of collapse*). I accept your sentence, Candida.

CANDIDA. Do you understand, Eugene?

MARCHBANKS. Oh, I feel I'm lost. He cannot bear the burden.

MORELL (*incredulously, raising his head with prosaic abruptness*). Do you mean me, Candida?

CANDIDA (*smiling a little*). Let us sit and talk comfortably over it like three friends. (*To Morell.*) Sit down, dear. (*Morell takes the chair from the fireside—the children's chair.*) Bring me that chair, Eugene. (*She indicates the easy chair. He fetches it silently, even with something like cold strength, and places it next to Morell, a little behind him. She sits down. He goes to the sofa and sits there, still silent and inscrutable. When they are all settled she begins, throwing a spell of quietness on them by her calm, sane, tender tone.*) You remember what you told me about yourself, Eugene: how nobody has cared for you since your old nurse died: how those clever, fashionable sisters and successful brothers of yours were your mother's and father's pets: how miserable you were at Eton: how your father is trying to starve you into returning to Oxford: how you have had to live without comfort or welcome or refuge, always lonely, and nearly always disliked and misunderstood, poor boy!

MARCHBANKS (*faithful to the nobility of his lot*). I had my books. I had Nature. And at last I met you.

CANDIDA. Never mind that just at present. Now I want you to look at this other boy here—my boy—spoiled from his cradle. We go once a fortnight to see his parents. You should come with us, Eugene, and see the pictures of the hero of that household. James as a baby! the most wonderful of all babies. James holding his first school prize, won at the ripe age of eight! James as the captain of his eleven! James in his first frock coat! James under all sorts of glorious circumstances! You know how strong he is (I hope he didn't hurt you)—

how clever he is—how happy! (*With deepening gravity.*) Ask James's mother and his three sisters what it cost to save James the trouble of doing anything but be strong and clever and happy. Ask me what it costs to be James's mother and three sisters and wife and mother to his children all in one. Ask Prossy and Maria how troublesome the house is even when we have no visitors to help us to slice the onions. Ask the tradesmen who want to worry James and spoil his beautiful sermons who it is that puts them off. When there is money to give, he gives it: when there is money to refuse, I refuse it. I build a castle of comfort and indulgence and love for him, and stand sentinel always to keep little vulgar cares out. I make him master here, though he does not know it, and could not tell you a moment ago how it came to be so. (*With sweet irony.*) And when he thought I might go away with you, his only anxiety was what should become of me! And to tempt me to stay he offered me (*leaning forward to stroke his hair caressingly at each phrase*) his strength for my defence, his industry for my livelihood, his position for my dignity, his— (*Relenting.*) Ah, I am mixing up your beautiful sentences and spoiling them, am I not, darling? (*She lays her cheek fondly against his.*)

MORELL (*quite overcome, kneeling beside her chair and embracing her with boyish ingenuousness*). It's all true, every word. What I am you have made me with the labor of your hands and the love of your heart! You are my wife, my mother, my sisters: you are the sum of all loving care to me.

CANDIDA (*in his arms, smiling, to Eugene*). Am I your mother and sisters to you, Eugene?

MARCHBANKS (*rising with a fierce gesture of disgust*). Ah, never. Out, then, into the night with me!

CANDIDA (*rising quickly and intercepting him*). You are not going like that, Eugene?

MARCHBANKS (*with the ring of a man's voice—no longer a boy's—in the words*). I know the hour when it strikes. I am impatient to do what must be done.

MORELL (*rising from his knee, alarmed*). Candida: don't let him do anything rash.

CANDIDA (*confident, smiling at Eugene*). Oh, there is no fear. He has learnt to live without happiness.

MARCHBANKS. I no longer desire happiness: life is nobler than that. Parson James: I give you my happiness with both hands: I love you because you have filled the heart of the woman I loved. Good-bye. (*He goes towards the door.*)

CANDIDA. One last word. (*He stops, but without turning to her.*) How old are you, Eugene?

MARCHBANKS. As old as the world now. This morning I was eighteen.

CANDIDA (*going to him, and standing behind him with one hand caressingly on his shoulder*). Eighteen! Will you, for my sake, make a little poem out of the two sentences I am going to say to you? And will you promise to repeat it to yourself whenever you think of me?

MARCHBANKS (*without moving*). Say the sentences.

CANDIDA. When I am thirty, she will be forty-five. When I am sixty, she will be seventy-five.

MARCHBANKS (*turning to her*). In a hundred years, we shall be the same age. But I have a better secret than that in my heart. Let me go now. The night outside grows impatient.

CANDIDA. Good-bye. (*She takes his face in her hands; and as he divines her intention and bends his knee, she kisses his forehead. Then he flies out into the night. She turns to Morell, holding out her arms to him.*) Ah, James! (*They embrace. But they do not know the secret in the poet's heart.*)

Caesar and Cleopatra
A History

INTRODUCTORY NOTE TO *CAESAR AND CLEOPATRA*

In 1898, the year of his marriage, Shaw at forty-two wrote *Caesar and Cleopatra,* his ninth play and the first to bring him fame and wealth. With it Shaw created another revolution in theatre and literature by treating a popular hero as an ordinary man who possesses extraordinary common sense. Shakespeare made Caesar a tragic hero but Shaw made him a comic hero, bald and middle-aged, conquering Egypt by trickery while tutoring a teen-age Cleopatra in the duties and privileges of being a queen. Shaw obviously did not follow the familiar sources for his story but used instead the writings of Mommsen, a nineteenth-century German historian, and the ideas of Carlyle on heroes who were free of illusions.

In the play we watch Caesar describe his fallibility, make cool decisions in the midst of turmoil, display his inner authority to win the respect of enemies, jump into the ocean to escape an army and finally leave Egypt and Cleopatra after promising to send Marc Antony back.

Caesar, the demagogue, had all the qualities in a leader which Shaw most admired. He was ruthless, unsentimental, the source of wit in others, scrupulously if annoyingly fair, and supremely egotistical. There is no character development in Caesar during the play, only a rich and glorious unfolding of layer after layer of an amazing character.

Cleopatra, however, grows before our eyes from a spoiled child to a young woman with the authority to rule a nation. Apollodorus presents the artist's point of view in a barbaric empire and Ftatateeta that of a devoted slave; both are vivid creations of Shaw's imagination.

ACT I

An October night on the Syrian border of Egypt towards the end of the XXXIII Dynasty, in the year 706 by Roman computation, afterwards reckoned by Christian computation as 48 B.C. A great radiance of silver fire, the dawn of a moon-lit night, is rising in the east. The stars and the cloudless sky are our own contemporaries, nineteen and a half centuries younger than we know them; but you would not guess that from their appearance. Below them are two notable draw-backs of civilization: a palace, and soldiers. The palace, an old, low, Syrian building of whitened mud, is not so ugly as Buckingham Palace; and the officers in the courtyard are more highly civilized than modern English officers: for example, they do not dig up the corpses of their dead enemies and muti-late them, as we dug up Cromwell and the Mahdi. They are in two groups: one intent on the gambling of their captain Belzanor, a warrior of fifty, who, with his spear on the ground beside his knee, is stooping to throw dice with a sly-looking young Persian recruit; the other gathered about a guardsman who has just finished telling a naughty story (still current in English barracks) at which they are laughing uproariously. They are about a dozen in number, all highly aristocratic young Egyptian guardsmen, handsomely equipped with weapons and armor, very un-English in point of not being ashamed of and uncomfortable in their professional dress; on the contrary, rather ostentatiously and arrogantly warlike, as valuing themselves on their military caste.

Belzanor is a typical veteran, tough and wilful; prompt, capable and crafty where brute force will serve; helpless and boyish when it will not: an effective sergeant, an incompetent general, a deplorable dictator. Would, if influentially con-nected, be employed in the two last capacities by a modern European State on the strength of his success in the first. Is rather to be pitied just now in view of the fact that Julius Cæsar is invading his country. Not knowing this, is intent on

151

his game with the Persian, whom, as a foreigner, he considers quite capable of cheating him.

His subalterns are mostly handsome young fellows whose interest in the game and the story symbolizes with tolerable completeness the main interests in life of which they are conscious. Their spears are leaning against the walls, or lying on the ground ready to their hands. The corner of the court-yard forms a triangle of which one side is the front of the palace, with a doorway, the other a wall with a gateway. The storytellers are on the palace side: the gamblers, on the gate-way side. Close to the gateway, against the wall, is a stone block high enough to enable a Nubian sentinel, standing on it, to look over the wall. The yard is lighted by a torch stuck in the wall. As the laughter from the group round the storyteller dies away, the kneeling Persian, winning the throw, snatches up the stake from the ground.

BELZANOR. By Apis, Persian, thy gods are good to thee.

THE PERSIAN. Try yet again, O captain. Double or quits!

BELZANOR. No more. I am not in the vein.

THE SENTINEL (*poising his javelin as he peers over the wall*). Stand. Who goes there?

They all start, listening. A strange voice replies from without.

VOICE. The bearer of evil tidings.

BELZANOR (*calling to the sentry*). Pass him.

THE SENTINEL (*grounding his javelin*). Draw near, O bearer of evil tidings.

BELZANOR (*pocketing the dice and picking up his spear*). Let us receive this man with honor. He bears evil tidings.

The guardsmen seize their spears and gather about the gate, leaving a way through for the newcomer.

PERSIAN (*rising from his knee*). Are evil tidings, then, so honorable?

BELZANOR. O barbarous Persian, hear my instruction. In Egypt the bearer of good tidings is sacrificed to the gods as a thank offering; but no god will accept the blood of the mes-senger of evil. When we have good tidings, we are careful to send them in the mouth of the cheapest slave we can find. Evil tidings are borne by young noblemen who desire to bring themselves into notice. (*They join the rest at the gate.*)

THE SENTINEL. Pass, O young captain; and bow the head in the House of the Queen.

VOICE. Go anoint thy javelin with fat of swine, O Black-amoor; for before morning the Romans will make thee eat it to the very butt.

The owner of the voice, a fairhaired dandy, dressed in a different fashion to that affected by the guardsmen, but no less extravagantly, comes through the gateway laughing. He is somewhat battlestained; and his left forearm, bandaged, comes through a torn sleeve. In his right hand he carries a Roman sword in its sheath. He swaggers down the courtyard, the Persian on his right, Belzanor on his left, and the guardsmen crowding down behind him.

BELZANOR. Who art thou that laughest in the House of Cleopatra the Queen, and in the teeth of Belzanor, the captain of her guard?

THE NEW COMER. I am Bel Affris, descended from the gods.

BELZANOR (*ceremoniously*). Hail, cousin!

ALL (*except the Persian*). Hail, cousin!

PERSIAN. All the Queen's guards are descended from the gods, O stranger, save myself. I am Persian, and descended from many kings.

BEL AFFRIS (*to the guardsmen*). Hail, cousin! (*To the Persian, condescendingly.*) Hail, mortal!

BELZANOR. You have been in battle, Bel Affris; and you are a soldier among soldiers. You will not let the Queen's women have the first of your tidings.

BEL AFFRIS. I have no tidings, except that we shall have our throats cut presently, women, soldiers, and all.

PERSIAN (*to Belzanor*). I told you so.

THE SENTINEL (*who has been listening*). Woe, alas!

BEL AFFRIS (*calling to him*). Peace, peace, poor Ethiop: destiny is with the gods who painted thee black. (*To Belzanor.*) What has this mortal (*indicating the Persian*) told you?

BELZANOR. He says that the Roman Julius Cæsar, who has landed on our shores with a handful of followers, will make himself master of Egypt. He is afraid of the Roman soldiers. (*The guardsmen laugh with boisterous scorn.*) Peasants, brought up to scare crows and follow the plough. Sons of smiths and millers and tanners! And we nobles, consecrated to arms, descended from the gods!

PERSIAN. Belzanor: the gods are not always good to their poor relations.

BELZANOR (*hotly, to the Persian*). Man to man, are we worse than the slaves of Cæsar?

BEL AFFRIS (*stepping between them*). Listen, cousin. Man to man, we Egyptians are as gods above the Romans.

THE GUARDSMEN (*exultingly*). Aha!

BEL AFFRIS. But this Cæsar does not pit man against man: he throws a legion at you where you are weakest as he throws a stone from a catapult; and that legion is as a man with one head, a thousand arms, and no religion. I have fought against them; and I know.

BELZANOR (*derisively*). Were you frightened, cousin?

The guardsmen roar with laughter, their eyes sparkling at the wit of their captain.

BEL AFFRIS. No, cousin; but I was beaten. They were frightened (perhaps); but they scattered us like chaff.

The guardsmen, much damped, utter a growl of contemptuous disgust.

BELZANOR. Could you not die?

BEL AFFRIS. No: that was too easy to be worthy of a descendant of the gods. Besides, there was no time: all was over in a moment. The attack came just where we least expected it.

BELZANOR. That shews that the Romans are cowards.

BEL AFFRIS. They care nothing about cowardice, these Romans: they fight to win. The pride and honor of war are nothing to them.

PERSIAN. Tell us the tale of the battle. What befell?

THE GUARDSMEN (*gathering eagerly round Bel Affris*). Ay: the tale of the battle.

BEL AFFRIS. Know then, that I am a novice in the guard of the temple of Ra in Memphis, serving neither Cleopatra nor her brother Ptolemy, but only the high gods. We went a journey to inquire of Ptolemy why he had driven Cleopatra into Syria, and how we of Egypt should deal with the Roman Pompey, newly come to our shores after his defeat by Cæsar at Pharsalia. What, think ye, did we learn? Even that Cæsar is coming also in hot pursuit of his foe, and that Ptolemy has slain Pompey, whose severed head he holds in readiness to present to the conqueror. (*Sensation among the guardsmen.*) Nay, more: we found that Cæsar is already come; for we had not made half a day's journey on our way back when we came upon a city rabble flying from his legions, whose landing they had gone out to withstand.

BELZANOR. And ye, the temple guard! did ye not withstand these legions?

BEL AFFRIS. What man could, that we did. But there came the sound of a trumpet whose voice was as the cursing of a black mountain. Then saw we a moving wall of shields coming towards us. You know how the heart burns when you charge a fortified wall; but how if the fortified wall were to charge you?

THE PERSIAN (*exulting in having told them so*). Did I not say it?

BEL AFFRIS. When the wall came nigh, it changed into a line of men—common fellows enough, with helmets, leather tunics, and breastplates. Every man of them flung his javelin: the one that came my way drove through my shield as through a papyrus—lo there! (*he points to the bandage on his left arm*) and would have gone through my neck had I not stooped. They were charging at the double then, and were upon us with short swords almost as soon as their javelins. When a man is close to you with such a sword, you can do nothing with our weapons: they are all too long.

THE PERSIAN. What did you do?

BEL AFFRIS. Doubled my fist and smote my Roman on the sharpness of his jaw. He was but mortal after all: he lay down in a stupor; and I took his sword and laid it on. (*Drawing the sword.*) Lo! a Roman sword with Roman blood on it!

THE GUARDSMEN (*approvingly*). Good! (*They take the sword and hand it round, examining it curiously.*)

THE PERSIAN. And your men?

BEL AFFRIS. Fled. Scattered like sheep.

BELZANOR (*furiously*). The cowardly slaves! Leaving the descendants of the gods to be butchered!

BEL AFFRIS (*with acid coolness*). The descendants of the gods did not stay to be butchered, cousin. The battle was not to the strong; but the race was to the swift. The Romans, who have no chariots, sent a cloud of horsemen in pursuit, and slew multitudes. Then our high priest's captain rallied a dozen descendants of the gods and exhorted us to die fighting. I said to myself: surely it is safer to stand than to lose my breath and be stabbed in the back; so I joined our captain and stood. Then the Romans treated us with respect; for no man attacks a lion when the field is full of sheep, except for the pride and honor of war, of which these Romans know nothing. So we escaped with our lives; and I am come to warn you that you must open your gates to Cæsar; for his advance guard is scarce an hour behind me; and not an Egyptian warrior is left standing between you and his legions.

THE SENTINEL. Woe, alas! (*He throws down his javelin and flies into the palace.*)

BELZANOR. Nail him to the door, quick! (*The guardsmen rush for him with their spears; but he is too quick for them.*) Now this news will run through the palace like fire through stubble.

BEL AFFRIS. What shall we do to save the women from the Romans?

BELZANOR. Why not kill them?

PERSIAN. Because we should have to pay blood money for some of them. Better let the Romans kill them: it is cheaper.

BELZANOR (*awestruck at his brain power*). O subtle one! O serpent!

BEL AFFRIS. But your Queen?

BELZANOR. True: we must carry off Cleopatra.

BEL AFFRIS. Will ye not await her command?

BELZANOR. Command! a girl of sixteen! Not we. At Memphis ye deem her a Queen: here we know better. I will take her on the crupper of my horse. When we soldiers have carried her out of Cæsar's reach, then the priests and the nurses and the rest of them can pretend she is a queen again, and put their commands into her mouth.

PERSIAN. Listen to me, Belzanor.

BELZANOR. Speak, O subtle beyond thy years.

THE PERSIAN. Cleopatra's brother Ptolemy is at war with her. Let us sell her to him.

THE GUARDSMEN. O subtle one! O serpent!

BELZANOR. We dare not. We are descended from the gods; but Cleopatra is descended from the river Nile; and the lands of our fathers will grow no grain if the Nile rises not to water them. Without our father's gifts we should live the lives of dogs.

PERSIAN. It is true: the Queen's guard cannot live on its pay. But hear me further, O ye kinsmen of Osiris.

THE GUARDSMEN. Speak, O subtle one. Hear the serpent begotten!

PERSIAN. Have I heretofore spoken truly to you of Cæsar, when you thought I mocked you?

GUARDSMEN. Truly, truly.

BELZANOR (*reluctantly admitting it*). So Bel Affris says.

PERSIAN. Hear more of him, then. This Cæsar is a great lover of women: he makes them his friends and counsellors.

BELZANOR. Faugh! This rule of women will be the ruin of Egypt.

THE PERSIAN. Let it rather be the ruin of Rome! Cæsar grows old now: he is past fifty and full of labors and battles. He is too old for the young women; and the old women are too wise to worship him.

BEL AFFRIS. Take heed, Persian. Cæsar is by this time almost within earshot.

PERSIAN. Cleopatra is not yet a woman: neither is she wise. But she already troubles men's wisdom.

BELZANOR. Ay: that is because she is descended from the river Nile and a black kitten of the sacred White Cat. What then?

PERSIAN. Why, sell her secretly to Ptolemy, and then offer ourselves to Cæsar as volunteers to fight for the overthrow of her brother and the rescue of our Queen, the Great Granddaughter of the Nile.

THE GUARDSMEN. O serpent!

PERSIAN. He will listen to us if we come with her picture in our mouths. He will conquer and kill her brother, and reign in Egypt with Cleopatra for his Queen. And we shall be her guard.

GUARDSMEN. O subtlest of all the serpents! O admiration! O wisdom!

BEL AFFRIS. He will also have arrived before you have done talking. O word spinner.

BELZANOR. That is true. (*An affrighted uproar in the palace interrupts him.*) Quick: the flight has begun: guard the door. (*They rush to the door and form a cordon before it with their spears. A mob of women-servants and nurses surges out. Those in front recoil from the spears, screaming to those behind to keep back. Belzanor's voice dominates the disturbance as he shouts.*) Back there. In again, unprofitable cattle.

THE GUARDSMEN. Back, unprofitable cattle.

BELZANOR. Send us out Ftatateeta, the Queen's chief nurse.

THE WOMEN (*calling into the palace*). Ftatateeta, Ftatateeta. Come, come. Speak to Belzanor.

A WOMAN. Oh, keep back. You are thrusting me on the
spearheads.

*A huge grim woman, her face covered with a network of
tiny wrinkles, and her eyes old, large, and wise; sinewy
handed, very tall, very strong; with the mouth of a bloodhound
and the jaws of a bulldog, appears on the threshold. She is
dressed like a person of consequence in the palace, and confronts the guardsmen insolently.*

FTATATEETA. Make way for the Queen's chief nurse.

BELZANOR (*with solemn arrogance*). Ftatateeta: I am Belzanor, the captain of the Queen's guard, descended from the
gods.

FTATATEETA (*retorting his arrogance with interest*). Belzanor: I am Ftatateeta, the Queen's chief nurse; and your
divine ancestors were proud to be painted on the wall in the
pyramids of the kings whom my fathers served.

The women laugh triumphantly.

BELZANOR (*with grim humor*). Ftatateeta: daughter of a
long-tongued, swivel-eyed chameleon, the Romans are at
hand. (*A cry of terror from the women: they would fly but
for the spears.*) Not even the descendants of the gods can
resist them; for they have each man seven arms, each carrying
seven spears. The blood in their veins is boiling quicksilver;
and their wives become mothers in three hours, and are slain
and eaten the next day.

*A shudder of horror from the women. Ftatateeta, despising
them and scorning the soldiers, pushes her way through the
crowd and confronts the spear points undismayed.*

FTATATEETA. Then fly and save yourselves, O cowardly
sons of the cheap clay gods that are sold to fish porters; and
leave us to shift for ourselves.

BELZANOR. Not until you have first done our bidding, O
terror of manhood. Bring out Cleopatra the Queen to us
and then go whither you will.

FTATATEETA (*with a derisive laugh*). Now I know why
the gods have taken her out of our hands. (*The guardsmen
start and look at one another.*) Know, thou foolish soldier,
that the Queen has been missing since an hour past sundown.

BELZANOR (*furiously*). Hag: you have hidden her to sell
to Cæsar or her brother. (*He grasps her by the left wrist,*

and drags her, helped by a few of the guard, to the middle of the courtyard, where, as they fling her on her knees, he draws a murderous looking knife.) Where is she? Where is she? or— (*He threatens to cut her throat.*)

FTATATEETA (*savagely*). Touch me, dog; and the Nile will not rise on your fields for seven times seven years of famine.

BELZANOR (*frightened, but desperate*). I will sacrifice: I will pay. Or stay. (*To the Persian.*) You, O subtle one: your father's lands lie far from the Nile. Slay her.

PERSIAN (*threatening her with his knife*). Persia has but one god; yet he loves the blood of old women. Where is Cleopatra?

FTATATEETA. Persian: as Osiris lives, I do not know. I chid her for bringing evil days upon us by talking to the sacred cats of the priests, and carrying them in her arms. I told her she would be left alone here when the Romans came as a punishment for her disobedience. And now she is gone—run away—hidden. I speak the truth. I call Osiris to witness——

THE WOMEN (*protesting officiously*). She speaks the truth, Belzanor.

BELZANOR. You have frightened the child: she is hiding. Search—quick—into the palace—search every corner.

The guards, led by Belzanor, shoulder their way into the palace through the flying crowd of women, who escape through the courtyard gate.

FTATATEETA (*screaming*). Sacrilege! Men in the Queen's chambers! Sa— (*Her voice dies away as the Persian puts his knife to her throat.*)

BEL AFFRIS (*laying a hand on Ftatateeta's left shoulder*). Forbear her yet a moment, Persian. (*To Ftatateeta, very significantly.*) Mother: your gods are asleep or away hunting; and the sword is at your throat. Bring us to where the Queen is hid, and you shall live.

FTATATEETA (*contemptuously*). Who shall stay the sword in the hand of a fool, if the high gods put it there? Listen to me, ye young men without understanding. Cleopatra fears me; but she fears the Romans more. There is but one power greater in her eyes than the wrath of the Queen's nurse and the cruelty of Cæsar; and that is the power of the Sphinx that sits in the desert watching the way to the sea.

What she would have it know, she tells into the ears of the
sacred cats; and on her birthday she sacrifices to it and decks
it with poppies. Go ye therefore into the desert and seek
Cleopatra in the shadow of the Sphinx; and on your heads
see to it that no harm comes to her.

BEL AFFRIS (*to the Persian*). May we believe this, O subtle
one?

PERSIAN. Which way come the Romans?

BEL AFFRIS. Over the desert, from the sea, by this very
Sphinx.

PERSIAN (*to Ftatateeta*). O mother of guile! O aspic's
tongue! You have made up this tale so that we two may go
into the desert and perish on the spears of the Romans.
(*Lifting his knife.*) Taste death.

FTATATEETA. Not from thee, baby. (*She snatches his
ankle from under him and flies stooping along the palace wall,
vanishing in the darkness within its precinct. Bel Affris
roars with laughter as the Persian tumbles. The guardsmen
rush out of the palace with Belzanor and a mob of fugitives,
mostly carrying bundles.*)

PERSIAN. Have you found Cleopatra?

BELZANOR. She is gone. We have searched every corner.

THE NUBIAN SENTINEL (*appearing at the door of the palace*).
Woe! Alas! Fly, fly!

BELZANOR. What is the matter now?

THE NUBIAN SENTINEL. The sacred white cat has been
stolen.

ALL. Woe! Woe! (*General panic. They all fly with
cries of consternation. The torch is thrown down and extinguished in the rush. Darkness. The noise of the fugitives
dies away. Dead silence. Suspense. Then the blackness
and stillness break softly into silver mist and strange airs as
the windswept harp of Memnon plays at the dawning of the
moon. It rises full over the desert; and a vast horizon comes
into relief, broken by a huge shape which soon reveals itself
in the spreading radiance as a Sphinx pedestalled on the
sands. The light still clears, until the upraised eyes of the
image are distinguished looking straight forward and upward
in infinite fearless vigil, and a mass of color between its great
paws defines itself as a heap of red poppies on which a girl
lies motionless, her silken vest heaving gently and regularly*

*with the breathing of a dreamless sleeper, and her braided hair
glittering in a shaft of moonlight like a bird's wing.*

*Suddenly there comes from afar a vaguely fearful sound [it
might be the bellow of a Minotaur softened by great distance]
and Memnon's music stops. Silence: then a few faint high-
ringing trumpet notes. Then silence again. Then a man comes
from the south with stealing steps, ravished by the mystery of
the night, all wonder, and halts, lost in contemplation, opposite
the left flank of the Sphinx, whose bosom, with its burden, is
hidden from him by its massive shoulder.)*

THE MAN. Hail, Sphinx: salutation from Julius Cæsar!
I have wandered in many lands, seeking the lost regions
from which my birth into this world exiled me, and the company of creatures such as I myself. I have found flocks and
pastures, men and cities, but no other Cæsar, no air native to
me, no man kindred to me, none who can do my day's deed,
and think my night's thought. In the little world yonder,
Sphinx, my place is as high as yours in this great desert; only I
wander, and you sit still; I conquer, and you endure; I work
and wonder, you watch and wait; I look up and am dazzled,
look down and am darkened, look round and am puzzled,
whilst your eyes never turn from looking out—out of the
world—to the lost region—the home from which we have
strayed. Sphinx, you and I, strangers to the race of men, are
no strangers to one another: have I not been conscious of you
and of this place since I was born? Rome is a madman's
dream: this is my Reality. These starry lamps of yours I have
seen from afar in Gaul, in Britain, in Spain, in Thessaly, sig-
nalling great secrets to some eternal sentinel below, whose post
I never could find. And here at last is their sentinel—an image
of the constant and immortal part of my life, silent, full of
thoughts, alone in the silver desert. Sphinx, Sphinx: I have
climbed mountains at night to hear in the distance the stealthy
footfall of the winds that chase your sands in forbidden play—
our invisible children, O Sphinx, laughing in whispers. My
way hither was the way of destiny: for I am he of whose genius
you are the symbol: part brute, part woman, and part God—
nothing of man in me at all. Have I read your riddle, Sphinx?

THE GIRL (*who has wakened, and peeped cautiously from
her nest to see who is speaking*). Old gentleman.

CÆSAR (*starting violently, and clutching his sword*). Immortal gods!

THE GIRL. Old gentleman: don't run away.

CÆSAR (*stupefied*). "Old gentleman: don't run away!!!" This! to Julius Cæsar!

THE GIRL (*urgently*). Old gentleman.

CÆSAR. Sphinx: you presume on your centuries. I am younger than you, though your voice is but a girl's voice as yet.

THE GIRL. Climb up here, quickly; or the Romans will come and eat you.

CÆSAR (*running forward past the Sphinx's shoulder, and seeing her*). A child at its breast! a divine child!

THE GIRL. Come up quickly. You must get up at its side and creep round.

CÆSAR (*amazed*). Who are you?

THE GIRL. Cleopatra, Queen of Egypt.

CÆSAR. Queen of the Gypsies, you mean.

CLEOPATRA. You must not be disrespectful to me, or the Sphinx will let the Romans eat you. Come up. It is quite cosy here.

CÆSAR (*to himself*). What a dream! What a magnificent dream! Only let me not wake, and I will conquer ten continents to pay for dreaming it out to the end. (*He climbs to the Sphinx's flank, and presently reappears to her on the pedestal, stepping round its right shoulder.*)

CLEOPATRA. Take care. That's right. Now sit down: you may have its other paw. (*She seats herself comfortably on its left paw.*) It is very powerful and will protect us; but (*shivering, and with plaintive loneliness*) it would not take any notice of me or keep me company. I am glad you have come: I was very lonely. Did you happen to see a white cat anywhere?

CÆSAR (*sitting slowly down on the right paw in extreme wonderment*). Have you lost one?

CLEOPATRA. Yes: the sacred white cat: is it not dreadful? I brought him here to sacrifice him to the Sphinx; but when we got a little way from the city a black cat called him, and he jumped out of my arms and ran away to it. Do you think that the black cat can have been my great-great-great-grandmother?

CÆSAR (*staring at her*). Your great-great-great-grandmother! Well, why not? Nothing would surprise me on this night of nights.

CLEOPATRA. I think it must have been. My great-grandmother's great-grandmother was a black kitten of the sacred white cat; and the river Nile made her his seventh wife. That is why my hair is so wavy. And I always want to be let do as I like, no matter whether it is the will of the gods or not: that is because my blood is made with Nile water.

CÆSAR. What are you doing here at this time of night? Do you live here?

CLEOPATRA. Of course not: I am the Queen; and I shall live in the palace at Alexandria when I have killed my brother, who drove me out of it. When I am old enough I shall do just what I like. I shall be able to poison the slaves and see them wriggle, and pretend to Ftatateeta that she is going to be put into the fiery furnace.

CÆSAR. Hm! Meanwhile why are you not at home and in bed?

CLEOPATRA. Because the Romans are coming to eat us all. You are not at home and in bed either.

CÆSAR (with conviction). Yes I am. I live in a tent; and I am now in that tent, fast asleep and dreaming. Do you suppose that I believe you are real, you impossible little dream witch?

CLEOPATRA (giggling and leaning trustfully towards him). You are a funny old gentleman. I like you.

CÆSAR. Ah, that spoils the dream. Why don't you dream that I am young?

CLEOPATRA. I wish you were; only I think I should be more afraid of you. I like men, especially young men with round strong arms; but I am afraid of them. You are old and rather thin and stringy; but you have a nice voice; and I like to have somebody to talk to, though I think you are a little mad. It is the moon that makes you talk to yourself in that silly way.

CÆSAR. What! you heard that, did you? I was saying my prayers to the great Sphinx.

CLEOPATRA. But this isn't the great Sphinx.

CÆSAR (much disappointed, looking up at the statue). What!

CLEOPATRA. This is only a dear little kitten of the Sphinx. Why, the great Sphinx is so big that it has a temple between its paws. This is my pet Sphinx. Tell me: do you think the

Romans have any sorcerers who could take us away from the Sphinx by magic?

CÆSAR. Why? Are you afraid of the Romans?

CLEOPATRA (*very seriously*). Oh, they would eat us if they caught us. They are barbarians. Their chief is called Julius Cæsar. His father was a tiger and his mother a burning mountain; and his nose is like an elephant's trunk. (*Cæsar involuntarily rubs his nose.*) They all have long noses, and ivory tusks, and little tails, and seven arms with a hundred arrows in each; and they live on human flesh.

CÆSAR. Would you like me to show you a real Roman?

CLEOPATRA (*terrified*). No. You are frightening me.

CÆSAR. No matter: this is only a dream——

CLEOPATRA (*excitedly*). It is not a dream: it is not a dream. See, see. (*She plucks a pin from her hair and jabs it repeatedly into his arm.*)

CÆSAR. Ffff—Stop. (*Wrathfully.*) How dare you?

CLEOPATRA (*abashed*). You said you were dreaming. (*Whimpering.*) I only wanted to shew you——

CÆSAR (*gently*). Come, come: don't cry. A queen mustn't cry. (*He rubs his arm, wondering at the reality of the smart.*) Am I awake? (*He strikes his hand against the Sphinx to test its solidity. It feels so real that he begins to be alarmed, and says perplexedly.*) Yes, I—(*quite panicstricken*) no: impossible: madness, madness! (*Desperately.*) Back to camp— to camp. (*He rises to spring down from the pedestal.*)

CLEOPATRA (*flinging her arms in terror round him*). No: you shan't leave me. No, no, no: don't go. I'm afraid—afraid of the Romans.

CÆSAR (*as the conviction that he is really awake forces itself on him*). Cleopatra: can you see my face well?

CLEOPATRA. Yes. It is so white in the moonlight.

CÆSAR. Are you sure it is the moonlight that makes me look whiter than an Egyptian? (*Grimly.*) Do you notice that I have a rather long nose?

CLEOPATRA (*recoiling, paralyzed by a terrible suspicion*). Oh!

CÆSAR. It is a Roman nose, Cleopatra.

CLEOPATRA. Ah! (*With a piercing scream she springs up; darts round the left shoulder of the Sphinx; scrambles down to the sand; and falls on her knees in frantic supplication, shrieking.*) Bite him in two, Sphinx: bite him in two. I meant to sacrifice the white cat—I did indeed—I—(*Cæsar, who has slipped down from the pedestal, touches her on the shoulder.*) Ah! (*She buries her head in her arms.*)

CÆSAR. Cleopatra: shall I teach you a way to prevent Cæsar from eating you?

CLEOPATRA (*clinging to him piteously*). Oh do, do, do. I will steal Ftatateeta's jewels and give them to you. I will make the river Nile water your lands twice a year.

CÆSAR. Peace, peace, my child. Your gods are afraid of the Romans: you see the Sphinx dare not bite me, nor prevent me carrying you off to Julius Cæsar.

CLEOPATRA (*in pleading murmurings*). You won't, you won't. You said you wouldn't.

CÆSAR. Cæsar never eats women.

CLEOPATRA (*springing up full of hope*). What!

CÆSAR (*impressively*). But he eats girls (*she relapses*) and cats. Now you are a silly little girl; and you are descended from the black kitten. You are both a girl and a cat.

CLEOPATRA (*trembling*). And will he eat me?

CÆSAR. Yes; unless you make him believe that you are a woman.

CLEOPATRA. Oh, you must get a sorcerer to make a woman of me. Are you a sorcerer?

CÆSAR. Perhaps. But it will take a long time; and this very night you must stand face to face with Cæsar in the palace of your fathers.

CLEOPATRA. No, no. I daren't.

CÆSAR. Whatever dread may be in your soul—however terrible Cæsar may be to you—you must confront him as a brave woman and a great queen; and you must feel no fear. If your hand shakes: if your voice quavers; then—night and death! (*She moans.*) But if he thinks you worthy to rule, he will set you on the throne by his side and make you the real ruler of Egypt.

CLEOPATRA (*despairingly*). No: he will find me out: he will find me out.

CÆSAR (*rather mournfully*). He is easily deceived by women. Their eyes dazzle him; and he sees them not as they are, but as he wishes them to appear to him.

CLEOPATRA (*hopefully*). Then we will cheat him. I will put on Ftatateeta's head-dress; and he will think me quite an old woman.

CÆSAR. If you do that he will eat you at one mouthful.

CLEOPATRA. But I will give him a cake with my magic opal and seven hairs of the white cat baked in it; and——

CÆSAR (*abruptly*). Pah! you are a little fool. He will eat your cake and you too. (*He turns contemptuously from her.*)

CLEOPATRA (*running after him and clinging to him*). Oh, please, please! I will do whatever you tell me. I will be good! I will be your slave. (*Again the terrible bellowing note sounds across the desert, now closer at hand. It is the bucina, the Roman war trumpet.*)

CÆSAR. Hark!

CLEOPATRA (*trembling*). What was that?

CÆSAR. Cæsar's voice.

CLEOPATRA (*pulling at his hand*). Let us run away. Come. Oh, come.

CÆSAR. You are safe with me until you stand on your throne to receive Cæsar. Now lead me thither.

CLEOPATRA (*only too glad to get away*). I will, I will. (*Again the bucina.*) Oh, come, come, come: the gods are angry. Do you feel the earth shaking?

CÆSAR. It is the tread of Cæsar's legions.

CLEOPATRA (*drawing him away*). This way, quickly. And let us look for the white cat as we go. It is he that has turned you into a Roman.

CÆSAR. Incorrigible, oh, incorrigible! Away! (*He follows her, the bucina sounding louder as they steal across the desert. The moonlight wanes: the horizon again shows black against the sky, broken only by the fantastic silhouette of the Sphinx. The sky itself vanishes in darkness, from which there is no relief until the gleam of a distant torch falls on great Egyptian pillars supporting the roof of a majestic corridor. At the farther end of this corridor a Nubian slave appears carrying the torch. Cæsar, still led by Cleopatra, follows him. They come down the corridor, Cæsar peering keenly about at the strange architecture, and at the pillar shadows between which, as the passing torch makes them hurry noiselessly backwards, figures of men with wings and hawks' heads, and vast black marble cats, seem to flit in and out of ambush. Farther along, the wall turns a corner and makes a spacious transept in which Cæsar sees, on his right, a throne, and behind the throne a door. On each side of the throne is a slender pillar with a lamp on it.*)

CÆSAR. What place is this?

CLEOPATRA. This is where I sit on the throne when I am allowed to wear my crown and robes. (*The slave holds his torch to shew the throne.*)

CÆSAR. Order the slave to light the lamps.

CLEOPATRA (*shyly*). Do you think I may?

CÆSAR. Of course. You are the Queen. (*She hesitates.*) Go on.

CLEOPATRA (*timidly, to the slave*). Light all the lamps.

FTATATEETA (*suddenly coming from behind the throne*). Stop. (*The slave stops. She turns sternly to Cleopatra, who quails like a naughty child.*) Who is this you have with you; and how dare you order the lamps to be lighted without my permission? (*Cleopatra is dumb with apprehension.*)

CÆSAR. Who is she?

CLEOPATRA. Ftatateeta.

FTATATEETA (*arrogantly*). Chief nurse to——

CÆSAR (*cutting her short*). I speak to the Queen. Be silent. (*To Cleopatra.*) Is this how your servants know their places? Send her away; and do you (*to the slave*) do as the Queen has bidden. (*The slave lights the lamps. Meanwhile Cleopatra stands hesitating, afraid of Ftatateeta.*) You are the Queen: send her away.

CLEOPATRA (*cajoling*). Ftatateeta, dear: you must go away —just for a little.

CÆSAR. You are not commanding her to go away: you are begging her. You are no Queen. You will be eaten. Farewell. (*He turns to go.*)

CLEOPATRA (*clutching him*). No, no, no. Don't leave me.

CÆSAR. A Roman does not stay with queens who are afraid of their slaves.

CLEOPATRA. I am not afraid. Indeed I am not afraid.

FTATATEETA. We shall see who is afraid here. (*Menacingly.*) Cleopatra——

CÆSAR. On your knees, woman: am I also a child that you dare trifle with me? (*He points to the floor at Cleopatra's feet. Ftatateeta, half cowed, half savage, hesitates. Cæsar calls to the Nubian.*) Slave. (*The Nubian comes to him.*) Can you cut off a head? (*The Nubian nods and grins ecstatically, showing all his teeth. Cæsar takes his sword by the scabbard, ready to offer the hilt to the Nubian, and turns again to Ftatateeta, repeating his gesture.*) Have you remembered yourself, mistress?

Ftatateeta, crushed, kneels before Cleopatra, who can hardly believe her eyes.

FTATATEETA (*hoarsely*). O Queen, forget not thy servant in the days of thy greatness.

CLEOPATRA (*blazing with excitement*). Go. Begone. Go away. (*Ftatateeta rises with stooped head, and moves backwards towards the door. Cleopatra watches her submission eagerly, almost clapping her hands, which are trembling. Suddenly she cries.*) Give me something to beat her with. (*She snatches a snake-skin from the throne and dashes after Ftatateeta, whirling it like a scourge in the air. Cæsar makes a bound and manages to catch her and hold her while Ftatateeta escapes.*)

CÆSAR. You scratch, kitten, do you?

CLEOPATRA (*breaking from him*). I will beat somebody. I will beat him. (*She attacks the slave.*) There, there, there! (*The slave flies for his life up the corridor and vanishes. She throws the snake-skin away and jumps on the step of the throne with her arms waving, crying.*) I am a real Queen at last—a real, real Queen! Cleopatra the Queen! (*Cæsar shakes his head dubiously, the advantage of the change seeming open to question from the point of view of the general welfare of Egypt. She turns and looks at him exultantly. Then she jumps down from the step, runs to him, and flings her arms round him rapturously, crying.*) Oh, I love you for making me a Queen.

CÆSAR. But queens love only kings.

CLEOPATRA. I will make all the men I love kings. I will make you a king. I will have many young kings, with round, strong arms; and when I am tired of them I will whip them to death; but you shall always be my king: my nice, kind, wise, good old king.

CÆSAR. Oh, my wrinkles, my wrinkles! And my child's heart! You will be the most dangerous of all Cæsar's conquests.

CLEOPATRA (*appalled*). Cæsar! I forgot Cæsar. (*Anxiously.*) You will tell him that I am a Queen, will you not?—a real Queen. Listen! (*stealthily coaxing him*) let us run away and hide until Cæsar is gone.

CÆSAR. If you fear Cæsar, you are no true Queen; and though you were to hide beneath a pyramid, he would go straight to it and lift it with one hand. And then—! (*He chops his teeth together.*)

CLEOPATRA (*trembling*). Oh!

CÆSAR. Be afraid if you dare. (*The note of the bucina resounds again in the distance. She moans with fear. Cæsar exults in it, exclaiming.*) Aha! Cæsar approaches the throne of Cleopatra. Come: take your place. (*He takes her hand and leads her to the throne. She is too downcast to speak.*) Ho, there, Teetatota. How do you call your slaves?

CLEOPATRA (*spiritlessly, as she sinks on the throne and cowers there, shaking*). Clap your hands.

He claps his hands. Ftatateeta returns.

CÆSAR. Bring the Queen's robes, and her crown, and her women; and prepare her.

CLEOPATRA (*eagerly—recovering herself a little*). Yes, the crown, Ftatateeta: I shall wear the crown.

FTATATEETA. For whom must the Queen put on her state?

CÆSAR. For a citizen of Rome. A king of kings, Totateeta.

CLEOPATRA (*stamping at her*). How dare you ask questions? Go and do as you are told. (*Ftatateeta goes out with a grim smile. Cleopatra goes on eagerly, to Cæsar.*) Cæsar will know that I am a Queen when he sees my crown and robes, will he not?

CÆSAR. No. How shall he know that you are not a slave dressed up in the Queen's ornaments?

CLEOPATRA. You must tell him.

CÆSAR. He will not ask me. He will know Cleopatra by her pride, her courage, her majesty, and her beauty. (*She looks very doubtful.*) Are you trembling?

CLEOPATRA (*shivering with dread*). No, I—I—(*In a very sickly voice.*) No.

Ftatateeta and three women come in with the regalia.

FTATATEETA. Of all the Queen's women, these three alone are left. The rest are fled. (*They begin to deck Cleopatra, who submits, pale and motionless.*)

CÆSAR. Good, good. Three are enough. Poor Cæsar generally has to dress himself.

FTATATEETA (*contemptuously*). The Queen of Egypt is not a Roman barbarian. (*To Cleopatra.*) Be brave, my nursling. Hold up your head before this stranger.

CÆSAR (*admiring Cleopatra, and placing the crown on her head*). Is it sweet or bitter to be a Queen, Cleopatra?

CLEOPATRA. Bitter.

CÆSAR. Cast out fear; and you will conquer Cæsar. Tota: are the Romans at hand?

FTATATEETA. They are at hand; and the guard has fled.

THE WOMEN (*wailing subduedly*). Woe to us!

The Nubian comes running down the hall.

NUBIAN. The Romans are in the courtyard. (*He bolts through the door. With a shriek, the women fly after him. Ftatateeta's jaw expresses savage resolution: she does not budge. Cleopatra can hardly restrain herself from following them. Cæsar grips her wrist, and looks steadfastly at her. She stands like a martyr.*)

CÆSAR. The Queen must face Cæsar alone. Answer "So be it."

CLEOPATRA (*white*). So be it.

CÆSAR (*releasing her*). Good.

A tramp and tumult of armed men is heard. Cleopatra's terror increases. The bucina sounds close at hand, followed by a formidable clangor of trumpets. This is too much for Cleopatra: she utters a cry and darts towards the door. Ftatateeta stops her ruthlessly.

FTATATEETA. You are my nursling. You have said "So be it"; and if you die for it, you must make the Queen's word good. (*She hands Cleopatra to Cæsar, who takes her back, almost beside herself with apprehension, to the throne.*)

CÆSAR. Now, if you quail——! (*He seats himself on the throne.*)

She stands on the step, all but unconscious, waiting for death. The Roman soldiers troop in tumultuously through the corridor, headed by their ensign with his eagle, and their bucinator, a burly fellow with his instrument coiled round his body, its brazen bell shaped like the head of a howling wolf. When they reach the transept, they stare in amazement at the throne; dress into ordered rank opposite it; draw their swords and lift them in the air with a shout of Hail, Cæsar. Cleopatra turns and stares wildly at Cæsar; grasps the situation; and, with a great sob of relief, falls into his arms.

ACT II

Alexandria. A hall on the first floor of the Palace, ending in a loggia approached by two steps. Through the arches of the loggia the Mediterranean can be seen, bright in the morning sun. The clean lofty walls, painted with a procession of the Egyptian theocracy, presented in profile as flat ornament, and the absence of mirrors, sham perspectives, stuffy upholstery and textiles, make the place handsome, wholesome, simple and cool, or, as a rich English manufacturer would express it, poor, bare, ridiculous and unhomely. For Tottenham Court Road civilization is to this Egyptian civilization as glass bead and tattoo civilization is to Tottenham Court Road.

The young king Ptolemy Dionysus (aged ten) is at the top of the steps, on his way in through the loggia, led by his guardian Pothinus, who has him by the hand. The court is assembled to receive him. It is made up of men and women (some of the women being officials) of various complexions and races, mostly Egyptian; some of them, comparatively fair, from lower Egypt; some, much darker, from upper Egypt; with a few Greeks and Jews. Prominent in a group on Ptolemy's right hand is Theodotus, Ptolemy's tutor. Another group, on Ptolemy's left, is headed by Achillas, the general of Ptolemy's troops. Theodotus is a little old man, whose features are as cramped and wizened as his limbs, except his tall straight forehead, which occupies more space than all the rest of his face. He maintains an air of magpie keenness and profundity, listening to what the others say with the sarcastic vigilance of a philosopher listening to the exercises of his disciples. Achillas is a tall handsome man of thirty-five, with a fine black beard curled like the coat of a poodle. Apparently not a clever man, but distinguished and dignified. Pothinus is a vigorous man of fifty, a eunuch, passionate, energetic and quick witted, but of common mind and character; impatient and unable to control his temper. He has fine tawny hair, like fur. Ptolemy, the King, looks much older than an Eng-

171

*lish boy of ten; but he has the childish air, the habit of being
in leading strings, the mixture of impotence and petulance,
the appearance of being excessively washed, combed and
dressed by other hands, which is exhibited by court-bred
princes of all ages.*

*All receive the King with reverences. He comes down the
steps to a chair of state which stands a little to his right, the
only seat in the hall. Taking his place before it, he looks
nervously for instructions to Pothinus, who places himself at
his left hand.*

POTHINUS. The King of Egypt has a word to speak.

THEODOTUS (*in a squeak which he makes impressive by
sheer self-opinionativeness*). Peace for the King's word!

PTOLEMY (*without any vocal inflexions: he is evidently repeating a lesson*). Take notice of this all of you. I am the first-
born son of Auletes the Flute Blower who was your King. My
sister Berenice drove him from his throne and reigned in his
stead but—but (*he hesitates*)——

POTHINUS (*stealthily prompting*). —but the gods would not
suffer——

PTOLEMY. Yes—the gods would not suffer—not suffer—
(*He stops; then, crestfallen.*) I forget what the gods would
not suffer.

THEODOTUS. Let Pothinus, the King's guardian, speak for
the King.

POTHINUS (*suppressing his impatience with difficulty*). The
King wished to say that the gods would not suffer the impiety
of his sister to go unpunished.

PTOLEMY (*hastily*). Yes: I remember the rest of it. (*He resumes his monotone.*) Therefore the gods sent a stranger, one
Mark Antony, a Roman captain of horsemen, across the sands
of the desert and he set my father again upon the throne. And
my father took Berenice my sister and struck her head off.
And now that my father is dead yet another of his daughters,
my sister Cleopatra, would snatch the kingdom from me and
reign in my place. But the gods would not suffer (*Pothinus
coughs admonitorily*)—the gods—the gods would not
suffer——

POTHINUS (*prompting*)—will not maintain——

PTOLEMY. Oh yes—will not maintain such iniquity, they
will give her head to the axe even as her sister's. But with the

help of the witch Ftatateeta she hath cast a spell on the Roman Julius Cæsar to make him uphold her false pretence to rule in Egypt. Take notice then that I will not suffer—that I will not suffer—(*Pettishly, to Pothinus.*) What is it that I will not suffer?

POTHINUS (*suddenly exploding with all the force and emphasis of political passion*). The King will not suffer a foreigner to take from him the throne of our Egypt. (*A shout of applause.*) Tell the King, Achillas, how many soldiers and horsemen follow the Roman?

THEODOTUS. Let the King's general speak!

ACHILLAS. But two Roman legions, O King. Three thousand soldiers and scarce a thousand horsemen.

The court breaks into derisive laughter; and a great chattering begins, amid which Rufio, a Roman officer, appears in the loggia. He is a burly, black-bearded man of middle age, very blunt, prompt and rough, with small clear eyes, and plump nose and cheeks, which, however, like the rest of his flesh, are in ironhard condition.

RUFIO (*from the steps*). Peace, ho! (*The laughter and chatter cease abruptly.*) Cæsar approaches.

THEODOTUS (*with much presence of mind*). The King permits the Roman commander to enter!

Cæsar, plainly dressed, but wearing an oak wreath to conceal his baldness, enters from the loggia, attended by Britannus, his secretary, a Briton, about forty, tall, solemn, and already slightly bald, with a heavy, drooping, hazel-colored moustache trained so as to lose its ends in a pair of trim whiskers. He is carefully dressed in blue, with portfolio, inkhorn, and reed pen at his girdle. His serious air and sense of the importance of the business in hand is in marked contrast to the kindly interest of Cæsar, who looks at the scene, which is new to him, with the frank curiosity of a child, and then turns to the King's chair: Britannus and Rufio posting themselves near the steps at the other side.

CÆSAR (*looking at Pothinus and Ptolemy*). Which is the King? the man or the boy?

POTHINUS. I am Pothinus, the guardian of my lord the King.

CÆSAR (*patting Ptolemy kindly on the shoulder*). So you are the King. Dull work at your age, eh? (*To Pothinus.*) Your servant, Pothinus. (*He turns away unconcernedly and comes slowly along the middle of the hall, looking from side to side at the courtiers until he reaches Achillas.*) And this gentleman?

THEODOTUS. Achillas, the King's general.

CÆSAR (*to Achillas, very friendly*). A general, eh? I am a general myself. But I began too old, too old. Health and many victories, Achillas!

ACHILLAS. As the gods will, Cæsar.

CÆSAR (*turning to Theodotus*). And you, sir, are———?

THEODOTUS. Theodotus, the King's tutor.

CÆSAR. You teach men how to be kings, Theodotus. That is very clever of you. (*Looking at the gods on the walls as he turns away from Theodotus and goes up again to Pothinus*). And this place?

POTHINUS. The council chamber of the chancellors of the King's treasury, Cæsar.

CÆSAR. Ah! that reminds me. I want some money.

POTHINUS. The King's treasury is poor, Cæsar.

CÆSAR. Yes: I notice that there is but one chair in it.

RUFIO (*shouting gruffly*). Bring a chair there, some of you, for Cæsar.

PTOLEMY (*rising shyly to offer his chair*). Cæsar———

CÆSAR (*kindly*). No, no, my boy: that is your chair of state. Sit down.

He makes Ptolemy sit down again. Meanwhile Rufio, looking about him, sees in the nearest corner an image of the god Ra, represented as a seated man with the head of a hawk. Before the image is a bronze tripod, about as large as a three-legged stool, with a stick of incense burning on it. Rufio, with Roman resourcefulness and indifference to foreign superstitions, promptly seizes the tripod; shakes off the incense; blows away the ash; and dumps it down behind Cæsar, nearly in the middle of the hall.

RUFIO. Sit on that, Cæsar.

A shiver runs through the court, followed by a hissing whisper of Sacrilege!

CÆSAR (*seating himself*). Now, Pothinus, to business. I am badly in want of money.

BRITANNUS (*disapproving of these informal expressions*). My master would say that there is a lawful debt due to Rome by Egypt, contracted by the King's deceased father to the Triumvirate; and that it is Cæsar's duty to his country to require immediate payment.

CÆSAR (*blandly*). Ah. I forgot. I have not made my companions known here. Pothinus: this is Britannus, my secretary. He is an islander from the western end of the world, a day's voyage from Gaul. (*Britannus bows stiffly.*) This gentleman is Rufio, my comrade in arms. (*Rufio nods.*) Pothinus: I want 1,600 talents.

The courtiers, appalled, murmur loudly, and Theodotus and Achillas appeal mutely to one another against so monstrous a demand.

POTHINUS (*aghast*). Forty million sesterces! Impossible. There is not so much money in the King's treasury.

CÆSAR (*encouragingly*). Only sixteen hundred talents, Pothinus. Why count it in sesterces? A sestertius is only worth a loaf of bread.

POTHINUS. And a talent is worth a racehorse. I say it is impossible. We have been at strife here, because the King's sister Cleopatra falsely claims his throne. The King's taxes have not been collected for a whole year.

CÆSAR. Yes they have, Pothinus. My officers have been collecting them all the morning. (*Renewed whisper and sensation, not without some stifled laughter, among the courtiers.*)

RUFIO (*bluntly*). You must pay, Pothinus. Why waste words? You are getting off cheaply enough.

POTHINUS (*bitterly*). Is it possible that Cæsar, the conqueror of the world, has time to occupy himself with such a trifle as our taxes?

CÆSAR. My friend: taxes are the chief business of a conqueror of the world.

POTHINUS. Then take warning, Cæsar. This day, the treasures of the temples and the gold of the King's treasury shall be sent to the mint to be melted down for our ransom in the sight of the people. They shall see us sitting under bare walls and drinking from wooden cups. And their wrath be on your head, Cæsar, if you force us to this sacrilege!

CÆSAR. Do not fear, Pothinus: the people know how well wine tastes in wooden cups. In return for your bounty, I will settle this dispute about the throne for you, if you will. What say you?

POTHINUS. If I say no, will that hinder you?

RUFIO (*defiantly*). No.

CÆSAR. You say the matter has been at issue for a year, Pothinus. May I have ten minutes at it?

POTHINUS. You will do your pleasure, doubtless.

CÆSAR. Good! But first, let us have Cleopatra here.

THEODOTUS. She is not in Alexandria: she is fled into Syria.

CÆSAR. I think not. (*To Rufio.*) Call Totateeta.

RUFIO (*calling*). Ho there, Teetatota.

Ftatateeta enters the loggia, and stands arrogantly at the top of the steps.

FTATATEETA. Who pronounces the name of Ftatateeta, the Queen's chief nurse?

CÆSAR. Nobody can pronounce it, Tota, except yourself. Where is your mistress?

Cleopatra, who is hiding behind Ftatateeta, peeps out at them, laughing. Cæsar rises.

CÆSAR. Will the Queen favor us with her presence for a moment?

CLEOPATRA (*pushing Ftatateeta aside and standing haughtily on the brink of the steps*). Am I to behave like a Queen?

CÆSAR. Yes.

Cleopatra immediately comes down to the chair of state; seizes Ptolemy and drags him out of his seat; then takes his place in the chair. Ftatateeta seats herself on the step of the loggia, and sits there, watching the scene with sybilline intensity.

PTOLEMY (*mortified, and struggling with his tears*). Cæsar: this is how she treats me always. If I am a king why is she allowed to take everything from me?

CLEOPATRA. You are not to be King, you little cry-baby. You are to be eaten by the Romans.

CÆSAR (*touched by Ptolemy's distress*). Come here, my boy, and stand by me.

Ptolemy goes over to Cæsar, who, resuming his seat on the tripod, takes the boy's hand to encourage him. Cleopatra, furiously jealous, rises and glares at them.

CLEOPATRA (*with flaming cheeks*). Take your throne: I don't want it. (*She flings away from the chair, and approaches Ptolemy, who shrinks from her.*) Go this instant and sit down in your place.

CÆSAR. Go, Ptolemy. Always take a throne when it is offered to you.

RUFIO. I hope you will have the good sense to follow your own advice when we return to Rome, Cæsar.

Ptolemy slowly goes back to the throne, giving Cleopatra a wide berth, in evident fear of her hands. She takes his place beside Cæsar.

CÆSAR. Pothinus——

CLEOPATRA (*interrupting him*). Are you not going to speak to me?

CÆSAR. Be quiet. Open your mouth again before I give you leave; and you shall be eaten.

CLEOPATRA. I am not afraid. A queen must not be afraid. Eat my husband there, if you like: he is afraid.

CÆSAR (*starting*). Your husband! What do you mean?

CLEOPATRA (*pointing to Ptolemy*). That little thing.

The two Romans and the Briton stare at one another in amazement.

THEODOTUS. Cæsar: you are a stranger here, and not conversant with our laws. The kings and queens of Egypt may not marry except with their own royal blood. Ptolemy and Cleopatra are born king and consort just as they are born brother and sister.

BRITANNUS (*shocked*). Cæsar: this is not proper.

THEODOTUS (*outraged*). How!

CÆSAR (*recovering his self-possession*). Pardon him, Theodotus: he is a barbarian, and thinks that the customs of his tribe and island are the laws of nature.

BRITANNUS. On the contrary, Cæsar, it is these Egyptians who are barbarians; and you do wrong to encourage them. I say it is a scandal.

CÆSAR. Scandal or not, my friend, it opens the gate of peace. (*He rises and addresses Pothinus seriously.*) Pothinus: hear what I propose.

RUFIO. Hear Cæsar there.

CÆSAR. Ptolemy and Cleopatra shall reign jointly in Egypt.

ACHILLAS. What of the King's younger brother and Cleopatra's younger sister?

RUFIO (*explaining*). There is another little Ptolemy, Cæsar: so they tell me.

CÆSAR. Well, the little Ptolemy can marry the other sister; and we will make them both a present of Cyprus.

POTHINUS (*impatiently*). Cyprus is of no use to anybody.

CÆSAR. No matter: you shall have it for the sake of peace.

BRITANNUS (*unconsciously anticipating a later statesman*). Peace with honor, Pothinus.

POTHINUS (*mutinously*). Cæsar: be honest. The money you

demand is the price of our freedom. Take it; and leave us to settle our own affairs.

THE BOLDER COURTIERS (*encouraged by Pothinus's tone and Cæsar's quietness*). Yes, yes. Egypt for the Egyptians!

The conference now becomes an altercation, the Egyptians becoming more and more heated. Cæsar remains unruffled; but Rufio grows fiercer and doggeder, and Britannus haughtily indignant.

RUFIO (*contemptuously*). Egypt for the Egyptians! Do you forget that there is a Roman army of occupation here, left by Aulus Gabinius when he set up your toy king for you?

ACHILLAS (*suddenly asserting himself*). And now under my command. *I* am the Roman general here, Cæsar.

CÆSAR (*tickled by the humor of the situation*). And also the Egyptian general, eh?

POTHINUS (*triumphantly*). That is so, Cæsar.

CÆSAR (*to Achillas*). So you can make war on the Egyptians in the name of Rome, and on the Romans—on me, if necessary—in the name of Egypt?

ACHILLAS. That is so, Cæsar.

CÆSAR. And which side are you on at present, if I may presume to ask, general?

ACHILLAS. On the side of the right and of the gods.

CÆSAR. Hm! How many men have you?

ACHILLAS. That will appear when I take the field.

RUFIO (*truculently*). Are your men Romans? If not, it matters not how many there are, provided you are no stronger than 500 to ten.

POTHINUS. It is useless to try to bluff us, Rufio. Cæsar has been defeated before and may be defeated again. A few weeks ago Cæsar was flying for his life before Pompey: a few months hence he may be flying for his life before Cato and Juba of Numidia, the African King.

ACHILLAS (*following up Pothinus's speech menacingly*). What can you do with 4,000 men?

THEODOTUS (*following up Achillas's speech with a raucous squeak*). And without money? Away with you.

ALL THE COURTIERS (*shouting fiercely and crowding towards Cæsar*). Away with you. Egypt for the Egyptians! Begone.

Rufio bites his beard, too angry to speak. Cæsar sits as

comfortably as if he were at breakfast, and the cat were clamoring for a piece of Finnan-haddie.

CLEOPATRA. Why do you let them talk to you like that, Cæsar? Are you afraid?

CÆSAR. Why, my dear, what they say is quite true.

CLEOPATRA. But if you go away, I shall not be Queen.

CÆSAR. I shall not go away until you are Queen.

POTHINUS. Achillas: if you are not a fool, you will take that girl whilst she is under your hand.

RUFIO (*daring them*). Why not take Cæsar as well, Achillas?

POTHINUS (*retorting the defiance with interest*). Well said, Rufio. Why not?

RUFIO. Try, Achillas. (*Calling.*) Guard there.

The loggia immediately fills with Cæsar's soldiers, who stand, sword in hand, at the top of the steps, waiting the word to charge from their centurion, who carries a cudgel. For a moment the Egyptians face them proudly: then they retire sullenly to their former places.

BRITANNUS. You are Cæsar's prisoners, all of you.

CÆSAR (*benevolently*). Oh no, no, no. By no means. Cæsar's guests, gentlemen.

CLEOPATRA. Won't you cut their heads off?

CÆSAR. What! Cut off your brother's head?

CLEOPATRA. Why not! He would cut off mine, if he got the chance. Wouldn't you, Ptolemy?

PTOLEMY (*pale and obstinate*). I would. I will, too, when I grow up.

Cleopatra is rent by a struggle between her newly acquired dignity as a queen, and a strong impulse to put out her tongue at him. She takes no part in the scene which follows, but watches it with curiosity and wonder, fidgeting with the restlessness of a child, and sitting down on Cæsar's tripod when he rises.

POTHINUS. Cæsar: if you attempt to detain us——

RUFIO. He will succeed, Egyptian: make up your mind to that. We hold the palace, the beach, and the eastern harbor. The road to Rome is open; and you shall travel it if Cæsar chooses.

CÆSAR (*courteously*). I could do no less, Pothinus, to secure the retreat of my own soldiers. I am accountable for every life among them. But you are free to go. So are all here, and in the palace.

RUFIO (*aghast at this clemency*). What! Renegades and all?

CÆSAR (*softening the expression*). Roman army of occupation and all, Rufio.

POTHINUS (*desperately*). Then I make a last appeal to Cæsar's justice. I shall call a witness to prove that but for us, the Roman army of occupation, led by the greatest soldier in the world, would now have Cæsar at its mercy. (*Calling through the loggia.*) Ho, there, Lucius Septimius (*Cæsar starts, deeply moved*): if my voice can reach you, come forth and testify before Cæsar.

CÆSAR (*shrinking*). No, no.

THEODOTUS. Yes, I say. Let the military tribune bear witness.

Lucius Septimius, a clean-shaven, trim athlete of about forty, with symmetrical features, resolute mouth, and handsome, thin Roman nose, in the dress of a Roman officer, comes in through the loggia and confronts Cæsar, who hides his face with his robe for a moment; then, mastering himself, drops it, and confronts the tribune with dignity.

POTHINUS. Bear witness, Lucius Septimius. Cæsar came hither in pursuit of his foe. Did we shelter his foe?

LUCIUS. As Pompey's foot touched the Egyptian shore, his head fell by the stroke of my sword.

THEODOTUS (*with viperish relish*). Under the eyes of his wife and child! Remember that, Cæsar! They saw it from the ship he had just left. We have given you a full and sweet measure of vengeance.

CÆSAR (*with horror*). Vengeance!

POTHINUS. Our first gift to you, as your galley came into the roadstead, was the head of your rival for the empire of the world. Bear witness, Lucius Septimius: is it not so?

LUCIUS. It is so. With this hand, that slew Pompey, I placed his head at the feet of Cæsar.

CÆSAR. Murderer! So would you have slain Cæsar, had Pompey been victorious at Pharsalia.

LUCIUS. Woe to the vanquished, Cæsar! When I served Pompey, I slew as good men as he, only because he conquered them. His turn came at last.

THEODOTUS (*flatteringly*). The deed was not yours, Cæsar,

but ours—nay, mine; for it was done by my counsel. Thanks to us, you keep your reputation for clemency, and have your vengeance too.

CÆSAR. Vengeance! Vengeance!! Oh, if I could stoop to vengeance, what would I not exact from you as the price of this murdered man's blood. (*They shrink back, appalled and disconcerted.*) Was he not my son-in-law, my ancient friend, for 20 years the master of great Rome, for 30 years the compeller of victory? Did not I, as a Roman, share his glory? Was the Fate that forced us to fight for the mastery of the world, of our making? Am I Julius Cæsar, or am I a wolf, that you fling to me the grey head of the old soldier, the laurelled conquerer, the mighty Roman, treacherously struck down by this callous ruffian, and then claim my gratitude for it! (*To Lucius Septimius.*) Begone: you fill me with horror.

LUCIUS (*cold and undaunted*). Pshaw! you have seen severed heads before, Cæsar, and severed right hands too, I think; some thousands of them, in Gaul, after you vanquished Vercingetorix. Did you spare him, with all your clemency? Was that vengeance?

CÆSAR. No, by the gods! would that it had been! Vengeance at least is human. No, I say: those severed right hands, and the brave Vercingetorix basely strangled in a vault beneath the Capitol, were (*with shuddering satire*) a wise severity, a necessary protection to the commonwealth, a duty of statesmanship—follies and fictions ten times bloodier than honest vengeance! What a fool was I then! To think that men's lives should be at the mercy of such fools! (*Humbly.*) Lucius Septimius, pardon me: why should the slayer of Vercingetorix rebuke the slayer of Pompey? You are free to go with the rest. Or stay if you will: I will find a place for you in my service.

LUCIUS. The odds are against you, Cæsar. I go. (*He turns to go out through the loggia.*)

RUFIO (*full of wrath at seeing his prey escaping*). That means that he is a Republican.

LUCIUS (*turning defiantly on the loggia steps*). And what are you?

RUFIO. A Cæsarian, like all Cæsar's soldiers.

CÆSAR (*courteously*). Lucius: believe me, Cæsar is no Cæsarian. Were Rome a true republic, then were Cæsar the first of Republicans. But you have made your choice. Farewell.

LUCIUS. Farewell. Come, Achillas, whilst there is yet time.

Cæsar, seeing that Rufio's temper threatens to get the worse of him, puts his hand on his shoulder and brings him down the hall out of harm's way, Britannus accompanying them and posting himself on Cæsar's right hand. This movement brings the three in a little group to the place occupied by Achillas, who moves haughtily away and joins Theodotus on the other side. Lucius Septimius goes out through the soldiers in the loggia. Pothinus, Theodotus and Achillas follow him with the courtiers, very mistrustful of the soldiers, who close up in their rear and go out after them, keeping them moving without much ceremony. The King is left in his chair, piteous, obstinate, with twitching face and fingers. During these movements Rufio maintains an energetic grumbling, as follows:—

RUFIO (*as Lucius departs*). Do you suppose he would let us go if he had our heads in his hands?

CÆSAR. I have no right to suppose that his ways are any baser than mine.

RUFIO. Psha!

CÆSAR. Rufio: if I take Lucius Septimius for my model, and become exactly like him, ceasing to be Cæsar, will you serve me still?

BRITANNUS. Cæsar: this is not good sense. Your duty to Rome demands that her enemies should be prevented from doing further mischief. (*Cæsar, whose delight in the moral eye-to-business of his British secretary is inexhaustible, smiles indulgently.*)

RUFIO. It is no use talking to him, Britannus: you may save your breath to cool your porridge. But mark this, Cæsar. Clemency is very well for you; but what is it for your soldiers, who have to fight to-morrow the men you spared yesterday? You may give what orders you please; but I tell you that your next victory will be a massacre, thanks to your clemency. *I,* for one, will take no prisoners. I will kill my enemies in the field; and then you can preach as much clemency as you please: I shall never have to fight them again. And now, with your leave, I will see these gentry off the premises. (*He turns to go.*)

CÆSAR (*turning also and seeing Ptolemy*). What! have they left the boy alone! Oh shame, shame!

RUFIO (*taking Ptolemy's hand and making him rise*). Come, your majesty!

PTOLEMY (*to Cæsar, drawing away his hand from Rufio*). Is he turning me out of my palace?

RUFIO (*grimly*). You are welcome to stay if you wish.

CÆSAR (*kindly*). Go, my boy. I will not harm you; but you will be safer away, among your friends. Here you are in the lion's mouth.

PTOLEMY (*turning to go*). It is not the lion I fear, but (*looking at Rufio*) the jackal. (*He goes out through the loggia.*)

CÆSAR (*laughing approvingly*). Brave boy!

CLEOPATRA (*jealous of Cæsar's approbation, calling after Ptolemy*). Little silly. You think that very clever.

CÆSAR. Britannus: attend the King. Give him in charge to that Pothinus fellow. (*Britannus goes out after Ptolemy.*)

RUFIO (*pointing to Cleopatra*). And this piece of goods? What is to be done with her? However, I suppose I may leave that to you. (*He goes out through the loggia.*)

CLEOPATRA (*flushing suddenly and turning on Cæsar*). Did you mean me to go with the rest?

CÆSAR (*a little preoccupied, goes with a sigh to Ptolemy's chair, whilst she waits for his answer with red cheeks and clenched fists*). You are free to do just as you please, Cleopatra.

CLEOPATRA. Then you do not care whether I stay or not?

CÆSAR (*smiling*). Of course I had rather you stayed.

CLEOPATRA. Much, much rather?

CÆSAR (*nodding*). Much, much rather.

CLEOPATRA. Then I consent to stay, because I am asked. But I do not want to, mind.

CÆSAR. That is quite understood. (*Calling.*) Totateeta.

Ftatateeta, still seated, turns her eyes on him with a sinister expression, but does not move.

CLEOPATRA (*with a splutter of laughter*). Her name is not Totateeta: it is Ftatateeta. (*Calling.*) Ftatateeta. (*Ftatateeta instantly rises and comes to Cleopatra.*)

CÆSAR (*stumbling over the name*). Tfatafeeta will forgive the erring tongue of a Roman. Tota: the Queen will hold her state here in Alexandria. Engage women to attend upon her; and do all that is needful.

FTATATEETA. Am I then the mistress of the Queen's household?

CLEOPATRA (*sharply*). No: I am the mistress of the Queen's household. Go and do as you are told, or I will have you thrown into the Nile this very afternoon, to poison the poor crocodiles.

CÆSAR (*shocked*). Oh no, no.

CLEOPATRA. Oh yes, yes. You are very sentimental, Cæsar; but you are clever; and if you do as I tell you, you will soon learn to govern.

Cæsar, quite dumbfounded by this impertinence, turns in his chair and stares at her.

Ftatateeta, smiling grimly, and showing a splendid set of teeth, goes, leaving them alone together.

CÆSAR. Cleopatra: I really think I must eat you, after all.

CLEOPATRA (*kneeling beside him and looking at him with eager interest, half real, half affected to shew how intelligent she is*). You must not talk to me now as if I were a child.

CÆSAR. You have been growing up since the Sphinx introduced us the other night; and you think you know more than I do already.

CLEOPATRA (*taken down, and anxious to justify herself*). No: that would be very silly of me: of course I know that. But— (*suddenly*) are you angry with me?

CÆSAR. No.

CLEOPATRA (*only half believing him*). Then why are you so thoughtful?

CÆSAR (*rising*). I have work to do, Cleopatra.

CLEOPATRA (*drawing back*). Work! (*Offended.*) You are tired of talking to me; and that is your excuse to get away from me.

CÆSAR (*sitting down again to appease her*). Well, well: another minute. But then—work!

CLEOPATRA. Work! what nonsense! You must remember that you are a king now: I have made you one. Kings don't work.

CÆSAR. Oh! Who told you that, little kitten? Eh?

CLEOPATRA. My father was King of Egypt; and he never worked. But he was a great king, and cut off my sister's head because she rebelled against him and took the throne from him.

CÆSAR. Well; and how did he get his throne back again?

CLEOPATRA (*eagerly, her eyes lighting up*). I will tell you. A beautiful young man, with strong round arms, came over the desert with many horsemen, and slew my sister's husband and gave my father back his throne. (*Wistfully.*) I was only twelve then. Oh, I wish he would come again, now that I am a queen. I would make him my husband.

CÆSAR. It might be managed, perhaps; for it was I who sent that beautiful young man to help your father.

CLEOPATRA (*enraptured*). You know him!

CÆSAR (*nodding*). I do.

CLEOPATRA. Has he come with you? (*Cæsar shakes his head: she is cruelly disappointed.*) Oh, I wish he had, I wish he had. If only I were a little older; so that he might not think me a mere kitten, as you do! But perhaps that is because you are old. He is many, many years younger than you, is he not?

CÆSAR (*as if swallowing a pill*). He is somewhat younger.

CLEOPATRA. Would he be my husband, do you think, if I asked him?

CÆSAR. Very likely.

CLEOPATRA. But I should not like to ask him. Could you not persuade him to ask me—without knowing that I wanted him to?

CÆSAR (*touched by her innocence of the beautiful young man's character*). My poor child!

CLEOPATRA. Why do you say that as if you were sorry for me? Does he love anyone else?

CÆSAR. I am afraid so.

CLEOPATRA (*tearfully*). Then I shall not be his first love.

CÆSAR. Not quite the first. He is greatly admired by women.

CLEOPATRA. I wish I could be the first. But if he loves me, I will make him kill all the rest. Tell me: is he still beautiful? Do his strong round arms shine in the sun like marble?

CÆSAR. He is in excellent condition—considering how much he eats and drinks.

CLEOPATRA. Oh, you must not say common, earthly things about him; for I love him. He is a god.

CÆSAR. He is a great captain of horsemen, and swifter of foot than any other Roman.

CLEOPATRA. What is his real name?

CÆSAR (*puzzled*). His real name?

CLEOPATRA. Yes. I always call him Horus, because Horus is the most beautiful of our gods. But I want to know his real name.

CÆSAR. His name is Mark Antony.

CLEOPATRA (*musically*). Mark Antony, Mark Antony, Mark Antony! What a beautiful name! (*She throws her arms round Cæsar's neck.*) Oh, how I love you for sending him to help my father! Did you love my father very much?

CÆSAR. No, my child; but your father, as you say, never worked. I always work. So when he lost his crown he had to promise me 16,000 talents to get it back for him.

CLEOPATRA. Did he ever pay you?

CÆSAR. Not in full.

CLEOPATRA. He was quite right: it was too dear. The whole world is not worth 16,000 talents.

CÆSAR. That is perhaps true, Cleopatra. Those Egyptians who work paid as much of it as he could drag from them. The rest is still due. But as I most likely shall not get it, I must go back to my work. So you must run away for a little and send my secretary to me.

CLEOPATRA (*coaxing*). No: I want to stay and hear you talk about Mark Antony.

CÆSAR. But if I do not get to work, Pothinus and the rest of them will cut us off from the harbor; and then the way from Rome will be blocked.

CLEOPATRA. No matter: I don't want you to go back to Rome.

CÆSAR. But you want Mark Antony to come from it.

CLEOPATRA (*springing up*). Oh yes, yes, yes: I forgot. Go quickly and work, Cæsar; and keep the way over the sea open for my Mark Antony. (*She runs out through the loggia, kissing her hand to Mark Antony across the sea.*)

CÆSAR (*going briskly up the middle of the hall to the loggia steps*). Ho, Britannus. (*He is startled by the entry of a wounded Roman soldier, who confronts him from the upper step.*) What now?

SOLDIER (*pointing to his bandaged head*). This, Cæsar; and two of my comrades killed in the market place.

CÆSAR (*quiet, but attending*). Ay. Why?

SOLDIER. There is an army come to Alexandria, calling itself the Roman army.

CÆSAR. The Roman army of occupation. Ay?

SOLDIER. Commanded by one Achillas.

CÆSAR. Well?

SOLDIER. The citizens rose against us when the army entered the gates. I was with two others in the market place when the news came. They set upon us. I cut my way out; and here I am.

CÆSAR. Good. I am glad to see you alive. (*Rufio enters the loggia hastily, passing behind the soldier to look out through one of the arches of the quay beneath.*) Rufio, we are besieged.

RUFIO. What! Already?

CÆSAR. Now or to-morrow: what does it matter? We shall be besieged.

Britannus runs in.

BRITANNUS. Cæsar——

CÆSAR (*anticipating him*). Yes: I know. (*Rufio and Britannus come down the hall from the loggia at opposite sides, past Cæsar, who waits for a moment near the step to say to the soldier.*) Comrade: give the word to turn out on the beach and stand by the boats. Get your wound attended to. Go. (*The soldier hurries out. Cæsar comes down the hall between Rufio and Britannus.*) Rufio: we have some ships in the west harbor. Burn them.

RUFIO (*staring*). Burn them!!

CÆSAR. Take every boat we have in the east harbor, and seize the Pharos—that island with the lighthouse. Leave half our men behind to hold the beach and the quay outside this palace: that is the way home.

RUFIO (*disapproving strongly*). Are we to give up the city?

CÆSAR. We have not got it, Rufio. This palace we have; and—what is that building next door?

RUFIO. The theatre.

CÆSAR. We will have that too: it commands the strand. For the rest, Egypt for the Egyptians!

RUFIO. Well, you know best, I suppose. Is that all?

CÆSAR. That is all. Are those ships burnt yet?

RUFIO. Be easy: I shall waste no more time. (*He runs out.*)

BRITANNUS. Cæsar: Pothinus demands speech of you. In my opinion he needs a lesson. His manner is most insolent.

CÆSAR. Where is he?

BRITANNUS. He waits without.

CÆSAR. Ho there! admit Pothinus.

Pothinus appears in the loggia, and comes down the hall very haughtily to Cæsar's left hand.

CÆSAR. Well, Pothinus?

POTHINUS. I have brought you our ultimatum, Cæsar.

CÆSAR. Ultimatum! The door was open: you should have gone out through it before you declared war. You are my prisoner now. (*He goes to the chair and loosens his toga.*)

POTHINUS (*scornfully*). I your prisoner! Do you know that you are in Alexandria, and that King Ptolemy, with an army outnumbering your little troop a hundred to one, is in possession of Alexandria?

CÆSAR (*unconcernedly taking off his toga and throwing it on the chair*). Well, my friend, get out if you can. And tell your friends not to kill any more Romans in the market place. Otherwise my soldiers, who do not share my celebrated clemency, will probably kill you. Britannus: pass the word to the guard; and fetch my armor. (*Britannus runs out. Rufio returns.*) Well?

RUFIO (*pointing from the loggia to a cloud of smoke drifting over the harbor*). See there! (*Pothinus runs eagerly up the steps to look out.*)

CÆSAR. What, ablaze already! Impossible!

RUFIO. Yes, five good ships, and a barge laden with oil grappled to each. But it is not my doing: the Egyptians have saved me the trouble. They have captured the west harbor.

CÆSAR (*anxiously*). And the east harbor? The lighthouse, Rufio?

RUFIO (*with a sudden splutter of raging ill usage, coming down to Cæsar and scolding him*). Can I embark a legion in five minutes? The first cohort is already on the beach. We can do no more. If you want faster work, come and do it yourself.

CÆSAR (*soothing him*). Good, good. Patience, Rufio, patience.

RUFIO. Patience! Who is impatient here, you or I? Would I be here, if I could not oversee them from that balcony?

CÆSAR. Forgive me, Rufio; and (*anxiously*) hurry them as much as——

He is interrupted by an outcry as of an old man in the extremity of misfortune. It draws near rapidly; and Theodotus rushes in, tearing his hair, and squeaking the most lamentable exclamations. Rufio steps back to stare at him, amazed at his frantic condition. Pothinus turns to listen.

THEODOTUS (*on the steps, with uplifted arms*). Horror unspeakable! Woe, alas! Help!

RUFIO. What now?

CÆSAR (*frowning*). Who is slain?

THEODOTUS. Slain! Oh, worse than the death of ten thousand men! Loss irreparable to mankind!

RUFIO. What has happened, man?

THEODOTUS (*rushing down the hall between them*). The fire has spread from your ships. The first of the seven wonders of the world perishes. The library of Alexandria is in flames.

RUFIO. Psha! (*Quite relieved, he goes up to the loggia and watches the preparations of the troops on the beach.*)

CÆSAR. Is that all?

THEODOTUS (*unable to believe his senses*). All! Cæsar: will you go down to posterity as a barbarous soldier too ignorant to know the value of books?

CÆSAR. Theodotus: I am an author myself; and I tell you it is better that the Egyptians should live their lives than dream them away with the help of books.

THEODOTUS (*kneeling, with genuine literary emotion: the passion of the pedant*). Cæsar: once in ten generations of men, the world gains an immortal book.

CÆSAR (*inflexible*). If it did not flatter mankind, the common executioner would burn it.

THEODOTUS. Without history, death would lay you beside your meanest soldier.

CÆSAR. Death will do that in any case. I ask no better grave.

THEODOTUS. What is burning there is the memory of mankind.

CÆSAR. A shameful memory. Let it burn.

THEODOTUS (*wildly*). Will you destroy the past?

CÆSAR. Ay, and build the future with its ruins. (*Theodotus, in despair, strikes himself on the temples with his fists.*)

But harken, Theodotus, teacher of kings: you who valued
Pompey's head no more than a shepherd values an onion,
and who now kneel to me, with tears in your old eyes, to
plead for a few sheepskins scrawled with errors. I cannot
spare you a man or a bucket of water just now; but you shall
pass freely out of the palace. Now, away with you to Achillas;
and borrow his legions to put out the fire. (*He hurries him
to the steps.*)

POTHINUS (*significantly*). You understand, Theodotus: I
remain a prisoner.

THEODOTUS. A prisoner!

CÆSAR. Will you stay to talk whilst the memory of mankind is burning? (*Calling through the loggia.*) Ho there! Pass
Theodotus out. (*To Theodotus.*) Away with you.

THEODOTUS (*to Pothinus*). I must go to save the library.
(*He hurries out.*)

CÆSAR. Follow him to the gate, Pothinus. Bid him urge
your people to kill no more of my soldiers, for your sake.

POTHINUS. My life will cost you dear if you take it, Cæsar.
(*He goes out after Theodotus.*)

*Rufio, absorbed in watching the embarkation, does not no-
tice the departure of the two Egyptians.*

RUFIO (*shouting from the loggia to the beach*). All ready,
there?

A CENTURION (*from below*). All ready. We wait for
Cæsar.

CÆSAR. Tell them Cæsar is coming—the rogues! (*Calling.*)
Britannicus. (*This magniloquent version of his secretary's
name is one of Cæsar's jokes. In later years it would have
meant, quite seriously and officially, Conqueror of Britain.*)

RUFIO (*calling down*). Push off, all except the longboat.
Stand by it to embark, Cæsar's guard there. (*He leaves the
balcony and comes down into the hall.*) Where are those
Egyptians? Is this more clemency? Have you let them go?

CÆSAR (*chuckling*). I have let Theodotus go to save the
library. We must respect literature, Rufio.

RUFIO (*raging*). Folly on folly's head! I believe if you
could bring back all the dead of Spain, Gaul and Thessaly
to life, you would do it that we might have the trouble of
fighting them over again.

CÆSAR. Might not the gods destroy the world if their only
thought were to be at peace next year? (*Rufio, out of all*

*patience, turns away in anger. Cæsar suddenly grips his
sleeve, and adds slyly in his ear.*) Besides, my friend: every
Egyptian we imprison means imprisoning two Roman soldiers
to guard him. Eh?

RUFIO. Agh! I might have known there was some fox's
trick behind your fine talking. (*He gets away from Cæsar
with an ill-humored shrug, and goes to the balcony for another look at the preparations; finally goes out.*)

CÆSAR. Is Britannus asleep? I sent him for my armor an
hour ago. (*Calling.*) Britannicus, thou British islander. Britannicus!

*Cleopatra runs in through the loggia with Cæsar's helmet
and sword, snatched from Britannus, who follows her with a
cuirass and greaves. They come down to Cæsar, she to his
left hand, Britannus to his right.*

CLEOPATRA. I am going to dress you, Cæsar. Sit down. (*He
obeys.*) These Roman helmets are so becoming! (*She takes
off his wreath.*) Oh! (*She bursts out laughing at him.*)

CÆSAR. What are you laughing at?

CLEOPATRA. You're bald (*beginning with a big B, and
ending with a splutter*).

CÆSAR (*almost annoyed*). Cleopatra! (*He rises, for the
convenience of Britannus, who puts the cuirass on him.*)

CLEOPATRA. So that is why you wear the wreath—to hide
it.

BRITANNUS. Peace, Egyptian: they are the bays of the
conqueror. (*He buckles the cuirass.*)

CLEOPATRA. Peace, thou: islander! (*To Cæsar.*) You should
rub your head with strong spirits of sugar, Cæsar. That will
make it grow.

CÆSAR (*with a wry face*). Cleopatra: do you like to be
reminded that you are very young?

CLEOPATRA (*pouting*). No.

CÆSAR (*sitting down again, and setting out his leg for
Britannus, who kneels to put on his greaves*). Neither do I
like to be reminded that I am—middle aged. Let me give
you ten of my superfluous years. That will make you twenty-
six, and leave me only—no matter. Is it a bargain?

CLEOPATRA. Agreed. Twenty-six, mind. (*She puts the helmet on him.*) Oh! How nice! You look only about fifty in it!

BRITANNUS (*looking up severely at Cleopatra*). You must
not speak in this manner to Cæsar.

CLEOPATRA. Is it true that when Cæsar caught you on that island, you were painted all over blue?

BRITANNUS. Blue is the color worn by all Britons of good standing. In war we stain our bodies blue; so that though our enemies may strip us of our clothes and our lives, they cannot strip us of our responsibility. (*He rises.*)

CLEOPATRA (*with Cæsar's sword*). Let me hang this on. Now you look splendid. Have they made any statues of you in Rome?

CÆSAR. Yes, many statues.

CLEOPATRA. You must send for one and give it to me.

RUFIO (*coming back into the loggia, more impatient than ever*). Now Cæsar: have you done talking? The moment your foot is aboard there will be no holding our men back: the boats will race one another for the lighthouse.

CÆSAR (*drawing his sword and trying the edge*). Is this well set to-day, Britannicus? At Pharsalia it was as blunt as a barrel-hoop.

BRITANNUS. It will split one of the Egyptian's hairs to-day, Cæsar. I have set it myself.

CLEOPATRA (*suddenly throwing her arms in terror round Cæsar*). Oh, you are not really going into battle to be killed?

CÆSAR. No, Cleopatra. No man goes to battle to be killed.

CLEOPATRA. But they do get killed. My sister's husband was killed in battle. You must not go. Let him go. (*Pointing to Rufio. They all laugh at her.*) Oh please, please don't go. What will happen to me if you never come back?

CÆSAR (*gravely*). Are you afraid?

CLEOPATRA (*shrinking*). No.

CÆSAR (*with quiet authority*). Go to the balcony; and you shall see us take the Pharos. You must learn to look on battles. Go. (*She goes, downcast, and looks out from the balcony.*) That is well. Now, Rufio. March.

CLEOPATRA (*suddenly clapping her hands*). Oh, you will not be able to go!

CÆSAR. Why? What now?

CLEOPATRA. They are drying up the harbor with buckets —a multitude of soldiers—over there (*pointing out across the sea to her left*)—they are dipping up the water.

RUFIO (*hastening to look*). It is true. The Egyptian army! Crawling over the edge of the west harbor like locusts. (*With*

sudden anger he strides down to Cæsar.) This is your accursed clemency, Cæsar. Theodotus has brought them.

CÆSAR (*delighted at his own cleverness*). I meant him to,
Rufio. They have come to put out the fire. The library will
keep them busy whilst we seize the lighthouse. Eh? (*He
rushes out buoyantly through the loggia, followed by
Britannus.*)

RUFIO (*disgustedly*). More foxing! Agh! (*He rushes off. A
shout from the soldiers announces the appearance of Cæsar
below.*)

CENTURION (*below*). All aboard. Give way there. (*Another
shout.*)

CLEOPATRA (*waving her scarf through the loggia arch*).
Goodbye, goodbye, dear Cæsar. Come back safe. Goodbye!

ACT III

The edge of the quay in front of the palace, looking out west over the east harbor of Alexandria to Pharos island, just off the end of which, and connected with it by a narrow mole, is the famous lighthouse, a gigantic square tower of white marble diminishing in size storey by storey to the top, on which stands a cresset beacon. The island is joined to the main land by the Heptastadium, a great mole or causeway five miles long bounding the harbor on the south.

In the middle of the quay a Roman sentinel stands on guard, pilum in hand, looking out to the lighthouse with strained attention, his left hand shading his eyes. The pilum is a stout wooden shaft 4½ feet long, with an iron spit about three feet long fixed in it. The sentinel is so absorbed that he does not notice the approach from the north end of the quay of four Egyptian market porters carrying rolls of carpet, preceded by Ftatateeta and Apollodorus the Sicilian. Apollodorus is a dashing young man of about twenty-four, handsome and debonair, dressed with deliberate æstheticism in the most delicate purples and dove greys, with ornaments of bronze, oxydized silver, and stones of jade and agate. His sword, designed as carefully as a medieval cross, has a blued blade showing through an openwork scabbard of purple leather and filigree. The porters, conducted by Ftatateeta, pass along the quay behind the sentinel to the steps of the palace, where they put down their bales and squat on the ground. Apollodorus does not pass along with them: he halts, amused by the preoccupation of the sentinel.

APOLLODORUS (calling to the sentinel). Who goes there, eh?

SENTINEL (starting violently and turning with his pilum at the charge, revealing himself as a small, wiry, sandy-haired, conscientious young man with an elderly face.) What's this? Stand. Who are you?

APOLLODORUS. I am Apollodorus the Sicilian. Why, man, what are you dreaming of? Since I came through the lines

194

beyond the theatre there, I have brought my caravan past three sentinels, all so busy staring at the lighthouse that not one of them challenged me. Is this Roman discipline?

SENTINEL. We are not here to watch the land but the sea. Cæsar has just landed on the Pharos. (*Looking at Ftatateeta.*) What have you here? Who is this piece of Egyptian crockery?

FTATATEETA. Apollodorus: rebuke this Roman dog; and bid him bridle his tongue in the presence of Ftatateeta, the mistress of the Queen's household.

APOLLODORUS. My friend: this is a great lady, who stands high with Cæsar.

SENTINEL (*not at all impressed, pointing to the carpets*). And what is all this truck?

APOLLODORUS. Carpets for the furnishing of the Queen's apartments in the palace. I have picked them from the best carpets in the world; and the Queen shall choose the best of my choosing.

SENTINEL. So you are the carpet merchant?

APOLLODORUS (*hurt*). My friend: I am a patrician.

SENTINEL. A patrician! A patrician keeping a shop instead of following arms!

APOLLODORUS. I do not keep a shop. Mine is a temple of the arts. I am a worshipper of beauty. My calling is to choose beautiful things for beautiful Queens. My motto is Art for Art's sake.

SENTINEL. That is not the password.

APOLLODORUS. It is a universal password.

SENTINEL. I know nothing about universal passwords. Either give me the password for the day or get back to your shop.

Ftatateeta, roused by his hostile tone, steals towards the edge of the quay with the step of a panther, and gets behind him.

APOLLODORUS. How if I do neither?

SENTINEL. Then I will drive this pilum through you.

APOLLODORUS. At your service, my friend. (*He draws his sword, and springs to his guard with unruffled grace.*)

FTATATEETA (*suddenly seizing the sentinel's arms from behind*). Thrust your knife into the dog's throat, Apollodorus. (*The chivalrous Apollodorus laughingly shakes his head; breaks ground away from the sentinel towards the palace; and lowers his point.*)

SENTINEL (*struggling vainly*). Curse on you! Let me go. Help ho!

FTATATEETA (*lifting him from the ground*). Stab the little Roman reptile. Spit him on your sword.

A couple of Roman soldiers, with a centurion, come running along the edge of the quay from the north end. They rescue their comrade, and throw off Ftatateeta, who is sent reeling away on the left hand of the sentinel.

CENTURION (*an unattractive man of fifty, short in his speech and manners, with a vine wood cudgel in his hand*). How now? What is all this?

FTATATEETA (*to Apollodorus*). Why did you not stab him? There was time!

APOLLODORUS. Centurion: I am here by order of the Queen to——

CENTURION (*interrupting him*). The Queen! Yes, yes: (*to the sentinel*) pass him in. Pass all these bazaar people in to the Queen, with their goods. But mind you pass no one out that you have not passed in—not even the Queen herself.

SENTINEL. This old woman is dangerous: she is as strong as three men. She wanted the merchant to stab me.

APOLLODORUS. Centurion: I am not a merchant. I am a patrician and a votary of art.

CENTURION. Is the woman your wife?

APOLLODORUS (*horrified*). No, no! (*Correcting himself politely.*) Not that the lady is not a striking figure in her own way. But (*emphatically*) she is not my wife.

FTATATEETA (*to the Centurion*). Roman: I am Ftatateeta, the mistress of the Queen's household.

CENTURION. Keep your hands off our men, mistress; or I will have you pitched into the harbor, though you were as strong as ten men. (*To his men.*) To your posts: march! (*He returns with his men the way they came.*)

FTATATEETA (*looking malignantly after him*). We shall see whom Isis loves best: her servant Ftatateeta or a dog of a Roman.

SENTINEL (*to Apollodorus, with a wave of his pilum towards the palace*). Pass in there; and keep your distance. (*Turning to Ftatateeta.*) Come within a yard of me, you old crocodile; and I will give you this (*the pilum*) in your jaws.

CLEOPATRA (*calling from the palace*). Ftatateeta, Ftatateeta.

FTATATEETA (*looking up, scandalized*). Go from the window, go from the window. There are men here.

CLEOPATRA. I am coming down.

FTATATEETA (*distracted*). No, no. What are you dreaming of? O ye gods, ye gods! Apollodorus: bid your men pick up your bales; and in with me quickly.

APOLLODORUS. Obey the mistress of the Queen's household.

FTATATEETA (*impatiently, as the porters stoop to lift the bales*). Quick, quick: she will be out upon us. (*Cleopatra comes from the palace and runs across the quay to Ftatateeta.*) Oh that ever I was born!

CLEOPATRA (*eagerly*). Ftatateeta: I have thought of something. I want a boat—at once.

FTATATEETA. A boat! No, no: you cannot. Apollodorus: speak to the Queen.

APOLLODORUS (*gallantly*). Beautiful queen: I am Apollodorus the Sicilian, your servant, from the bazaar. I have brought you the three most beautiful Persian carpets in the world to choose from.

CLEOPATRA. I have no time for carpets to-day. Get me a boat.

FTATATEETA. What whim is this? You cannot go on the water except in the royal barge.

APOLLODORUS. Royalty, Ftatateeta, lies not in the barge but in the Queen. (*To Cleopatra.*) The touch of your majesty's foot on the gunwale of the meanest boat in the harbor will make it royal. (*He turns to the harbor and calls seaward.*) Ho there, boatman! Pull in to the steps.

CLEOPATRA. Apollodorus: you are my perfect knight; and I will always buy my carpets through you. (*Apollodorus bows joyously. An oar appears above the quay; and the boatman, a bullet-headed, vivacious, grinning fellow, burnt almost black by the sun, comes up a flight of steps from the water on the sentinel's right, oar in hand, and waits at the top.*) Can you row, Apollodorus?

APOLLODORUS. My oars shall be your majesty's wings. Whither shall I row my Queen?

CLEOPATRA. To the lighthouse. Come. (*She makes for the steps.*)

SENTINEL (*opposing her with his pilum at the charge*). Stand. You cannot pass.

CLEOPATRA (*flushing angrily*). How dare you? Do you know that I am the Queen?

SENTINEL. I have my orders. You cannot pass.

CLEOPATRA. I will make Cæsar have you killed if you do not obey me.

SENTINEL. He will do worse to me if I disobey my officer. Stand back.

CLEOPATRA. Ftatateeta: strangle him.

SENTINEL (*alarmed—looking apprehensively at Ftatateeta, and brandishing his pilum*). Keep off, there.

CLEOPATRA (*running to Apollodorus*). Apollodorus: make your slaves help us.

APOLLODORUS. I shall not need their help, lady. (*He draws his sword.*) Now, soldier: choose which weapon you will defend yourself with. Shall it be sword against pilum, or sword against sword?

SENTINEL. Roman against Sicilian, curse you. Take that. (*He hurls his pilum at Apollodorus, who drops expertly on one knee. The pilum passes whizzing over his head and falls harmless. Apollodorus, with a cry of triumph, springs up and attacks the sentinel, who draws his sword and defends himself, crying.*) Ho there, guard. Help!

Cleopatra, half frightened, half delighted, takes refuge near the palace, where the porters are squatting among the bales. The boatman, alarmed, hurries down the steps out of harm's way, but stops, with his head just visible above the edge of the quay, to watch the fight. The sentinel is handicapped by his fear of an attack in the rear from Ftatateeta. His swordsmanship, which is of a rough and ready sort, is heavily taxed, as he has occasionally to strike at her to keep her off between a blow and a guard with Apollodorus. The Centurion returns with several soldiers. Apollodorus springs back towards Cleopatra as this reinforcement confronts him.

CENTURION (*coming to the sentinel's right hand*). What is this? What now?

SENTINEL (*panting*). I could do well enough by myself if it weren't for the old woman. Keep her off me: that is all the help I need.

CENTURION. Make your report, soldier. What has happened?

FTATATEETA. Centurion: he would have slain the Queen.

SENTINEL (*bluntly*). I would, sooner than let her pass. She wanted to take a boat, and go—so she said—to the lighthouse.

I stopped her, as I was ordered to; and she set this fellow on me. (*He goes to pick up his pilum and returns to his place with it.*)

CENTURION (*turning to Cleopatra*). Cleopatra: I am loth to offend you; but without Cæsar's express order we dare not let you pass beyond the Roman lines.

APOLLODORUS. Well, Centurion; and has not the lighthouse been within the Roman lines since Cæsar landed there?

CLEOPATRA. Yes, yes. Answer that, if you can.

CENTURION (*to Apollodorus*). As for you, Apollodorus, you may thank the gods that you are not nailed to the palace door with a pilum for your meddling.

APOLLODORUS (*urbanely*). My military friend, I was not born to be slain by so ugly a weapon. When I fall, it will be (*holding up his sword*) by this white queen of arms, the only weapon fit for an artist. And now that you are convinced that we do not want to go beyond the lines, let me finish killing your sentinel and depart with the Queen.

CENTURION (*as the sentinel makes an angry demonstration*). Peace there. Cleopatra. I must abide by my orders, and not by the subtleties of this Sicilian. You must withdraw into the palace and examine your carpets there.

CLEOPATRA (*pouting*). I will not: I am the Queen. Cæsar does not speak to me as you do. Have Cæsar's centurions changed manners with his scullions?

CENTURION (*sulkily*). I do my duty. That is enough for me.

APOLLODORUS. Majesty: when a stupid man is doing something he is ashamed of, he always declares that it is his duty.

CENTURION (*angry*). Apollodorus——

APOLLODORUS (*interrupting him with defiant elegance*). I will make amends for that insult with my sword at fitting time and place. Who says artist, says duellist. (*To Cleopatra.*) Hear my counsel, star of the east. Until word comes to these soldiers from Cæsar himself, you are a prisoner. Let me go to him with a message from you, and a present; and before the sun has stooped half way to the arms of the sea, I will bring you back Cæsar's order of release.

CENTURION (*sneering at him*). And you will sell the Queen the present, no doubt.

APOLLODORUS. Centurion: the Queen shall have from me, without payment, as the unforced tribute of Sicilian taste to

Egyptian beauty, the richest of these carpets for her present
to Cæsar.

CLEOPATRA (*exultantly, to the Centurion*). Now you see
what an ignorant common creature you are!

CENTURION (*curtly*). Well, a fool and his wares are soon
parted. (*He turns to his men.*) Two more men to this post
here; and see that no one leaves the palace but this man and
his merchandize. If he draws his sword again inside the lines,
kill him. To your posts. March.

He goes out, leaving two auxiliary sentinels with the other.

APOLLODORUS (*with polite goodfellowship*). My friends:
will you not enter the palace and bury our quarrel in a bowl
of wine? (*He takes out his purse, jingling the coins in it.*)
The Queen has presents for you all.

SENTINEL (*very sulky*). You heard our orders. Get about
your business.

FIRST AUXILIARY. Yes: you ought to know better. Off with
you.

SECOND AUXILIARY (*looking longingly at the purse—this
sentinel is a hooknosed man, unlike his comrade, who is squab
faced*). Do not tantalize a poor man.

APOLLODORUS (*to Cleopatra*). Pearl of Queens: the Centurion is at hand; and the Roman soldier is incorruptible
when his officer is looking. I must carry your word to
Cæsar.

CLEOPATRA (*who has been meditating among the carpets*).
Are these carpets very heavy?

APOLLODORUS. It matters not how heavy. There are plenty
of porters.

CLEOPATRA. How do they put the carpets into boats? Do
they throw them down?

APOLLODORUS. Not into small boats, majesty. It would sink
them.

CLEOPATRA. Not into that man's boat, for instance? (*Pointing to the boatman.*)

APOLLODORUS. No. Too small.

CLEOPATRA. But you can take a carpet to Cæsar in it if
I send one?

APOLLODORUS. Assuredly.

CLEOPATRA. And you will have it carried gently down the
steps and take great care of it?

APOLLODORUS. Depend on me.

CLEOPATRA. Great, great care?

APOLLODORUS. More than of my own body.

CLEOPATRA. You will promise me not to let the porters drop it or throw it about?

APOLLODORUS. Place the most delicate glass goblet in the palace in the heart of the roll, Queen; and if it be broken, my head shall pay for it.

CLEOPATRA. Good. Come, Ftatateeta. (*Ftatateeta comes to her. Apollodorus offers to squire them into the palace.*) No, Apollodorus, you must not come. I will choose a carpet for myself. You must wait here. (*She runs into the palace.*)

APOLLODORUS (*to the porters*). Follow this lady (*indicating Ftatateeta*); and obey her.

The porters rise and take up their bales.

FTATATEETA (*addressing the porters as if they were vermin*). This way. And take your shoes off before you put your feet on those stairs.

She goes in, followed by the porters with the carpets. Meanwhile Apollodorus goes to the edge of the quay and looks out over the harbor. The sentinels keep their eyes on him malignantly.

APOLLODORUS (*addressing the sentinel*). My friend——

SENTINEL (*rudely*). Silence there.

FIRST AUXILIARY. Shut your muzzle, you.

SECOND AUXILIARY (*in a half whisper, glancing apprehensively towards the north end of the quay*). Can't you wait a bit?

APOLLODORUS. Patience, worthy three-headed donkey. (*They mutter ferociously; but he is not at all intimidated.*) Listen: were you set here to watch me, or to watch the Egyptians?

SENTINEL. We know our duty.

APOLLODORUS. Then why don't you do it? There is something going on over there. (*Pointing southwestward to the mole.*)

SENTINEL (*sulkily*). I do not need to be told what to do by the like of you.

APOLLODORUS. Blockhead. (*He begins shouting.*) Ho there, Centurion. Hoiho!

SENTINEL. Curse your meddling. (*Shouting.*) Hoiho! Alarm! Alarm!

FIRST AND SECOND AUXILIARIES. Alarm! alarm! Hoiho!

The Centurion comes running in with his guard.

CENTURION. What now? Has the old woman attacked you again? (*Seeing Apollodorus.*) Are you here still?

APOLLODORUS (*pointing as before*). See there. The Egyptians are moving. They are going to recapture the Pharos. They will attack by sea and land: by land along the great mole; by sea from the west harbor. Stir yourselves, my military friends: the hunt is up. (*A clangor of trumpets from several points along the quay.*) Aha! I told you so.

CENTURION (*quickly*). The two extra men pass the alarm to the south posts. One man keep guard here. The rest with me—quick.

The two auxiliary sentinels run off to the south. The Centurion and his guard run off northward; and immediately afterwards the bucina sounds. The four porters come from the palace carrying a carpet, followed by Ftatateeta.

SENTINEL (*handling his pilum apprehensively*). You again! (*The porters stop.*)

FTATATEETA. Peace, Roman fellow: you are now single-handed. Apollodorus: this carpet is Cleopatra's present to Cæsar. It has rolled up in it ten precious goblets of the thinnest Iberian crystal, and a hundred eggs of the sacred blue pigeon. On your honor, let not one of them be broken.

APOLLODORUS. On my head be it. (*To the porters.*) Into the boat with them carefully.

The porters carry the carpet to the steps.

FIRST PORTER (*looking down at the boat*). Beware what you do, sir. Those eggs of which the lady speaks must weigh more than a pound apiece. This boat is too small for such a load.

BOATMAN (*excitedly rushing up the steps*). Oh thou injurious porter! Oh thou unnatural son of a she-camel! (*To Apollodorus.*) My boat, sir, hath often carried five men. Shall it not carry your lordship and a bale of pigeons' eggs? (*To the porter.*) Thou mangy dromedary, the gods shall punish thee for this envious wickedness.

FIRST PORTER (*stolidly*). I cannot quit this bale now to beat thee; but another day I will lie in wait for thee.

APOLLODORUS (*going between them*). Peace there. If the boat were but a single plank, I would get to Cæsar on it.

FTATATEETA (*anxiously*). In the name of the gods, Apollodorus, run no risks with that bale.

APOLLODORUS. Fear not, thou venerable grotesque: I guess its great worth. (*To the porters.*) Down with it, I say; and gently; or ye shall eat nothing but stick for ten days.

The boatman goes down the steps, followed by the porters with the bale: Ftatateeta and Apollodorus watching from the edge.

APOLLODORUS. Gently, my sons, my children—(*with sudden alarm*) gently, ye dogs. Lay it level in the stern—so—'tis well.

FTATATEETA (*screaming down at one of the porters*). Do not step on it, do not step on it. Oh thou brute beast!

FIRST PORTER (*ascending*). Be not excited, mistress: all is well.

FTATATEETA (*panting*). All well! Oh, thou has given my heart a turn! (*She clutches her side, gasping*).

The four porters have now come up and are waiting at the stairhead to be paid.

APOLLODORUS. Here, ye hungry ones. (*He gives money to the first porter, who holds it in his hand to shew to the others. They crowd greedily to see how much it is, quite prepared, after the Eastern fashion, to protest to heaven against their patron's stinginess. But his liberality overpowers them.*)

FIRST PORTER. O bounteous prince!

SECOND PORTER. O lord of the bazaar!

THIRD PORTER. O favored of the gods!

FOURTH PORTER. O father to all the porters of the market!

SENTINEL (*enviously, threatening them fiercely with his pilum*). Hence, dogs: off. Out of this. (*They fly before him northward along the quay.*)

APOLLODORUS. Farewell, Ftatateeta. I shall be at the lighthouse before the Egyptians. (*He descends the steps.*)

FTATATEETA. The gods speed thee and protect my nursling!

The sentry returns from chasing the porters and looks down at the boat, standing near the stairhead lest Ftatateeta should attempt to escape.

APOLLODORUS (*from beneath, as the boat moves off*). Farewell, valiant pilum pitcher.

SENTINEL. Farewell, shopkeeper.

APOLLODORUS. Ha, ha! Pull, thou brave boatman, pull. Soho-o-o-o-o! (*He begins to sing in barcarolle measure to the rhythm of the oars.*)

> My heart, my heart, spread out thy wings:
> Shake off thy heavy load of love—

Give me the oars, O son of a snail.

SENTINEL (*threatening Ftatateeta*). Now, mistress: back to your henhouse. In with you.

FTATATEETA (*falling on her knees and stretching her hands over the waters*). Gods of the seas, bear her safely to the shore!

SENTINEL. Bear who safely? What do you mean?

FTATATEETA (*looking darkly at him*). Gods of Egypt and of Vengeance, let this Roman fool be beaten like a dog by his captain for suffering her to be taken over the waters.

SENTINEL. Accursed one: is she then in the boat? (*He calls over the sea.*) Hoiho, there, boatman! Hoiho!

APOLLODORUS (*singing in the distance*).

> My heart, my heart, be whole and free:
> Love is thine only enemy.

Meanwhile Rufio, the morning's fighting done, sits munching dates on a faggot of brushwood outside the door of the lighthouse, which towers gigantic to the clouds on his left. His helmet, full of dates, is between his knees; and a leathern bottle of wine is by his side. Behind him the great stone pedestal of the lighthouse is shut in from the open sea by a low stone parapet, with a couple of steps in the middle to the broad coping. A huge chain with a hook hangs down from the lighthouse crane above his head. Faggots like the one he sits on lie beneath it ready to be drawn up to feed the beacon.

Cæsar is standing on the step at the parapet looking out anxiously, evidently ill at ease. Britannus comes out of the lighthouse door.

RUFIO. Well, my British islander. Have you been up to the top?

BRITANNUS. I have. I reckon it at 200 feet high.

RUFIO. Anybody up there?

BRITANNUS. One elderly Tyrian to work the crane; and his son, a well-conducted youth of 14.

RUFIO (*looking at the chain*). What! An old man and a boy work that! Twenty men, you mean.

BRITANNUS. Two only, I assure you. They have counterweights, and a machine with boiling water in it which I do not understand: it is not of British design. They use it to haul up barrels of oil and faggots to burn in the brazier on the roof.

RUFIO. But——

BRITANNUS. Excuse me: I came down because there are messengers coming along the mole to us from the island. I must see what their business is. (*He hurries out past the lighthouse.*)

CÆSAR (*coming away from the parapet, shivering and out of sorts*). Rufio: this has been a mad expedition. We shall be beaten. I wish I knew how our men are getting on with that barricade across the great mole.

RUFIO (*angrily*). Must I leave my food and go starving to bring you a report?

CÆSAR (*soothing him nervously*). No, Rufio, no. Eat, my son, eat. (*He takes another turn, Rufio chewing dates meanwhile.*) The Egyptians cannot be such fools as not to storm the barricade and swoop down on us here before it is finished. It is the first time I have ever run an avoidable risk. I should not have come to Egypt.

RUFIO. An hour ago you were all for victory.

CÆSAR (*apologetically*). Yes: I was a fool—rash, Rufio—boyish.

RUFIO. Boyish! Not a bit of it. Here. (*Offering him a handful of dates.*)

CÆSAR. What are these for?

RUFIO. To eat. That's what's the matter with you. When a man comes to your age, he runs down before his midday meal. Eat and drink; and then have another look at our chances.

CÆSAR (*taking the dates*). My age! (*He shakes his head and bites a date.*) Yes, Rufio: I am an old man—worn out now—true, quite true. (*He gives way to melancholy contemplation, and eats another date.*) Achillas is still in his prime: Ptolemy is a boy. (*He eats another date, and plucks up a little.*) Well, every dog has his day; and I have had mine: I cannot complain. (*With sudden cheerfulness.*) These dates are not bad, Rufio. (*Britannus returns, greatly excited, with a leathern bag. Cæsar is himself again in a moment.*) What now?

BRITANNUS (*triumphantly*). Our brave Rhodian mariners

have captured a treasure. There! (*He throws the bag down at Cæsar's feet.*) Our enemies are delivered into our hands.

CÆSAR. In that bag?

BRITANNUS. Wait till you hear, Cæsar. This bag contains all the letters which have passed between Pompey's party and the army of occupation here.

CÆSAR. Well?

BRITANNUS (*impatient of Cæsar's slowness to grasp the situation*). Well, we shall now know who your foes are. The name of every man who has plotted against you since you crossed the Rubicon may be in these papers, for all we know.

CÆSAR. Put them in the fire.

BRITANNUS. Put them—!!!! (*He gasps.*)

CÆSAR. In the fire. Would you have me waste the next three years of my life in proscribing and condemning men who will be my friends when I have proved that my friendship is worth more than Pompey's was—than Cato's is. O incorrigible British islander: am I a bull dog, to seek quarrels merely to shew how stubborn my jaws are?

BRITANNUS. But your honor—the honor of Rome——

CÆSAR. I do not make human sacrifices to my honor, as your Druids do. Since you will not burn these, at least I can drown them. (*He picks up the bag and throws it over the parapet into the sea.*)

BRITANNUS. Cæsar: this is mere eccentricity. Are traitors to be allowed to go free for the sake of a paradox?

RUFIO (*rising*). Cæsar: when the islander has finished preaching, call me again. I am going to have a look at the boiling water machine. (*He goes into the lighthouse.*)

BRITANNUS (*with genuine feeling*). O Cæsar, my great master, if I could but persuade you to regard life seriously, as men do in my country!

CÆSAR. Do they truly do so, Britannus?

BRITANNUS. Have you not been there? Have you not seen them? What Briton speaks as you do in your moments of levity? What Briton neglects to attend the services at the sacred grove? What Briton wears clothes of many colors as you do, instead of plain blue, as all solid, well-esteemed men should? These are moral questions with us.

CÆSAR. Well, well, my friend: some day I shall settle down and have a blue toga, perhaps. Meanwhile, I must get on as best I can in my flippant Roman way. (*Apollodorus comes past the lighthouse.*) What now?

BRITANNUS (*turning quickly, and challenging the stranger with official haughtiness*). What is this? Who are you? How did you come here?

APOLLODORUS. Calm yourself, my friend: I am not going to eat you. I have come by boat, from Alexandria, with precious gifts for Cæsar.

CÆSAR. From Alexandria!

BRITANNUS (*severely*). That is Cæsar, sir.

RUFIO (*appearing at the lighthouse door*). What's the matter now?

APOLLODORUS. Hail, great Cæsar! I am Apollodorus the Sicilian, an artist.

BRITANNUS. An artist! Why have they admitted this vagabond?

CÆSAR. Peace, man. Apollodorus is a famous patrician amateur.

BRITANNUS (*disconcerted*). I crave the gentleman's pardon. (*To Cæsar.*) I understood him to say that he was a professional. (*Somewhat out of countenance, he allows Apollodorus to approach Cæsar, changing places with him. Rufio, after looking Apollodorus up and down with marked disparagement, goes to the other side of the platform.*)

CÆSAR. You are welcome, Apollodorus. What is your business?

APOLLODORUS. First, to deliver to you a present from the Queen of Queens.

CÆSAR. Who is that?

APOLLODORUS. Cleopatra of Egypt.

CÆSAR (*taking him into his confidence in his most winning manner*). Apollodorus: this is no time for playing with presents. Pray you, go back to the Queen, and tell her that if all goes well I shall return to the palace this evening.

APOLLODORUS. Cæsar: I cannot return. As I approached the lighthouse, some fool threw a great leathern bag into the sea. It broke the nose of my boat; and I had hardly time to get myself and my charge to the shore before the poor little cockleshell sank.

CÆSAR. I am sorry, Apollodorus. The fool shall be rebuked. Well, well: what have you brought me? The Queen will be hurt if I do not look at it.

RUFIO. Have we time to waste on this trumpery? The Queen is only a child.

CÆSAR. Just so: that is why we must not disappoint her. What is the present, Apollodorus?

APOLLODORUS. Cæsar: it is a Persian carpet—a beauty! And in it are—so I am told—pigeons' eggs and crystal goblets and fragile precious things. I dare not for my head have it carried up that narrow ladder from the causeway.

RUFIO. Swing it up by the crane, then. We will send the eggs to the cook; drink our wine from the goblets; and the carpet will make a bed for Cæsar.

APOLLODORUS. The crane! Cæsar: I have sworn to tender this bale of carpet as I tender my own life.

CÆSAR (*cheerfully*). Then let them swing you up at the same time; and if the chain breaks, you and the pigeons' eggs will perish together. (*He goes to the chain and looks up along it, examining it curiously.*)

APOLLODORUS (*to Britannus*). Is Cæsar serious?

BRITANNUS. His manner is frivolous because he is an Italian; but he means what he says.

APOLLODORUS. Serious or not, he spake well. Give me a squad of soldiers to work the crane.

BRITANNUS. Leave the crane to me. Go and await the descent of the chain.

APOLLODORUS. Good. You will presently see me there (*turning to them all and pointing with an eloquent gesture to the sky above the parapet*) rising like the sun with my treasure.

He goes back the way he came. Britannus goes into the lighthouse.

RUFIO (*ill-humoredly*). Are you really going to wait here for this foolery, Cæsar?

CÆSAR (*backing away from the crane as it gives signs of working*). Why not?

RUFIO. The Egyptians will let you know why not if they have the sense to make a rush from the shore end of the mole before our barricade is finished. And here we are waiting like children to see a carpet full of pigeons' eggs.

The chain rattles, and is drawn up high enough to clear the parapet. It then swings round out of sight behind the lighthouse.

CÆSAR. Fear not, my son Rufio. When the first Egyptian takes his first step along the mole, the alarm will sound; and we two will reach the barricade from our end before the Egyptians reach it from their end—we two, Rufio: I, the old man, and you, his biggest boy. And the old man will be there first. So peace; and give me some more dates.

APOLLODORUS (*from the causeway below*). Soho, haul away. So-ho-o-o-o! (*The chain is drawn up and comes round again from behind the lighthouse. Apollodorus is swinging in the air with his bale of carpet at the end of it. He breaks into song as he soars above the parapet.*)

> Aloft, aloft, behold the blue
> That never shone in woman's eyes—

Easy there: stop her. (*He ceases to rise.*) Farther round! (*The chain comes forward above the platform.*)

RUFIO (*calling up*). Lower away there. (*The chain and its load begin to descend.*)

APOLLODORUS (*calling up*). Gently—slowly—mind the eggs.

RUFIO (*calling up*). Easy there—slowly—slowly.

Apollodorus and the bale are deposited safely on the flags in the middle of the platform. Rufio and Cæsar help Apollodorus to cast off the chain from the bale.

RUFIO. Haul up.

The chain rises clear of their heads with a rattle. Britannus comes from the lighthouse and helps them to uncord the carpet.

APOLLODORUS (*when the cords are loose*). Stand off, my friends: let Cæsar see. (*He throws the carpet open.*)

RUFIO. Nothing but a heap of shawls. Where are the pigeons' eggs?

APOLLODORUS. Approach, Cæsar; and search for them among the shawls.

RUFIO (*drawing his sword*). Ha, treachery! Keep back, Cæsar: I saw the shawl move: there is something alive there.

BRITANNUS (*drawing his sword*). It is a serpent.

APOLLODORUS. Dares Cæsar thrust his hand into the sack where the serpent moves?

RUFIO (*turning on him*). Treacherous dog——

CÆSAR. Peace. Put up your swords. Apollodorus: your serpent seems to breathe very regularly. (*He thrusts his hand under the shawls and draws out a bare arm.*) This is a pretty little snake.

RUFIO (*drawing out the other arm*). Let us have the rest of you.

They pull Cleopatra up by the wrists into a sitting position. Britannus, scandalized, sheathes his sword with a drive of protest.

CLEOPATRA (*gasping*). Oh, I'm smothered. Oh, Cæsar; a man stood on me in the boat; and a great sack of something fell upon me out of the sky; and then the boat sank, and then I was swung up into the air and bumped down.

CÆSAR (*petting her as she rises and takes refuge on his breast*). Well, never mind: here you are safe and sound at last.

RUFIO. Ay; and now that she is here, what are we to do with her?

BRITANNUS. She cannot stay here, Cæsar, without the companionship of some matron.

CLEOPATRA (*jealously, to Cæsar, who is obviously perplexed*). Aren't you glad to see me?

CÆSAR. Yes, yes; I am very glad. But Rufio is very angry; and Britannus is shocked.

CLEOPATRA (*contemptuously*). You can have their heads cut off, can you not?

CÆSAR. They would not be so useful with their heads cut off as they are now, my sea bird.

RUFIO (*to Cleopatra*). We shall have to go away presently and cut some of your Egyptians' heads off. How will you like being left here with the chance of being captured by that little brother of yours if we are beaten?

CLEOPATRA. But you mustn't leave me alone. Cæsar, you will not leave me alone, will you?

RUFIO. What! not when the trumpet sounds and all our lives depend on Cæsar's being at the barricade before the Egyptians reach it? Eh?

CLEOPATRA. Let them lose their lives: they are only soldiers.

CÆSAR (*gravely*). Cleopatra: when that trumpet sounds, we must take every man his life in his hand, and throw it in the face of Death. And of my soldiers who have trusted me there is not one whose hand I shall not hold more sacred than your head. (*Cleopatra is overwhelmed. Her eyes fill with tears.*) Apollodorus: you must take her back to the palace.

APOLLODORUS. Am I a dolphin, Cæsar, to cross the seas with young ladies on my back? My boat is sunk: all yours are either at the barricade or have returned to the city. I will hail one if I can: that is all I can do. (*He goes back to the causeway.*)

CLEOPATRA (*struggling with her tears*). It does not matter. I will not go back. Nobody cares for me.

CÆSAR. Cleopatra——

CLEOPATRA. You want me to be killed.

CÆSAR (*still more gravely*). My poor child: your life matters little here to anyone but yourself. (*She gives way altogether at this, casting herself down on the faggots weeping. Suddenly a great tumult is heard in the distance, bucinas and trumpets sounding through a storm of shouting. Britannus rushes to the parapet and looks along the mole. Cæsar and Rufio turn to one another with quick intelligence.*)

CÆSAR. Come, Rufio.

CLEOPATRA (*scrambling to her knees and clinging to him*). No, no. Do not leave me, Cæsar. (*He snatches his skirt from her clutch.*) Oh!

BRITANNUS (*from the parapet*). Cæsar: we are cut off. The Egyptians have landed from the west harbor between us and the barricade!!!

RUFIO (*running to see*). Curses! It is true. We are caught like rats in a trap.

CÆSAR (*truthfully*). Rufio, Rufio: my men at the barricade are between the sea party and the shore party. I have murdered them.

RUFIO (*coming back from the parapet to Cæsar's right hand*). Ay: that comes of fooling with this girl here.

APOLLODORUS (*coming up quickly from the causeway*). Look over the parapet, Cæsar.

CÆSAR. We have looked, my friend. We must defend ourselves here.

APOLLODORUS. I have thrown the ladder into the sea. They cannot get in without it.

RUFIO. Ay; and we cannot get out. Have you thought of that?

APOLLODORUS. Not get out! Why not? You have ships in the east harbor.

BRITANNUS (*hopefully, at the parapet*). The Rhodian galleys are standing in towards us already. (*Cæsar quickly joins Britannus at the parapet.*)

RUFIO (*to Apollodorus, impatiently*). And by what road are we to walk to the galleys, pray?

APOLLODORUS (*with gay, defiant rhetoric*). By the road that leads everywhere—the diamond path of the sun and moon. Have you never seen the child's shadow play of The Broken Bridge? "Ducks and geese with ease get over"—eh? (*He throws away his cloak and cap, and binds his sword on his back.*)

RUFIO. What are you talking about?

APOLLODORUS. I will shew you. (*Calling to Britannus.*) How far off is the nearest galley?

BRITANNUS. Fifty fathoms.

CÆSAR. No, no: they are farther off than they seem in this clear air to your British eyes. Nearly quarter of a mile, Apollodorus.

APOLLODORUS. Good. Defend yourselves here until I send you a boat from that galley.

RUFIO. Have you wings, perhaps?

APOLLODORUS. Water wings, soldier. Behold!

He runs up the steps between Cæsar and Britannus to the coping of the parapet; springs into the air; and plunges head foremost into the sea.

CÆSAR (*like a schoolboy—wildly excited*). Bravo, bravo! (*Throwing off his cloak.*) By Jupiter, I will do that too.

RUFIO (*seizing him*). You are mad. You shall not.

CÆSAR. Why not? Can I not swim as well as he?

RUFIO (*frantic*). Can an old fool dive and swim like a young one? He is twenty-five and you are fifty.

CÆSAR (*breaking loose from Rufio*). Old!!!

BRITANNUS (*shocked*). Rufio: you forget yourself.

CÆSAR. I will race you to the galley for a week's pay, father Rufio.

CLEOPATRA. But me! me!! me!!! what is to become of me?

CÆSAR. I will carry you on my back to the galley like a dolphin. Rufio: when you see me rise to the surface, throw her in: I will answer for her. And then in with you after her, both of you.

CLEOPATRA. No, no, NO. I shall be drowned.

BRITANNUS. Cæsar: I am a man and a Briton, not a fish. I must have a boat. I cannot swim.

CLEOPATRA. Neither can I.

CÆSAR (to Britannus). Stay here, then, alone, until I recapture the lighthouse: I will not forget you. Now, Rufio.

RUFIO. You have made up your mind to this folly?

CÆSAR. The Egyptians have made it up for me. What else is there to do? And mind where you jump: I do not want to get your fourteen stone in the small of my back as I come up. (He runs up the steps and stands on the coping.)

BRITANNUS (anxiously). One last word, Cæsar. Do not let yourself be seen in the fashionable part of Alexandria until you have changed your clothes.

CÆSAR (calling over the sea). Ho, Apollodorus: (he points skyward and quotes the barcarolle)

The white upon the blue above—

APOLLODORUS (swimming in the distance).

Is purple on the green below—

CÆSAR (exultantly). Aha! (He plunges into the sea.)

CLEOPATRA (running excitedly to the steps). Oh, let me see. He will be drowned. (Rufio seizes her.) Ah—ah—ah—ah! (He pitches her screaming into the sea. Rufio and Britannus roar with laughter.)

RUFIO (looking down after her). He has got her. (To Britannus.) Hold the fort, Briton. Cæsar will not forget you. (He springs off.)

BRITANNUS (running to the steps to watch them as they swim). All safe, Rufio?

RUFIO (swimming). All safe.

CÆSAR (swimming farther off). Take refuge up there by the beacon; and pile the fuel on the trap door, Britannus.

BRITANNUS (calling in reply). I will first do so, and then commend myself to my country's gods. (A sound of cheering from the sea. Britannus gives full vent to his excitement.) The boat has reached him: Hip, hip, hip, hurrah!

ACT IV

Cleopatra's sousing in the east harbor of Alexandria was in October 48 B.C. In March 47 she is passing the afternoon in her boudoir in the palace, among a bevy of her ladies, listening to a slave girl who is playing the harp in the middle of the room. The harpist's master, an old musician, with a lined face, prominent brows, white beard, moustache and eyebrows twisted and horned at the ends, and a consciously keen and pretentious expression, is squatting on the floor close to her on her right, watching her performance. Ftatateeta is in attendance near the door, in front of a group of female slaves. Except the harp player all are seated: Cleopatra in a chair opposite the door on the other side of the room; the rest on the ground. Cleopatra's ladies are all young, the most conspicuous being Charmian and Iras, her favorites. Charmian is a hatched faced, terra cotta colored little goblin, swift in her movements, and neatly finished at the hands and feet. Iras is a plump, goodnatured creature, rather fatuous, with a profusion of red hair, and a tendency to giggle on the slightest provocation.

CLEOPATRA. Can I——

FTATATEETA (*insolently, to the player*). Please, thou! The Queen speaks. (*The player stops.*)

CLEOPATRA (*to the old musician*). I want to learn to play the harp with my own hands. Cæsar loves music. Can you teach me?

MUSICIAN. Assuredly I and no one else can teach the Queen. Have I not discovered the lost method of the ancient Egyptians, who could make a pyramid tremble by touching a bass string? All the other teachers are quacks: I have exposed them repeatedly.

CLEOPATRA. Good: you shall teach me. How long will it take?

MUSICIAN. Not very long: only four years. Your Majesty

214

must first become proficient in the philosophy of Pythagoras.

CLEOPATRA. Has she (*indicating the slave*) become proficient in the philosophy of Pythagoras?

MUSICIAN. Oh, she is but a slave. She learns as a dog learns.

CLEOPATRA. Well, then, I will learn as a dog learns; for she plays better than you. You shall give me a lesson every day for a fortnight. (*The musician hastily scrambles to his feet and bows profoundly.*) After that, whenever I strike a false note you shall be flogged; and if I strike so many that there is not time to flog you, you shall be thrown into the Nile to feed the crocodiles. Give the girl a piece of gold; and send them away.

MUSICIAN (*much taken aback*). But true art will not be thus forced.

FTATATEETA (*pushing him out*). What is this? Answering the Queen, forsooth. Out with you.

He is pushed out by Ftatateeta, the girl following with her harp, amid the laughter of the ladies and slaves.

CLEOPATRA. Now, can any of you amuse me? Have you any stories or any news?

IRAS. Ftatateeta——

CLEOPATRA. Oh, Ftatateeta, Ftatateeta, always Ftatateeta. Some new tale to set me against her.

IRAS. No: this time Ftatateeta has been virtuous. (*All the ladies laugh—not the slaves.*) Pothinus has been trying to bribe her to let him speak with you.

CLEOPATRA (*wrathfully*). Ha! you all sell audiences with me, as if I saw whom you please, and not whom I please. I should like to know how much of her gold piece that harp girl will have to give up before she leaves the palace.

IRAS. We can easily find out that for you.

The ladies laugh.

CLEOPATRA (*frowning*). You laugh; but take care, take care. I will find out some day how to make myself served as Cæsar is served.

CHARMIAN. Old hooknose! (*They laugh again.*)

CLEOPATRA (*revolted*). Silence. Charmian: do not you be a silly little Egyptian fool. Do you know why I allow you all to chatter impertinently just as you please, instead of treating you as Ftatateeta would treat you if she were Queen?

CHARMIAN. Because you try to imitate Cæsar in everything; and he lets everybody say what they please to him.

CLEOPATRA. No; but because I asked him one day why he did so; and he said "Let your women talk; and you will learn something from them." What have I to learn from them? I said. "What they are," said he; and oh! you should have seen his eye as he said it. You would have curled up, you shallow things. (*They laugh. She turns fiercely on Iras.*) At whom are you laughing—at me or at Cæsar?

IRAS. At Cæsar.

CLEOPATRA. If you were not a fool, you would laugh at me; and if you were not a coward you would not be afraid to tell me so. (*Ftatateeta returns.*) Ftatateeta: they tell me that Pothinus has offered you a bribe to admit him to my presence.

FTATATEETA (*protesting*). Now by my father's gods——

CLEOPATRA (*cutting her short despotically*). Have I not told you not to deny things? You would spend the day calling your father's gods to witness to your virtues if I let you. Go take the bribe; and bring in Pothinus. (*Ftatateeta is about to reply.*) Don't answer me. Go.

Ftatateeta goes out; and Cleopatra rises and begins to prowl to and fro between her chair and the door, meditating. All rise and stand.

IRAS (*as she reluctantly rises*). Heigho! I wish Cæsar were back in Rome.

CLEOPATRA (*threateningly*). It will be a bad day for you all when he goes. Oh, if I were not ashamed to let him see that I am as cruel at heart as my father, I would make you repent that speech! Why do you wish him away?

CHARMIAN. He makes you so terribly prosy and serious and learned and philosophical. It is worse than being religious, at our ages. (*The ladies laugh.*)

CLEOPATRA. Cease that endless cackling, will you. Hold your tongues.

CHARMIAN (*with mock resignation*). Well, well: we must try to live up to Cæsar.

They laughed again. Cleopatra rages silently as she continues to prowl to and fro. Ftatateeta comes back with Pothinus, who halts on the threshold.

FTATATEETA (*at the door*). Pothinus craves the ear of the——

CLEOPATRA. There, there: that will do: let him come in. (*She resumes her seat. All sit down except Pothinus, who advances to the middle of the room. Ftatateeta takes her former place.*) Well, Pothinus: what is the latest news from your rebel friends?

POTHINUS (*haughtily*). I am no friend of rebellion. And a prisoner does not receive news.

CLEOPATRA. You are no more a prisoner than I am—than Cæsar is. These six months we have been besieged in this palace by my subjects. You are allowed to walk on the beach among the soldiers. Can I go farther myself, or can Cæsar?

POTHINUS. You are but a child, Cleopatra, and do not understand these matters.

The ladies laugh. Cleopatra looks inscrutably at him.

CHARMIAN. I see you do not know the latest news, Pothinus.

POTHINUS. What is that?

CHARMIAN. That Cleopatra is no longer a child. Shall I tell you how to grow much older, and much, much wiser in one day?

POTHINUS. I should prefer to grow wiser without growing older.

CHARMIAN. Well, go up to the top of the lighthouse; and get somebody to take you by the hair and throw you into the sea. (*The ladies laugh.*)

CLEOPATRA. She is right, Pothinus: you will come to the shore with much conceit washed out of you. (*The ladies laugh. Cleopatra rises impatiently.*) Begone, all of you. I will speak with Pothinus alone. Drive them out, Ftatateeta. (*They run out laughing. Ftatateeta shuts the door on them.*) What are you waiting for?

FTATATEETA. It is not meet that the Queen remain alone with——

CLEOPATRA (*interrupting her*). Ftatateeta: must I sacrifice you to your father's gods to teach you that *I* am Queen of Egypt, and not you?

FTATATEETA (*indignantly*). You are like the rest of them. You want to be what these Romans call a New Woman. (*She goes out, banging the door.*)

CLEOPATRA (*sitting down again*). Now, Pothinus: why did you bribe Ftatateeta to bring you hither?

POTHINUS (*studying her gravely*). Cleopatra: what they tell me is true. You are changed.

CLEOPATRA. Do you speak with Cæsar every day for six months: and you will be changed.

POTHINUS. It is the common talk that you are infatuated with this old man.

CLEOPATRA. Infatuated? What does that mean? Made foolish, is it not? Oh no: I wish I were.

POTHINUS. You wish you were made foolish? How so?

CLEOPATRA. When I was foolish, I did what I liked, except when Ftatateeta beat me; and even then I cheated her and did it by stealth. Now that Cæsar has made me wise, it is no use my liking or disliking; I do what must be done, and have no time to attend to myself. That is not happiness; but it is greatness. If Cæsar were gone, I think I could govern the Egyptians; for what Cæsar is to me, I am to the fools around me.

POTHINUS (*looking hard at her*). Cleopatra: this may be the vanity of youth.

CLEOPATRA. No, no: it is not that I am so clever, but that the others are so stupid.

POTHINUS (*musingly*). Truly, that is the great secret.

CLEOPATRA. Well, now tell me what you came to say?

POTHINUS (*embarrassed*). I! Nothing.

CLEOPATRA. Nothing!

POTHINUS. At least—to beg for my liberty: that is all.

CLEOPATRA. For that you would have knelt to Cæsar. No, Pothinus: you came with some plan that depended on Cleopatra being a little nursery kitten. Now that Cleopatra is a Queen, the plan is upset.

POTHINUS (*bowing his head submissively*). It is so.

CLEOPATRA (*exultant*). Aha!

POTHINUS (*raising his eyes keenly to hers*). Is Cleopatra then indeed a Queen, and no longer Cæsar's prisoner and slave?

CLEOPATRA. Pothinus: we are all Cæsar's slaves—all we in this land of Egypt—whether we will or no. And she who is wise enough to know this will reign when Cæsar departs.

POTHINUS. You harp on Cæsar's departure.

CLEOPATRA. What if I do?

POTHINUS. Does he not love you?

CLEOPATRA. Love me! Pothinus: Cæsar loves no one. Who are those we love? Only those whom we do not hate: all people are strangers and enemies to us except those we love. But it is not so with Cæsar. He has no hatred in him: he makes friends with everyone as he does with dogs and children. His kindness to me is a wonder: neither mother, father, nor nurse have ever taken so much care for me, or thrown open their thoughts to me so freely.

POTHINUS. Well: is not this love?

CLEOPATRA. What! When he will do as much for the first girl he meets on his way back to Rome? Ask his slave, Britannus: he has been just as good to him. Nay, ask his very horse! His kindness is not for anything in me: it is in his own nature.

POTHINUS. But how can you be sure that he does not love you as men love women?

CLEOPATRA. Because I cannot make him jealous. I have tried.

POTHINUS. Hm! Perhaps I should have asked, then, do you love him?

CLEOPATRA. Can one love a god? Besides, I love another Roman: one whom I saw long before Cæsar—no god, but a man—one who can love and hate—one whom I can hurt and who would hurt me.

POTHINUS. Does Cæsar know this?

CLEOPATRA. Yes.

POTHINUS. And he is not angry?

CLEOPATRA. He promises to send him to Egypt to please me!

POTHINUS. I do not understand this man.

CLEOPATRA (with superb contempt). You understand Cæsar! How could you? (Proudly.) I do—by instinct.

POTHINUS (deferentially, after a moment's thought). Your Majesty caused me to be admitted to-day. What message has the Queen for me?

CLEOPATRA. This. You think that by making my brother king, you will rule in Egypt, because you are his guardian and he is a little silly.

POTHINUS. The Queen is pleased to say so.

CLEOPATRA. The Queen is pleased to say this also. That Cæsar will eat up you, and Achillas, and my brother, as a cat eats up mice; and that he will put on this land of Egypt as a shepherd puts on his garment. And when he has done that, he will return to Rome, and leave Cleopatra here as his viceroy.

POTHINUS (*breaking out wrathfully*). That he will never do. We have a thousand men to his ten; and we will drive him and his beggarly legions into the sea.

CLEOPATRA (*with scorn, getting up to go*). You rant like any common fellow. Go, then, and marshal your thousands; and make haste; for Mithridates of Pergamos is at hand with reinforcements for Cæsar. Cæsar has held you at bay with two legions: we shall see what he will do with twenty.

POTHINUS. Cleopatra——

CLEOPATRA. Enough, enough: Cæsar has spoiled me for talking to weak things like you. (*She goes out. Pothinus, with a gesture of rage, is following, when Ftatateeta enters and stops him.*)

POTHINUS. Let me go forth from this hateful place.

FTATATEETA. What angers you?

POTHINUS. The curse of all the gods of Egypt be upon her! She has sold her country to the Roman, that she may buy it back from him with her kisses.

FTATATEETA. Fool: did she not tell you that she would have Cæsar gone?

POTHINUS. You listened?

FTATATEETA. I took care that some honest woman should be at hand whilst you were with her.

POTHINUS. Now by the gods——

FTATATEETA. Enough of your gods! Cæsar's gods are all powerful here. It is no use you coming to Cleopatra: you are only an Egyptian. She will not listen to any of her own race: she treats us all as children.

POTHINUS. May she perish for it!

FTATATEETA (*balefully*). May your tongue wither for that wish! Go! send for Lucius Septimius, the slayer of Pompey. He is a Roman: may be she will listen to him. Begone!

POTHINUS (*darkly*). I know to whom I must go now.

FTATATEETA (*suspiciously*). To whom, then?

POTHINUS. To a greater Roman than Lucius. And mark this, mistress. You thought, before Cæsar came, that Egypt should presently be ruled by you and your crew in the name of Cleopatra. I set myself against it——

FTATATEETA (*interrupting him—wrangling*). Ay; that it might be ruled by you and your crew in the name of Ptolemy.

POTHINUS. Better me, or even you, than a woman with a Roman heart; and that is what Cleopatra is now become. Whilst I live, she shall never rule. So guide yourself accordingly. (*He goes out.*)

It is by this time drawing on to dinner time. The table is laid on the roof of the palace; and thither Rufio is now climbing, ushered by a majestic palace official, wand of office in hand, and followed by a slave carrying an inlaid stool. After many stairs they emerge at last into a massive colonnade on the roof. Light curtains are drawn between the columns on the north and east to soften the westering sun. The official leads Rufio to one of these shaded sections. A cord for pulling the curtains apart hangs down between the pillars.

THE OFFICIAL (*bowing*). The Roman commander will await Cæsar here.

The slave sets down the stool near the southernmost column, and slips out through the curtains.

RUFIO (*sitting down, a little blown*). Pouf! That was a climb. How high have we come?

THE OFFICIAL. We are on the palace roof, O Beloved of Victory!

RUFIO. Good! the Beloved of Victory has no more stairs to get up.

A second official enters from the opposite end, walking backwards.

THE SECOND OFFICIAL. Cæsar approaches.

Cæsar, fresh from the bath, clad in a new tunic of purple silk, comes in, beaming and festive, followed by two slaves carrying a light couch, which is hardly more than an elaborately designed bench. They place it near the northmost of the two curtained columns. When this is done they slip out through the curtains; and the two officials, formally bowing, follow them. Rufio rises to receive Cæsar.

CÆSAR (*coming over to him*). Why, Rufio! (*Surveying his dress with an air of admiring astonishment.*) A new baldrick! A new golden pommel to your sword! And you have had your hair cut! But not your beard—? impossible! (*He sniffs at Rufio's beard.*) Yes, perfumed, by Jupiter Olympus!

Rufio (*growling*). Well: is it to please myself?

Cæsar (*affectionately*). No, my son Rufio, but to please me—to celebrate my birthday.

Rufio (*contemptuously*). Your birthday! You always have a birthday when there is a pretty girl to be flattered or an ambassador to be conciliated. We had seven of them in ten months last year.

Cæsar (*contritely*). It is true, Rufio! I shall never break myself of these petty deceits.

Rufio. Who is to dine with us—besides Cleopatra?

Cæsar. Apollodorus the Sicilian.

Rufio. That popinjay!

Cæsar. Come! the popinjay is an amusing dog—tells a story; sings a song; and saves us the trouble of flattering the Queen. What does she care for old politicians and camp-fed bears like us? No: Apollodorus is good company, Rufio, good company.

Rufio. Well, he can swim a bit and fence a bit: he might be worse, if he only knew how to hold his tongue.

Cæsar. The gods forbid he should ever learn! Oh, this military life! this tedious, brutal life of action! That is the worst of us Romans: we are mere doers and drudgers: a swarm of bees turned into men. Give me a good talker—one with wit and imagination enough to live without continually doing something!

Rufio. Ay! a nice time he would have of it with you when dinner was over! Have you noticed that I am before my time?

Cæsar. Aha! I thought that meant something. What is it?

Rufio. Can we be overheard here?

Cæsar. Our privacy invites eavesdropping. I can remedy that. (*He claps his hands twice. The curtains are drawn, revealing the roof garden with a banqueting table set across in the middle for four persons, one at each end, and two side by side. The seat next Cæsar and Rufio is blocked with golden wine vessels and basins. A gorgeous major-domo is superintending the laying of the table by a staff of slaves. The colonnade goes round the garden at both sides to the farther end, where a gap in it, like a great gateway, leaves the view open to the sky beyond the western edge of the roof, except in the middle, where a life size image of Ra, seated on a huge plinth, towers up, with hawk head and crown of asp and disk. His altar, which stands at his feet, is a single white stone.*)

Now everybody can see us, nobody will think of listening to us. (*He sits down on the bench left by the two slaves.*)

RUFIO (*sitting down on his stool*). Pothinus wants to speak to you. I advise you to see him: there is some plotting going on here among the women.

CÆSAR. Who is Pothinus?

RUFIO. The fellow with hair like squirrel's fur—the little King's bear leader, whom you kept prisoner.

CÆSAR (*annoyed*). And has he not escaped?

RUFIO. No.

CÆSAR (*rising imperiously*). Why not? You have been guarding this man instead of watching the enemy. Have I not told you always to let prisoners escape unless there are special orders to the contrary? Are there not enough mouths to be fed without him?

RUFIO. Yes; and if you would have a little sense and let me cut his throat, you would save his rations. Anyhow, he won't escape. Three sentries have told him they would put a pilum through him if they saw him again. What more can they do? He prefers to stay and spy on us. So would I if I had to do with generals subject to fits of clemency.

CÆSAR (*resuming his seat, argued down*). Hm! And so he wants to see me.

RUFIO. Ay. I have brought him with me. He is waiting there (*jerking his thumb over his shoulder*) under guard.

CÆSAR. And you want me to see him?

RUFIO (*obstinately*). I don't want anything. I daresay you will do what you like. Don't put it on to me.

CÆSAR (*with an air of doing it expressly to indulge Rufio*). Well, well: let us have him.

RUFIO (*calling*). Ho there, guard! Release your man and send him up. (*Beckoning.*) Come along!

Pothinus enters and stops mistrustfully between the two, looking from one to the other.

CÆSAR (*graciously*). Ah, Pothinus! You are welcome. And what is the news this afternoon?

POTHINUS. Cæsar: I come to warn you of a danger, and to make you an offer.

CÆSAR. Never mind the danger. Make the offer.

RUFIO. Never mind the offer. What's the danger?

POTHINUS. Cæsar: you think that Cleopatra is devoted to you.

CÆSAR (*gravely*). My friend: I already know what I think. Come to your offer.

POTHINUS. I will deal plainly. I know not by what strange gods you have been enabled to defend a palace and a few yards of beach against a city and an army. Since we cut you off from Lake Mareotis, and you dug wells in the salt sea sand and brought up buckets of fresh water from them, we have known that your gods are irresistible, and that you are a worker of miracles. I no longer threaten you——

RUFIO (*sarcastically*). Very handsome of you, indeed.

POTHINUS. So be it: you are the master. Our gods sent the northwest winds to keep you in our hands; but you have been too strong for them.

CÆSAR (*gently urging him to come to the point*). Yes, yes, my friend. But what then?

RUFIO. Spit it out, man. What have you to say?

POTHINUS. I have to say that you have a traitress in your camp. Cleopatra——

THE MAJOR-DOMO (*at the table, announcing*). The Queen! (*Cæsar and Rufio rise.*)

RUFIO (*aside to Pothinus*). You should have spat it out sooner, you fool. Now it is too late.

Cleopatra, in gorgeous raiment, enters in state through the gap in the colonnade, and comes down past the image of Ra and past the table to Cæsar. Her retinue, headed by Ftatateeta, joins the staff at the table. Cæsar gives Cleopatra his seat, which she takes.

CLEOPATRA (*quickly, seeing Pothinus*). What is he doing here?

CÆSAR (*seating himself beside her, in the most amiable of tempers*). Just going to tell me something about you. You shall hear it. Proceed, Pothinus.

POTHINUS (*disconcerted*). Cæsar— (*He stammers.*)

CÆSAR. Well, out with it.

POTHINUS. What I have to say is for your ear, not for the Queen's.

CLEOPATRA (*with subdued ferocity*). There are means of making you speak. Take care.

POTHINUS (*defiantly*). Cæsar does not employ those means.

CÆSAR. My friend: when a man has anything to tell in this world, the difficulty is not to make him tell it, but to prevent him from telling it too often. Let me celebrate my birthday by setting you free. Farewell: we shall not meet again.

CLEOPATRA (*angrily*). Cæsar: this mercy is foolish.

POTHINUS (*to Cæsar*). Will you not give me a private audience? Your life may depend on it. (*Cæsar rises loftily.*)

RUFIO (*aside to Pothinus*). Ass! Now we shall have some heroics.

CÆSAR (*oratorically*). Pothinus——

RUFIO (*interrupting him*). Cæsar: the dinner will spoil if you begin preaching your favorite sermon about life and death.

CLEOPATRA (*priggishly*). Peace, Rufio. I desire to hear Cæsar.

RUFIO (*bluntly*). Your Majesty has heard it before. You repeated it to Apollodorus last week; and he thought it was all your own. (*Cæsar's dignity collapses. Much tickled, he sits down again and looks roguishly at Cleopatra, who is furious. Rufio calls as before.*) Ho there, guard! Pass the prisoner out. He is released. (*To Pothinus.*) Now off with you. You have lost your chance.

POTHINUS (*his temper overcoming his prudence*). I will speak.

CÆSAR (*to Cleopatra*). You see. Torture would not have wrung a word from him.

POTHINUS. Cæsar: you have taught Cleopatra the arts by which the Romans govern the world.

CÆSAR. Alas! they cannot even govern themselves. What then?

POTHINUS. What then? Are you so besotted with her beauty that you do not see that she is impatient to reign in Egypt alone, and that her heart is set on your departure?

CLEOPATRA (*rising*). Liar!

CÆSAR (*shocked*). What! Protestations! Contradictions!

CLEOPATRA (*ashamed, but trembling with suppressed rage*). No. I do not deign to contradict. Let him talk. (*She sits down again.*)

POTHINUS. From her own lips I have heard it. You are to be her cat's-paw; you are to tear the crown from her brother's head and set it on her own, delivering us all into her hand —delivering yourself also. And then Cæsar can return to Rome, or depart through the gate of death, which is nearer and surer.

CÆSAR (*calmly*). Well, my friend; and is not this very natural?

POTHINUS (*astonished*). Natural! Then you do not resent treachery?

CÆSAR. Resent! O thou foolish Egyptian, what have I to do with resentment? Do I resent the wind when it chills me, or the night when it makes me stumble in the darkness? Shall I resent youth when it turns from age, and ambition when it turns from servitude? To tell me such a story as this is but to tell me that the sun will rise to-morrow.

CLEOPATRA (*unable to contain herself*). But it is false— false. I swear it.

CÆSAR. It is true, though you swore it a thousand times, and believed all you swore. (*She is convulsed with emotion. To screen her, he rises and takes Pothinus to Rufio, saying.*) Come, Rufio: let us see Pothinus past the guard. I have a word to say to him. (*Aside to them.*) We must give the Queen a moment to recover herself. (*Aloud.*) Come. (*He takes Pothinus and Rufio out with him, conversing with them meanwhile.*) Tell your friends, Pothinus, that they must not think I am opposed to a reasonable settlement of the country's affairs— (*They pass out of hearing.*)

CLEOPATRA (*in a stifled whisper*). Ftatateeta, Ftatateeta.

FTATATEETA (*hurrying to her from the table and petting her*). Peace, child: be comforted——

CLEOPATRA (*interrupting her*). Can they hear us?

FTATATEETA. No, dear heart, no.

CLEOPATRA. Listen to me. If he leaves the Palace alive, never see my face again.

FTATATEETA. He? Poth——

CLEOPATRA (*striking her on the mouth*). Strike his life out as I strike his name from your lips. Dash him down from the wall. Break him on the stones. Kill, kill, kill him.

FTATATEETA (*shewing all her teeth*). The dog shall perish.

CLEOPATRA. Fail in this, and you go out from before me forever.

FTATATEETA (*resolutely*). So be it. You shall not see my face until his eyes are darkened.

Cæsar comes back, with Apollodorus, exquisitely dressed, and Rufio.

CLEOPATRA (*to Ftatateeta*). Come soon—soon. (*Ftatateeta turns her meaning eyes for a moment on her mistress; then goes grimly away past Ra and out. Cleopatra runs like a gazelle to Cæsar.*) So you have come back to me, Cæsar. (*Caressingly.*) I thought you were angry. Welcome, Apollodorus. (*She gives him her hand to kiss, with her other arm about Cæsar.*)

APOLLODORUS. Cleopatra grows more womanly beautiful from week to week.

CLEOPATRA. Truth, Apollodorus?

APOLLODORUS. Far, far short of the truth! Friend Rufio threw a pearl into the sea: Cæsar fished up a diamond.

CÆSAR. Cæsar fished up a touch of rheumatism, my friend. Come: to dinner! to dinner! (*They move towards the table.*)

CLEOPATRA (*skipping like a young fawn*). Yes, to dinner. I have ordered such a dinner for you, Cæsar!

CÆSAR. Ay? What are we to have?

CLEOPATRA. Peacocks' brains.

CÆSAR (*as if his mouth watered*). Peacocks' brains, Apollodorus!

APOLLODORUS. Not for me. I prefer nightingales' tongues. (*He goes to one of the two covers set side by side.*)

CLEOPATRA. Roast boar, Rufio!

RUFIO (*gluttonously*). Good! (*He goes to the seat next to Apollodorus, on his left.*)

CÆSAR (*looking at his seat, which is at the end of the table, to Ra's left hand*). What has become of my leathern cushion?

CLEOPATRA (*at the opposite end*). I have got new ones for you.

THE MAJOR-DOMO. These cushions, Cæsar, are of Maltese gauze, stuffed with rose leaves.

CÆSAR. Rose leaves! Am I a caterpillar? (*He throws the cushions away and seats himself on the leather mattress underneath.*)

CLEOPATRA. What a shame! My new cushions!

THE MAJOR-DOMO (*at Cæsar's elbow*). What shall we serve to whet Cæsar's appetite?

CÆSAR. What have you got?

THE MAJOR-DOMO. Sea hedgehogs, black and white sea acorns, sea nettles, beccaficoes, purple shellfish——

CÆSAR. Any oysters?

THE MAJOR-DOMO. Assuredly.

CÆSAR. British oysters?

THE MAJOR-DOMO (*assenting*). British oysters, Cæsar.

CÆSAR. Oysters, then. (*The Major-Domo signs to a slave at each order; and the slave goes out to execute it.*) I have been in Britain—that western land of romance—the last piece of earth on the edge of the ocean that surrounds the world. I went there in search of its famous pearls. The British pearl was a fable; but in searching for it I found the British oyster.

APOLLODORUS. All posterity will bless you for it. (*To the Major-Domo.*) Sea hedgehogs for me.

RUFIO. Is there nothing solid to begin with?

THE MAJOR-DOMO. Fieldfares with asparagus——

CLEOPATRA (*interrupting*). Fattened fowls! have some fattened fowls, Rufio.

RUFIO. Ay, that will do.

CLEOPATRA (*greedily*). Fieldfares for me.

THE MAJOR-DOMO. Cæsar will deign to choose his wine? Sicilian, Lesbian, Chian——

RUFIO (*contemptuously*). All Greek.

APOLLODORUS. Who would drink Roman wine when he could get Greek? Try the Lesbian, Cæsar.

CÆSAR. Bring me my barley water.

RUFIO (*with intense disgust*). Ugh! Bring me my Falernian. (*The Falernian is presently brought to him.*)

CLEOPATRA (*pouting*). It is waste of time giving you dinners, Cæsar. My scullions would not condescend to your diet.

CÆSAR (*relenting*). Well, well: let us try the Lesbian. (*The Major-Domo fills Cæsar's goblet; then Cleopatra's and Apollodorus's.*) But when I return to Rome, I will make laws against these extravagances. I will even get the laws carried out.

CLEOPATRA (*coaxingly*). Never mind. To-day you are to be like other people: idle, luxurious, and kind. (*She stretches her hand to him along the table.*)

CÆSAR. Well, for once I will sacrifice my comfort— (*kissing her hand*) there! (*He takes a draught of wine.*) Now are you satisfied?

CLEOPATRA. And you no longer believe that I long for your departure for Rome?

CÆSAR. I no longer believe anything. My brains are asleep. Besides, who knows whether I shall return to Rome?

RUFIO (*alarmed*). How? Eh? What?

CÆSAR. What has Rome to shew me that I have not seen already? One year of Rome is like another, except that I grow older, whilst the crowd in the Appian Way is always the same age.

APOLLODORUS. It is no better here in Egypt. The old men, when they are tired of life, say "We have seen everything except the source of the Nile."

CÆSAR (*his imagination catching fire*). And why not see that? Cleopatra: will you come with me and track the flood to its cradle in the heart of the regions of mystery? Shall we leave Rome behind us—Rome, that has achieved greatness only to learn how greatness destroys nations of men who are not great! Shall I make you a new kingdom, and build you a holy city there in the great unknown?

CLEOPATRA (*rapturously*). Yes, yes. You shall.

RUFIO. Ay: now he will conquer Africa with two legions before we come to the roast boar.

APOLLODORUS. Come: no scoffing. This is a noble scheme: in it Cæsar is no longer merely the conquering soldier, but the creative poet-artist. Let us name the holy city, and consecrate it with Lesbian wine.

CÆSAR. Cleopatra shall name it herself.

CLEOPATRA. It shall be called Cæsar's Gift to his Beloved.

APOLLODORUS. No, no. Something vaster than that—something universal, like the starry firmament.

CÆSAR (*prosaically*). Why not simply The Cradle of the Nile?

CLEOPATRA. No: the Nile is my ancestor; and he is a god. Oh! I have thought of something. The Nile shall name it himself. Let us call upon him. (*To the Major-Domo.*) Send for him. (*The three men stare at one another; but the Major-Domo goes out as if he had received the most matter-of-fact order.*) And (*to the retinue*) away with you all.

The retinue withdraws, making obeisance.

A priest enters, carrying a miniature sphinx with a tiny tripod before it. A morsel of incense is smoking in the tripod. The priest comes to the table and places the image in the middle of it. The light begins to change to the magenta purple of the Egyptian sunset, as if the god had brought a strange-colored shadow with him. The three men are determined not to be impressed; but they feel curious in spite of themselves.

CÆSAR. What hocus-pocus is this?

CLEOPATRA. You shall see. And it is not hocus-pocus. To do it properly, we should kill something to please him; but perhaps he will answer Cæsar without that if we spill some wine to him.

APOLLODORUS (*turning his head to look up over his shoulder at Ra*). Why not appeal to our hawkheaded friend here?

CLEOPATRA (*nervously*). Sh! He will hear you and be angry.

RUFIO (*phlegmatically*). The source of the Nile is out of his district, I expect.

CLEOPATRA. No: I will have my city named by nobody but my dear little sphinx, because it was in its arms that Cæsar found me asleep. (*She languishes at Cæsar; then turns curtly to the priest.*) Go. I am a priestess, and have power to take your charge from you. (*The priest makes a reverence and goes out.*) Now let us call on the Nile all together. Perhaps he will rap on the table.

CÆSAR. What! table rapping! Are such superstitions still believed in this year 707 of the Republic?

CLEOPATRA. It is no superstition: our priests learn lots of things from the tables. Is it not so, Apollodorus?

APOLLODORUS. Yes: I profess myself a converted man. When Cleopatra is priestess, Apollodorus is devotee. Propose the conjuration.

CLEOPATRA. You must say with me "Send us thy voice, Father Nile."

ALL FOUR (*holding their glasses together before the idol*). Send us thy voice, Father Nile.

The death cry of a man in mortal terror and agony answers them. Appalled, the men set down their glasses, and listen. Silence. The purple deepens in the sky. Cæsar, glancing at Cleopatra, catches her pouring out her wine before the god, with gleaming eyes, and mute assurances of gratitude and worship. Apollodorus springs up and runs to the edge of the roof to peer down and listen.

CÆSAR (*looking piercingly at Cleopatra*). What was that?

CLEOPATRA (*petulantly*). Nothing. They are beating some slave.

CÆSAR. Nothing!

RUFIO. A man with a knife in him, I'll swear.

CÆSAR (*rising*). A murder!

APOLLODORUS (*at the back, waving his hand for silence*). S-sh! Silence. Did you hear that?

CÆSAR. Another cry?

APOLLODORUS (*returning to the table*). No, a thud. Something fell on the beach, I think.

RUFIO (*grimly, as he rises*). Something with bones in it, eh?

CÆSAR (*shuddering*). Hush, hush, Rufio. (*He leaves the table and returns to the colonnade: Rufio following at his left elbow, and Apollodorus at the other side.*)

CLEOPATRA (*still in her place at the table*). Will you leave me, Cæsar? Apollodorus: are you going?

APOLLODORUS. Faith, dearest Queen, my appetite is gone.

CÆSAR. Go down to the courtyard, Apollodorus; and find out what has happened.

Apollodorus nods and goes out, making for the staircase by which Rufio ascended.

CLEOPATRA. Your soldiers have killed somebody, perhaps. What does it matter?

The murmur of a crowd rises from the beach below. Cæsar and Rufio look at one another.

CÆSAR. This must be seen to. (*He is about to follow Apollodorus when Rufio stops him with a hand on his arm as Ftatateeta comes back by the far end of the roof, with dragging steps, a drowsy satiety in her eyes and in the corners of the bloodhound lips. For a moment Cæsar suspects that she is drunk with wine. Not so Rufio: he knows well the red vintage that has inebriated her.*)

RUFIO (*in a low tone*). There is some mischief between those two.

FTATATEETA. The Queen looks again on the face of her servant.

Cleopatra looks at her for a moment with an exultant reflection of her murderous expression. Then she flings her arms round her; kisses her repeatedly and savagely; and tears off her jewels and heaps them on her. The two men turn from the spectacle to look at one another. Ftatateeta drags herself sleepily to the altar; kneels before Ra; and remains there in prayer. Cæsar goes to Cleopatra, leaving Rufio in the colonnade.

CÆSAR (*with searching earnestness*). Cleopatra: what has happened?

CLEOPATRA (*in mortal dread of him, but with her utmost cajolery*). Nothing, dearest Cæsar. (*With sickly sweetness, her voice almost failing.*) Nothing. I am innocent. (*She approaches him affectionately.*) Dear Cæsar: are you angry with me? Why do you look at me so? I have been here with you all the time. How can I know what has happened?

CÆSAR (*reflectively*). That is true.

CLEOPATRA (*greatly relieved, trying to caress him*). Of course it is true. (*He does not respond to the caress.*) You know it is true, Rufio.

The murmur without suddenly swells to a roar and subsides.

RUFIO. I shall know presently. (*He makes for the altar in the burly trot that serves him for a stride, and touches Ftatateeta on the shoulder.*) Now, mistress: I shall want you. (*He orders her, with a gesture, to go before him.*)

FTATATEETA (*rising and glowering at him*). My place is with the Queen.

CLEOPATRA. She has done no harm, Rufio.

CÆSAR (*to Rufio*). Let her stay.

RUFIO (*sitting down on the altar*). Very well. Then my place is here too; and you can see what is the matter for yourself. The city is in a pretty uproar, it seems.

CÆSAR (*with grave displeasure*). Rufio: there is a time for obedience.

RUFIO. And there is a time for obstinacy. (*He folds his arms doggedly.*)

CÆSAR (*to Cleopatra*). Send her away.

CLEOPATRA (*whining in her eagerness to propitiate him*). Yes, I will. I will do whatever you ask me, Cæsar, always, because I love you. Ftatateeta: go away.

FTATATEETA. The Queen's word is my will. I shall be at hand for the Queen's call. (*She goes out past Ra, as she came.*)

RUFIO (*following her*). Remember, Cæsar, your bodyguard also is within call. (*He follows her out.*)

Cleopatra, presuming upon Cæsar's submission to Rufio, leaves the table and sits down on the bench in the colonnade.

CLEOPATRA. Why do you allow Rufio to treat you so? You should teach him his place.

CÆSAR. Teach him to be my enemy, and to hide his thoughts from me as you are now hiding yours.

CLEOPATRA (*her fears returning*). Why do you say that, Cæsar? Indeed, indeed, I am not hiding anything. You are wrong to treat me like this. (*She stifles a sob.*) I am only a child; and you turn into stone because you think some one has been killed. I cannot bear it. I cannot bear it. (*She purposely breaks down and weeps. He looks at her with profound*

*sadness and complete coldness. She looks up to see what effect
she is producing. Seeing that he is unmoved, she sits up, pretending to struggle with her emotion and to put it bravely
away.*) But there: I know you hate tears: you shall not be
troubled with them. I know you are not angry, but only sad;
only I am so silly, I cannot help being hurt when you speak
coldly. Of course you are quite right: it is dreadful to think of
anyone being killed or even hurt; and I hope nothing really
serious has— (*Her voice dies away under his contemptuous
penetration.*)

CÆSAR. What has frightened you into this? What have you
done? (*A trumpet sounds on the beach below.*) Aha! that
sounds like the answer.

CLEOPATRA (*sinking back trembling on the bench and covering her face with her hands*). I have not betrayed you,
Cæsar: I swear it.

CÆSAR. I know that. I have not trusted you. (*He turns
from her, and is about to go out when Apollodorus and Britannus drag in Lucius Septimius to him. Rufio follows. Cæsar
shudders.*) Again, Pompey's murderer!

RUFIO. The town has gone mad, I think. They are for tearing the palace down and driving us into the sea straight away.
We laid hold of this renegade in clearing them out of the
courtyard.

CÆSAR. Release him. (*They let go his arms.*) What has
offended the citizens, Lucius Septimius?

LUCIUS. What did you expect, Cæsar? Pothinus was a favorite of theirs.

CÆSAR. What has happened to Pothinus? I set him free,
here, not half an hour ago. Did they not pass him out?

LUCIUS. Ay, through the gallery arch sixty feet above
ground, with three inches of steel in his ribs. He is as dead
as Pompey. We are quits now, as to killing—you and I.

CÆSAR (*shocked*). Assassinated!—our prisoner, our guest!
(*He turns reproachfully on Rufio.*) Rufio——

RUFIO (*emphatically—anticipating the question*). Whoever
did it was a wise man and a friend of yours (*Cleopatra is
greatly emboldened*); but none of us had a hand in it. So it is
no use to frown at me. (*Cæsar turns and looks at Cleopatra.*)

CLEOPATRA (*violently—rising*). He was slain by order of
the Queen of Egypt. I am not Julius Cæsar the dreamer, who
allows every slave to insult him. Rufio has said I did well:

now the others shall judge me too. (*She turns to the others.*) This Pothinus sought to make me conspire with him to betray Cæsar to Achillas and Ptolemy. I refused; and he cursed me and came privily to Cæsar to accuse me of his own treachery. I caught him in the act; and he insulted me—me, the Queen! to my face. Cæsar would not avenge me: he spoke him fair and set him free. Was I right to avenge myself? Speak, Lucius.

LUCIUS. I do not gainsay it. But you will get little thanks from Cæsar for it.

CLEOPATRA. Speak, Apollodorus. Was I wrong?

APOLLODORUS. I have only one word of blame, most beautiful. You should have called upon me, your knight; and in fair duel I should have slain the slanderer.

CLEOPATRA (*passionately*). I will be judged by your very slave, Cæsar. Britannus: speak. Was I wrong?

BRITANNUS. Were treachery, falsehood, and disloyalty left unpunished, society must become like an arena full of wild beasts, tearing one another to pieces. Cæsar is in the wrong.

CÆSAR (*with quiet bitterness*). And so the verdict is against me, it seems.

CLEOPATRA (*vehemently*). Listen to me, Cæsar. If one man in all Alexandria can be found to say that I did wrong, I swear to have myself crucified on the door of the palace by my own slaves.

CÆSAR. If one man in all the world can be found, now or forever, to know that you did wrong, that man will have either to conquer the world as I have, or be crucified by it. (*The uproar in the streets again reaches them.*) Do you hear? These knockers at your gate are also believers in vengeance and in stabbing. You have slain their leader: it is right that they shall slay you. If you doubt it, ask your four counsellors here. And then in the name of that right (*he emphasizes the word with great scorn*) shall I not slay them for murdering their Queen, and be slain in my turn by their countrymen as the invader of their fatherland? Can Rome do less then than slay these slayers too, to shew the world how Rome avenges her sons and her honor? And so, to the end of history, murder shall breed murder, always in the name of right and honor and peace, until the gods are tired of blood and create a race that can understand. (*Fierce uproar. Cleopatra becomes white with terror.*) Hearken, you who must not be insulted. Go near enough to catch their words: you will find them bitterer than the tongue of Pothinus. (*Loftily wrapping himself up in an impenetrable dignity.*) Let the Queen of Egypt now give her orders for vengeance, and take her measures for defence; for she has renounced Cæsar. (*He turns to go.*)

CLEOPATRA (*terrified, running to him and falling on her knees*). You will not desert me, Cæsar. You will defend the palace.

CÆSAR. You have taken the powers of life and death upon you. I am only a dreamer.

CLEOPATRA. But they will kill me.

CÆSAR. And why not?

CLEOPATRA. In pity——

CÆSAR. Pity! What! has it come to this so suddenly, that nothing can save you now but pity? Did it save Potninus?

She rises, wringing her hands, and goes back to the bench in despair. Apollodorus shews his sympathy with her by quietly posting himself behind the bench. The sky has by this time become the most vivid purple, and soon begins to change to a glowing pale orange, against which the colonnade and the great image show darklier and darklier.

RUFIO. Cæsar: enough of preaching. The enemy is at the gate.

CÆSAR (*turning on him and giving way to his wrath*). Ay; and what has held him battled at the gate all these months? Was it my folly, as you deem it, or your wisdom? In this Egyptian Red Sea of blood, whose hand has held all your heads above the waves? (*Turning on Cleopatra.*) And yet, when Cæsar says to such an one, "Friend, go free," you, clinging for your little life to my sword, dare steal out and stab him in the back? And you, soldiers and gentlemen, and honest servants as you forget that you are, applaud this as-sassination, and say "Cæsar is in the wrong. By the gods, I am tempted to open my hand and let you all sink into the flood.

CLEOPATRA (*with a ray of cunning hope*). But, Cæsar, if you do, you will perish yourself.

Cæsar's eyes blaze.

RUFIO (*greatly alarmed*). Now, by great Jove, you filthy little Egyptian rat, that is the very word to make him walk out alone into the city and leave us here to be cut to pieces. (*Desperately, to Cæsar.*) Will you desert us because we are a parcel of fools? I mean no harm by killing: I do it as a dog kills a cat, by instinct. We are all dogs at your heels; but we have served you faithfully.

CÆSAR (*relenting*). Alas, Rufio, my son, my son: as dogs we are like to perish now in the streets.

APOLLODORUS (*at his post behind Cleopatra's seat*). Cæsar, what you say has an Olympian ring in it: it must be right; for it is fine art. But I am still on the side of Cleopatra. If we must die, she shall not want the devotion of a man's heart nor the strength of a man's arm.

CLEOPATRA (*sobbing*). But I don't want to die.

CÆSAR (*sadly*). Oh, ignoble, ignoble!

LUCIUS (*coming forward between Cæsar and Cleopatra*). Hearken to me, Cæsar. It may be ignoble; but I also mean to live as long as I can.

CÆSAR. Well, my friend, you are likely to outlive Cæsar. Is it any magic of mine, think you, that has kept your army and this whole city at bay for so long? Yesterday, what quarrel had they with me that they should risk their lives against me? But to-day we have flung them down their hero, murdered; and now every man of them is set upon clearing out this nest of assassins—for such we are and no more. Take courage then; and sharpen your sword. Pompey's head has fallen; and Cæsar's head is ripe.

APOLLODORUS. Does Cæsar despair?

CÆSAR (*with infinite pride*). He who has never hoped can never despair. Cæsar, in good or bad fortune, looks his fate in the face.

LUCIUS. Look it in the face, then; and it will smile as it always has on Cæsar.

CÆSAR (*with involuntary haughtiness*). Do you presume to encourage me?

LUCIUS. I offer you my services. I will change sides if you will have me.

CÆSAR (*suddenly coming down to earth again, and looking sharply at him, divining that there is something behind the offer*). What! At this point?

LUCIUS (*firmly*). At this point.

RUFIO. Do you suppose Cæsar is mad, to trust you?

LUCIUS. I do not ask him to trust me until he is victorious. I ask for my life, and for a command in Cæsar's army. And since Cæsar is a fair dealer, I will pay in advance.

CÆSAR. Pay! How?

LUCIUS. With a piece of good news for you.

Cæsar divines the news in a flash.

RUFIO. What news?

CÆSAR (*with an elate and buoyant energy which makes Cleopatra sit up and stare*). What news! What news, did you say, my son Rufio? The relief has arrived: what other news remains for us? Is it not so, Lucius Septimius? Mithridates of Pergamos is on the march.

LUCIUS. He has taken Pelusium.

CÆSAR (*delighted*). Lucius Septimius: you are henceforth my officer. Rufio: the Egyptians must have sent every soldier from the city to prevent Mithridates crossing the Nile. There is nothing in the streets now but mob—mob!

LUCIUS. It is so. Mithridates is marching by the great road to Memphis to cross above the Delta. Achillas will fight him there.

CAESAR (*all audacity*). Achillas shall fight Cæsar there. See, Rufio. (*He runs to the table; snatches a napkin; and draws a plan on it with his finger dipped in wine, whilst Rufio and Lucius Septimius crowd about him to watch, all looking closely, for the light is now almost gone.*) Here is the palace (*pointing to his plan*): here is the theatre. You (*to Rufio*) take twenty men and pretend to go by that street (*pointing it out*); and whilst they are stoning you, out go all cohorts by this and this. My streets are right, are they, Lucius?

LUCIUS. Ay, that is the fig market——

CÆSAR (*too much excited to listen to him*). I saw them the day we arrived. Good! (*He throws the napkin on the table and comes down again into the colonnade.*) Away, Britannus: tell Petronius that within an hour half our forces must take ship for the western lake. See to my horse and armor. (*Britannus runs out.*) With the rest, *I* shall march round the lake and up the Nile to meet Mithridates. Away, Lucius; and give the word.

Lucius hurries out after Britannus.

RUFIO. Come: this is something like business.

CÆSAR (*buoyantly*). Is it not, my only son? (*He claps his hands. The slaves hurry in to the table.*) No more of this mawkish revelling: away with all this stuff: shut it out of my sight and be off with you. (*The slaves begin to remove the table; and the curtains are drawn, shutting in the colonnade.*) You understand about the streets, Rufio?

RUFIO. Ay, I think I do. I will get through them, at all events.

The bucina sounds busily in the courtyard beneath.

CÆSAR. Come, then: we must talk to the troops and hearten them. You down to the beach: I to the courtyard. (*He makes for the staircase.*)

CLEOPATRA (*rising from her seat, where she has been quite neglected all this time, and stretching out her hands timidly to him*). Cæsar.

CÆSAR (*turning*). Eh?

CLEOPATRA. Have you forgotten me?

CÆSAR (*indulgently*). I am busy now, my child, busy. When I return your affairs shall be settled. Farewell; and be good and patient.

He goes, preoccupied and quite indifferent. She stands with clenched fists, in speechless rage and humiliation.

RUFIO. That game is played and lost, Cleopatra. The woman always gets the worst of it.

CLEOPATRA (*haughtily*). Go. Follow your master.

RUFIO (*in her ear, with rough familiarity*). A word first. Tell your executioner that if Pothinus had been properly killed—in the throat—he would not have called out. Your man bungled his work.

CLEOPATRA (*enigmatically*). How do you know it was a man?

RUFIO (*startled, and puzzled*). It was not you: you were with us when it happened. (*She turns her back scornfully on him. He shakes his head, and draws the curtains to go out. It is now a magnificent moonlit night. The table has been removed. Ftatateeta is seen in the light of the moon and stars, again in prayer before the white altar-stone of Ra. Rufio starts; closes the curtains again softly; and says in a low voice to Cleopatra.*) Was it she? with her own hand?

CLEOPATRA (*threateningly*). Whoever it was, let my enemies beware of her. Look to it, Rufio, you who dare make the Queen of Egypt a fool before Cæsar.

RUFIO (*looking grimly at her*). I will look to it, Cleopatra. (*He nods in confirmation of the promise, and slips out through the curtains, loosening his sword in its sheath as he goes.*)

ROMAN SOLDIERS (*in the courtyard below*). Hail, Cæsar! Hail, hail!

Cleopatra listens. The bucina sounds again, followed by several trumpets.

CLEOPATRA (*wringing her hands and calling*). Ftatateeta. Ftatateeta. It is dark; and I am alone. Come to me. (*Silence.*) Ftatateeta. (*Louder.*) Ftatateeta. (*Silence. In a panic she snatches the cord and pulls the curtains apart.*)

Ftatateeta is lying dead on the altar of Ra, with her throat cut. Her blood deluges the white stone.

ACT V

High noon. Festival and military pageant on the esplanade
before the palace. In the east harbor Cæsar's galley, so gor-
geously decorated that it seems to be rigged with flowers,
is alongside the quay, close to the steps Apollodorus descended when he embarked with the carpet. A Roman guard
is posted there in charge of a gangway, whence a red floor-
cloth is laid down the middle of the esplanade, turning off
to the north opposite the central gate in the palace front,
which shuts in the esplanade on the south side. The broad
steps of the gate, crowded with Cleopatra's ladies, all in their
gayest attire, are like a flower garden. The façade is lined by
her guard, officered by the same gallants to whom Bel Affris
announced the coming of Cæsar six months before in the old
palace on the Syrian border. The north side is lined by Roman
soldiers, with the townsfolk on tiptoe behind them, peering
over their heads at the cleared esplanade, in which the officers
stroll about, chatting. Among these are Belzanor and the
Persian; also the Centurion, vinewood cudgel in hand, battle
worn, thick-booted, and much outshone, both socially and
decoratively, by the Egyptian officers.

Apollodorus makes his way through the townsfolk and calls
to the officers from behind the Roman line.

APOLLODORUS. Hullo! May I pass?

CENTURION. Pass Apollodorus the Sicilian there! (The soldiers let him through.)

BELZANOR. Is Cæsar at hand?

APOLLODORUS. Not yet. He is still in the market place. I
could not stand any more of the roaring of the soldiers! After
half an hour of the enthusiasm of an army, one feels the need
of a little sea air.

PERSIAN. Tell us the news. Hath he slain the priests?

APOLLODORUS. Not he. They met him in the market place
with ashes on their heads and their gods in their hands. They

placed the gods at his feet. The only one that was worth looking at was Apis: a miracle of gold and ivory work. By my advice he offered the chief priest two talents for it.

BELZANOR (*appalled*). Apis the all-knowing for two talents! What said the chief priest?

APOLLODORUS. He invoked the mercy of Apis, and asked for five.

BELZANOR. There will be famine and tempest in the land for this.

PERSIAN. Pooh! Why did not Apis cause Cæsar to be vanquished by Achillas? Any fresh news from the war, Apollodorus?

APOLLODORUS. The little King Ptolemy was drowned.

BELZANOR. Drowned! How?

APOLLODORUS. With the rest of them. Cæsar attacked them from three sides at once and swept them into the Nile. Ptolemy's barge sank.

BELZANOR. A marvelous man, this Cæsar! Will he come soon, think you?

APOLLODORUS. He was settling the Jewish question when I left.

A flourish of trumpets from the north, and commotion among the townsfolk, announces the approach of Cæsar.

PERSIAN. He has made short work of them. Here he comes. (*He hurries to his post in front of the Egyptian lines.*)

BELZANOR (*following him*). Ho there! Cæsar comes.

The soldiers stand at attention, and dress their lines. Apollodorus goes to the Egyptian line.

CENTURION (*hurrying to the gangway guard*). Attention there! Cæsar comes.

Cæsar arrives in state with Rufio: Britannus following. The soldiers receive him with enthusiastic shouting.

CÆSAR. I see my ship awaits me. The hour of Cæsar's farewell to Egypt has arrived. And now, Rufio, what remains to be done before I go?

RUFIO (*at his left hand*). You have not yet appointed a Roman governor for this province.

CÆSAR (*looking whimsically at him, but speaking with perfect gravity*). What say you to Mithridates of Pergamos, my reliever and rescuer, the great son of Eupator?

RUFIO. Why, that you will want him elsewhere. Do you

forget that you have some three or four armies to conquer on your way home?

CÆSAR. Indeed! Well, what say you to yourself?

RUFIO (*incredulously*). I! I a governor! What are you dreaming of? Do you not know that I am only the son of a freedman?

CÆSAR (*affectionately*). Has not Cæsar called you his son? (*Calling to the whole assembly.*) Peace awhile there; and hear me.

THE ROMAN SOLDIERS. Hear Cæsar.

CÆSAR. Hear the service, quality, rank and name of the Roman governor. By service, Cæsar's shield; by quality, Cæsar's friend; by rank, a Roman soldier. (*The Roman soldiers give a triumphant shout.*) By name, Rufio. (*They shout again.*)

RUFIO (*kissing Cæsar's hand*). Ay: I am Cæsar's shield; but of what use shall I be when I am no longer on Cæsar's arm? Well, no matter— (*He becomes husky, and turns away to recover himself.*)

CÆSAR. Where is that British Islander of mine?

BRITANNUS (*coming forward on Cæsar's right hand*). Here, Cæsar.

CÆSAR. Who bade you, pray, thrust yourself into the battle of the Delta, uttering the barbarous cries of your native land, and affirming yourself a match for any four of the Egyptians, to whom you applied unseemly epithets?

BRITANNUS. Cæsar: I ask you to excuse the language that escaped me in the heat of the moment.

CÆSAR. And how did you, who cannot swim, cross the canal with us when we stormed the camp?

BRITANNUS. Cæsar: I clung to the tail of your horse.

CÆSAR. These are not the deeds of a slave, Britannicus, but of a free man.

BRITANNUS. Cæsar: I was born free.

CÆSAR. But they call you Cæsar's slave.

BRITANNUS. Only as Cæsar's slave have I found real freedom.

CÆSAR (*moved*). Well said. Ungrateful that I am, I was about to set you free; but now I will not part from you for a million talents. (*He claps him friendly on the shoulder. Britannus, gratified, but a trifle shamefaced, takes his hand and kisses it sheepishly.*)

BELZANOR (*to the Persian*). This Roman knows how to make men serve him.

PERSIAN. Ay: men too humble to become dangerous rivals to him.

BELZANOR. O subtle one! O cynic!

CÆSAR (*seeing Apollodorus in the Egyptian corner and calling to him*). Apollodorus: I leave the art of Egypt in your charge. Remember: Rome loves art and will encourage it ungrudgingly.

APOLLODORUS. I understand, Cæsar. Rome will produce no art itself; but it will buy up and take away whatever the other nations produce.

CÆSAR. What! Rome produce no art! Is peace not an art? is war not an art? is government not an art? is civilization not an art? All these we give you in exchange for a few ornaments. You will have the best of the bargain. (*Turning to Rufio.*) And now, what else have I to do before I embark? (*Trying to recollect.*) There is something I cannot remember: what can it be? Well, well: it must remain undone: we must not waste this favorable wind. Farewell, Rufio.

RUFIO. Cæsar: I am loth to let you go to Rome without your shield. There are too many daggers there.

CÆSAR. It matters not: I shall finish my life's work on my way back; and then I shall have lived long enough. Besides: I have always disliked the idea of dying: I had rather be killed. Farewell.

RUFIO (*with a sigh, raising his hands and giving Cæsar up as incorrigible*). Farewell. (*They shake hands.*)

CÆSAR (*waving his hands to Apollodorus*). Farewell, Apollodorus, and my friends, all of you. Aboard!

The gangway is run out from the quay to the ship. As Cæsar moves towards it, Cleopatra, cold and tragic, cunningly dressed in black, without ornaments or decoration of any kind, and thus making a striking figure among the brilliantly dressed bevy of ladies as she passes through it, comes from the palace and stands on the steps. Cæsar does not see her until she speaks.

CLEOPATRA. Has Cleopatra no part in this leave taking?

CÆSAR (*enlightened*). Ah, I knew there was something. (*To Rufio.*) How could you let me forget her, Rufio? (*Hastening to her.*) Had I gone without seeing you, I should never have forgiven myself. (*He takes her hands, and brings*

her into the middle of the esplanade. She submits stonily.)
Is this mourning for me?

CLEOPATRA. No.

CÆSAR (*remorsefully*). Ah, that was thoughtless of me!
It is for your brother.

CLEOPATRA. No.

CÆSAR. For whom, then?

CLEOPATRA. Ask the Roman governor whom you have
left us.

CÆSAR. Rufio?

CLEOPATRA. Yes: Rufio. (*She points at him with deadly
scorn.*) He who is to rule here in Cæsar's name, in Cæsar's
way, according to Cæsar's boasted laws of life.

CÆSAR (*dubiously*). He is to rule as he can, Cleopatra. He
has taken the work upon him, and will do it in his own way.

CLEOPATRA. Not in your way, then?

CÆSAR (*puzzled*). What do you mean by my way?

CLEOPATRA. Without punishment. Without revenge. Without judgment.

CÆSAR (*approvingly*). Ay: that is the right way, the great
way, the only possible way in the end. (*To Rufio.*) Believe
it, Rufio, if you can.

RUFIO. Why, I believe it, Cæsar. You have convinced me
of it long ago. But look you. You are sailing for Numidia
to-day. Now tell me: if you meet a hungry lion there, you
will not punish it for wanting to eat you?

CÆSAR (*wondering what he is driving at*). No.

RUFIO. Nor revenge upon it the blood of those it has already eaten.

CÆSAR. No.

RUFIO. Nor judge it for its guiltiness.

CÆSAR. No.

RUFIO. What, then, will you do to save your life from it?

CÆSAR (*promptly*). Kill it, man, without malice, just as
it would kill me. What does this parable of the lion mean?

RUFIO. Why, Cleopatra had a tigress that killed men at
her bidding. I thought she might bid it kill you some day.
Well, had I not been Cæsar's pupil, what pious things might
I not have done to that tigress? I might have punished it.
I might have revenged Pothinus on it.

CÆSAR (*interjects*). Pothinus!

RUFIO (*continuing*). I might have judged it. But I put

all these follies behind me; and, without malice, only cut its throat. And that is why Cleopatra comes to you in mourning.

CLEOPATRA (*vehemently*). He has shed the blood of my servant Ftatateeta. On your head be it as upon his, Cæsar, if you hold him free of it.

CÆSAR (*energetically*). On my head be it, then; for it was well done. Rufio: had you set yourself in the seat of the judge, and with hateful ceremonies and appeals to the gods handed that woman over to some hired executioner to be slain before the people in the name of justice, never again would I have touched your hand without a shudder. But this was natural slaying: I feel no horror at it.

Rufio, satisfied, nods at Cleopatra, mutely inviting her to mark that.

CLEOPATRA (*pettish and childish in her impotence*). No: not when a Roman slays an Egyptian. All the world will now see how unjust and corrupt Cæsar is.

CÆSAR (*taking her hands coaxingly*). Come: do not be angry with me. I am sorry for that poor Totateeta. (*She laughs in spite of herself.*) Aha! you are laughing. Does that mean reconciliation?

CLEOPATRA (*angry with herself for laughing*). No, no, NO!! But it is so ridiculous to hear you call her Totateeta.

CÆSAR. What! As much a child as ever, Cleopatra! Have I not made a woman of you after all?

CLEOPATRA. Oh, it is you who are a great baby: you make me seem silly because you will not behave seriously. But you have treated me badly; and I do not forgive you.

CÆSAR. Bid me farewell.

CLEOPATRA. I will not.

CÆSAR (*coaxing*). I will send you a beautiful present from Rome.

CLEOPATRA (*proudly*). Beauty from Rome to Egypt indeed! What can Rome give me that Egypt cannot give me?

APOLLODORUS. That is true, Cæsar. If the present is to be really beautiful, I shall have to buy it for you in Alexandria.

CÆSAR. You are forgetting the treasures for which Rome is most famous, my friend. You cannot buy them in Alexandria.

APOLLODORUS. What are they, Cæsar?

CÆSAR. Her sons. Come, Cleopatra: forgive me and bid me farewell; and I will send you a man, Roman from head to heel and Roman of the noblest; not old and ripe for the knife; not lean in the arms and cold in the heart; not hiding a bald head under his conqueror's laurels; not stooped with the weight of the world on his shoulders; but brisk and fresh, strong and young, hoping in the morning, fighting in the day, and revelling in the evening. Will you take such an one in exchange for Cæsar?

CLEOPATRA (*palpitating*). His name, his name?

CÆSAR. Shall it be Mark Antony? (*She throws herself into his arms.*)

RUFIO. You are a bad hand at a bargain, mistress, if you will swap Cæsar for Antony.

CÆSAR. So now you are satisfied.

CLEOPATRA. You will not forget.

CÆSAR. I will not forget. Farewell: I do not think we shall meet again. Farewell. (*He kisses her on the forehead. She is much affected and begins to sniff. He embarks.*)

THE ROMAN SOLDIERS (*as he sets his foot on the gangway*). Hail, Cæsar; and farewell!

He reaches the ship and returns Rufio's wave of the hand.

APOLLODORUS (*to Cleopatra*). No tears, dearest Queen: they stab your servant to the heart. He will return some day.

CLEOPATRA. I hope not. But I can't help crying, all the same. (*She waves her handkerchief to Cæsar; and the ship begins to move.*)

THE ROMAN SOLDIERS (*drawing their swords and raising them in the air*). Hail, Cæsar!

NOTES TO CÆSAR AND CLEOPATRA

CLEOPATRA'S CURE FOR BALDNESS

For the sake of conciseness in a hurried situation I have made Cleopatra recommend rum. This, I am afraid, is an anachronism: the only real one in the play. To balance it, I give a couple of the remedies she actually believed in. They are quoted by Galen from Cleopatra's book on Cosmetic.

"For bald patches, powder red sulphuret of arsenic and take it up with oak gum, as much as it will bear. Put on a rag and apply, having soaped the place well first. I have mixed the above with a foam of nitre, and it worked well."

Several other receipts follow, ending with: "The following is the best of all, acting for fallen hairs, when applied with oil or pomatum; acts also for falling off of eyelashes or for people getting bald all over. It is wonderful. Of domestic mice burnt, one part; of vine rag burnt, one part; of horse's teeth burnt, one part; of bear's grease, one; of deer's marrow, one; of reed bark, one. To be pounded when dry, and mixed with plenty of honey till it gets the consistency of honey; then the bear's grease and marrow to be mixed (when melted), the medicine to be put in a brass flask, and the bald part rubbed till it sprouts."

Concerning these ingredients, my fellow-dramatist, Gilbert Murray, who, as a Professor of Greek, has applied to classical antiquity the methods of high scholarship (my own method is pure divination), writes to me as follows: "Some of this I don't understand, and possibly Galen did not, as he quotes your heroine's own language. Foam of nitre is, I think, something like soapsuds. Reed bark is an old expression. It might mean the outside membrane of a reed: I do not know what it ought to be called. In the burnt mice receipt I take it that you first mixed the solid powders with honey, and then added the grease. I expect Cleopatra preferred it because in most of the others you have to lacerate the skin, prick it, or rub it till it bleeds. I do not know what vine rag is. I translate literally.".

APPARENT ANACHRONISMS

The only way to write a play which shall convey to the general public an impression of antiquity is to make the characters speak blank verse and abstain from reference to steam, telegraphy, or any of the material conditions of their existence. The more ignorant men are, the more convinced are they that their little parish and their little chapel is an apex to which civilization and philosophy have painfully struggled up the pyramid of time from a desert of savagery. Savagery, they think, became barbarism; barbarism became ancient civilization; ancient civilization became Pauline Christianity; Pauline Christianity became Roman Catholicism; Roman Catholicism became the Dark Ages; and the Dark Ages were finally enlightened by the Protestant instincts of the English race. The whole process is summed up as Progress with a capital P. And any elderly gentleman of Progressive temperament will testify that the improvement since he was a boy is enormous.

Now if we count the generations of Progressive elderly gentlemen since, say, Plato, and add together the successive enormous improvements to which each of them has testified, it will strike us at once as an unaccountable fact that the world, instead of having been improved in 67 generations out of all recognition, presents, on the whole, a rather less digni-fied appearance in Ibsen's Enemy of the People than in Plato's Republic. And in truth, the period of time covered by history is far too short to allow of any perceptible progress in the popular sense of Evolution of the Human Species. The notion that there has been any such Progress since Cæsar's time (less than 20 centuries) is too absurd for dis-cussion. All the savagery, barbarism, dark ages and the rest of it of which we have any record as existing in the past, exists at the present moment. A British carpenter or stone-mason may point out that he gets twice as much money for his labor as his father did in the same trade, and that his suburban house, with its bath, its cottage piano, its drawing-room suite, and its album of photographs, would have shamed the plainness of his grandmother's. But the descendants of feudal barons, living in squalid lodgings on a salary of fifteen shillings a week instead of in castles on princely revenues, do not congratulate the world on the change. Such changes, in

fact, are not to the point. It has been known, as far back as
our records go, that man running wild in the woods is different
to man kennelled in a city slum; that a dog seems to understand a shepherd better than a hewer of wood and drawer of
water can understand an astronomer; and that breeding, gentle
nurture and luxurious food and shelter will produce a kind of
man with whom the common laborer is socially incompatible.
The same thing is true of horses and dogs. Now there is
clearly room for great changes in the world by increasing the
percentage of individuals who are carefully bred and gently
nurtured, even to finally making the most of every man and
woman born. But that possibility existed in the days of the
Hittites as much as it does to-day. It does not give the slightest real support to the common assumption that the civilized
contemporaries of the Hittites were unlike their civilized
descendants to-day.

This would appear the tritest commonplace if it were not
that the ordinary citizen's ignorance of the past combines
with his idealization of the present to mislead and flatter him.
Our latest book on the new railway across Asia describes the
dulness of the Siberian farmer and the vulgar pursepride of
the Siberian man of business without the least consciousness
that the sting of contemptuous instances given might have
been saved by writing simply "Farmers and provincial pluto-
crats in Siberia are exactly what they are in England." The
latest professor descanting on the civilization of the Western
Empire in the fifth century feels bound to assume, in the teeth
of his own researches, that the Christian was one sort of
animal and the Pagan another. It might as well be assumed,
as indeed it generally is assumed by implication, that a murder committed with a poisoned arrow is different to a murder
committed with a Mauser rifle. All such notions are illusions.
Go back to the first syllable of recorded time, and there you
will find your Christian and your Pagan, your yokel and your
poet, helot and hero, Don Quixote and Sancho, Tamino and
Papageno, Newton and bushman unable to count eleven, all
alive and contemporaneous, and all convinced that they are
the heirs of all the ages and the privileged recipients of THE
truth (all others damnable heresies), just as you have them
to-day, flourishing in countries each of which is the bravest
and best that ever sprang at Heaven's command from out
the azure main.

Again, there is the illusion of "increased command over Nature," meaning that cotton is cheap and that ten miles of country road on a bicycle have replaced four on foot. But even if man's increased command over Nature included any increased command over himself (the only sort of command relevant to his evolution into a higher being), the fact remains that it is only by running away from the increased command over Nature to country places where Nature is still in primitive command over Man that he can recover from the effects of the smoke, the stench, the foul air, the overcrowding, the racket, the ugliness, the dirt which the cheap cotton costs us. If manufacturing activity means Progress, the town must be more advanced than the country; and the field laborers and village artizans of to-day must be much less changed from the servants of Job than the proletariat of modern London from the proletariat of Cæsar's Rome. Yet the cockney proletarian is so inferior to the village laborer that it is only by steady recruiting from the country that London is kept alive. This does not seem as if the change since Job's time were Progress in the popular sense: quite the reverse. The common stock of discoveries in physics has accumulated a little: that is all.

One more illustration. Is the Englishman prepared to admit that the American is his superior as a human being? I ask this question because the scarcity of labor in America relatively to the demand for it has led to a development of machinery there, and a consequent "increase of command over Nature" which makes many of our English methods appear almost medieval to the up-to-date Chicagoan. This means that the American has an advantage over the Englishman of exactly the same nature that the Englishman has over the contemporaries of Cicero. Is the Englishman prepared to draw the same conclusion in both cases? I think not. The American, of course, will draw it cheerfully; but I must then ask him whether, since a modern Negro has a greater "command over Nature" than Washington had, we are also to accept the conclusion, involved in his former one, that humanity has progressed from Washington to the *fin de siècle* Negro.

Finally, I would point out that if life is crowned by its success and devotion in industrial organization and ingenuity, we had better worship the ant and the bee (as moralists urge us to do in our childhood), and humble ourselves before the arrogance of the birds of Aristophanes.

My reason then for ignoring the popular conception of Progress in Cæsar and Cleopatra is that there is no reason to suppose that any Progress has taken place since their time. But even if I shared the popular delusion, I do not see that I could have made any essential difference in the play. I can only imitate humanity as I know it. Nobody knows whether Shakespeare thought that ancient Athenian joiners, weavers, or bellows menders were any different from Elizabethan ones; but it is quite certain that he could not have made them so, unless, indeed, he had played the literary man and made Quince say, not "Is all our company here?" but "Bottom: was not that Socrates that passed us at the Piræus with Glaucon and Polemarchus on his way to the house of Kephalus." And so on.

CLEOPATRA

Cleopatra was only sixteen when Cæsar went to Egypt; but in Egypt sixteen is a riper age than it is in England. The childishness I have ascribed to her, as far as it is childishness of character and not lack of experience, is not a matter of years. It may be observed in our own climate at the present day in many women of fifty. It is a mistake to suppose that the difference between wisdom and folly has anything to do with the difference between physical age and physical youth. Some women are younger at seventy than most women at seventeen.

It must be borne in mind, too, that Cleopatra was a queen, and was therefore not the typical Greek-cultured, educated Egyptian lady of her time. To represent her by any such type would be as absurd as to represent George IV by a type founded on the attainments of Sir Isaac Newton. It is true that an ordinarily well-educated Alexandrian girl of her time would no more have believed bogey stories about the Romans than the daughter of a modern Oxford professor would believe them about the Germans (though, by the way, it is possible to talk great nonsense at Oxford about foreigners when we are at war with them). But I do not feel bound to believe that Cleopatra was well educated. Her father, the illustrious Flute Blower, was not at all a parent of the Oxford professor type. And Cleopatra was a chip of the old block.

BRITANNUS

I find among those who have read this play in manuscript a strong conviction that an ancient Briton could not possibly have been like a modern one. I see no reason to adopt this curious view. It is true that the Roman and Norman conquests must have for a time disturbed the normal British type produced by the climate. But Britannus, born before these events, represents the unadulterated Briton who fought Cæsar and impressed Roman observers much as we should expect the ancestors of Mr. Podsnap to impress the cultivated Italians of their time.

I am told that it is not scientific to treat national character as a product of climate. This only shews the wide difference between common knowledge and the intellectual game called science. We have men of exactly the same stock, and speaking the same language, growing in Great Britain, in Ireland, and in America. The result is three of the most distinctly marked nationalities under the sun. Racial characteristics are quite another matter. The difference between a Jew and a Gentile has nothing to do with the difference between an Englishman and a German. The characteristics of Britannus are local characteristics, not race characteristics. In an ancient Briton they would, I take it, be exaggerated, since modern Britain, disforested, drained, urbanified and consequently cosmopolized, is presumably less characteristically British than Cæsar's Britain.

And again I ask does anyone who, in the light of a competent knowledge of his own age, has studied history from contemporary documents, believe that 67 generations of promiscuous marriage have made any appreciable difference in the human fauna of these isles? Certainly I do not.

JULIUS CÆSAR

As to Cæsar himself, I have purposely avoided the usual anachronism of going to Cæsar's books, and concluding that the style is the man. That is only true of authors who have the specific literary genius, and have practiced long enough to attain complete self-expression in letters. It is not true even on these conditions in an age when literature is conceived as a game of style, and not as a vehicle of self-expression by the author. Now Cæsar was an amateur stylist writing books of travel and campaign histories in a style so impersonal that the authenticity of the later volumes is disputed. They reveal some of his qualities just as the Voyage of a Naturalist Round the World reveals some of Darwin's, without expressing his private personality. An Englishman reading them would say that Cæsar was a man of great common sense and good taste, meaning thereby a man without originality or moral courage.

In exhibiting Cæsar as a much more various person than the historian of the Gallic wars, I hope I have not succumbed unconsciously to the dramatic illusion to which all great men owe part of their reputation and some the whole of it. I admit that reputations gained in war are specially questionable. Able civilians taking up the profession of arms, like Cæsar and Cromwell, in middle age, have snatched all its laurels from opponent commanders bred to it, apparently because capable persons engaged in military pursuits are so scarce that the existence of two of them at the same time in the same hemisphere is extremely rare. The capacity of any conqueror is therefore more likely than not to be an illusion produced by the incapacity of his adversary. At all events, Cæsar might have won his battles without being wiser than Charles XII or Nelson or Joan of Arc, who were, like most modern "self-made" millionaires, half-witted geniuses, enjoying the worship accorded by all races to certain forms of insanity. But Cæsar's victories were only advertisements for an eminence that would never have become popular without them. Cæsar is greater off the battle field than on it. Nelson off his quarterdeck was so quaintly out of the question that when his head was injured at the battle of the Nile, and his conduct became for some years openly scandalous, the difference was not important enough to be noticed. It may, however, be said that peace hath her illusory reputations no less than war. And it is certainly true that in civil life mere capacity for work—the power of killing a dozen secretaries under you, so to speak, as a life-or-death courier kills horses—enables men with common ideas and superstitions to distance all competitors in the strife of political ambition. It was this power of work that astonished Cicero as the most prodigious of Cæsar's gifts, as it astonished later observers in Napoleon before it wore him out. How if Cæsar were nothing but a Nelson and a Gladstone combined! a prodigy of vitality without any special quality of mind! nay, with ideas that were worn out before he was born, as Nelson's and Gladstone's were! I have considered that possibility too, and rejected it. I cannot cite all the stories about Cæsar which seem to me to shew that he was genuinely original; but let me at least point out that I have been careful to attribute nothing but originality to him. Originality gives a man an air of frankness, generosity, and magnanimity by enabling him to estimate the value of truth, money, or success in any particular instance quite independently of convention and moral generalization. He therefore will not, in the ordinary Treasury bench fashion, tell a lie which everybody knows to be a lie (and consequently expects him as a matter of good taste to tell). His lies are not found out: they pass for candors. He understands the paradox of money, and gives it away when he can get most for it: in other words, when its value is least, which is just when a common man tries hardest to get it. He knows that the real moment of success is not the moment apparent to the crowd. Hence, in order to produce an impression of complete disinterestedness and magnanimity, he has only to act with entire selfishness; and this is perhaps the only sense in which a man can be said to be *naturally* great. It is in this sense that I have represented Cæsar as great. Having virtue, he has no need of goodness. He is neither forgiving, frank, nor generous, because a man who is too great to resent has nothing to forgive; a man who says things that other people are afraid to say need be no more frank than Bismarck was; and there is no generosity in giving things you do not want to people of whom you intend to make use. This distinction between virtue and goodness is not understood in England: hence the poverty of our drama in heroes. Our stage attempts at them are mere goody-goodies. Goodness, in its popular British sense of self-denial, implies that man is vicious by nature, and that supreme goodness is supreme martyrdom. Not sharing that pious opinion, I have not given countenance to it in any of my plays. In this I follow the precedent of the ancient myths, which represent the hero as vanquishing his enemies, not in fair fight, but with enchanted sword, superequine horse and magical invulnerability, the possession of which, from the vulgar moral-istic point of view, robs his exploits of any merit whatever.

As to Cæsar's sense of humor, there is no more reason to assume that he lacked it than to assume that he was deaf or blind. It is said that on the occasion of his assassination by a conspiracy of moralists (it is always your moralist who makes assassination a duty, on the scaffold or off it), he de-fended himself until the good Brutus struck him, when he exclaimed "What! you too, Brutus!" and disdained further fight. If this be true, he must have been an incorrigible comedian. But even if we waive this story, or accept the tradi-tional sentimental interpretation of it, there is still abundant evidence of his lightheartedness and adventurousness. Indeed it is clear from his whole history that what has been called his ambition was an instinct for exploration. He had much more of Columbus and Franklin in him than of Henry V.

However, nobody need deny Cæsar a share, at least, of the qualities I have attributed to him. All men, much more Julius Cæsars, possess all qualities in some degree. The really interesting question is whether I am right in assuming that the way to produce an impression of greatness is by exhibiting a man, not as mortifying his nature by doing his duty, in the manner which our system of putting little men into great posi-tions (not having enough great men in our influential families to go round) forces us to inculcate, but as simply doing what he naturally wants to do. For this raises the question whether our world has not been wrong in its moral theory for the last 2,500 years or so. It must be a constant puzzle to many of us that the Christian era, so excellent in its intentions, should have been practically such a very discreditable episode in the history of the race. I doubt if this is altogether due to the vulgar and sanguinary sensationalism of our religious legends, with their substitution of gross physical torments and public executions for the passion of humanity. Islam, substituting voluptuousness for torment (a merely superficial difference, it is true), has done no better. It may have been the failure of Christianity to emancipate itself from expiatory theories of moral responsibility, guilt, innocence, reward, punishment, and the rest of it, that baffled its intention of changing the world. But these are bound up in all philosophies of creation as opposed to cosmism. They may therefore be regarded as the price we pay for popular religion.

Man and Superman

A Comedy and a Philosophy

~~~~~~~~~~~~~~~~~~~~~~~~~~~~~~~~~

INTRODUCTORY NOTE TO *MAN AND SUPERMAN*

Man and Superman, begun in 1901 and finished in 1903, is considered by many critics to be one of Shaw's greatest works, ranking with *Saint Joan, Back to Methuselah* and *Heartbreak House.* The play is impressive in concept, treatment and length. Subtitled "A Comedy and a Philosophy," one might suppose that the John Tanner–Ann Whitefield plot in Acts I, II and IV is the comedy and the Don Juan in Hell episode in Act III is the philosophy. But the two are combined adroitly in this double play and reinforced with more cogent reasoning in the remarkable Preface and an appendix, "The Revolutionist's Handbook and Pocket Companion," which Shaw prepared for the play.

In this magnum opus, Shaw presents his ideas on creative evolution and the Life Force. He believed that if man used his brains and creative evolution he could create a race of supermen to meet the demands and expectations of the Life Force (or God). He believed, too, that women alone understand the Life Force and seek the best man they can find to produce the healthiest and brightest children possible.

Shaw warned that if the human race did not achieve its potential, the Life Force (or God) would erase it and start anew with another and higher breed of animal. Shaw dramatizes his thesis brilliantly in *Man and Superman* by making the age-old struggle between the mother-woman and the artist-man a hilarious one; in *Don Juan in Hell,* Shaw shows the Don as a man who runs away from love, heaven as a dull place, and hell as a popular locality ruled by a charming Devil.

By upsetting audience expectations about Don Juan and the usual theatrical treatment of sexual attraction, Shaw drove home his ideas on the new woman (Ann and Violet), the new man (Straker), sex ("moral passion is the only real passion"), the futility of romanticism (Octavius) and the death grip of Puritanism (Ramsden).

259

Rarely are the two parts of the play performed in the same evening. Similarly, the reader is advised to read Acts I, II, and IV of *Man and Superman* before he reads Act III, the Don Juan story. The italicized stage directions deserve careful reading in this play because of the extra vitality they add to the characters. Even the one that tells the actor to "look at her with an eloquent blush, and run off" is as stimulating to the reader as to the performer.

TO
ARTHUR BINGHAM WALKLEY

My dear Walkley

You once asked me why I did not write a Don Juan play. The levity with which you assumed this frightful responsibility has probably by this time enabled you to forget it; but the day of reckoning has arrived: here is your play! I say your play, because *qui facit per alium facit per se.* Its profits, like its labor, belong to me: its morals, its manners, its philosophy, its influence on the young, are for you to justify. You were of mature age when you made the suggestion; and you knew your man. It is hardly fifteen years since, as twin pioneers of the New Journalism of that time, we two, cradled in the same new sheets, made an epoch in the criticism of the theatre and the opera house by making it a pretext for a propaganda of our own views of life. So you cannot plead ignorance of the character of the force you set in motion. You meant me to *épater le bourgeois;* and if he protests, I hereby refer him to you as the accountable party.

I warn you that if you attempt to repudiate your responsibility, I shall suspect you of finding the play too decorous for your taste. The fifteen years have made me older and graver. In you I can detect no such becoming change. Your levities and audacities are like the loves and comforts prayed for by Desdemona: they increase, even as your days do grow. No mere pioneering journal dares meddle with them now: the stately Times itself is alone sufficiently above suspicion to act as your chaperone; and even the Times must sometimes thank its stars that new plays are not produced every day, since after each such event its gravity is compromised, its platitude turned to epigram, its portentousness to wit, its propriety to elegance, and even its decorum into naughtiness by criticisms which the traditions of the paper do not allow you to sign at the end, but which you take care to sign with the most extravagant flourishes between the lines. I am not sure that this is not a portent of Revolution. In eighteenth-century France the end was at hand when men bought the Encyclopedia and found Diderot there. When I buy the Times and find you there, my prophetic ear catches a rattle of twentieth-century tumbrils.

However, that is not my present anxiety. The question is, will you not be disappointed with a Don Juan play in which not one of that hero's *mille etre adventures* is brought upon the stage? To propitiate you, let me explain myself. You will retort that I never do anything else: it is your favorite jibe at me that what I call drama is nothing but explanation. But you must not expect me to adopt your inexplicable, fantastic, petulant, fastidious ways: you must take me as I am, a reasonable, patient, consistent, apologetic, laborious person, with the temperament of a schoolmaster and the pursuits of a vestryman. No doubt that literary knack of mine which happens to amuse the British public distracts attention from my character; but the character is there none the less, solid as bricks. I have a conscience; and conscience is always anxiously explanatory. You, on the contrary, feel that a man who discusses his conscience is much like a woman who discusses her modesty. The only moral force you condescend to parade is the force of your wit: the only demand you make in public is the demand of your artistic temperament for symmetry, elegance, style, grace, refinement, and the cleanliness which comes next to godliness if not before it. But my conscience is the genuine pulpit article: it annoys me to see people comfortable when they ought to be uncomfortable; and I insist on making them think in order to bring them to conviction of sin. If you don't like my preaching you must lump it. I really cannot help it.

In the preface to my Plays for Puritans I explained the predicament of our contemporary English drama, forced to deal almost exclusively with cases of sexual attraction, and yet forbidden to exhibit the incidents of that attraction or even to discuss its nature. Your suggestion that I should write a Don Juan play was virtually a challenge to me to treat this subject myself dramatically. The challenge was difficult enough to be worth accepting, because, when you come to think of it, though we have plenty of dramas with heroes and heroines who are in love and must accordingly marry or perish at the end of the play, or about people whose relations with one another have been complicated by the marriage laws, not to mention the looser sort of plays which trade on the tradition that illicit love affairs are at once vicious and delightful, we have no modern English plays in which the natural attraction of the sexes for one another is made the mainspring of the action. That is why we insist on beauty in our performers, differing herein from the countries our friend William Archer holds up as examples of seriousness to our childish theatres. There the Juliets and Isoldes, the Romeos and Tristans, might be our mothers and fathers. Not so the English actress. The heroine she impersonates is not allowed to discuss the elemental relations of men and women: all her romantic twaddle about novelet-made love, all her purely legal dilemmas as to whether she was married or "betrayed," quite miss our hearts and worry our minds. To console ourselves we must just look at her. We do so; and her beauty feeds our starving emotions. Sometimes we grumble ungallantly at the lady because she does not act as well as she looks. But in a drama which, with all its preoccupation with sex, is really void of sexual interest, good looks are more desired than histrionic skill.

Let me press this point on you, since you are too clever to raise the fool's cry of paradox whenever I take hold of a stick by the right instead of the wrong end. Why are our occasional attempts to deal with the sex problem on the stage so repulsive and dreary that even those who are most determined that sex questions shall be held open and their discussion kept free, cannot pretend to relish these joyless attempts at social sanitation? Is it not because at bottom they are utterly sexless? What is the usual formula for such plays? A woman has, on some past occasion, been brought into conflict with the law which regulates the relations of the sexes. A man, by falling in love with her, or marrying her, is brought into conflict with the social convention which discountenances the woman. Now the conflicts of individuals with law and convention can be dramatized like all other human conflicts; but they are purely judicial; and the fact that we are much more curious about the suppressed relations between the man and the woman than about the relations between both and our courts of law and private juries of matrons, produces that sensation of evasion, of dissatisfaction, of fundamental irrelevance, of shallowness, of useless disagreeableness, of total failure to edify and partial failure to interest, which is as familiar to you in the

theatres as it was to me when I, too, frequented those uncomfortable buildings, and found our popular playwrights
in the mind to (as they thought) emulate Ibsen.

I take it that when you asked me for a Don Juan play you
did not want that sort of thing. Nobody does: the successes
such plays sometimes obtain are due to the incidental conventional melodrama with which the experienced popular
author instinctively saves himself from failure. But what did
you want? Owing to your unfortunate habit—you now, I
hope, feel its inconvenience—of not explaining yourself, I
have had to discover this for myself. First, then, I have had
to ask myself, what is a Don Juan? Vulgarly, a libertine. But
your dislike of vulgarity is pushed to the length of a defect
(universality of character is impossible without a share of vulgarity); and even if you could acquire the taste, you would
find yourself overfed from ordinary sources without troubling
me. So I took it that you demanded a Don Juan in the philosophic sense.

Philosophically, Don Juan is a man who, though gifted
enough to be exceptionally capable of distinguishing between
good and evil, follows his own instincts without regard to the
common, statute, or canon law; and therefore, whilst gaining
the ardent sympathy of our rebellious instincts (which are
flattered by the brilliancies with which Don Juan associates
them), finds himself in mortal conflict with existing institutions, and defends himself by fraud and force as unscrupulously as a farmer defends his crops by the same means against vermin. The prototypic Don Juan, invented early in the XVI century by a Spanish monk, was presented, according to the ideas
of that time, as the enemy of God, the approach of whose vengeance is felt throughout the drama, growing in menace from
minute to minute. No anxiety is caused on Don Juan's account
by any minor antagonist: he easily eludes the police, temporal
and spiritual; and when an indignant father seeks private
redress with the sword, Don Juan kills him without an effort.
Not until the slain father returns from heaven as the agent of
God, in the form of his own statue, does he prevail against
his slayer and cast him into hell. The moral is a monkish one:
repent and reform now; for to-morrow it may be too late.
This is really the only point on which Don Juan is sceptical;
for he is a devout believer in an ultimate hell, and risks damnation only because, as he is young, it seems so far off that

repentance can be postponed until he has amused himself to his heart's content.

But the lesson intended by an author is hardly ever the lesson the world chooses to learn from his book. What attracts and impresses us in El Burlador de Sevilla is not the immediate urgency of repentance, but the heroism of daring to be the enemy of God. From Prometheus to my own Devil's Disciple, such enemies have always been popular. Don Juan became such a pet that the world could not bear his damnation. It reconciled him sentimentally to God in a second version, and clamored for his canonization for a whole century, thus treating him as English journalism has treated that comic foe of the gods, Punch. Molière's Don Juan casts back to the original in point of impenitence; but in piety he falls off greatly. True, he also proposes to repent; but in what terms! "Oui, ma foi! il faut s'amender. Encore vingt ou trente ans de cette vie-ci, et puis nous songerons à nous." After Molière comes the artist-enchanter, the master of masters, Mozart, who reveals the hero's spirit in magical harmonies, elfin tones, and elate darting rhythms as of summer lightning made audible. Here you have freedom in love and in morality mocking exquisitely at slavery to them, and interesting you, attracting you, tempting you, inexplicably forcing you to range the hero with his enemy the statue on a transcendent plane, leaving the prudish daughter and her priggish lover on a crockery shelf below to live piously ever after.

After these completed works Byron's fragment does not count for much philosophically. Our vagabond libertines are no more interesting from that point of view than the sailor who has a wife in every port; and Byron's hero is, after all, only a vagabond libertine. And he is dumb: he does not discuss himself with a Sganarelle-Leporello or with the fathers or brothers of his mistresses: he does not even, like Casanova, tell his own story. In fact he is not a true Don Juan at all; for he is no more an enemy of God than any romantic and adventurous young sower of wild oats. Had you and I been in his place at his age, who knows whether we might not have done as he did, unless indeed your fastidiousness had saved you from the empress Catherine. Byron was as little of a philosopher as Peter the Great: both were instances of that rare and useful, but unedifying variation, an energetic genius born without the prejudices or superstitions of his contemporaries. The resultant unscrupulous freedom of thought made Byron a greater poet than Wordsworth just as it made Peter a greater king than George III; but as it was, after all, only a negative qualification, it did not prevent Peter from being an appalling blackguard and an arrant poltroon, nor did it enable Byron to become a religious force like Shelley. Let us, then, leave Byron's Don Juan out of account. Mozart's is the last of the true Don Juans; for by the time he was of age, his cousin Faust had, in the hands of Goethe, taken his place and carried both his warfare and his reconciliation with the gods far beyond mere lovemaking into politics, high art, schemes for reclaiming new continents from the ocean, and recognition of an eternal womanly principle in the universe. Goethe's Faust and Mozart's Don Juan were the last words of the XVIII century on the subject; and by the time the polite critics of the XIX century, ignoring William Blake as superficially as the XVIII had ignored Hogarth or the XVII Bunyan, had got past the Dickens-Macaulay Dumas-Guizot stage and the Stendhal-Meredith-Turgenieff stage, and were confronted with philosophic fiction by such pens as Ibsen's and Tolstoy's, Don Juan had changed his sex and become Doña Juana, breaking out of the Doll's House and asserting herself as an individual instead of a mere item in a moral pageant.

Now it is all very well for you at the beginning of the XX century to ask me for a Don Juan play; but you will see from the foregoing survey that Don Juan is a full century out of date for you and for me; and if there are millions of less literate people who are still in the eighteenth century, have they not Molière and Mozart, upon whose art no human hand can improve? You would laugh at me if at this time of day I dealt in duels and ghosts and "womanly" women. As to mere libertinism, you would be the first to remind me that the Festin de Pierre of Molière is not a play for amorists, and that one bar of the voluptuous sentimentality of Gounod or Bizet would appear as a licentious stain on the score of Don Giovanni. Even the more abstract parts of the Don Juan play are dilapidated past use: for instance, Don Juan's supernatural antagonist hurled those who refuse to repent into lakes of burning brimstone, there to be tormented by devils with horns and tails. Of that antagonist, and of that conception of repentance, how much is left that could be used in a play by me dedicated to you? On the other hand, those forces of middle-class public opinion which hardly existed for a Spanish nobleman in the days of the first Don Juan, are now triumphant everywhere. Civilized society is one huge bourgeoisie: no nobleman dares now shock his greengrocer. The women, "marchesane, principesse, cameriere, cittadine" and all, are become equally dangerous: the sex is aggresive, powerful: when women are wronged they do not group themselves pathetically to sing "Protegga il giusto cielo": they grasp formidable legal and social weapons, and retaliate. Political parties are wrecked and public careers undone by a single indiscretion. A man had better have all the statues in London to supper with him, ugly as they are, than be brought to the bar of the Nonconformist Conscience by Donna Elvira. Excommunication has become almost as serious a business as it was in the X century.

As a result, Man is no longer, like Don Juan, victor in the duel of sex. Whether he has ever really been may be doubted: at all events the enormous superiority of Woman's natural position in this matter is telling with greater and greater force. As to pulling the Nonconformist Conscience by the beard as Don Juan plucked the beard of the Commandant's statue in the convent of San Francisco, that is out of the question nowadays: prudence and good manners alike forbid it to a hero with any mind. Besides, it is Don Juan's own beard that is in danger of plucking. Far from relapsing into hypocrisy, as Sganarelle feared, he has unexpectedly discovered a moral in his immorality. The growing recognition of his new point of view is heaping responsibility on him. His former jests he has had to take as seriously as I have had to take some of the jests of Mr. W. S. Gilbert. His scepticism, once his least tolerated quality, has now triumphed so completely that he can no longer assert himself by witty negations, and must, to save himself from cipherdom, find an affirmative position. His thousand and three affairs of gallantry, after becoming, at most, two immature intrigues leading to sordid and prolonged complications and humiliations, have been discarded altogether as unworthy of his philosophic dignity and compromising to his newly acknowledged position as the founder of a school. Instead of pretending to read Ovid he does actually read Schopenhaur and Nietzsche, studies Westermarck, and is concerned for the future of the race instead of for the freedom of his own instincts. Thus his profligacy and his daredevil airs have gone the way of his sword and mandolin into the rag shop of anachronisms and superstitions. In fact, he is now more Hamlet than Don Juan; for though the lines put into the actor's mouth to indicate to the pit that Hamlet is a philosopher are for the most part mere harmonious platitude which, with a little debasement of the word-music, would be properer to Pecksniff, yet if you separate the real hero, inarticulate and unintelligible to himself except in flashes of inspiration, from the performer who has to talk at any cost through five acts; and if you also do what you must always do in Shakespear's tragedies: that is, dissect out the absurd sensational incidents and physical violences of the borrowed story from the genuine Shakespearian tissue, you will get a true Promethean foe of the gods, whose instinctive attitude towards women much resembles that to which Don Juan is now driven. From this point of view Hamlet was a developed Don Juan whom Shakespear palmed off as a reputable man just as he palmed poor Macbeth off as a murderer. To-day the palming off is no longer necessary (at least on your plane and mine) because Don Juanism is no longer misunderstood as mere Casanovism. Don Juan himself is almost ascetic in his desire to avoid that misunderstanding; and so my attempt to bring him up to date by launching him as a modern Englishman into a modern English environment has produced a figure superficially quite unlike the hero of Mozart.

And yet I have not the heart to disappoint you wholly of another glimpse of the Mozartian *dissoluto punito* and his antagonist the statue. I feel sure you would like to know more of that statue—to draw him out when he is off duty, so to speak. To gratify you, I have resorted to the trick of the strolling theatrical manager who advertizes the pantomime of Sinbad the Sailor with a stock of second-hand picture posters designed for Ali Baba. He simply thrusts a few oil jars into the valley of diamonds, and so fulfils the promise held out by the hoardings to the public eye. I have adapted this simple device to our occasion by thrusting into my perfectly modern three-act play a totally extraneous act in which my hero, enchanted by the air of the Sierra, has a dream in which his Mozartian ancestor appears and philosophizes at great length in a Shavio-Socratic dialogue with the lady, the statue, and the devil.

But this pleasantry is not the essence of the play. Over

this essence I have no control. You propound a certain social substance, sexual attraction to wit, for dramatic distillation; and I distil it for you. I do not adulterate the product with aphrodisiacs nor dilute it with romance and water; for I am merely executing your commission, not producing a popular play for the market. You must therefore (unless, like most wise men, you read the play first and the preface afterwards) prepare yourself to face a trumpery story of modern London life, a life in which, as you know, the ordinary man's main business is to get means to keep up the position and habits of a gentleman, and the ordinary woman's business is to get married. In 9,999 cases out of 10,000, you can count on their doing nothing, whether noble or base, that conflicts with these ends; and that assurance is what you rely on as their religion, their morality, their principles, their patriotism, their reputation, their honor and so forth.

On the whole, this is a sensible and satisfactory foundation for society. Money means nourishment and marriage means children; and that men should put nourishment first and women children first is, broadly speaking, the law of Nature and not the dictate of personal ambition. The secret of the prosaic man's success, such as it is, is the simplicity with which he pursues these ends: the secret of the artistic man's failure, such as that is, is the versatility with which he strays in all directions after secondary ideals. The artist is either a poet or a scallawag: as poet, he cannot see, as the prosaic man does, that chivalry is at bottom only romantic suicide: as scallawag, he cannot see that it does not pay to sponge and beg and lie and brag and neglect his person. Therefore do not misunderstand my plain statement of the fundamental constitution of London society as an Irishman's reproach to your nation. From the day I first set foot on this foreign soil I knew the value of the prosaic qualities of which Irishmen teach Englishmen to be ashamed as well as I knew the vanity of the poetic qualities of which Englishmen teach Irishmen to be proud. For the Irishman instinctively disparages the quality which makes the Englishman dangerous to him; and the Englishman instinctively flatters the fault that makes the Irishman harmless and amusing to him. What is wrong with the prosaic Englishman is what is wrong with the prosaic men of all countries: stupidity. The vitality which places nourishment and children first, heaven and hell a somewhat remote second, and the health of society as an organic whole nowhere, may muddle successfully through the comparatively tribal stages of gregariousness; but in nineteenth-century nations and twentieth-century empires the determination of every man to be rich at all costs, and of every woman to be married at all costs, must, without a highly scientific social organization, produce a ruinous development of poverty, celibacy, prostitution, infant mortality, adult degeneracy, and everything that wise men most dread. In short, there is no future for men, however brimming with crude vitality, who are neither intelligent nor politically educated enough to be Socialists. So do not misunderstand me in the other direction either: if I appreciate the vital qualities of the Englishman as I appreciate the vital qualities of the bee, I do not guarantee the Englishman against being, like the bee (or the Canaanite), smoked out and unloaded of his honey by beings inferior to himself in simple acquisitiveness, combativeness, and fecundity, but superior to him in imagination and cunning.

The Don Juan play, however, is to deal with sexual attraction, and not with nutrition, and to deal with it in a society in which the serious business of sex is left by men to women, as the serious business of nutrition is left by women to men. That the men, to protect themselves against a too aggressive prosecution of the women's business, have set up a feeble romantic convention that the initiative in sex business must always come from the man, is true; but the pretence is so shallow that even in the theatre, that last sanctuary of unreality, it imposes only on the inexperienced. In Shakespear's plays the woman always takes the initiative. In his problem plays and his popular plays alike the love interest is the interest of seeing the woman hunt the man down. She may do it by blandishment, like Rosalind, or by stratagem, like Mariana; but in every case the relation between the woman and the man is the same: she is the pursuer and contriver, he the pursued and disposed of. When she is baffled, like Ophelia, she goes mad and commits suicide; and the man goes straight from her funeral to a fencing match. No doubt Nature, with very young creatures, may save the woman the trouble of scheming: Prospero knows that he has only to throw Ferdinand and Miranda together and they will mate like a pair of doves; and there is no need for Perdita to capture Florizel as the lady doctor in All's Well That Ends Well (an early Ibsenite heroine) captures Bertram. But the mature cases all illustrate the Shakespearian law. The one apparent exception, Petruchio, is not a real one: he is most carefully characterized as a purely commercial matrimonial adventurer. Once he is assured that Katharine has money, he undertakes to marry her before he has seen her. In real life we find not only Petruchios, but Mantalinis and Dobbins who pursue women with appeals to their pity or jealousy or vanity, or cling to them in a romantically infatuated way. Such effeminates do not count in the world scheme: even Bunsby dropping like a fascinated bird into the jaws of Mrs. MacStinger is by comparison a true tragic object of pity and terror. I find in my own plays that Woman, projecting herself dramatically by my hands (a process over which I assure you I have no more real control than I have over my wife), behaves just as Woman did in the plays of Shakespear.

And so your Don Juan has come to birth as a stage projection of the tragi-comic love chase of the man by the woman; and my Don Juan is the quarry instead of the huntsman. Yet he is a true Don Juan, with a sense of reality that disables convention, defying to the last the fate which finally overtakes him. The woman's need of him to enable her to carry on Nature's most urgent work, does not prevail against him until his resistance gathers her energy to a climax at which she dares to throw away her customary exploitations of the conventional affectionate and dutiful poses, and claim him by natural right for a purpose that far transcends their mortal personal purposes.

Among the friends to whom I have read this play in manuscript are some of our own sex who are shocked at the "unscrupulousness," meaning the total disregard of masculine fastidiousness, with which the woman pursues her purpose. It does not occur to them that if women were as fastidious as men, morally or physically, there would be an end of the race. Is there anything meaner than to throw necessary work upon other people and then disparage it as unworthy and indelicate. We laugh at the haughty American nation because it makes the Negro clean its boots and then proves the moral and physical inferiority of the Negro by the fact that he is a shoeblack; but we ourselves throw the whole drudgery of creation on one sex, and then imply that no female of any womanliness or delicacy would initiate any effort in that direction. There

are no limits to male hypocrisy in this matter. No doubt there
are moments when man's sexual immunities are made acutely
humiliating to him. When the terrible moment of birth arrives,
its supreme importance and its superhuman effort and peril,
in which the father has no part, dwarf him into the meanest
insignificance: he slinks out of the way of the humblest petticoat, happy if he be poor enough to be pushed out of the
house to outface his ignominy by drunken rejoicings. But
when the crisis is over he takes his revenge, swaggering as
the breadwinner, and speaking of Woman's "sphere" with
condescension, even with chivalry, as if the kitchen and the
nursery were less important than the office in the city. When
his swagger is exhausted he drivels into erotic poetry or sentimental uxoriousness; and the Tennysonian King Arthur posing
at Guinevere becomes Don Quixote grovelling before Dul-
cinea. You must admit that here Nature beats Comedy out of
the field: the wildest hominist or feminist farce is insipid after
the most commonplace "slice of life." The pretence that women
do not take the initiative is part of the farce. Why, the whole
world is strewn with snares, traps, gins and pitfalls for the
capture of men by women. Give women the vote, and in five
years there will be a crushing tax on bachelors. Men, on the
other hand, attach penalties to marriage, depriving women of
property, of the franchise, of the free use of their limbs, of
that ancient symbol of immortality, the right to make oneself
at home in the house of God by taking off the hat, of everything that he can force Woman to dispense with without compelling himself to dispense with her. All in vain. Woman must
marry because the race must perish without her travail: if the
risk of death and the certainty of pain, danger and unutterable
discomforts cannot deter her, slavery and swaddled ankles
will not. And yet we assume that the force that carries women
through all these perils and hardships stops abashed before
the primnesses of our behavior for young ladies. It is assumed
that the woman must wait, motionless, until she is wooed. Nay,
she often does wait motionless. That is how the spider waits
for the fly. But the spider spins her web. And if the fly, like
my hero, shews a strength that promises to extricate him, how
swiftly does she abandon her pretence of passiveness, and
openly fling coil after coil about him until he is secured for
ever!

If the really impressive books and other art-works of the

world were produced by ordinary men, they would express more fear of women's pursuit than love of their illusory beauty. But ordinary men cannot produce really impressive art-works. Those who can are men of genius: that is, men selected by Nature to carry on the work of building up an intellectual consciousness of her own instinctive purpose. Accordingly, we observe in the man of genius all the unscrupulousness and all the "self-sacrifice" (the two things are the same) of Woman. He will risk the stake and the cross; starve, when necessary, in a garret all his life; study women and live on their work and care as Darwin studied worms and lived upon sheep; work his nerves into rags without payment, a sublime altruist in his disregard of himself, an atrocious egotist in his disregard of others. Here Woman meets a purpose as impersonal, as irresistible as her own; and the clash is sometimes tragic. When it is complicated by the genius being a woman, then the game is one for a king of critics: your George Sand becomes a mother to gain experience for the novelist and to develop her, and gobbles up men of genius, Chopins, Mussets and the like, as mere hors d'œuvres.

I state the extreme case, of course; but what is true of the great man who incarnates the philosophic consciousness of Life and the woman who incarnates its fecundity, is true in some degree of all geniuses and all women. Hence it is that the world's books get written, its pictures painted, its statues modelled, its symphonies composed, by people who are free of the otherwise universal dominion of the tyranny of sex. Which leads us to the conclusion, astonishing to the vulgar, that art, instead of being before all things the expression of the normal sexual situation, is really the only department in which sex is a superseded and secondary power, with its consciousness so confused and its purpose so perverted, that its ideas are mere fantasy to common men. Whether the artist becomes poet or philosopher, moralist or founder of a religion, his sexual doctrine is nothing but a barren special pleading for pleasure, excitement, and knowledge when he is young, and for contemplative tranquillity when he is old and satiated. Romance and Asceticism, Amorism and Puritanism are equally unreal in the great Philistine world. The world shewn us in books, whether the books be confessed epics or professed gospels, or in codes, or in political orations, or in philosophic systems, is not the main world at all: it is only the self-

consciousness of certain abnormal people who have the specific
artistic talent and temperament. A serious matter this for you
and me, because the man whose consciousness does not cor-
respond to that of the majority is a madman; and the old
habit of worshipping madmen is giving way to the new habit
of locking them up. And since what we call education and
culture is for the most part nothing but the substitution of
reading for experience, of literature for life, of the obsolete
fictitious for the contemporary real, education, as you no doubt
observed at Oxford, destroys, by supplantation, every mind
that is not strong enough to see through the imposture and to
use the great Masters of Arts as what they really are and no
more: that is, patentees of highly questionable methods of
thinking, and manufacturers of highly questionable, and for
the majority but half valid representations of life. The schoolboy who uses his Homer to throw at his fellow's head makes
perhaps the safest and most rational use of him; and I observe
with reassurance that you occasionally do the same, in your
prime, with your Aristotle.

Fortunately for us, whose minds have been so overwhelm-
ingly sophisticated by literature, what produces all these
treatises and poems and scriptures of one sort or another is
the struggle of Life to become divinely conscious of itself
instead of blindly stumbling hither and thither in the line of
least resistance. Hence there is a driving towards truth in all
books on matters where the writer, though exceptionally
gifted, is normally constituted, and has no private axe to
grind. Copernicus had no motive for misleading his fellowmen
as to the place of the sun in the solar system: he looked for it
as honestly as a shepherd seeks his path in a mist. But Copernicus would not have written love stories scientifically. When
it comes to sex relations, the man of genius does not share the
common man's danger of capture, nor the woman of genius
the common woman's overwhelming specialization. And that
is why our scriptures and other art works, when they deal
with love, turn from honest attempts at science in physics
to romantic nonsense, erotic ecstasy, or the stern asceticism
of satiety ("the road of excess leads to the palace of wisdom"
said William Blake; for "you never know what is enough unless
you know what is more than enough").

There is a political aspect of this sex question which is
too big for my comedy, and too momentous to be passed

over without culpable frivolity. It is impossible to demonstrate
that the initiative in sex transactions remains with Woman,
and has been confirmed to her, so far, more and more by the
suppression of rapine and discouragement of importunity,
without being driven to very serious reflections on the fact
that this initiative is politically the most important of all the
initiatives, because our political experiment of democracy, the
last refuge of cheap misgovernment, will ruin us if our citizens
are ill bred.

When we two were born, this country was still dominated
by a selected class bred by political marriages. The commercial class had not then completed the first twenty-five
years of its new share of political power; and it was itself
selected by money qualification, and bred, if not by political
marriage, at least by a pretty rigorous class marriage. Aristocracy and plutocracy still furnish the figureheads of politics;
but they are now dependent on the votes of the promiscuously
bred masses. And this, if you please, at the very moment when
the political problem, having suddenly ceased to mean a very
limited and occasional interference, mostly by way of jobbing
public appointments, in the mismanagement of a tight but
parochial little island, with occasional meaningless prosecution of dynastic wars, has become the industrial reorganization
of Britain, the construction of a practically international Commonwealth, and the partition of the whole of Africa and perhaps the whole of Asia by the civilized Powers. Can you believe that the people whose conceptions of society and conduct,
whose power of attention and scope of interest, are measured
by the British theatre as you know it to-day, can either handle
this colossal task themselves, or understand and support the
sort of mind and character that is (at least comparatively)
capable of handling it? For remember: what our voters are
in the pit and gallery they are also in the polling booth. We
are all now under what Burke called "the hoofs of the swinish
multitude." Burke's language gave great offence because the
implied exceptions to its universal application made it a class
insult; and it certainly was not for the pot to call the kettle
black. The aristocracy he defended, in spite of the political
marriages by which it tried to secure breeding for itself, had
its mind undertrained by silly schoolmasters and governesses,
its character corrupted by gratuitous luxury, its self-respect
adulterated to complete spuriousness by flattery and flunkey-

ism. It is no better to-day and never will be any better: our very peasants have something morally hardier in them that culminates occasionally in a Bunyan, a Burns, or a Carlyle. But observe, this aristocracy, which was overpowered from 1832 to 1885 by the middle class, has come back to power by the votes of "the swinish multitude." Tom Paine has triumphed over Edmund Burke; and the swine are now courted electors. How many of their own class have these electors sent to parliament? Hardly a dozen out of 670, and these only under the persuasion of conspicuous personal qualifications and popular eloquence. The multitude thus pronounces judgment on its own units: it admits itself unfit to govern, and will vote only for a man morphologically and generically transfigured by palatial residence and equipage, by transcendent tailoring, by the glamor of aristocratic kinship. Well, we two know these transfigured persons, these college passmen, these well-groomed monocular Algys and Bobbies, these cricketers to whom age brings golf instead of wisdom, these plutocratic products of "the nail and sarspan business as he got his money by." Do you know whether to laugh or cry at the notion that they, poor devils! will drive a team of continents as they drive a four-in-hand; turn a jostling anarchy of casual trade and speculation into an ordered productivity; and federate our colonies into a world-Power of the first magnitude? Give these people the most perfect political constitution and the soundest political program that benevolent omniscience can devise for them, and they will interpret it into mere fashionable folly or canting charity as infallibly as a savage converts the philosophical theology of a Scotch missionary into crude African idolatry.

I do not know whether you have any illusions left on the subject of education, progress, and so forth. I have none. Any pamphleteer can shew the way to better things; but when there is no will there is no way. My nurse was fond of remarking that you cannot make a silk purse out of a sow's ear; and the more I see of the efforts of our churches and universities and literary sages to raise the mass above its own level, the more convinced I am that my nurse was right. Progress can do nothing but make the most of us all as we are, and that most would clearly not be enough even if those who are already raised out of the lowest abysses would allow the others a chance. The bubble of Heredity has been pricked: the certainty that acquirements are negligible as elements in practical heredity has demolished the hopes of the educationists as well as the terrors of the degeneracy mongers; and we know now that there is no hereditary "governing class" any more than a hereditary hooliganism. We must either breed political capacity or be ruined by Democracy, which was forced on us by the failure of the older alternatives. Yet if Despotism failed only for want of a capable benevolent despot, what chance has Democracy, which requires a whole population of capable voters: that is, of political critics who, if they cannot govern in person for lack of spare energy or specific talent for administration, can at least recognize and appreciate capacity and benevolence in others, and so govern through capably benevolent representatives? Where are such voters to be found to-day? Nowhere. Promiscuous breeding has produced a weakness of character that is too timid to face the full stringency of a thoroughly competitive struggle for existence and too lazy and petty to organize the commonwealth co-operatively. Being cowards, we defeat natural selection under cover of philanthropy: being sluggards, we neglect artificial selection under cover of delicacy and morality.

Yet we must get an electorate of capable critics or collapse as Rome and Egypt collapsed. At this moment the Roman decadent phase of *panem et circenses* is being inaugurated under our eyes. Our newspapers and melodramas are blustering about our imperial destiny; but our eyes and hearts turn eagerly to the American millionaire. As his hand goes down to his pocket, our fingers go up to the brims of our hats by instinct. Our ideal prosperity is not the prosperity of the industrial north, but the prosperity of the Isle of Wight, of Folkestone and Ramsgate, of Nice and Monte Carlo. That is the only prosperity you see on the stage, where the workers are all footmen, parlormaids, comic lodging-letters and fashionable professional men, whilst the heroes and heroines are miraculously provided with unlimited dividends, and eat gratuitously, like the knights in Don Quixote's books of chivalry. The city papers prate of the competition of Bombay with Manchester and the like. The real competition is the competition of Regent Street with the Rue de Rivoli, of Brighton and the south coast with the Riviera, for the spending money of the American Trusts. What is all this growing love of pageantry, this effusive loyalty, this officious rising and uncovering at a wave from a flag or a blast from a brass band? Imperialism? Not a bit of it. Obsequiousness, servility, cupidity roused by the prevailing smell of money. When Mr. Carnegie rattled his millions in his pockets all England became one rapacious cringe. Only, when Rhodes (who had probably been reading my Socialism for Millionaires) left word that no idler was to inherit his estate, the bent backs straightened mistrustfully for a moment. Could it be that the Diamond King was no gentleman after all? However, it was easy to ignore a rich man's solecism. The ungentlemanly clause was not mentioned again; and the backs soon bowed themselves back into their natural shape.

But I hear you asking me in alarm whether I have actually put all this tub thumping into a Don Juan comedy. I have not. I have only made my Don Juan a political pamphleteer, and given you his pamphlet in full by way of appendix. You will find it at the end of the book. I am sorry to say that it is a common practice with romancers to announce their hero as a man of extraordinary genius, and to leave his works entirely to the reader's imagination; so that at the end of the book you whisper to yourself ruefully that but for the author's solemn preliminary assurance you should hardly have given the gentleman credit for ordinary good sense. You cannot accuse me of this pitiable barrenness, this feeble evasion. I not only tell you that my hero wrote a revolutionists' handbook: I give you the handbook at full length for your edification if you care to read it. And in that handbook you will find the politics of the sex question as I conceive Don Juan's descendant to understand them. Not that I disclaim the fullest responsibility for his opinions and for those of all my characters, pleasant and unpleasant. They are all right from their several points of view; and their points of view are, for the dramatic moment, mine also. This may puzzle the people who believe that there is such a thing as an absolutely right point of view, usually their own. It may seem to them that nobody who doubts this can be in a state of grace. However that may be, it is certainly true that nobody who agrees with them can possibly be a dramatist, or indeed anything else that turns upon a knowledge of mankind. Hence it has been pointed out that Shakespear had no conscience. Neither have I, in that sense.

You may, however, remind me that this digression of mine

into politics was preceded by a very convincing demonstration that the artist never catches the point of view of the common man on the question of sex, because he is not in the same predicament. I first prove that anything I write on the relation of the sexes is sure to be misleading; and then I proceed to write a Don Juan play. Well, if you insist on asking me why I behave in this absurd way, I can only reply that you asked me to, and that in any case my treatment of the subject may be valid for the artist, amusing to the amateur, and at least intelligible and therefore possibly suggestive to the Philistine. Every man who records his illusions is providing data for the genuinely scientific psychology which the world still waits for. I plank down my view of the existing relations of men to women in the most highly civilized society for what it is worth. It is a view like any other view and no more, neither true nor false, but, I hope, a way of looking at the subject which throws into the familiar order of cause and effect a sufficient body of fact and experience to be interesting to you, if not to the playgoing public of London. I have certainly shewn little consideration for that public in this enterprise; but I know that it has the friendliest disposition towards you and me as far as it has any consciousness of our existence, and quite understands that what I write for you must pass at a considerable height over its simple romantic head. It will take my books as read and my genius for granted, trusting me to put forth work of such quality as shall bear out its verdict. So we may disport ourselves on our own plane to the top of our bent; and if any gentleman points out that neither this epistle dedicatory nor the dream of Don Juan in the third act of the ensuing comedy is suitable for immediate production at a popular theatre we need not contradict him. Napoleon provided Talma with a pit of kings, with what effect on Talma's acting is not recorded. As for me, what I have always wanted is a pit of philosophers; and this is a play for such a pit.

I should make formal acknowledgment to the authors whom I have pillaged in the following pages if I could recollect them all. The theft of the brigand-poetaster from Sir Arthur Conan Doyle is deliberate; and the metamorphosis of Leporello into Enry Straker, motor engineer and New Man, is an intentional dramatic sketch for the contemporary embryo of Mr. H. G. Wells's anticipation of the efficient engineering class which will, he hopes, finally sweep the jabberers out of the way of civilization. Mr. Barrie has also, whilst I am correcting my proofs, delighted London with a servant who knows more than his masters. The conception of Mendoza Limited I trace back to a certain West Indian colonial secretary, who, at a period when he and I and Mr. Sidney Webb were sowing our political wild oats as a sort of Fabian Three Musketeers, without any prevision of the surprising respectability of the crop that followed, recommended Webb, the encyclopedic and inexhaustible, to form himself into a company for the benefit of the shareholders. Octavius I take over unaltered from Mozart; and I hereby authorize any actor who impersonates him, to sing "Dalla sua pace" (if he can) at any convenient moment during the representation. Ann was suggested to me by the fifteenth-century Dutch morality called Everyman, which Mr. William Poel has lately resuscitated so triumphantly. I trust he will work that vein further, and recognize that Elizabethan Renascence fustian is no more bearable after medieval poesy than Scribe after Ibsen. As I sat watching Everyman at the Charterhouse, I said to myself Why not Everywoman? Ann was the result: every woman is not Ann; but Ann is Everywoman.

That the author of Everyman was no mere artist, but an artist-philosopher, and that the artist-philosophers are the only sort of artists I take quite seriously, will be no news to you. Even Plato and Boswell, as the dramatists who invented Socrates and Dr. Johnson, impress me more deeply than the romantic playwrights. Ever since, as a boy, I first breathed the air of the transcendental regions at a performance of Mozart's Zauberflöte, I have been proof against the garish splendors and alcoholic excitements of the ordinary stage combinations of Tappertitian romance with the police intelligence. Bunyan, Blake, Hogarth and Turner (these four apart and above all the English classics), Goethe, Shelley, Schopenhaur, Wagner, Ibsen, Morris, Tolstoy, and Nietzsche are among the writers whose peculiar sense of the world I recognize as more or less akin to my own. Mark the word peculiar. I read Dickens and Shakespear without shame or stint; but their pregnant observations and demonstrations of life are not coordinated into any philosophy or religion: on the contrary, Dickens's sentimental assumptions are violently contradicted by his observations; and Shakespear's pessimism is only his

wounded humanity. Both have the specific genius of the
fictionist and the common sympathies of human feeling and
thought in pre-eminent degree. They are often saner and
shrewder than the philosophers just as Sancho-Panza was
often saner and shrewder than Don Quixote. They clear away
vast masses of oppressive gravity by their sense of the ridiculous, which is at bottom a combination of sound moral judgment with lighthearted good humor. But they are concerned
with the diversities of the world instead of with its unities:
they are so irreligious that they exploit popular religion for
professional purposes without delicacy or scruple (for example, Sydney Carton and the ghost in Hamlet!): they are
anarchical, and cannot balance their exposures of Angelo and
Dogberry, Sir Leicester Dedlock and Mr. Tite Barnacle, with
any portrait of a prophet or a worthy leader: they have no
constructive ideas: they regard those who have them as dangerous fanatics: in all their fictions there is no leading thought
or inspiration for which any man could conceivably risk the
spoiling of his hat in a shower, much less his life. Both are
alike forced to borrow motives for the more strenuous actions of their personages from the common stockpot of melodramatic plots; so that Hamlet has to be stimulated by the
prejudices of a policeman and Macbeth by the cupidities of a
bushranger. Dickens, without the excuse of having to manu-
facture motives for Hamlets and Macbeths, superfluously
punts his crew down the stream of his monthly parts by
mechanical devices which I leave you to describe, my own
memory being quite baffled by the simplest question as to
Monks in Oliver Twist, or the long lost parentage of Smike,
or the relations between the Dorrit and Clennam families so
inopportunely discovered by Monsieur Rigaud Blandois. The
truth is, the world was to Shakespear a great "stage of fools"
on which he was utterly bewildered. He could see no sort of
sense in living at all; and Dickens saved himself from the
despair of the dream in The Chimes by taking the world for
granted and busying himself with its details. Neither of them
could do anything with a serious positive character: they
could place a human figure before you with perfect verisimili-
tude; but when the moment came for making it live and
move, they found, unless it made them laugh, that they had
a puppet on their hands, and had to invent some artificial
external stimulus to make it work. This is what is the matter

with Hamlet all through: he has no will except in his bursts
of temper. Foolish Bardolaters make a virtue of this after
their fashion: they declare that the play is the tragedy of
irresolution; but all Shakespear's projections of the deepest
humanity he knew have the same defect: their characters and
manners are lifelike; but their actions are forced on them from
without, and the external force is grotesquely inappropriate
except when it is quite conventional, as in the case of Henry
V. Falstaff is more vivid than any of these serious reflective
characters, because he is self-acting: his motives are his own
appetites and instincts and humors. Richard III, too, is delightful as the whimsical comedian who stops a funeral to
make love to the corpse's widow; but when, in the next act,
he is replaced by a stage villain who smothers babies and
offs with people's heads, we are revolted at the imposture and
repudiate the changeling. Faulconbridge, Coriolanus, Leontes
are admirable descriptions of instinctive temperaments: indeed
the play of Coriolanus is the greatest of Shakespear's comedies; but description is not philosophy; and comedy neither
compromises the author nor reveals him. He must be judged
by those characters into which he puts what he knows of
himself, his Hamlets and Macbeths and Lears and Prosperos.
If these characters are agonizing in a void about factitious
melodramatic murders and revenges and the like, whilst the
comic characters walk with their feet on solid ground, vivid
and amusing, you know that the author has much to shew
and nothing to teach. The comparison between Falstaff and
Prospero is like the comparison between Micawber and David
Copperfield. At the end of the book you know Micawber,
whereas you only know what has happened to David, and are
not interested enough in him to wonder what his politics or
religion might be if anything so stupendous as a religious or
political idea, or a general idea of any sort, were to occur
to him. He is tolerable as a child; but he never becomes a
man, and might be left out of his own biography altogether
but for his usefulness as a stage confidant, a Horatio or
"Charles his friend"—what they call on the stage a feeder.

Now you cannot say this of the works of the artist-philosophers. You cannot say it, for instance, of The Pilgrim's Progress. Put your Shakespearian hero and coward, Henry V and
Pistol or Parolles, beside Mr. Valiant and Mr. Fearing, and
you have a sudden revelation of the abyss that lies between

the fashionable author who could see nothing in the world but personal aims and the tragedy of their disappointment or the comedy of their incongruity, and the field preacher who achieved virtue and courage by identifying himself with the purpose of the world as he understood it. The contrast is enormous: Bunyan's coward stirs your blood more than Shakespear's hero, who actually leaves you cold and secretly hostile. You suddenly see that Shakespear, with all his flashes and divinations, never understood virtue and courage, never conceived how any man who was not a fool could, like Bunyan's hero, look back from the brink of the river of death over the strife and labor of his pilgrimage, and say "yet do I not repent me"; or, with the panache of a millionaire, bequeath "my sword to him that shall succeed me in my pilgrimage, and my courage and skill to him that can get it." This is the true joy in life, the being used for a purpose recognized by yourself as a mighty one; the being thoroughly worn out before you are thrown on the scrap heap; the being a force of Nature instead of a feverish selfish little clod of ailments and grievances complaining that the world will not devote itself to making you happy. And also the only real tragedy in life is the being used by personally minded men for purposes which you recognize to be base. All the rest is at worst mere misfortune or mortality: this alone is misery, slavery, hell on earth; and the revolt against it is the only force that offers a man's work to the poor artist, whom our personally minded rich people would so willingly employ as pander, buffoon, beauty monger, sentimentalizer and the like.

It may seem a long step from Bunyan to Nietzsche; but the difference between their conclusions is purely formal. Bunyan's perception that righteousness is filthy rags, his scorn for Mr. Legality in the village of Morality, his defiance of the Church as the supplanter of religion, his insistence on courage as the virtue of virtues, his estimate of the career of the conventionally respectable and sensible Worldly Wiseman as no better at bottom than the life and death of Mr. Badman: all this, expressed by Bunyan in the terms of a tinker's theology, is what Nietzsche has expressed in terms of post-Darwinian, post-Schopenhaurian philosophy; Wagner in terms of polytheistic mythology; and Ibsen in terms of mid-XIX-century Parisian dramaturgy. Nothing is new in these matters except their novelties: for instance, it is a novelty to call Justification by Faith "Wille," and Justification by Works "Vorstellung." The sole use of the novelty is that you and I buy and read Schopenhaur's treatise on Will and Representation when we should not dream of buying a set of sermons on Faith versus Works. At bottom the controversy is the same, and the dramatic results are the same. Bunyan makes no attempt to present his pilgrims as more sensible or better conducted than Mr. Worldly Wiseman. Mr. W. W.'s worst enemies, as Mr. Embezzler, Mr. Never-go-to-Church-on-Sunday, Mr. Bad Form, Mr. Murderer, Mr. Burglar, Mr. Co-respondent, Mr. Blackmailer, Mr. Cad, Mr. Drunkard, Mr. Labor Agitator and so forth, can read the Pilgrim's Progress without finding a word said against them; whereas the respectable people who snub them and put them in prison, such as Mr. W. W. himself and his young friend Civility; Formalist and Hypocrisy; Wildhead, Inconsiderate, and Pragmatick (who were clearly young university men of good family and high feeding); that brisk lad Ignorance, Talkative, By-Ends of Fairspeech and his mother-in-law Lady Feigning, and other reputable gentlemen and citizens, catch it very severely. Even Little Faith, though he gets to heaven at last, is given to understand that it served him right to be mobbed by the brothers Faint Heart, Mistrust, and Guilt, all three recognized members of respectable society and veritable pillars of the law. The whole allegory is a consistent attack on morality and respectability, without a word that one can remember against vice and crime. Exactly what is complained of in Nietzsche and Ibsen, is it not? And also exactly what would be complained of in all the literature which is great enough and old enough to have attained canonical rank, officially or unofficially, were it not that books are admitted to the canon by a compact which confesses their greatness in consideration of abrogating their meaning; so that the reverend rector can agree with the prophet Micah as to his inspired style without being committed to any complicity in Micah's furiously Radical opinions. Why, even I, as I force myself, pen in hand, into recognition and civility, find all the force of my onslaught destroyed by a simple policy of nonresistance. In vain do I redouble the violence of the language in which I proclaim my heterodoxies. I rail at the theistic credulity of Voltaire, the amoristic superstition of Shelley, the revival of tribal soothsaying and idolatrous rites which Huxley called Science and mistook for an advance on the Pentateuch, no less than at the welter of ecclesiastical and professional humbug which saves the face of the stupid system of violence and robbery which we call Law and Industry. Even atheists reproach me with infidelity and anarchists with nihilism because I cannot endure their moral tirades. And yet, instead of exclaiming "Send this inconceivable Satanist to the stake," the respectable newspapers pith me by announcing "another book by this brilliant and thoughtful writer." And the ordinary citizen, knowing that an author who is well spoken of by a respectable newspaper must be all right, reads me, as he reads Micah, with undisturbed edification from his own point of view. It is narrated that in the eighteen-seventies an old lady, a very devout Methodist, moved from Colchester to a house in the neighborhood of the City Road, in London, where, mistaking the Hall of Science for a chapel, she sat at the feet of Charles Bradlaugh for many years, entranced by his eloquence, without questioning his orthodoxy or moulting a feather of her faith. I fear I shall be defrauded of my just martyrdom in the same way.

However, I am digressing, as a man with a grievance always does. And after all, the main thing in determining the artistic quality of a book is not the opinions it propagates, but the fact that the writer has opinions. The old lady from Colchester was right to sun her simple soul in the energetic radiance of Bradlaugh's genuine beliefs and disbeliefs rather than in the chill of such mere painting of light and heat as elocution and convention can achieve. My contempt for belles lettres, and for amateurs who become the heroes of the fanciers of literary virtuosity, is not founded on any illusion of mind as to the permanence of those forms of thought (call them opinions) by which I strive to communicate my bent to my fellows. To younger men they are already outmoded; for though they have no more lost their logic than an eighteenth-century pastel has lost its drawing or its color, yet, like the pastel, they grow indefinably shabby, and will grow shabbier until they cease to count at all, when my books will either perish, or, if the world is still poor enough to want them, will have to stand, with Bunyan's, by quite amorphous qualities of temper and energy. With this conviction I cannot be a bellettrist. No doubt I must recognize, as even the Ancient Mariner did, that I must tell my story en-

tertainingly if I am to hold the wedding guest spellbound
in spite of the siren sounds of the loud bassoon. But "for
art's sake" alone I would not face the toil of writing a single
sentence. I know that there are men who, having nothing to
say and nothing to write, are nevertheless so in love with
oratory and with literature that they keep desperately repeating as much as they can understand of what others have said
or written aforetime. I know that the leisurely tricks which
their want of conviction leaves them free to play with the
diluted and misapprehended message supply them with a
pleasant parlor game which they call style. I can pity their
dotage and even sympathize with their fancy. But a true
original style is never achieved for its own sake: a man may
pay from a shilling to a guinea, according to his means, to see,
hear, or read another man's act of genius; but he will not
pay with his whole life and soul to become a mere virtuoso
in literature, exhibiting an accomplishment which will not
even make money for him, like fiddle playing. Effectiveness
of assertion is the Alpha and Omega of style. He who has
nothing to assert has no style and can have none: he who
has something to assert will go as far in power of style as its
momentousness and his conviction will carry him. Disprove
his assertion after it is made, yet its style remains. Darwin
has no more destroyed the style of Job nor of Handel than
Martin Luther destroyed the style of Giotto. All the asser-
tions get disproved sooner or later; and so we find the world
full of a magnificent débris of artistic fossils, with the matter-
of-fact credibility gone clean out of them, but the form still
splendid. And that is why the old masters play the deuce
with our mere susceptibles. Your Royal Academician thinks
he can get the style of Giotto without Giotto's beliefs, and correct his perspective into the bargain. Your man of letters
thinks he can get Bunyan's or Shakespear's style without
Bunyan's conviction or Shakespear's apprehension, especially
if he takes care not to split his infinitives. And so with your
Doctors of Music, who, with their collections of discords
duly prepared and resolved or retarded or anticipated in
the manner of the great composers, think they can learn the
art of Palestrina from Cherubini's treatise. All this academic
art is far worse than the trade in sham antique furniture; for
the man who sells me an oaken chest which he swears was
made in the XIII century, though as a matter of fact he made

it himself only yesterday, at least does not pretend that there are any modern ideas in it, whereas your academic copier of fossils offers them to you as the latest outpouring of the human spirit, and, worst of all, kidnaps young people as pupils and persuades them that his limitations are rules, his observances dexterities, his timidities good taste, and his emptinesses purities. And when he declares that art should not be didactic, all the people who have nothing to teach and all the people who don't want to learn agree with him emphatically.

I pride myself on not being one of these susceptibles. If you study the electric light with which I supply you in that Bumbledonian public capacity of mine over which you make merry from time to time, you will find that your house contains a great quantity of highly susceptible copper wire which gorges itself with electricity and gives you no light whatever. But here and there occurs a scrap of intensely insusceptible, intensely resistant material; and that stubborn scrap grapples with the current and will not let it through until it has made itself useful to you as those two vital qualities of literature, light and heat. Now if I am to be no mere copper wire amateur but a luminous author, I must also be a most intensely refractory person, liable to go out and to go wrong at inconvenient moments, and with incendiary possibilities. These are the faults of my qualities; and I assure you that I sometimes dislike myself so much that when some irritable reviewer chances at that moment to pitch into me with zest, I feel unspeakably relieved and obliged. But I never dream of reforming, knowing that I must take myself as I am and get what work I can out of myself. All this you will understand; for there is community of material between us: we are both critics of life as well as of art; and you have perhaps said to yourself when I have passed your windows "There, but for the grace of God, go I." An awful and chastening reflection, which shall be the closing cadence of this immoderately long letter from yours faithfully,

G. BERNARD SHAW.

WOKING, 1903.

ACT I

Roebuck Ramsden is in his study, opening the morning's letters. The study, handsomely and solidly furnished, proclaims the man of means. Not a speck of dust is visible: it is clear that there are at least two housemaids and a parlormaid downstairs, and a housekeeper upstairs who does not let them spare elbow-grease. Even the top of Roebuck's head is polished: on a sunshiny day he could heliograph his orders to distant camps by merely nodding. In no other respect, however, does he suggest the military man. It is in active civil life that men get his broad air of importance, his dignified expectation of deference, his determinate mouth disarmed and refined since the hour of his success by the withdrawal of opposition and the concession of comfort and precedence and power. He is more than a highly respectable man: he is marked out as a president of highly respectable men, a chairman among directors, an alderman among councillors, a mayor among aldermen. Four tufts of iron-grey hair, which will soon be as white as isinglass, and are in other respects not at all unlike it, grow in two symmetrical pairs above his ears and at the angles of his spreading jaws. He wears a black frock coat, a white waistcoat (it is bright spring weather), and trousers, neither black nor perceptibly blue, of one of those indefinitely mixed hues which the modern clothier has produced to harmonize with the religions of respectable men. He has not been out of doors yet to-day; so he still wears his slippers, his boots being ready for him on the hearthrug. Surmising that he has no valet, and seeing that he has no secretary with a shorthand notebook and a typewriter, one meditates on how little our great burgess domesticity has been disturbed by new fashions and methods, or by the enterprise of the railway and hotel companies which sell you a Saturday to Monday of life at Folkestone as a real gentleman for two guineas, first-class fares both ways included.

How old is Roebuck? The question is important on the

*threshold of a drama of ideas; for under such circumstances
everything depends on whether his adolescence belonged to
the sixties or to the eighties. He was born, as a matter of fact,
in 1839, and was a Unitarian and Free Trader from his boy-
hood, and an Evolutionist from the publication of the Origin
of Species. Consequently he has always classed himself as an
advanced thinker and fearlessly outspoken reformer.*

*Sitting at his writing table, he has on his right the windows
giving on Portland Place. Through these, as through a proscen-
ium, the curious spectator may contemplate his profile as well
as the blinds will permit. On his left is the inner wall, with a
stately bookcase, and the door not quite in the middle, but
somewhat farther from him. Against the wall opposite him are
two busts on pillars: one, to his left, of John Bright; the other,
to his right, of Mr. Herbert Spencer. Between them hang an
engraved portrait of Richard Cobden; enlarged photographs
of Martineau, Huxley, and George Eliot; autotypes of alle-
gories by Mr. G. F. Watts (for Roebuck believes in the fine
arts with all the earnestness of a man who does not understand them), and an impression of Dupont's engraving of
Delaroche's Beaux Arts hemicycle, representing the great men
of all ages. On the wall behind him, above the mantleshelf,
is a family portrait of impenetrable obscurity.*

*A chair stands near the writing table for the convenience
of business visitors. Two other chairs are against the wall between the busts.*

*A parlormaid enters with a visitor's card. Roebuck takes
it, and nods, pleased. Evidently a welcome caller.*

RAMSDEN. Shew him up.

The parlormaid goes out and returns with the visitor.

THE MAID. Mr. Robinson.

*Mr. Robinson is really an uncommonly nice looking young
fellow. He must, one thinks, be the jeune premier; for it is
not in reason to suppose that a second such attractive male
figure should appear in one story. The slim, shapely frame,
the elegant suit of new mourning, the small head and regular
features, the pretty little moustache, the frank clear eyes, the
wholesome bloom on the youthful complexion, the well
brushed glossy hair, not curly, but of fine texture and good
dark color, the arch of good nature in the eyebrows, the erect
forehead and neatly pointed chin, all announce the man who*

*will love and suffer later on. And that he will not do so
without sympathy is guaranteed by an engaging sincerity and
eager modest serviceableness which stamp him as a man of
amiable nature. The moment he appears, Ramsden's face ex-
pands into fatherly liking and welcome, an expression which
drops into one of decorous grief as the young man approaches
him with sorrow in his face as well as in his black clothes.
Ramsden seems to know the nature of the bereavement. As
the visitor advances silently to the writing table, the old man
rises and shakes his hand across it without a word: a long,
affectionate shake which tells the story of a recent sorrow
common to both.*

RAMSDEN (*concluding the handshake and cheering up*).
Well, well, Octavius, it's the common lot. We must all face it
some day. Sit down.

*Octavius takes the visitor's chair. Ramsden replaces him-
self in his own.*

OCTAVIUS. Yes: we must face it, Mr. Ramsden. But I
owed him a great deal. He did everything for me that my
father could have done if he had lived.

RAMSDEN. He had no son of his own, you see.

OCTAVIUS. But he had daughters; and yet he was as good
to my sister as to me. And his death was so sudden! I always
intended to thank him—to let him know that I had not taken
all his care of me as a matter of course, as any boy takes his
father's care. But I waited for an opportunity; and now he is
dead—dropped without a moment's warning. He will never
know what I felt. (*He takes out his handkerchief and cries
unaffectedly.*)

RAMSDEN. How do we know that, Octavius? He may know
it: we cannot tell. Come! don't grieve. (*Octavius masters
himself and puts up his handkerchief.*) That's right. Now
let me tell you something to console you. The last time I saw
him—it was in this very room—he said to me: "Tavy is a
generous lad and the soul of honor; and when I see how little
consideration other men get from their sons, I realize how
much better than a son he's been to me." There! Doesn't that
do you good?

OCTAVIUS. Mr. Ramsden: he used to say to me that he
had met only one man in the world who was the soul of
honor, and that was Roebuck Ramsden.

RAMSDEN. Oh, that was his partiality: we were very old

friends, you know. But there was something else he used to say about you. I wonder whether I ought to tell you or not!

OCTAVIUS. You know best.

RAMSDEN. It was something about his daughter.

OCTAVIUS (*eagerly*). About Ann! Oh, do tell me that, Mr. Ramsden.

RAMSDEN. Well, he said he was glad, after all, you were not his son, because he thought that someday Annie and you—(*Octavius blushes vividly.*) Well, perhaps I shouldn't have told you. But he was in earnest.

OCTAVIUS. Oh, if only I thought I had a chance! You know, Mr. Ramsden, I don't care about money or about what people call position; and I can't bring myself to take an interest in the business of struggling for them. Well, Ann has a most exquisite nature; but she is so accustomed to be in the thick of that sort of thing that she thinks a man's character incomplete if he is not ambitious. She knows that if she married me she would have to reason herself out of being ashamed of me for not being a big success of some kind.

RAMSDEN (*getting up and planting himself with his back to the fireplace*). Nonsense, my boy, nonsense! You're too modest. What does she know about the real value of men at her age? (*More seriously.*) Besides, she's a wonderfully dutiful girl. Her father's wish would be sacred to her. Do you know that since she grew up to years of discretion, I don't believe she has ever once given her own wish as a reason for doing anything or not doing it. It's always "Father wishes me to," or "Mother wouldn't like it." It's really almost a fault in her. I have often told her she must learn to think for herself.

OCTAVIUS (*shaking his head*). I couldn't ask her to marry me because her father wished it, Mr. Ramsden.

RAMSDEN. Well, perhaps not. No: of course not. I see that. No: you certainly couldn't. But when you win her on your own merits, it will be a great happiness to her to fulfil her father's desire as well as her own. Eh? Come! you'll ask her, won't you?

OCTAVIUS (*with sad gaiety*). At all events I promise you I shall never ask anyone else.

RAMSDEN. Oh, you shan't need to. She'll accept you, my boy—although (*here he suddenly becomes very serious indeed*) you have one great drawback.

OCTAVIUS (*anxiously*). What drawback is that, Mr. Ramsden? I should rather say which of my many drawbacks?

RAMSDEN. I'll tell you, Octavius. (*He takes from the table a book bound in red cloth.*) I have in my hand a copy of the most infamous, the most scandalous, the most michievous, the most blackguardly book that ever escaped burning at the hands of the common hangman. I have not read it: I would not soil my mind with such filth; but I have read what the papers say of it. The title is quite enough for me. (*He reads it.*) The Revolutionist's Handbook and Pocket Companion. By John Tanner, M.I.R.C., Member of the Idle Rich Class.

OCTAVIUS (*smiling*). But Jack—

RAMSDEN (*testily*). For goodness' sake, don't call him Jack under my roof. (*He throws the book violently down on the table. Then, somewhat relieved, he comes past the table to Octavius, and addresses him at close quarters with impressive gravity.*) Now, Octavius, I know that my dead friend was right when he said you were a generous lad. I know that this man was your schoolfellow, and that you feel bound to stand by him because there was a boyish friendship between you. But I ask you to consider the altered circumstances. You were treated as a son in my friend's house. You lived there; and your friends could not be turned from the door. This man Tanner was in and out there on your account almost from his childhood. He addresses Annie by her Christian name as freely as you do. Well, while her father was alive, that was her father's business, not mine. This man Tanner was only a boy to him: his opinions were something to be laughed at, like a man's hat on a child's head. But now Tanner is a grown man and Annie a grown woman. And her father is gone. We don't as yet know the exact terms of his will; but he often talked it over with me; and I have no more doubt than I have that you're sitting there that the will appoints me Annie's trustee and guardian. (*Forcibly.*) Now I tell you, once for all, I can't and I won't have Annie placed in such a position that she must, out of regard for you, suffer the intimacy of this fellow Tanner. It's not fair: it's not right: it's not kind. What are you going to do about it?

OCTAVIUS. But Ann herself has told Jack that whatever his opinions are, he will always be welcome because he knew her dear father.

RAMSDEN (*out of patience*). That girl's mad about her

duty to her parents. (*He starts off like a goaded ox in the direction of John Bright, in whose expression there is no sympathy for him. As he speaks he fumes down to Herbert Spencer, who receives him still more coldly.*) Excuse me, Octavius; but there are limits to social toleration. You know that I am not a bigoted or prejudiced man. You know that I am plain Roebuck Ramsden when other men who have done less have got handles to their names, because I have stood for equality and liberty of conscience while they were truckling to the Church and to the aristocracy. Whitefield and I lost chance after chance through our advanced opinions. But I draw the line at Anarchism and Free Love and that sort of thing. If I am to be Annie's guardian, she will have to learn that she has a duty to me. I won't have it: I will not have it. She must forbid John Tanner the house; and so must you.

The parlormaid returns.

OCTAVIUS. But—

RAMSDEN (*calling his attention to the servant*). Ssh! Well?

THE MAID. Mr. Tanner wishes to see you, sir.

RAMSDEN. Mr. Tanner!

OCTAVIUS. Jack!

RAMSDEN. How dare Mr. Tanner call on me! Say I cannot see him.

OCTAVIUS (*hurt*). I am sorry you are turning my friend from your door like that.

THE MAID (*calmly*). He's not at the door, sir. He's upstairs in the drawing room with Miss Ramsden. He came with Mrs. Whitefield and Miss Ann and Miss Robinson, sir.

Ramsden's feelings are beyond words.

OCTAVIUS (*grinning*). That's very like Jack, Mr. Ramsden. You must see him, even if it's only to turn him out.

RAMSDEN (*hammering out his words with suppressed fury*). Go upstairs and ask Mr. Tanner to be good enough to step down here. (*The parlormaid goes out; and Ramsden returns to the fireplace, as to a fortified position.*) I must say that of all the confounded pieces of impertinence—well, if these are Anarchist manners, I hope you like them. And Annie with him! Annie! A— (*He chokes.*)

OCTAVIUS. Yes: that's what surprises me. He's so desperately afraid of Ann. There must be something the matter.

Mr. John Tanner suddenly opens the door and enters. He is too young to be described simply as a big man with a beard.

But it is already plain that middle life will find him in that category. He has still some of the slimness of youth; but youthfulness is not the effect he aims at: his frock coat would befit a prime minister; and a certain high chested carriage of the shoulders, a lofty pose of the head, and the Olympian majesty with which a mane, or rather a huge wisp, of hazel colored hair is thrown back from an imposing brow, suggest Jupiter rather than Apollo. He is prodigiously fluent of speech, restless, excitable (mark the snorting nostril and the restless blue eye, just the thirty-secondth of an inch too wide open), possibly a little mad. He is carefully dressed, not from the vanity that cannot resist finery, but from a sense of the importance of everything he does which leads him to make as much of paying a call as other men do of getting married or laying a foundation stone. A sensitive, susceptible, exaggerative, earnest man: a megalomaniac, who would be lost without a sense of humor.

Just at present the sense of humor is in abeyance. To say that he is excited is nothing: all his moods are phases of excitement. He is now in the panic-stricken phase; and he walks straight up to Ramsden as if with the fixed intention of shooting him on his own hearthrug. But what he pulls from his breast pocket is not a pistol, but a foolscap document which he thrusts under the indignant nose of Ramsden as he exclaims—

TANNER. Ramsden: do you know what that is?

RAMSDEN (*loftily*). No, sir.

TANNER. It's a copy of Whitefield's will. Ann got it this morning.

RAMSDEN. When you say Ann, you mean, I presume, Miss Whitefield.

TANNER. I mean our Ann, your Ann, Tavy's Ann, and now, Heaven help me, my Ann!

OCTAVIUS (*rising, very pale*). What do you mean?

TANNER. Mean! (*He holds up the will.*) Do you know who is appointed Ann's guardian by this will?

RAMSDEN (*coolly*). I believe I am.

TANNER. You! You and I, man. I! I!! I!!! Both of us! (*He flings the will down on the writing table.*)

RAMSDEN. You! Impossible.

TANNER. It's only too hideously true. (*He throws himself into Octavius's chair.*) Ramsden: get me out of it somehow.

You don't know Ann as well as I do. She'll commit every crime a respectable woman can; and she'll justify everyone of them by saying that it was the wish of her guardians. She'll put everything on us; and we shall have no more control over her than a couple of mice over a cat.

OCTAVIUS. Jack: I wish you wouldn't talk like that about Ann.

TANNER. This chap's in love with her: that's another complication. Well, she'll either jilt him and say I didn't approve of him, or marry him and say you ordered her to. I tell you, this is the most \staggering blow that has ever fallen on a man of my age and temperament.

RAMSDEN. Let me see that will, sir. (*He goes to the writing table and picks it up.*) I cannot believe that my old friend Whitefield would have shewn such a want of confidence in me as to associate me with—(*His countenance falls as he reads.*)

TANNER. It's all my own doing: that's the horrible irony of it. He told me one day that you were to be Ann's guardian; and like a fool I began arguing with him about the folly of leaving a young woman under the control of an old man with obsolete ideas.

RAMSDEN (*stupended*). My ideas obsolete! ! ! ! ! ! !

TANNER. Totally. I had just finished an essay called Down with Government by the Greyhaired; and I was full of arguments and illustrations. I said the proper thing was to combine the experience of an old hand with the vitality of a young one. Hang me if he didn't take me at my word and alter his will—it's dated only a fortnight after that conversation—appointing me as joint guardian with you!

RAMSDEN (*pale and determined*). I shall refuse to act.

TANNER. What's the good of that? I've been refusing all the way from Richmond; but Ann keeps on saying that of course she's only an orphan; and that she can't expect the people who were glad to come to the house in her father's time to trouble much about her now. That's the latest game. An orphan! It's like hearing an ironclad talk about being at the mercy of the winds and waves.

OCTAVIUS. This is not fair, Jack. She is an orphan. And you ought to stand by her.

TANNER. Stand by her! What danger is she in? She has the law on her side; she has popular sentiment on her side; she has plenty of money and no conscience. All she wants

with me is to load up all her moral responsibilities on me,
and do as she likes at the expense of my character. I can't
control her; and she can compromise me as much as she likes.
I might as well be her husband.

RAMSDEN. You can refuse to accept the guardianship. I
shall certainly refuse to hold it jointly with you.

TANNER. Yes; and what will she say to that? what does
she say to it? Just that her father's wishes are sacred to her,
and that she shall always look up to me as her guardian
whether I care to face the responsibility or not. Refuse! You
might as well refuse to accept the embraces of a boa constrictor when once it gets round your neck.

OCTAVIUS. This sort of talk is not kind to me, Jack.

TANNER (*rising and going to Octavius to console him, but
still lamenting*). If he wanted a young guardian, why didn't
he appoint Tavy?

RAMSDEN. Ah! why indeed?

OCTAVIUS. I will tell you. He sounded me about it; but
I refused the trust because I loved her. I had no right to let
myself be forced on her as a guardian by her father. He spoke
to her about it; and she said I was right. You know I love
her, Mr. Ramsden; and Jack knows it too. If Jack loved a
woman, I would not compare her to a boa constrictor in his
presence, however much I might dislike her. (*He sits down
between the busts and turns his face to the wall.*)

RAMSDEN. I do not believe that Whitefield was in his right
senses when he made that will. You have admitted that he
made it under your influence.

TANNER. You ought to be pretty well obliged to me for
my influence. He leaves you two thousand five hundred for
your trouble. He leaves Tavy a dowry for his sister and five
thousand for himself.

OCTAVIUS (*his tears flowing afresh*). Oh, I can't take it.
He was too good to us.

TANNER. You won't get it, my boy, if Ramsden upsets the
will.

RAMSDEN. Ha! I see. You have got me in a cleft stick.

TANNER. He leaves me nothing but the charge of Ann's
morals, on the ground that I have already more money than
is good for me. That shews that he had his wits about him,
doesn't it?

RAMSDEN (*grimly*). I admit that.

OCTAVIUS (*rising and coming from his refuge by the wall*). Mr. Ramsden: I think you are prejudiced against Jack. He is a man of honor, and incapable of abusing—

TANNER. Don't, Tavy: you'll make me ill. I am not a man of honor: I am a man struck down by a dead hand. Tavy: you must marry her after all and take her off my hands. And I had set my heart on saving you from her!

OCTAVIUS. Oh, Jack, you talk of saving me from my highest happiness.

TANNER. Yes, a lifetime of happiness. If it were only the first half hour's happiness, Tavy, I would buy it for you with my last penny. But a lifetime of happiness! No man alive could bear it: it would be hell on earth.

RAMSDEN (*violently*). Stuff, sir. Talk sense; or else go and waste someone else's time: I have something better to do than listen to your fooleries. (*He positively kicks his way to his table and resumes his seat.*)

TANNER. You hear him, Tavy! Not an idea in his head later than eighteen-sixty. We can't leave Ann with no other guardian to turn to.

RAMSDEN. I am proud of your contempt for my character and opinions, sir. Your own are set forth in that book, I believe.

TANNER (*eagerly going to the table*). What! You've got my book! What do you think of it?

RAMSDEN. Do you suppose I would read such a book, sir?

TANNER. Then why did you buy it?

RAMSDEN. I did not buy it, sir. It has been sent me by some foolish lady who seems to admire your views. I was about to dispose of it when Octavius interrupted me. I shall do so now, with your permission. (*He throws the book into the waste-paper basket with such vehemence that Tanner recoils under the impression that it is being thrown at his head.*)

TANNER. You have no more manners than I have myself. However, that saves ceremony between us. (*He sits down again.*) What do you intend to do about this will?

OCTAVIUS. May I make a suggestion?

RAMSDEN. Certainly, Octavius.

OCTAVIUS. Aren't we forgetting that Ann herself may have some wishes in this matter?

RAMSDEN. I quite intend that Annie's wishes shall be

consulted in every reasonable way. But she is only a woman, and a young and inexperienced woman at that.

TANNER. Ramsden: I begin to pity you.

RAMSDEN (*hotly*). I don't want to know how you feel towards me, Mr. Tanner.

TANNER. Ann will do just exactly what she likes. And what's more, she'll force us to advise her to do it; and she'll put the blame on us if it turns out badly. So, as Tavy is longing to see her—

OCTAVIUS (*shyly*). I am not, Jack.

TANNER. You lie, Tavy: you are. So let's have her down from the drawingroom and ask her what she intends us to do. Off with you, Tavy, and fetch her. (*Tavy turns to go.*) And don't be long; for the strained relations between myself and Ramsden will make the interval rather painful. (*Ramsden compresses his lips, but says nothing.*)

OCTAVIUS. Never mind him, Mr. Ramsden. He's not serious. (*He goes out.*)

RAMSDEN (*very deliberately*). Mr. Tanner: you are the most impudent person I have ever met.

TANNER (*seriously*). I know it, Ramsden. Yet even I cannot wholly conquer shame. We live in an atmosphere of shame. We are ashamed of everything that is real about us; ashamed of ourselves, of our relatives, of our incomes, of our accents, of our opinions, of our experience, just as we are ashamed of our naked skins. Good Lord, my dear Ramsden, we are ashamed to walk, ashamed to ride in an omnibus, ashamed to hire a hansom instead of keeping a carriage, ashamed of keeping one horse instead of two and a groom-gardener instead of a coachman and footman. The more things a man is ashamed of, the more respectable he is. Why, you're ashamed to buy my book, ashamed to read it; the only thing you're not ashamed of is to judge me for it without having read it; and even that only means that you're ashamed to have heterodox opinions. Look at the effect I produce because my fairy godmother withheld from me this gift of shame. I have every possible virtue that a man can have except—

RAMSDEN. I am glad you think so well of yourself.

TANNER. All you mean by that is that you think I ought to be ashamed of talking about my virtues. You don't mean that I haven't got them: you know perfectly well that I am as sober and honest a citizen as yourself, as truthful personally, and much more truthful politically and morally.

RAMSDEN (*touched on his most sensitive point*). I deny that. I will not allow you or any man to treat me as if I were a mere member of the British public. I detest its prejudices; I scorn its narrowness; I demand the right to think for myself. You pose as an advanced man. Let me tell you that I was an advanced man before you were born.

TANNER. I knew it was a long time ago.

RAMSDEN. I am as advanced as ever I was. I defy you to prove that I have ever hauled down the flag. I am more advanced than ever I was. I grow more advanced every day.

TANNER. More advanced in years, Polonius.

RAMSDEN. Polonius! So you are Hamlet, I suppose.

TANNER. No: I am only the most impudent person you've ever met. That's your notion of a thoroughly bad character. When you want to give me a piece of your mind, you ask yourself, as a just and upright man, what is the worst you can fairly say of me. Thief, liar, forger, adulterer, perjurer, glutton, drunkard? Not one of these names fit me. You have to fall back on my deficiency in shame. Well, I admit it. I even congratulate myself; for if I were ashamed of my real self, I should cut as stupid a figure as any of the rest of you. Cultivate a little impudence, Ramsden; and you will become quite a remarkable man.

RAMSDEN. I have no—

TANNER. You have no desire for that sort of notoriety. Bless you, I knew that answer would come as well as I know that a box of matches will come out of an automatic machine when I put a penny in the slot: you would be ashamed to say anything else.

The crushing retort for which Ramsden has been visibly collecting his forces is lost for ever; for at this point Octavius returns with Miss Ann Whitefield and her mother; and Ramsden springs up and hurries to the door to receive them. Whether Ann is good-looking or not depends upon your taste; also and perhaps chiefly on your age and sex. To Octavius she is an enchantingly beautiful woman, in whose presence the world becomes transfigured, and the puny lines of individual consciousness are suddenly made infinite by a mystic memory of the whole life of the race to its beginnings in the east, or even back to the paradise from which it fell. She is to him the

reality of romance, the inner good sense of nonsense, the un-
veiling of his eyes, the freeing of his soul, the abolition of
time, place and circumstance, the etherealization of his blood
into rapturous rivers of the very water of life itself, the revelation of all the mysteries and the sanctification of all the
dogmas. To her mother she is, to put it as moderately as
possible, nothing whatever of the kind. Not that Octavius's
admiration is in any way ridiculous or discreditable. Ann is a
well formed creature, as far as that goes; and she is perfectly
ladylike, graceful, and comely, with ensnaring eyes and hair.
Besides, instead of making herself an eyesore, like her
mother, she has devised a mourning costume of black and
violet silk which does honor to her late father and reveals the
family tradition of brave unconventionality by which Ramsden
sets such store.

But all this is beside the point as an explanation of Ann's
charm. Turn up her nose, give a cast to her eye, replace her
black and violet confection by the apron and feathers of a
flower girl, strike all the aitches out of her speech, and Ann
would still make men dream. Vitality is as common as humanity; but, like humanity, it sometimes rises to genius; and
Ann is one of the vital geniuses. Not at all, if you please, an
oversexed person: that is a vital defect, not a true excess. She
is a perfectly respectable, perfectly self-controlled woman,
and looks it; though her pose is fashionably frank and im-
pulsive. She inspires confidence as a person who will do
nothing she does not mean to do; also some fear, perhaps, as
a woman who will probably do everything she means to do
without taking more account of other people than may be
necessary and what she calls right. In short, what the weaker
of her own sex sometimes call a cat.

Nothing can be more decorous than her entry and her
reception by Ramsden, whom she kisses. The late Mr. Whitefield would be gratified almost to impatience by the long
faces of the men (except Tanner, who is fidgety), the silent
handgrasps, the sympathetic placing of chairs, the sniffing of
the widow, and the liquid eye of the daughter, whose heart,
apparently, will not let her control her tongue to speech.
Ramsden and Octavius take the two chairs from the wall, and
place them for the two ladies; but Ann comes to Tanner and
takes his chair, which he offers with a brusque gesture, sub-
sequently relieving his irritation by sitting down on the

corner of the writing table with studied indecorum. Octavius gives Mrs. Whitefield a chair next Ann, and himself takes the vacant one which Ramsden has placed under the nose of the effigy of Mr. Herbert Spencer.

Mrs. Whitefield, by the way, is a little woman, whose faded flaxen hair looks like straw on an egg. She has an expression of muddled shrewdness, a squeak of protest in her voice, and an odd air of continually elbowing away some larger person who is crushing her into a corner. One guesses her as one of those women who are conscious of being treated as silly and negligible, and who, without having strength enough to assert themselves effectually, at any rate never submit to their fate. There is a touch of chivalry in Octavius's scrupulous attention to her, even whilst his whole soul is absorbed by Ann.

Ramsden goes solemnly back to his magisterial seat at the writing table, ignoring Tanner, and opens the proceedings.

RAMSDEN. I am sorry, Annie, to force business on you at a sad time like the present. But your poor dear father's will has raised a very serious question. You have read it, I believe?

Ann assents with a nod and a catch of her breath, too much affected to speak.

I must say I am surprised to find Mr. Tanner named as joint guardian and trustee with myself of you and Rhoda. *(A pause. They all look portentous; but they have nothing to say. Ramsden, a little ruffled by the lack of any response, continues.)* I don't know that I can consent to act under such conditions. Mr. Tanner has, I understand, some objection also; but I do not profess to understand its nature: he will no doubt speak for himself. But we are agreed that we can decide nothing until we know your views. I am afraid I shall have to ask you to choose between my sole guardianship and that of Mr. Tanner; for I fear it is impossible for us to undertake a joint arrangement.

ANN *(in a low musical voice)*. Mamma—

MRS. WHITEFIELD *(hastily)*. Now, Ann, I do beg you not to put it on me. I have no opinion on the subject; and if I had, it would probably not be attended to. I am quite content with whatever you three think best.

Tanner turns his head and looks fixedly at Ramsden, who angrily refuses to receive this mute communication.

ANN *(resuming in the same gentle voice, ignoring her*

mother's bad taste). Mamma knows that she is not strong enough to bear the whole responsibility for me and Rhoda without some help and advice. Rhoda must have a guardian; and though I am older, I do not think any young unmarried woman should be left quite to her own guidance. I hope you agree with me, Granny?

TANNER (*starting*). Granny! Do you intend to call your guardians Granny?

ANN. Don't be foolish, Jack. Mr. Ramsden has always been Grandpapa Roebuck to me: I am Granny's Annie; and he is Annie's Granny. I christened him so when I first learned to speak.

RAMSDEN (*sarcastically*). I hope you are satisfied, Mr. Tanner. Go on, Annie: I quite agree with you.

ANN. Well, if I am to have a guardian, can I set aside anybody whom my dear father appointed for me?

RAMSDEN (*biting his lip*). You approve of your father's choice, then?

ANN. It is not for me to approve or disapprove. I accept it. My father loved me and knew best what was good for me.

RAMSDEN. Of course I understand your feeling, Annie. It is what I should have expected of you; and it does you credit. But it does not settle the question so completely as you think. Let me put a case to you. Suppose you were to discover that I had been guilty of some disgraceful action—that I was not the man your poor dead father took me for! Would you still consider it right that I should be Rhoda's guardian?

ANN. I can't imagine you doing anything disgraceful, Granny.

TANNER (*to Ramsden*). You haven't done anything of the sort, have you?

RAMSDEN (*indignantly*). No, sir.

MRS. WHITEFIELD (*placidly*). Well, then, why suppose it?

ANN. You see, Granny, Mamma would not like me to suppose it.

RAMSDEN (*much perplexed*). You are both so full of natural and affectionate feeling in these family matters that it is very hard to put the situation fairly before you.

TANNER. Besides, my friend, you are not putting the situation fairly before them.

RAMSDEN (*sulkily*). Put it yourself, then.

TANNER. I will. Ann: Ramsden thinks I am not fit to be your guardian; and I quite agree with him. He considers that if your father had read my book, he wouldn't have appointed me. That book is the disgraceful action he has been talking about. He thinks it's your duty for Rhoda's sake to ask him to act alone and to make me withdraw. Say the word; and I will.

ANN. But I haven't read your book, Jack.

TANNER (*diving at the waste-paper basket and fishing the book out for her*). Then read it at once and decide.

RAMSDEN (*vehemently*). If I am to be your guardian, I positively forbid you to read that book, Annie. (*He smites the table with his fist and rises.*)

ANN. Of course not if you don't wish it. (*She puts the book on the table.*)

TANNER. If one guardian is to forbid you to read the other guardian's book, how are we to settle it? Suppose I order you to read it! What about your duty to me?

ANN (*gently*). I am sure you would never purposely force me into a painful dilemma, Jack.

RAMSDEN (*irritably*). Yes, yes, Annie: this is all very well, and, as I said, quite natural and becoming. But you must make a choice one way or the other. We are as much in a dilemma as you.

ANN. I feel that I am too young, too inexperienced, to decide. My father's wishes are sacred to me.

MRS. WHITEFIELD. If you two men won't carry them out I must say it is rather hard that you should put the responsibility on Ann. It seems to me that people are always putting things on other people in this world.

RAMSDEN. I am sorry you take it in that way.

ANN (*touchingly*). Do you refuse to accept me as your ward, Granny?

RAMSDEN. No: I never said that. I greatly object to act with Mr. Tanner: that's all.

MRS. WHITEFIELD. Why? What's the matter with poor Jack?

TANNER. My views are too advanced for him.

RAMSDEN (*indignantly*). They are not. I deny it.

ANN. Of course not. What nonsense! Nobody is more advanced than Granny. I am sure it is Jack himself who has made all the difficulty. Come, Jack! be kind to me in my sorrow. You don't refuse to accept me as your ward, do you?

TANNER (*gloomily*). No. I let myself in for it; so I suppose I must face it. (*He turns away to the bookcase, and stands there, moodily studying the titles of the volumes.*)

ANN (*rising and expanding with subdued but gushing delight*). Then we are all agreed; and my dear father's will is to be carried out. You don't know what a joy that is to me and to my mother! (*She goes to Ramsden and presses both his hands, saying.*) And I shall have my dear Granny to help and advise me. (*She casts a glance at Tanner over her shoulder.*) And Jack the Giant Killer. (*She goes past her mother to Octavius.*) And Jack's inseparable friend Ricky-ticky-tavy. (*He blushes and looks inexpressibly foolish.*)

MRS. WHITEFIELD (*rising and shaking her widow's weeds straight*). Now that you are Ann's guardian, Mr. Ramsden, I wish you would speak to her about her habit of giving people nicknames. They can't be expected to like it. (*She moves towards the door.*)

ANN. How can you say such a thing, Mamma! (*Glowing with affectionate remorse.*) Oh, I wonder can you be right! Have I been inconsiderate? (*She turns to Octavius, who is sitting astride his chair with his elbows on the back of it. Putting her hand on his forehead she turns his face up suddenly.*) Do you want to be treated like a grown up man? Must I call you Mr. Robinson in future?

OCTAVIUS (*earnestly*). Oh please call me Ricky-ticky-tavy. "Mr. Robinson" would hurt me cruelly. (*She laughs and pats his cheek with her finger; then comes back to Ramsden.*) You know I'm beginning to think that Granny is rather a piece of impertinence. But I never dreamt of its hurting you.

RAMSDEN (*breezily, as he pats her affectionately on the back*). My dear Annie, nonsense. I insist on Granny. I won't answer to any other name than Annie's Granny.

ANN (*gratefully*). You all spoil me, except Jack.

TANNER (*over his shoulder, from the bookcase*). I think you ought to call me Mr. Tanner.

ANN (*gently*). No you don't, Jack. That's like the things you say on purpose to shock people: those who know you pay no attention to them. But, if you like, I'll call you after your famous ancestor Don Juan.

RAMSDEN. Don Juan!

ANN (*innocently*). Oh, is there any harm in it? I didn't

know. Then I certainly won't call you that. May I call you Jack until I can think of something else?

TANNER. Oh, for Heaven's sake don't try to invent anything worse. I capitulate. I consent to Jack. I embrace Jack. Here endeth my first and last attempt to assert my authority.

ANN. You see, Mamma, they all really like to have pet names.

MRS. WHITEFIELD. Well, I think you might at least drop them until we are out of mourning.

ANN (*reproachfully, stricken to the soul*). Oh, how could you remind me, mother? (*She hastily leaves the room to conceal her emotion.*)

MRS. WHITEFIELD. Of course. My fault as usual! (*She follows Ann.*)

TANNER (*coming from the bookcase*). Ramsden: we're beaten—smashed—nonentitized, like her mother.

RAMSDEN. Stuff, sir. (*He follows Mrs. Whitefield out of the room.*)

TANNER (*left alone with Octavius, stares whimsically at him*). Tavy: do you want to count for something in the world?

OCTAVIUS. I want to count for something as a poet: I want to write a great play.

TANNER. With Ann as the heroine?

OCTAVIUS. Yes: I confess it.

TANNER. Take care, Tavy. The play with Ann as the heroine is all right; but if you're not very careful, by Heaven she'll marry you.

OCTAVIUS (*sighing*). No such luck, Jack!

TANNER. Why, man, your head is in the lioness's mouth: you are half swallowed already—in three bites—Bite One, Ricky; Bite Two, Ticky; Bite Three, Tavy; and down you go.

OCTAVIUS. She is the same to everybody, Jack: you know her ways.

TANNER. Yes: she breaks everybody's back with the stroke of her paw; but the question is, which of us will she eat? My own opinion is that she means to eat you.

OCTAVIUS (*rising, pettishly*). It's horrible to talk like that about her when she is upstairs crying for her father. But I do so want her to eat me that I can bear your brutalities because they give me hope.

TANNER. Tavy; that's the devilish side of a woman's fascination: she makes you will your own destruction.

OCTAVIUS. But it's not destruction: it's fulfilment.

TANNER. Yes, of her purpose; and that purpose is neither her happiness nor yours, but Nature's. Vitality in a woman is a blind fury of creation. She sacrifices herself to it: do you think she will hesitate to sacrifice you?

OCTAVIUS. Why, it is just because she is self-sacrificing that she will not sacrifice those she loves.

TANNER. That is the profoundest of mistakes, Tavy. It is the self-sacrificing women that sacrifice others most recklessly. Because they are unselfish, they are kind in little things. Because they have a purpose which is not their own purpose, but that of the whole universe, a man is nothing to them but an instrument of that purpose.

OCTAVIUS. Don't be ungenerous, Jack. They take the tenderest care of us.

TANNER. Yes, as a soldier takes care of his rifle or a musician of his violin. But do they allow us any purpose or freedom of our own? Will they lend us to one another? Can the strongest man escape from them when once he is appropriated? They tremble when we are in danger, and weep when we die; but the tears are not for us, but for a father wasted, a son's breeding thrown away. They accuse us of treating them as a mere means to our pleasure; but how can so feeble and transient a folly as a man's selfish pleasure enslave a woman as the whole purpose of Nature embodied in a woman can enslave a man?

OCTAVIUS. What matter, if the slavery makes us happy?

TANNER. No matter at all if you have no purpose of your own, and are, like most men, a mere breadwinner. But you, Tavy, are an artist: that is, you have a purpose as absorbing and as unscrupulous as a woman's purpose.

OCTAVIUS. Not unscrupulous.

TANNER. Quite unscrupulous. The true artist will let his wife starve, his children go barefoot, his mother drudge for his living at seventy, sooner than work at anything but his art. To women he is half vivisector, half vampire. He gets into intimate relations with them to study them, to strip the mask of convention from them, to surprise their inmost secrets, knowing that they have the power to rouse his deepest creative energies, to rescue him from his cold reason, to make him see visions and dream dreams, to inspire him, as he calls it. He persuades women that they may do this for their own purpose whilst he really means them to do it for his. He steals the mother's milk and blackens it to make printer's ink to scoff at her and glorify ideal women with. He pretends to spare her the pangs of child-bearing so that he may have for himself the tenderness and fostering that belong of right to her children. Since marriage began, the great artist has been known as a bad husband. But he is worse: he is a child-robber, a blood-sucker, a hypocrite and a cheat. Perish the race and wither a thousand women if only the sacrifice of them enable him to act Hamlet better, to paint a finer picture, to write a deeper poem, a greater play, a profounder philosophy! For mark you, Tavy, the artist's work is to shew us ourselves as we really are. Our minds are nothing but this knowledge of our-selves; and he who adds a jot to such knowledge creates new mind as surely as any woman creates new men. In the rage of that creation he is as ruthless as the woman, as dangerous to her as she to him, and as horribly fascinating. Of all human struggles there is none so treacherous and remorseless as the struggle between the artist man and the mother woman. Which shall use up the other? that is the issue between them. And it is all the deadlier because, in your romanticist cant, they love one another.

OCTAVIUS. Even if it were so—and I don't admit it for a moment—it is out of the deadliest struggles that we get the noblest characters.

TANNER. Remember that the next time you meet a grizzly bear or a Bengal tiger, Tavy.

OCTAVIUS. I meant where there is love, Jack.

TANNER. Oh, the tiger will love you. There is no love sincerer than the love of food. I think Ann loves you that way: she patted your cheek as if it were a nicely underdone chop.

OCTAVIUS. You know, Jack, I should have to run away from you if I did not make it a fixed rule not to mind anything you say. You come out with perfectly revolting things some-times.

Ramsden returns, followed by Ann. They come in quickly, with their former leisurely air of decorous grief changed to one of genuine concern, and, on Ramsden's part, of worry. He comes between the two men, intending to address Octavius, but pulls himself up abruptly as he sees Tanner.

RAMSDEN. I hardly expected to find you still here, Mr. Tanner.

TANNER. Am I in the way? Good morning, fellow guardian. (*He goes towards the door.*)

ANN. Stop, Jack. Granny: he must know, sooner or later.

RAMSDEN. Octavius: I have a very serious piece of news for you. It is of the most private and delicate nature—of the most painful nature too, I am sorry to say. Do you wish Mr. Tanner to be present whilst I explain?

OCTAVIUS (*turning pale*). I have no secrets from Jack.

RAMSDEN. Before you decide that finally, let me say that the news concerns your sister, and that it is terrible news.

OCTAVIUS. Violet! What has happened? Is she—dead?

RAMSDEN. I am not sure that it is not even worse than that.

OCTAVIUS. Is she badly hurt? Has there been an accident?

RAMSDEN. No: nothing of that sort.

TANNER. Ann: will you have the common humanity to tell us what the matter is?

ANN (*half whispering*). I can't. Violet has done something dreadful. We shall have to get her away somewhere. (*She flutters to the writing table and sits in Ramsden's chair, leaving the three men to fight it out between them.*)

OCTAVIUS (*enlightened*). Is that what you meant, Mr. Ramsden?

RAMSDEN. Yes. (*Octavius sinks upon a chair, crushed.*) I am afraid there is no doubt that Violet did not really go to Eastbourne three weeks ago when we thought she was with the Parry Whitefields. And she called on a strange doctor yesterday with a wedding ring on her finger. Mrs. Parry Whitefield met her there by chance; and so the whole thing came out.

OCTAVIUS (*rising with his fists clenched*). Who is the scoundrel?

ANN. She won't tell us.

OCTAVIUS (*collapsing into the chair again*). What a frightful thing!

TANNER (*with angry sarcasm*). Dreadful. Appalling. Worse than death, as Ramsden says. (*He comes to Octavius.*) What would you not give, Tavy, to turn it into a railway accident, with all her bones broken, or something equally respectable and deserving of sympathy?

OCTAVIUS. Don't be brutal, Jack.

TANNER. Brutal! Good Heavens, man, what are you crying for? Here is a woman whom we all supposed to be making bad water color sketches, practising Grieg and Brahms, gadding about to concerts and parties, wasting her life and her money. We suddenly learn that she has turned from these sillinesses to the fulfilment of her highest purpose and greatest function—to increase, multiply and replenish the earth. And instead of admiring her courage and rejoicing in her instinct; instead of crowning the completed womanhood and raising the triumphal strain of "Unto us a child is born: unto us a son is given," here you are—you who have been as merry as grigs in your mourning for the dead—all pulling long faces and looking as ashamed and disgraced as if the girl had committed the vilest of crimes.

RAMSDEN (*roaring with rage*). I will not have these abominations uttered in my house. (*He smites the writing table with his fist.*)

TANNER. Look here: if you insult me again I'll take you at your word and leave your house. Ann: where is Violet now?

ANN. Why? Are you going to her?

TANNER. Of course I am going to her. She wants help; she wants money; she wants respect and congratulation; she wants every chance for her child. She does not seem likely to get it from you: she shall from me. Where is she?

ANN. Don't be so headstrong, Jack. She's upstairs.

TANNER. What! Under Ramsden's sacred roof! Go and do your miserable duty, Ramsden. Hunt her out into the street. Cleanse your threshold from her contamination. Vindicate the purity of your English home. I'll go for a cab.

ANN (*alarmed*). Oh, Granny, you mustn't do that.

OCTAVIUS (*broken-heartedly, rising*). I'll take her away, Mr. Ramsden. She had no right to come to your house.

RAMSDEN (*indignantly*). But I am only too anxious to help her. (*Turning on Tanner.*) How dare you, sir, impute such monstrous intentions to me? I protest against it. I am ready to put down my last penny to save her from being driven to run to you for protection.

TANNER (*subsiding*). It's all right, then. He's not going to act up to his principles. It's agreed that we all stand by Violet.

OCTAVIUS. But who is the man? He can make reparation by marrying her; and he shall, or he shall answer for it to me.

RAMSDEN. He shall, Octavius. There you speak like a man.

TANNER. Then you don't think him a scoundrel, after all?

OCTAVIUS. Not a scoundrel! He is a heartless scoundrel.

RAMSDEN. A damned scoundrel. I beg your pardon, Annie; but I can say no less.

TANNER. So we are to marry your sister to a damned scoundrel by way of reforming her character! On my soul, I think you are all mad.

ANN. Don't be absurd, Jack. Of course you are quite right, Tavy; but we don't know who he is: Violet won't tell us.

TANNER. What on earth does it matter who he is? He's done his part; and Violet must do the rest.

RAMSDEN (*beside himself*). Stuff! lunacy! There is a rascal in our midst, a libertine, a villain worse than a murderer; and we are not to learn who he is! In our ignorance we are to shake him by the hand; to introduce him into our homes; to trust our daughters with him; to—to—

ANN (*coaxingly*). There, Granny, don't talk so loud. It's most shocking: we must all admit that; but if Violet won't tell us, what can we do? Nothing. Simply nothing.

RAMSDEN. Hmph! I'm not so sure of that. If any man has paid Violet any special attention, we can easily find that out. If there is any man of notoriously loose principles among us—

TANNER. Ahem!

RAMSDEN (*raising his voice*). Yes sir, I repeat, if there is any man of notoriously loose principles among us—

TANNER. Or any man notoriously lacking in self-control.

RAMSDEN (*aghast*). Do you dare to suggest that *I* am capable of such an act?

TANNER. My dear Ramsden, this is an act of which every man is capable. That is what comes of getting at cross purposes with Nature. The suspicion you have just flung at me clings to us all. It's a sort of mud that sticks to the judge's ermine or the cardinal's robe as fast as to the rags of the tramp. Come, Tavy: don't look so bewildered: it might have been me: it might have been Ramsden; just as it might have been anybody. If it had, what could we do but lie and protest —as Ramsden is going to protest.

RAMSDEN (*choking*). I—I—I—

TANNER. Guilt itself could not stammer more confusedly. And yet you know perfectly well he's innocent, Tavy.

RAMSDEN (*exhausted*). I am glad you admit that, sir. I admit, myself, that there is an element of truth in what you say, grossly as you may distort it to gratify your malicious humor. I hope, Octavius, no suspicion of me is possible in your mind.

OCTAVIUS. Of you! No, not for a moment.

TANNER (*drily*). I think he suspects me just a little.

OCTAVIUS. Jack: you couldn't—you wouldn't—

TANNER. Why not?

OCTAVIUS (*appalled*). Why not!

TANNER. Oh, well, I'll tell you why not. First, you would feel bound to quarrel with me. Second, Violet doesn't like me. Third, if I had the honor of being the father of Violet's child, I should boast of it instead of denying it. So be easy: our friendship is not in danger.

OCTAVIUS. I should have put away the suspicion with horror if only you would think and feel naturally about it. I beg your pardon.

TANNER. My pardon! nonsense! And now let's sit down and have a family council. (*He sits down. The rest follow his example, more or less under protest.*) Violet is going to do the State a service; consequently she must be packed abroad like a criminal until it's over. What's happening upstairs?

ANN. Violet is in the housekeeper's room—by herself, of course.

TANNER. Why not in the drawingroom?

ANN. Don't be absurd, Jack. Miss Ramsden is in the drawingroom with my mother, considering what to do.

TANNER. Oh! the housekeeper's room is the penitentiary, I suppose; and the prisoner is waiting to be brought before her judges. The old cats!

ANN. Oh, Jack!

RAMSDEN. You are at present a guest beneath the roof of one of the old cats, sir. My sister is the mistress of this house.

TANNER. She would put me in the housekeeper's room, too, if she dared, Ramsden. However, I withdraw cats. Cats would have more sense. Ann: as your guardian, I order you to go to Violet at once and be particularly kind to her.

ANN. I have seen her, Jack. And I am sorry to say I am afraid she is going to be rather obstinate about going abroad. I think Tavy ought to speak to her about it.

OCTAVIUS. How can I speak to her about such a thing? (*He breaks down.*)

ANN. Don't break down, Ricky. Try to bear it for all our sakes.

RAMSDEN. Life is not all plays and poems, Octavius. Come! face it like a man.

TANNER (*chafing again*). Poor dear brother! Poor dear friends of the family! Poor dear Tabbies and Grimalkins! Poor dear everybody except the woman who is going to risk her life to create another life! Tavy: don't you be a selfish ass. Away with you and talk to Violet; and bring her down here if she cares to come. (*Octavius rises.*) Tell her we'll stand by her.

RAMSDEN (*rising*). No, sir—

TANNER (*rising also and interrupting him*). Oh, we understand: it's against your conscience; but still you'll do it.

OCTAVIUS. I assure you all, on my word, I never meant to be selfish. It's so hard to know what to do when one wishes earnestly to do right.

TANNER. My dear Tavy, your pious English habit of regarding the world as a moral gymnasium, built expressly to strengthen your character in, occasionally leads you to think about your own confounded principles when you should be thinking about other people's necessities. The need of the present hour is a happy mother and a healthy baby. Bend your energies on that; and you will see your way clearly enough.

Octavius, much perplexed, goes out.

RAMSDEN (*facing Tanner impressively*). And Morality, sir? What is to become of that?

TANNER. Meaning a weeping Magdalen and an innocent child branded with her shame. Not in our circle, thank you. Morality can go to its father the devil.

RAMSDEN. I thought so, sir. Morality sent to the devil to please our libertines, male and female. That is to be the future of England, is it?

TANNER. Oh, England will survive your disapproval. Meanwhile, I understand that you agree with me as to the practical course we are to take?

RAMSDEN. Not in your spirit, sir. Not for your reasons.

TANNER. You can explain that if anybody calls you to account, here or hereafter. (*He turns away, and plants himself in front of Mr. Herbert Spencer, at whom he stares gloomily.*)

ANN (*rising and coming to Ramsden*). Granny: hadn't you better go up to the drawingroom and tell them what we intend to do?

RAMSDEN (*looking pointedly at Tanner*). I hardly like to leave you alone with this gentleman. Will you not come with me?

ANN. Miss Ramsden would not like to speak about it before me, Granny. I ought not to be present.

RAMSDEN. You are right: I should have thought of that. You are a good girl, Annie.

He pats her on the shoulder. She looks up at him with beaming eyes; and he goes out, much moved. Having disposed of him, she looks at Tanner. His back being turned to her, she gives a moment's attention to her personal appearance, then softly goes to him and speaks almost into his ear.

ANN. Jack (*he turns with a start*): are you glad that you are my guardian? You don't mind being made responsible for me, I hope.

TANNER. The latest addition to your collection of scapegoats, eh?

ANN. Oh, that stupid old joke of yours about me! Do please drop it. Why do you say things that you know must pain me? I do my best to please you, Jack: I suppose I may tell you so now that you are my guardian. You will make me so unhappy if you refuse to be friends with me.

TANNER (*studying her as gloomily as he studied the bust*). You need not go begging for my regard. How unreal our judgments are! You seem to me to have absolutely no conscience—only hypocrisy; and you can't see the difference—yet there is a sort of fascination about you. I always attend to you, somehow. I should miss you if I lost you.

ANN (*tranquilly slipping her arm into his and walking about with him*). But isn't that only natural, Jack? We have known each other since we were children. Do you remember—

TANNER (*abruptly breaking loose*). Stop! I remember everything.

ANN. Oh, I daresay we were often very silly; but—

TANNER. I won't have it, Ann. I am no more that schoolboy now than I am the dotard of ninety I shall grow into if I live long enough. It is over: let me forget it.

ANN. Wasn't it a happy time? (*She attempts to take his arm again.*)

TANNER. Sit down and behave yourself. (*He makes her sit down in the chair next to the writing table.*) No doubt it was a happy time for you. You were a good girl and never compromised yourself. And yet the wickedest child that ever was slapped could hardly have had a better time. I can understand the success with which you bullied the other girls: your virtue imposed on them. But tell me this: did you ever know a good boy?

ANN. Of course. All boys are foolish sometimes; but Tavy was always a really good boy.

TANNER (*struck by this*). Yes: you're right. For some reason you never tempted Tavy.

ANN. Tempted! Jack!

TANNER. Yes, my dear Lady Mephistopheles, tempted. You were insatiably curious as to what a boy might be capable of, and diabolically clever at getting through his guard and surprising his inmost secrets.

ANN. What nonsense! All because you used to tell me long stories of the wicked things you had done—silly boys' tricks! And you call such things inmost secrets! Boys' secrets are just like men's; and you know what they are!

TANNER (*obstinately*). No I don't. What are they, pray?

ANN. Why, the things they tell everybody, of course.

TANNER. Now I swear I told you things I told no one else. You lured me into a compact by which we were to have no secrets from one another. We were to tell one another everything. I didn't notice that you never told me anything.

ANN. You didn't want to talk about me, Jack. You wanted to talk about yourself.

TANNER. Ah, true, horribly true. But what a devil of a child you must have been to know that weakness and to play on it for the satisfaction of your own curiosity! I wanted to brag to you, to make myself interesting. And I found myself doing all sorts of mischievous things simply to have something to tell you about. I fought with boys I didn't hate; I lied about things I might just as well have told the truth about; I stole things I didn't want; I kissed little girls I didn't care for. It was all bravado: passionless and therefore unreal.

ANN. I never told of you, Jack.

TANNER. No; but if you had wanted to stop me you would have told of me. You wanted me to go on.

ANN (*flashing out*). Oh, that's not true: it's not true, Jack. I never wanted you to do those dull, disappointing, brutal, stupid, vulgar things. I always hoped that it would be something really heroic at last. (*Recovering herself.*) Excuse me, Jack; but the things you did were never a bit like the things I wanted you to do. They often gave me great uneasiness; but I could not tell of you and get you into trouble. And you were only a boy. I knew you would grow out of them. Perhaps I was wrong.

TANNER (*sardonically*). Do not give way to remorse, Ann. At least nineteen twentieths of the exploits I confessed to you were pure lies. I soon noticed that you didn't like the true stories.

ANN. Of course I knew that some of the things couldn't have happened. But——

TANNER. You are going to remind me that some of the most disgraceful ones did.

ANN (*fondly, to his great terror*). I don't want to remind you of anything. But I knew the people they happened to, and heard about them.

TANNER. Yes; but even the true stories were touched up for telling. A sensitive boy's humiliations may be very good fun for ordinary thickskinned grown-ups; but to the boy himself they are so acute, so ignominious, that he cannot confess them—cannot but deny them passionately. However, perhaps it was as well for me that I romanced a bit; for, on the one occasion when I told you the truth, you threatened to tell of me.

ANN. Oh, never. Never once.

TANNER. Yes, you did. Do you remember a dark-eyed girl named Rachel Rosetree? (*Ann's brows contract for an instant involuntarily.*) I got up a love affair with her; and we met one night in the garden and walked about very uncomfortably with our arms round one another, and kissed at parting, and were most conscientiously romantic. If that love affair had gone on, it would have bored me to death; but it didn't go on; for the next thing that happened was that Rachel cut me because she found out that I had told you. How did she find it out? From you. You went to her and held the guilty secret over her head, leading her a life of abject terror and humiliation by threatening to tell on her.

ANN. And a very good thing for her, too. It was my duty to stop her misconduct; and she is thankful to me for it now.

TANNER. Is she?

ANN. She ought to be, at all events.

TANNER. It was not your duty to stop my misconduct, I suppose.

ANN. I did stop it by stopping her.

TANNER. Are you sure of that? You stopped my telling you about my adventures; but how do you know that you stopped the adventures?

ANN. Do you mean to say that you went on in the same way with other girls?

TANNER. No. I had enough of that sort of romantic tomfoolery with Rachel.

ANN (*unconvinced*). Then why did you break off our confidences and become quite strange to me?

TANNER (*enigmatically*). It happened just then that I got something that I wanted to keep all to myself instead of sharing it with you.

ANN. I am sure I shouldn't have asked for any of it if you had grudged it.

TANNER. It wasn't a box of sweets, Ann. It was something you'd never have let me call my own.

ANN (*incredulously*). What?

TANNER. My soul.

ANN. Oh, do be sensible, Jack. You know you're talking nonsense.

TANNER. The most solemn earnest, Ann. You didn't notice at that time that you were getting a soul too. But you were. It was not for nothing that you suddenly found you had a moral duty to chastise and reform Rachel. Up to that time you had traded pretty extensively in being a good child; but you had never set up a sense of duty to others. Well, I set one up too. Up to that time I had played the boy buccaneer with no more conscience than a fox in a poultry farm. But now I began to have scruples, to feel obligations, to find that veracity and honor were no longer goody-goody expressions in the mouths of grown up people, but compelling principles in myself.

ANN (*quietly*). Yes, I suppose you're right. You were beginning to be a man, and I to be a woman.

TANNER. Are you sure it was not that we were beginning to be something more? What does the beginning of manhood and womanhood mean in most people's mouths? You know: it means the beginning of love. But love began long before that for me. Love played its part in the earliest dreams and follies and romances I can remember—may I say the earliest follies and romances we can remember?—though we did not understand it at the time. No: the change that came to me was the birth in me of moral passion; and I declare that according to my experience moral passion is the only real passion.

ANN. All passions ought to be moral, Jack.

TANNER. Ought! Do you think that anything is strong enough to impose oughts on a passion except a stronger passion still?

ANN. Our moral sense controls passion, Jack. Don't be stupid.

TANNER. Our moral sense! And is that not a passion? Is the devil to have all the passions as well as all the good tunes? If it were not a passion—if it were not the mightiest of the passions, all the other passions would sweep it away like a leaf before a hurricane. It is the birth of that passion that turns a child into a man.

ANN. There are other passions, Jack. Very strong ones.

TANNER. All the other passions were in me before; but they were idle and aimless—mere childish greedinesses and cruelties, curiosities and fancies, habits and superstitions, grotesque and ridiculous to the mature intelligence. When they suddenly began to shine like newly lit flames it was by no light of their own, but by the radiance of the dawning moral passion. That passion dignified them, gave them conscience and meaning, found them a mob of appetites and organized them into an army of purposes and principles. My soul was born of that passion.

ANN. I noticed that you got more sense. You were a dreadfully destructive boy before that.

TANNER. Destructive! Stuff! I was only mischievous.

ANN. Oh Jack, you were very destructive. You ruined all the young fir trees by chopping off their leaders with a wooden sword. You broke all the cucumber frames with your catapult. You set fire to the common: the police arrested Tavy for it because he ran away when he couldn't stop you. You—

TANNER. Pooh! pooh! pooh! these were battles, bombardments, stratagems to save our scalps from the red Indians. You have no imagination, Ann. I am ten times more destructive now than I was then. The moral passion has taken my destructiveness in hand and directed it to moral ends. I have become a reformer, and, like all reformers, an iconoclast. I no longer break cucumber frames and burn gorse bushes: I shatter creeds and demolish idols.

ANN (*bored*). I am afraid I am too feminine to see any sense in destruction. Destruction can only destroy.

TANNER. Yes. That is why it is so useful. Construction cumbers the ground with institutions made by busybodies. Destruction clears it and gives us breathing space and liberty.

ANN. It's no use, Jack. No woman will agree with you there.

TANNER. That's because you confuse construction and destruction with creation and murder. They're quite different: I adore creation and abhor murder. Yes: I adore it in tree and flower, in bird and beast, even in you. (*A flush of interest and delight suddenly chases the growing perplexity and boredom from her face.*) It was the creative instinct that led you to attach me to you by bonds that have left their mark on me to this day. Yes, Ann: the old childish compact between us was an unconscious love compact—

ANN. Jack!

TANNER. Oh, don't be alarmed—

ANN. I am not alarmed.

TANNER (*whimsically*). Then you ought to be: where are your principles?

ANN. Jack: are you serious or are you not?

TANNER. Do you mean about the moral passion?

ANN. No, no; the other one. (*Confused.*) Oh! you are so silly: one never knows how to take you.

TANNER. You must take me quite seriously. I am your guardian; and it is my duty to improve your mind.

ANN. The love compact is over, then, is it? I suppose you grew tired of me?

TANNER. No; but the moral passion made our childish relations impossible. A jealous sense of my new individuality arose in me—

ANN. You hated to be treated as a boy any longer. Poor Jack!

TANNER. Yes, because to be treated as a boy was to be taken on the old footing. I had become a new person; and those who knew the old person laughed at me. The only man who behaved sensibly was my tailor: he took my measure anew every time he saw me, whilst all the rest went on with their old measurements and expected them to fit me.

ANN. You became frightfully self-conscious.

TANNER. When you go to heaven, Ann, you will be frightfully conscious of your wings for the first year or so. When you meet your relatives there, and they persist in treating you as if you were still a mortal, you will not be able to bear them. You will try to get into a circle which has never known you except as an angel.

ANN. So it was only your vanity that made you run away from us after all?

TANNER. Yes, only my vanity, as you call it.

ANN. You need not have kept away from me on that account.

TANNER. From you above all others. You fought harder than anybody against my emancipation.

ANN (*earnestly*). Oh, how wrong you are! I would have done anything for you.

TANNER. Anything except let me get loose from you. Even then you had acquired by instinct that damnable woman's trick of heaping obligations on a man, of placing yourself so entirely and helplessly at his mercy that at last he dare not take a step without running to you for leave. I know a poor wretch whose one desire in life is to run away from his wife. She prevents him by threatening to throw herself in front of the engine of the train he leaves her in. That is what all women do. If we try to go where you do not want us to go there is no law to prevent us; but when we take the first step your breasts are under our foot as it descends: your bodies are under our wheels as we start. No woman shall ever enslave me in that way.

ANN. But, Jack, you cannot get through life without considering other people a little.

TANNER. Ay; but what other people? It is this consideration of other people—or rather this cowardly fear of them which we call consideration—that makes us the sentimental slaves we are. To consider you, as you call it, is to substitute your will for my own. How if it be a baser will than mine? Are women taught better than men or worse? Are mobs of voters taught better than statesmen or worse? Worse, of course, in both cases. And then what sort of world are you going to get, with its public men considering its voting mobs, and its private men considering their wives? What does Church and State mean nowadays? The Woman and the Ratepayer.

ANN (*placidly*). I am so glad you understand politics, Jack: it will be most useful to you if you go into parliament. (*He collapses like a pricked bladder.*) But I am sorry you thought my influence a bad one.

TANNER. I don't say it was a bad one. But bad or good, I didn't choose to be cut to your measure. And I won't be cut to it.

ANN. Nobody wants you to, Jack. I assure you—really on my word—I don't mind your queer opinions one little bit. You know we have all been brought up to have advanced opinions. Why do you persist in thinking me so narrow minded?

TANNER. That's the danger of it. I know you don't mind, because you've found out that it doesn't matter. The boa constrictor doesn't mind the opinions of a stag one little bit when once she has got her coils round it.

ANN (*rising in sudden enlightenment*). O-o-o-o-oh! now I understand why you warned Tavy that I am a boa constrictor. Granny told me. (*She laughs and throws her boa round his neck.*) Doesn't it feel nice and soft, Jack?

TANNER (*in the coils*). You scandalous woman, will you throw away even your hypocrisy?

ANN. I am never hypocritical with you, Jack. Are you angry? (*She withdraws the boa and throws it on a chair.*) Perhaps I shouldn't have done that.

TANNER (*contemptuously*). Pooh, prudery! Why should you not, if it amuses you?

ANN (*shyly*). Well, because—because I suppose what you really meant by the boa constrictor was this. (*She puts her arms round his neck.*)

TANNER (*staring at her*). Magnificent audacity! (*She laughs and pats his cheeks.*) Now just to think that if I mentioned this episode not a soul would believe me except the people who would cut me for telling, whilst if you accused me of it nobody would believe my denial!

ANN (*taking her arms away with perfect dignity*). You are incorrigible, Jack. But you should not jest about our affection for one another. Nobody could possibly misunderstand it. You do not misunderstand it, I hope.

TANNER. My blood interprets for me, Ann. Poor Ricky Ticky Tavy!

ANN (*looking quickly at him as if this were a new light*). Surely you are not so absurd as to be jealous of Tavy.

TANNER. Jealous! Why should I be? But I don't wonder at your grip of him. I feel the coils tightening round my very self, though you are only playing with me.

ANN. Do you think I have designs on Tavy?

TANNER. I know you have.

ANN (*earnestly*). Take care, Jack. You may make Tavy very unhappy if you mislead him about me.

TANNER. Never fear: he will not escape you.

ANN. I wonder are you really a clever man!

TANNER. Why this sudden misgiving on the subject?

ANN. You seem to understand all the things I don't understand; but you are a perfect baby in the things I do understand.

TANNER. I understand how Tavy feels for you, Ann: you may depend on that, at all events.

ANN. And you think you understand how I feel for Tavy, don't you?

TANNER. I know only too well what is going to happen to poor Tavy.

ANN. I should laugh at you, Jack, if it were not for poor papa's death. Mind! Tavy will be very unhappy.

TANNER. Yes; but he won't know it, poor devil. He is a thousand times too good for you. That's why he is going to make the mistake of his life about you.

ANN. I think men make more mistakes by being too clever than by being too good. (*She sits down, with a trace of contempt for the whole male sex in the elegant carriage of her shoulders.*)

TANNER. Oh, I know you don't care very much about Tavy. But there is always one who kisses and one who only allows the kiss. Tavy will kiss; and you will only turn the cheek. And you will throw him over if anybody better turns up.

ANN (*offended*). You have no right to say such things, Jack. They are not true, and not delicate. If you and Tavy choose to be stupid about me, that is not my fault.

TANNER (*remorsefully*). Forgive my brutalities, Ann. They are levelled at this wicked world, not at you. (*She looks up at him, pleased and forgiving. He becomes cautious at once.*) All the same, I wish Ramsden would come back. I never feel safe with you: there is a devilish charm—or no: not a charm, a subtle interest (*she laughs*)—Just so: you know it; and you triumph in it. Openly and shamelessly triumph in it!

ANN. What a shocking flirt you are, Jack!

TANNER. A flirt!! I!!!

ANN. Yes, a flirt. You are always abusing and offending people; but you never really mean to let go your hold of them.

TANNER. I will ring the bell. This conversation has already gone further than I intended.

Ramsden and Octavius come back with Miss Ramsden, a hardheaded old maiden lady in a plain brown silk gown, with enough rings, chains and brooches to show that her plainness of dress is a matter of principle, not of poverty. She comes into the room very determinedly: the two men, perplexed and downcast, following her. Ann rises and goes eagerly to meet her. Tanner retreats to the wall between the busts and pretends to study the pictures. Ramsden goes to his table as usual; and Octavius clings to the neighborhood of Tanner.

MISS RAMSDEN (*almost pushing Ann aside as she comes to Mrs. Whitefield's chair and plants herself there resolutely*). I wash my hands of the whole affair.

OCTAVIUS (*very wretched*). I know you wish me to take Violet away, Miss Ramsden. I will. (*He turns irresolutely to the door.*)

RAMSDEN. No no—

MISS RAMSDEN. What is the use of saying no, Roebuck? Octavius knows that I would not turn any truly contrite and repentant woman from your doors. But when a woman is not only wicked, but intends to go on being wicked, she and I part company.

ANN. Oh, Miss Ramsden, what do you mean? What has Violet said?

RAMSDEN. Violet is certainly very obstinate. She won't leave London. I don't understand her.

MISS RAMSDEN. I do. It's as plain as the nose on your face, Roebuck, that she won't go because she doesn't want to be separated from this man, whoever he is.

ANN. Oh, surely, surely! Octavius: did you speak to her?

OCTAVIUS. She won't tell us anything. She won't make any arrangement until she has consulted somebody. It can't be anybody else than the scoundrel who has betrayed her.

TANNER (to Octavius). Well, let her consult him. He will be glad enough to have her sent abroad. Where is the difficulty?

MISS RAMSDEN (taking the answer out of Octavius's mouth). The difficulty, Mr. Jack, is that when I offered to help her I didn't offer to become her accomplice in her wickedness. She either pledges her word never to see that man again, or else she finds some new friends; and the sooner the better.

The parlormaid appears at the door. Ann hastily resumes her seat, and looks as unconcerned as possible. Octavius instinctively imitates her.

THE MAID. The cab is at the door, ma'am.

MISS RAMSDEN. What cab?

THE MAID. For Miss Robinson.

MISS RAMSDEN. Oh! (Recovering herself.) All right. (The maid withdraws.) She has sent for a cab.

TANNER. I wanted to send for that cab half an hour ago.

MISS RAMSDEN. I am glad she understands the position she has placed herself in.

RAMSDEN. I don't like her going away in this fashion, Susan. We had better not do anything harsh.

OCTAVIUS. No: thank you again and again; but Miss Ramsden is quite right. Violet cannot expect to stay.

ANN. Hadn't you better go with her, Tavy?

OCTAVIUS. She won't have me.

MISS RAMSDEN. Of course she won't. She's going straight to that man.

TANNER. As a natural result of her virtuous reception here.

RAMSDEN (much troubled). There, Susan! You hear! and there's some truth in it. I wish you could reconcile it with your principles to be a little patient with this poor girl. She's very young; and there's a time for everything.

MISS RAMSDEN. Oh, she will get all the sympathy she wants from the men. I'm surprised at you, Roebuck.

TANNER. So am I, Ramsden, most favorably.

Violet appears at the door. She is as impenitent and self-possessed a young lady as one would desire to see among the best behaved of her sex. Her small head and tiny resolute mouth and chin; her haughty crispness of speech and trimness of carriage; the ruthless elegance of her equipment, which includes a very smart hat with a dead bird in it, mark a personality which is as formidable as it is exquisitely pretty. She is not a siren, like Ann: admiration comes to her without any compulsion or even interest on her part; besides, there is some fun in Ann, but in this woman none, perhaps no mercy either: if anything restrains her, it is intelligence and pride, not compassion. Her voice might be the voice of a schoolmistress addressing a class of girls who had disgraced themselves, as she proceeds with complete composure and some disgust to say what she has come to say.

VIOLET. I have only looked in to tell Miss Ramsden that she will find her birthday present to me, the filagree bracelet, in the housekeeper's room.

TANNER. Do come in, Violet, and talk to us sensibly.

VIOLET. Thank you: I have had quite enough of the family conversation this morning. So has your mother, Ann: she has gone home crying. But at all events, I have found out what some of my pretended friends are worth. Good bye.

TANNER. No, no: one moment. I have something to say which I beg you to hear. (*She looks at him without the slightest curiosity, but waits, apparently as much to finish getting her glove on as to hear what he has to say.*) I am altogether on your side in this matter. I congratulate you, with the sincerest respect, on having the courage to do what you have done. You are entirely in the right; and the family is entirely in the wrong.

Sensation. Ann and Miss Ramsden rise and turn towards the two. Violet, more surprised than any of the others, forgets her glove, and comes forward into the middle of the room, both puzzled and displeased. Octavius alone does not move or raise his head: he is overwhelmed with shame.

ANN (*pleading to Tanner to be sensible*). Jack!

MISS RAMSDEN (*outraged*). Well, I must say!

VIOLET (*sharply to Tanner*). Who told you?

TANNER. Why, Ramsden and Tavy of course. Why should they not?

VIOLET. But they don't know.

TANNER. Don't know what?

VIOLET. They don't know that I am in the right, I mean.

TANNER. Oh, they know it in their hearts, though they think themselves bound to blame you by their silly superstitions about morality and propriety and so forth. But I know, and the whole world really knows, though it dare not say so, that you were right to follow your instinct; that vitality and bravery are the greatest qualities a woman can have, and motherhood her solemn initiation into womanhood; and that the fact of your not being legally married matters not one scrap either to your own worth or to our real regard for you.

VIOLET (*flushing with indignation*). Oh! You think me a wicked woman, like the rest. You think I have not only been vile, but that I share your abominable opinions. Miss Ramsden: I have borne your hard words because I knew you would be sorry for them when you found out the truth. But I won't bear such a horrible insult as to be complimented by Jack on being one of the wretches of whom he approves. I have kept my marriage a secret for my husband's sake. But now I claim my right as a married woman not to be insulted.

OCTAVIUS (*raising his head with inexpressible relief*). You are married!

VIOLET. Yes; and I think you might have guessed it. What business had you all to take it for granted that I had no right to wear my wedding ring? Not one of you even asked me: I cannot forget that.

TANNER (*in ruins*). I am utterly crushed. I meant well. I apologize—abjectly apologize.

VIOLET. I hope you will be more careful in future about the things you say. Of course one does not take them seriously; but they are very disagreeable, and rather in bad taste, I think.

TANNER (*bowing to the storm*). I have no defence: I shall know better in future than to take any woman's part. We have all disgraced ourselves in your eyes, I am afraid, except Ann. She befriended you. For Ann's sake, forgive us.

VIOLET. Yes: Ann has been very kind; but then Ann knew.

TANNER. Oh!

MISS RAMSDEN (*stiffly*). And who, pray, is the gentleman who does not acknowledge his wife?

VIOLET (*promptly*). That is my business, Miss Ramsden, and not yours. I have my reasons for keeping my marriage a secret for the present.

RAMSDEN. All I can say is that we are extremely sorry, Violet. I am shocked to think of how we have treated you.

OCTAVIUS (*awkwardly*). I beg your pardon, Violet. I can say no more.

MISS RAMSDEN (*still loth to surrender*). Of course what you say puts a very different complexion on the matter. All the same, I owe it to myself—

VIOLET (*cutting her short*). You owe me an apology, Miss Ramsden: that's what you owe both to yourself and to me. If you were a married woman you would not like sitting in the housekeeper's room and being treated like a naughty child by young girls and old ladies without any serious duties and responsibilities.

TANNER. Don't hit us when we're down, Violet. We seem to have made fools of ourselves; but really it was you who made fools of us.

VIOLET. It was no business of yours, Jack, in any case.

TANNER. No business of mine! Why, Ramsden as good as accused me of being the unknown gentleman.

Ramsden makes a frantic demonstration; but Violet's cool keen anger extinguishes it.

VIOLET. You! Oh, how infamous! how abominable! how disgracefully you have all been talking about me! If my husband knew it he would never let me speak to any of you again. (*To Ramsden.*) I think you might have spared me that, at least.

RAMSDEN. But I assure you I never—at least it is a monstrous perversion of something I said that—

MISS RAMSDEN. You needn't apologize, Roebuck. She brought it all on herself. It is for her to apologize for having deceived us.

VIOLET. I can make allowances for you, Miss Ramsden: you cannot understand how I feel on this subject, though I should have expected rather better taste from people of greater experience. However, I quite feel that you have all placed yourselves in a very painful position; and the most truly considerate thing for me to do is to go at once. Good morning.

She goes, leaving them staring.

MISS RAMSDEN. Well, I must say!

RAMSDEN (*plaintively*). I don't think she is quite fair to us.

TANNER. You must cower before the wedding ring like the rest of us, Ramsden. The cup of our ignominy is full.

ACT II

On the carriage drive in the park of a country house near Richmond a motor car has broken down. It stands in front of a clump of trees round which the drive sweeps to the house, which is partly visible through them: indeed Tanner, standing in the drive with the car on his right hand, could get an unobstructed view of the west corner of the house on his left were he not far too much interested in a pair of supine legs in blue serge trousers which protrude from beneath the machine. He is watching them intently with bent back and hands supported on his knees. His leathern overcoat and peaked cap proclaim him one of the dismounted passengers.

THE LEGS. Aha! I got him.

TANNER. All right now?

THE LEGS. Aw rawt nah.

Tanner stoops and takes the legs by the ankles, drawing their owner forth like a wheelbarrow, walking on his hands, with a hammer in his mouth. He is a young man in a neat suit of blue serge, clean shaven, dark eyed, square fingered, with short well brushed black hair and rather irregular sceptically turned eyebrows. When he is manipulating the car his movements are swift and sudden, yet attentive and deliberate. With Tanner and Tanner's friends his manner is not in the least deferential, but cool and reticent, keeping them quite effectually at a distance whilst giving them no excuse for complaining of him. Nevertheless he has a vigilant eye on them always, and that, too, rather cynically, like a man who knows the world well from its seamy side. He speaks slowly and with a touch of sarcasm; and as he does not at all affect the gentleman in his speech, it may be inferred that his smart appearance is a mark of respect to himself and his own class, not to that which employs him.

He now gets into the car to test his machinery and put his cap and overcoat on again. Tanner takes off his leathern overcoat and pitches it into the car. The chauffeur (or auto-mobilist or motoreer or whatever England may presently decide to call him) looks round inquiringly in the act of stowing away his hammer.

THE CHAUFFEUR. Had enough of it, eh?

TANNER. I may as well walk to the house and stretch my legs and calm my nerves a little. (*Looking at his watch.*) I suppose you know that we have come from Hyde Park Corner to Richmond in twenty-one minutes.

THE CHAUFFEUR. I'd ha done it under fifteen if I'd had a clear road all the way.

TANNER. Why do you do it? Is it for love of sport or for the fun of terrifying your unfortunate employer?

THE CHAUFFEUR. What are you afraid of?

TANNER. The police, and breaking my neck.

THE CHAUFFEUR. Well, if you like easy going, you can take a bus, you know. It's cheaper. You pay me to save your time and give you the value of your thousand pound car. (*He sits down calmly.*)

TANNER. I am the slave of that car and of you too. I dream of the accursed thing at night.

THE CHAUFFEUR. You'll get over that. If you're going up to the house, may I ask how long you're goin' to stay there? Because if you mean to put in the whole morning talkin' to the ladies, I'll put the car in the stables and make myself comfortable. If not, I'll keep the car on the go about here till you come.

TANNER. Better wait here. We shan't be long. There's a young American gentleman, a Mr. Malone, who is driving Mr. Robinson down in his new American steam car.

THE CHAUFFEUR (*springing up and coming hastily out of the car to Tanner*). American steam car! Wot! racin' us dahn from London!

TANNER. Perhaps they're here already.

THE CHAUFFEUR. If I'd known it! (*With deep reproach.*) Why didn't you tell me, Mr. Tanner?

TANNER. Because I've been told that this car is capable of 84 miles an hour; and I already know what you are capable of when there is a rival car on the road. No, Henry: there are things it is not good for you to know; and this was one of them. However, cheer up: we are going to have a day after your own heart. The American is to take Mr. Robinson and his sister and Miss Whitefield. We are to take Miss Rhoda.

THE CHAUFFEUR (*consoled, and musing on another matter*). That's Miss Whitefield's sister, isn't it?

TANNER. Yes.

THE CHAUFFEUR. And Miss Whitefield herself is goin' in the other car? Not with you?

TANNER. Why the devil should she come with me? Mr. Robinson will be in the other car. (*The Chauffeur looks at Tanner with cool incredulity, and turns to the car, whistling a popular air softly to himself. Tanner, a little annoyed, is about to pursue the subject when he hears the footsteps of Octavius on the gravel. Octavius is coming from the house, dressed for motoring, but without his overcoat.*) We've lost the race, thank Heaven: here's Mr. Robinson. Well, Tavy, is the steam car a success?

OCTAVIUS. I think so. We came from Hyde Park Corner here in seventeen minutes. (*The Chauffeur, furious, kicks the car with a groan of vexation.*) How long were you?

TANNER. Oh, about three quarters of an hour or so.

THE CHAUFFEUR (*remonstrating*). Now, now, Mr. Tanner, come now! We could ha' done it easy under fifteen.

TANNER. By the way, let me introduce you. Mr. Octavius Robinson: Mr. Enry Straker.

STRAKER. Pleased to meet you, sir. Mr. Tanner is gittin at you with 'is Enry Straker, you know. You call it Henery. But I don't mind, bless you.

TANNER. You think it's simply bad taste in me to chaff him, Tavy. But you're wrong. This man takes more trouble to drop his aitches than ever his father did to pick them up. It's a mark of caste to him. I have never met anybody more swollen with the pride of class than Enry is.

STRAKER. Easy, easy! A little moderation, Mr. Tanner.

TANNER. A little moderation, Tavy, you observe. You would tell me to draw it mild. But this chap has been educated. What's more, he knows that we haven't. What was that Board School of yours, Straker?

STRAKER. Sherbrooke Road.

TANNER. Sherbrooke Road! Would any of us say Rugby! Harrow! Eton! in that tone of intellectual snobbery? Sherbrooke Road is a place where boys learn something: Eton is a boy farm where we are sent because we are nuisances at home, and because in after life, whenever a Duke is mentioned, we can claim him as an old schoolfellow.

STRAKER. You don't know nothing about it, Mr. Tanner. It's not the Board School that does it: it's the Polytechnic.

TANNER. His university, Octavius. Not Oxford, Cambridge, Durham, Dublin or Glasgow. Not even those Nonconformist holes in Wales. No, Tavy. Regent Street, Chelsea, the Borough —I don't know half their confounded names: these are his universities, not mere shops for selling class limitations like ours. You despise Oxford, Enry, don't you?

STRAKER. No, I don't. Very nice sort of place, Oxford, I should think, for people that like that sort of place. They teach you to be a gentleman there. In the Polytechnic they teach you to be an engineer or such like. See?

TANNER. Sarcasm, Tavy, sarcasm! Oh, if you could only see into Enry's soul, the depth of his contempt for a gentleman, the arrogance of his pride in being an engineer, would appal you. He positively likes the car to break down because it brings out my gentlemanly helplessness and his workmanlike skill and resource.

STRAKER. Never you mind him, Mr. Robinson. He likes to talk. We know him, don't we?

OCTAVIUS (*earnestly*). But there's a great truth at the bottom of what he says. I believe most intensely in the dignity of labor.

STRAKER (*unimpressed*). That's because you never done any, Mr. Robinson. My business is to do away with labor. You'll get more out of me and a machine than you will out of twenty laborers, and not so much to drink either.

TANNER. For Heaven's sake, Tavy, don't start him on political economy. He knows all about it; and we don't. You're only a poetic Socialist, Tavy: he's a scientific one.

STRAKER (*unperturbed*). Yes. Well, this conversation is very improvin'; but I've got to look after the car; and you two want to talk about your ladies. *I* know. (*He retires to busy himself about the car; and presently saunters off towards the house.*)

TANNER. That's a very momentous social phenomenon.

OCTAVIUS. What is?

TANNER. Straker is. Here have we literary and cultured persons been for years setting up a cry of the New Woman whenever some unusually old fashioned female came along;

and never noticing the advent of the New Man. Straker's the
New Man.

OCTAVIUS. I see nothing new about him, except your way
of chaffing him. But I don't want to talk about him just now.
I want to speak to you about Ann.

TANNER. Straker knew even that. He learnt it at the Polytechnic, probably. Well, what about Ann? Have you proposed
to her?

OCTAVIUS (*self-reproachfully*). I was brute enough to do so
last night.

TANNER. Brute enough! What do you mean?

OCTAVIUS (*dithyrambically*). Jack: we men are all coarse:
we never understand how exquisite a woman's sensibilities
are. How could I have done such a thing!

TANNER. Done what, you maudlin idiot?

OCTAVIUS. Yes, I am an idiot. Jack: if you had heard her
voice! if you had seen her tears! I have lain awake all night
thinking of them. If she had reproached me, I could have
borne it better.

TANNER. Tears! that's dangerous. What did she say?

OCTAVIUS. She asked me how she could think of anything
now but her dear father. She stifled a sob—(*He breaks down.*)

TANNER (*patting him on the back*). Bear it like a man,
Tavy, even if you feel it like an ass. It's the old game: she's
not tired of playing with you yet.

OCTAVIUS (*impatiently*). Oh, don't be a fool, Jack. Do you
suppose this eternal shallow cynicism of yours has any real
bearing on a nature like hers?

TANNER. Hm! Did she say anything else?

OCTAVIUS. Yes; and that is why I expose myself and her
to your ridicule by telling you what passed.

TANNER (*remorsefully*). No, dear Tavy, not ridicule, on
my honor! However, no matter. Go on.

OCTAVIUS. Her sense of duty is so devout, so perfect, so—

TANNER. Yes: I know. Go on.

OCTAVIUS. You see, under this new arrangement, you and
Ramsden are her guardians; and she considers that all her duty
to her father is now transferred to you. She said she thought I
ought to have spoken to you both in the first instance. Of
course she is right; but somehow it seems rather absurd that
I am to come to you and formally ask to be received as a suitor
for your ward's hand.

TANNER. I am glad that love has not totally extinguished your sense of humor, Tavy.

OCTAVIUS. That answer won't satisfy her.

TANNER. My official answer is, obviously, Bless you, my children: may you be happy!

OCTAVIUS. I wish you would stop playing the fool about this. If it is not serious to you, it is to me, and to her.

TANNER. You know very well that she is as free to choose as you are.

OCTAVIUS. She does not think so.

TANNER. Oh, doesn't she! just! However, say what you want me to do?

OCTAVIUS. I want you to tell her sincerely and earnestly what you think about me. I want you to tell her that you can trust her to me—that is, if you feel you can.

TANNER. I have no doubt that I can trust her to you. What worries me is the idea of trusting you to her. Have you read Maeterlinck's book about the bee?

OCTAVIUS (keeping his temper with difficulty). I am not discussing literature at present.

TANNER. Be just a little patient with me. I am not discussing literature: the book about the bee is natural history. It's an awful lesson to mankind. You think that you are Ann's suitor; that you are the pursuer and she the pursued; that it is your part to woo, to persuade, to prevail, to overcome. Fool: it is you who are the pursued, the marked down quarry, the destined prey. You need not sit looking longingly at the bait through the wires of the trap: the door is open, and will remain so until it shuts behind you for ever.

OCTAVIUS. I wish I could believe that, vilely as you put it.

TANNER. Why, man, what other work has she in life but to get a husband? It is a woman's business to get married as soon as possible, and a man's to keep unmarried as long as he can. You have your poems and your tragedies to work at: Ann has nothing.

OCTAVIUS. I cannot write without inspiration. And nobody can give me that except Ann.

TANNER. Well, hadn't you better get it from her at a safe distance? Petrarch didn't see half as much of Laura, nor Dante of Beatrice, as you see of Ann now; and yet they wrote first-rate poetry—at least so I'm told. They never exposed their idolatry to the test of domestic familiarity; and it lasted them to their graves. Marry Ann; and at the end of a week you'll find no more inspiration in her than in a plate of muffins.

OCTAVIUS. You think I shall tire of her!

TANNER. Not at all: you don't get tired of muffins. But you don't find inspiration in them; and you won't in her when she ceases to be a poet's dream and becomes a solid eleven stone wife. You'll be forced to dream about somebody else; and then there will be a row.

OCTAVIUS. This sort of talk is no use, Jack. You don't understand. You have never been in love.

TANNER. I! I have never been out of it. Why, I am in love even with Ann. But I am neither the slave of love nor its dupe. Go to the bee, thou poet: consider her ways and be wise. By Heaven, Tavy, if women could do without our work, and we ate their children's bread instead of making it, they would kill us as the spider kills her mate or as the bees kill the drone. And they would be right if we were good for nothing but love.

OCTAVIUS. Ah, if we were only good enough for Love! There is nothing like Love: there is nothing else but Love: without it the world would be a dream of sordid horror.

TANNER. And this—this is the man who asks me to give him the hand of my ward! Tavy: I believe we were changed in our cradles, and that you are the real descendant of Don Juan.

OCTAVIUS. I beg you not to say anything like that to Ann.

TANNER. Don't be afraid. She has marked you for her own; and nothing will stop her now. You are doomed. (*Straker comes back with a newspaper.*) Here comes the New Man, demoralizing himself with a halfpenny paper as usual.

STRAKER. Now would you believe it, Mr. Robinson, when we're out motoring we take in two papers, the Times for him, the Leader or the Echo for me. And do you think I ever see my paper? Not much. He grabs the Leader and leaves me to stodge myself with his Times.

OCTAVIUS. Are there no winners in the Times?

TANNER. Enry don't 'old with bettin', Tavy. Motor records are his weakness. What's the latest?

STRAKER. Paris to Biskra at forty mile an hour average, not countin' the Mediterranean.

TANNER. How many killed?

STRAKER. Two silly sheep. What does it matter? Sheep don't cost such a lot: they were glad to 'ave the price without the trouble o' sellin' 'em to the butcher. All the same, d'y'see, there'll be a clamor agin it presently; and then the French Government'll stop it; an our chance'll be gone, see? That what makes me fairly mad: Mr. Tanner won't do a good run while he can.

TANNER. Tavy: do you remember my uncle James?

OCTAVIUS. Yes. Why?

TANNER. Uncle James had a first rate cook: he couldn't digest anything except what she cooked. Well, the poor man was shy and hated society. But his cook was proud of her skill, and wanted to serve up dinners to princes and ambassadors. To prevent her from leaving him, that poor old man had to give a big dinner twice a month, and suffer agonies of awkwardness. Now here am I; and here is this chap Enry Straker, the New Man. I loathe travelling; but I rather like Enry. He cares for nothing but tearing along in a leather coat and goggles, with two inches of dust all over him, at sixty miles an hour and the risk of his life and mine. Except, of course, when he is lying on his back in the mud under the machine trying to find out where it has given way. Well, if I don't give him a thousand mile run at least once a fortnight I shall lose him. He will give me the sack and go to some American millionaire; and I shall have to put up with a nice respectful groom-gardener-amateur, who will touch his hat and know his place. I am Enry's slave, just as Uncle James was his cook's slave.

STRAKER (exasperated). Garn! I wish I had a car that would go as fast as you can talk, Mr. Tanner. What I say is that you lose money by a motor car unless you keep it workin'. Might as well 'ave a pram and a nussmaid to wheel you in it as that car and me if you don't git the last inch out of us both.

TANNER (soothingly). All right, Henry, all right. We'll go out for half an hour presently.

STRAKER (in disgust). Arf an ahr! (He returns to his machine; seats himself in it; and turns up a fresh page of his paper in search of more news.)

OCTAVIUS. Oh, that reminds me. I have a note for you from Rhoda. (He gives Tanner a note.)

TANNER (opening it). I rather think Rhoda is heading for a row with Ann. As a rule there is only one person an English girl hates more than she hates her mother; and that's her eldest sister. But Rhoda positively prefers her mother to Ann. She—(*Indignantly.*) Oh, I say!

OCTAVIUS. What's the matter?

TANNER. Rhoda was to have come with me for a ride in the motor car. She says Ann has forbidden her to go out with me.

Straker suddenly begins whistling his favorite air with remarkable deliberation. Surprised by this burst of larklike melody, and jarred by a sardonic note in its cheerfulness, they turn and look inquiringly at him. But he is busy with his paper; and nothing comes of their movement.

OCTAVIUS (*recovering himself*). Does she give any reason?

TANNER. Reason! An insult is not a reason. Ann forbids her to be alone with me on any occasion. Says I am not a fit person for a young girl to be with. What do you think of your paragon now?

OCTAVIUS. You must remember that she has a very heavy responsibility now that her father is dead. Mrs. Whitefield is too weak to control Rhoda.

TANNER (*staring at him*). In short, you agree with Ann.

OCTAVIUS. No; but I think I understand her. You must admit that your views are hardly suited for the formation of a young girl's mind and character.

TANNER. I admit nothing of the sort. I admit that the formation of a young lady's mind and character usually consists in telling her lies; but I object to the particular lie that I am in the habit of abusing the confidence of girls.

OCTAVIUS. Ann doesn't say that, Jack.

TANNER. What else does she mean?

STRAKER (*catching sight of Ann coming from the house*). Miss Whitefield, gentlemen. (*He dismounts and strolls away down the avenue with the air of a man who knows he is no longer wanted.*)

ANN (*coming between Octavius and Tanner*). Good morning, Jack. I have come to tell you that poor Rhoda has got one of her headaches and cannot go out with you to-day in the car. It is a cruel disappointment to her, poor child!

TANNER. What do you say now, Tavy?

OCTAVIUS. Surely you cannot misunderstand, Jack. Ann is shewing you the kindest consideration, even at the cost of deceiving you.

ANN. What do you mean?

TANNER. Would you like to cure Rhoda's headache, Ann?

ANN. Of course.

TANNER. Then tell her what you said just now; and add that you arrived about two minutes after I had received her letter and read it.

ANN. Rhoda has written to you!

TANNER. With full particulars.

OCTAVIUS. Never mind him, Ann. You were right—quite right. Ann was only doing her duty, Jack; and you know it. Doing it in the kindest way, too.

ANN (going to Octavius). How kind you are, Tavy! How helpful! How well you understand!

Octavius beams.

TANNER. Ay: tighten the coils. You love her, Tavy, don't you?

OCTAVIUS. She knows I do.

ANN. Hush. For shame, Tavy!

TANNER. Oh, I give you leave. I am your guardian; and I commit you to Tavy's care for the next hour. I am off for a turn in the car.

ANN. No, Jack. I must speak to you about Rhoda. Ricky: will you go back to the house and entertain your American friend. He's rather on Mamma's hands so early in the morning. She wants to finish her housekeeping.

OCTAVIUS. I fly, dearest Ann. (He kisses her hand.)

ANN (tenderly). Ricky Ticky Tavy!

He looks at her with an eloquent blush, and runs off.

TANNER (bluntly). Now look here, Ann. This time you've landed yourself; and if Tavy were not in love with you past all salvation he'd have found out what an incorrigible liar you are.

ANN. You misunderstand, Jack. I didn't dare tell Tavy the truth.

TANNER. No: your daring is generally in the opposite direction. What the devil do you mean by telling Rhoda that I am too vicious to associate with her? How can I ever have any human or decent relations with her again, now that you have poisoned her mind in that abominable way?

ANN. I know you are incapable of behaving badly—

TANNER. Then why did you lie to her?

ANN. I had to.

TANNER. Had to!

ANN. Mother made me.

TANNER (*his eye flashing*). Ha! I might have known it. The mother! Always the mother!

ANN. It was that dreadful book of yours. You know how timid mother is. All timid women are conventional: we must be conventional. Even you, who are a man, cannot say what you think without being misunderstood and vilified—yes: I admit it: I have had to vilify you. Do you want to have poor Rhoda misunderstood and vilified in the same way? Would it be right for mother to let her expose herself to such treatment before she is old enough to judge for herself?

TANNER. In short, the way to avoid misunderstanding is for everybody to lie and slander and insinuate and pretend as hard as they can. That is what obeying your mother comes to.

ANN. I love my mother, Jack.

TANNER (*working himself up into a sociological rage*). Is that any reason why you are not to call your soul your own? Oh, I protest against this vile abjection of youth to age! Look at fashionable society as you know it. What does it pretend to be? An exquisite dance of nymphs. What is it? A horrible procession of wretched girls, each in the claws of a cynical, cunning, avaricious, disillusioned, ignorantly experienced, foul-minded old woman whom she calls mother, and whose duty it is to corrupt her mind and sell her to the highest bidder. Why do these unhappy slaves marry anybody, however old and vile, sooner than not marry at all? Because marriage is their only means of escape from these decrepit fiends who hide their selfish ambitions, their jealous hatreds of the young rivals who have supplanted them, under the mask of maternal duty and family affection. Such things are abominable: the voice of nature proclaims for the daughter a father's care and for the son a mother's. The law for father and son and mother and daughter is not the law of love: it is the law of revolution, of emancipation, of final supersession of the old and worn-out by the young and capable. I tell you, the first duty of manhood and womanhood is a Declaration of Independence: the man who pleads his father's authority is no man: the woman who pleads her mother's authority is unfit to bear citizens to a free people.

ANN (*watching him with quiet curiosity*). I suppose you will go in seriously for politics some day, Jack.

TANNER (*heavily let down*). Eh? What? Wh——? (*Collecting his scattered wits.*) What has that got to do with what I have been saying?

ANN. You talk so well.

TANNER. Talk! Talk! It means nothing to you but talk. Well, go back to your mother, and help her to poison Rhoda's imagination as she has poisoned yours. It is the tame elephants who enjoy capturing the wild ones.

ANN. I am getting on. Yesterday I was a boa constrictor: to-day I am an elephant.

TANNER. Yes. So pack your trunk and begone: I have no more to say to you.

ANN. You are so utterly unreasonable and impracticable. What can I do?

TANNER. Do! Break your chains. Go your way according to your own conscience and not according to your mother's. Get your mind clean and vigorous; and learn to enjoy a fast ride in a motor car instead of seeing nothing in it but an excuse for a detestable intrigue. Come with me to Marseilles and across to Algiers and to Biskra, at sixty miles an hour. Come right down to the Cape if you like. That will be a Declaration of Independence with a vengeance. You can write a book about it afterwards. That will finish your mother and make a woman of you.

ANN (*thoughtfully*). I don't think there would be any harm in that, Jack. You are my guardian: you stand in my father's place by his own wish. Nobody could say a word against our travelling together. It would be delightful: thank you a thousand times, Jack. I'll come.

TANNER (*aghast*). You'll come!!!

ANN. Of course.

TANNER. But—(*He stops, utterly appalled; then resumes feebly.*) No: look here, Ann: if there's no harm in it there's no point in doing it.

ANN. How absurd you are! You don't want to compromise me, do you?

TANNER. Yes: that's the whole sense of my proposal.

ANN. You are talking the greatest nonsense; and you know it. You would never do anything to hurt me.

TANNER. Well, if you don't want to be compromised, don't come.

ANN (*with simple earnestness*). Yes, I will come, Jack,

since you wish it. You are my guardian; and I think we ought to see more of one another and come to know one another better. (*Gratefully.*) It's very thoughtful and very kind of you, Jack, to offer me this lovely holiday, especially after what I said about Rhoda. You really are good—much better than you think. When do we start?

TANNER. But——

The conversation is interrupted by the arrival of Mrs. Whitefield from the house. She is accompanied by the American gentleman, and followed by Ramsden and Octavius.

Hector Malone is an Eastern American; but he is not at all ashamed of his nationality. This makes English people of fashion think well of him, as of a young fellow who is manly enough to confess to an obvious disadvantage without any attempt to conceal or extenuate it. They feel that he ought not to be made to suffer for what is clearly not his fault, and make a point of being specially kind to him. His chivalrous manners to women, and his elevated moral sentiments, being both gratuitous and unusual, strike them as being a little unfortunate; and though they find his vein of easy humor rather amusing when it has ceased to puzzle them (as it does at first), they have had to make him understand that he really must not tell anecdotes unless they are strictly personal and scandalous, and also that oratory is an accomplishment which belongs to a cruder stage of civilization than that in which his migration has landed him. On these points Hector is not quite convinced: he still thinks that the British are apt to make merits of their stupidities, and to represent their various incapacities as points of good breeding. English life seems to him to suffer from a lack of edifying rhetoric (which he calls moral tone); English behavior to shew a want of respect for womanhood; English pronunciation to fail very vulgarly in tackling such words as world, girl, bird, etc.; English society to be plain spoken to an extent which stretches occasionally to intolerable coarseness; and English intercourse to need enlivening by games and stories and other pastimes; so he does not feel called upon to acquire these defects after taking great pains to cultivate himself in a first rate manner before venturing across the Atlantic. To this culture he finds English people either totally indifferent, as they very commonly are to all culture, or else politely evasive, the truth being that Hector's culture is nothing but a state of saturation with our literary exports of thirty years ago, reimported by him to be unpacked at a moment's notice and hurled at the head of English literature, science and art, at every conversational opportunity. The dismay set up by these sallies encourages him in his belief that he is helping to educate England. When he finds people chattering harmlessly about Anatole France and Nietzsche, he devastates them with Matthew Arnold, the Autocrat of the Breakfast Table, and even Macauley; and as he is devoutly religious at bottom, he first leads the unwary, by humorous irreverences, to leave popular theology out of account in discussing moral questions with him, and then scatters them in confusion by demanding whether the carrying out of his ideals of conduct was not the manifest object of God Almighty in creating honest men and pure women. The engaging freshness of his personality and the dumbfounding staleness of his culture make it extremely difficult to decide whether he is worth knowing; for whilst his company is undeniably pleasant and enlivening, there is intellectually nothing new to be got out of him, especially as he despises politics, and is careful not to talk commercial shop, in which department he is probably much in advance of his English capitalist friends. He gets on best with romantic Christians of the amoristic sect: hence the friendship which has sprung up between him and Octavius.

In appearance Hector is a neatly built young man of twenty-four, with a short, smartly trimmed black beard, clear, well shaped eyes, and an ingratiating vivacity of expression. He is, from the fashionable point of view, faultlessly dressed. As he comes along the drive from the house with Mrs. Whitefield he is sedulously making himself agreeable and entertaining, and thereby placing on her slender wit a burden it is unable to bear. An Englishman would let her alone, accepting boredom and indifference as their common lot; and the poor lady wants to be either let alone or let prattle about the things that interest her.

Ramsden strolls over to inspect the motor car. Octavius joins Hector.

ANN (*pouncing on her mother joyously*). Oh, mamma, what do you think! Jack is going to take me to Nice in his motor car. Isn't it lovely? I am the happiest person in London.

TANNER (*desperately*). Mrs. Whitefield objects. I am sure she objects. Doesn't she, Ramsden?

RAMSDEN. I should think it very likely indeed.

ANN. You don't object, do you, mother?

MRS. WHITEFIELD. *I* object! Why should I? I think it will do you good, Ann. (*Trotting over to Tanner.*) I meant to ask you to take Rhoda out for a run occasionally: she is too much in the house; but it will do when you come back.

TANNER. Abyss beneath abyss of perfidy!

ANN (*hastily, to distract attention from this outburst*). Oh, I forgot: you have not met Mr. Malone. Mr. Tanner, my guardian: Mr. Hector Malone.

HECTOR. Pleased to meet you, Mr. Tanner. I should like to suggest an extension of the travelling party to Nice, if I may.

ANN. Oh, we're all coming. That's understood, isn't it?

HECTOR. I also am the modest possessor of a motor car. If Miss Robinson will allow me the privilege of taking her, my car is at her service.

OCTAVIUS. Violet!

General constraint.

ANN (*subduedly*). Come, mother: we must leave them to talk over the arrangements. I must see to my travelling kit.

Mrs. Whitefield looks bewildered; but Ann draws her discreetly away; and they disappear round the corner towards the house.

HECTOR. I think I may go so far as to say that I can depend on Miss Robinson's consent.

Continued embarrassment.

OCTAVIUS. I'm afraid we must leave Violet behind. There are circumstances which make it impossible for her to come on such an expedition.

HECTOR (*amused and not at all convinced*). Too American, eh? Must the young lady have a chaperone?

OCTAVIUS. It's not that, Malone—at least not altogether.

HECTOR. Indeed! May I ask what other objection applies?

TANNER (*impatiently*). Oh, tell him, tell him. We shall never be able to keep the secret unless everybody knows what it is. Mr. Malone: if you go to Nice with Violet, you go with another man's wife. She is married.

HECTOR (*thunderstruck*). You don't tell me so!

TANNER. We do. In confidence.

RAMSDEN (*with an air of importance, lest Malone should suspect a misalliance*). Her marriage has not yet been made known: she desires that it shall not be mentioned for the present.

HECTOR. I shall respect the lady's wishes. Would it be indiscreet to ask who her husband is, in case I should have an opportunity of consulting him about this trip?

TANNER. We don't know who he is.

HECTOR (*retiring into his shell in a very marked manner*). In that case, I have no more to say.

They become more embarrassed than ever.

OCTAVIUS. You must think this very strange.

HECTOR. A little singular. Pardon me for saying so.

RAMSDEN (*half apologetic, half huffy*). The young lady was married secretly; and her husband has forbidden her, it seems, to declare his name. It is only right to tell you, since you are interested in Miss—er—in Violet.

OCTAVIUS (*sympathetically*). I hope this is not a disappointment to you.

HECTOR (*softened, coming out of his shell again*). Well: it is a blow. I can hardly understand how a man can leave his wife in such a position. Surely it's not customary. It's not manly. It's not considerate.

OCTAVIUS. We feel that, as you may imagine, pretty deeply.

RAMSDEN (*testily*). It is some young fool who has not enough experience to know what mystifications of this kind lead to.

HECTOR (*with strong symptoms of moral repugnance*). I hope so. A man need be very young and pretty foolish too to be excused for such conduct. You take a very lenient view, Mr. Ramsden. Too lenient to my mind. Surely marriage should ennoble a man.

TANNER (*sardonically*). Ha!

HECTOR. Am I to gather from that cachination that you don't agree with me, Mr. Tanner?

TANNER (*drily*). Get married and try. You may find it delightful for a while: you certainly won't find it ennobling. The greatest common measure of a man and a woman is not necessarily greater than the man's single measure.

HECTOR. Well, we think in America that a woman's morl number is higher than a man's, and that the purer nature of a woman lifts a man right out of himself, and makes him better than he was.

OCTAVIUS (*with conviction*). So it does.

TANNER. No wonder American women prefer to live in Europe! It's more comfortable than standing all their lives on an altar to be worshipped. Anyhow, Violet's husband has not been ennobled. So what's to be done?

HECTOR (*shaking his head*). I can't dismiss that man's conduct as lightly as you do, Mr. Tanner. However, I'll say no more. Whoever he is, he's Miss Robinson's husband; and I should be glad for her sake to think better of him.

OCTAVIUS (*touched; for he divines a secret sorrow*). I'm very sorry, Malone. Very sorry.

HECTOR (*gratefully*). You're a good fellow, Robinson. Thank you.

TANNER. Talk about something else. Violet's coming from the house.

HECTOR. I should esteem it a very great favor, gentlemen, if you would take the opportunity to let me have a few words with the lady alone. I shall have to cry off this trip; and it's rather a delicate—

RAMSDEN (*glad to escape*). Say no more. Come, Tanner. Come, Tavy. (*He strolls away into the park with Octavius and Tanner, past the motor car.*)

Violet comes down the avenue to Hector.

VIOLET. Are they looking?

HECTOR. No.

She kisses him.

VIOLET. Have you been telling lies for my sake?

HECTOR. Lying! Lying hardly describes it. I overdo it. I get carried away in an ecstasy of mendacity. Violet: I wish you'd let me own up.

VIOLET (*instantly becoming serious and resolute*). No, no, Hector: you promised me not to.

HECTOR. I'll keep my promise until you release me from it. But I feel mean, lying to those men, and denying my wife. Just dastardly.

VIOLET. I wish your father were not so unreasonable.

HECTOR. He's not unreasonable. He's right from his point of view. He has a prejudice against the English middle class.

VIOLET. It's too ridiculous. You know how I dislike saying such things to you, Hector; but if I were to—oh, well, no matter.

HECTOR. I know. If you were to marry the son of an English manufacturer of office furniture, your friends would consider it a misalliance. And here's my silly old dad, who is the biggest office furniture man in the world, would shew me the door for marrying the most perfect lady in England merely because she has no handle to her name. Of course it's just absurd. But I tell you, Violet, I don't like deceiving him. I feel as if I was stealing his money. Why won't you let me own up?

VIOLET. We can't afford it. You can be as romantic as you please about love, Hector; but you mustn't be romantic about money.

HECTOR (*divided between his uxoriousness and his habitual elevation of moral sentiment*). That's very English. (*Appealing to her impulsively.*) Violet: dad's bound to find us out someday.

VIOLET. Oh yes, later on of course. But don't let's go over this every time we meet, dear. You promised—

HECTOR. All right, all right, I—

VIOLET (*not to be silenced*). It is I and not you who suffer by this concealment; and as to facing a struggle and poverty and all that sort of thing I simply will not do it. It's too silly.

HECTOR. You shall not. I'll sort of borrow the money from my dad until I get on my own feet; and then I can own up and pay up at the same time.

VIOLET (*alarmed and indignant*). Do you mean to work? Do you want to spoil our marriage?

HECTOR. Well, I don't mean to let marriage spoil my character. Your friend Mr. Tanner has got the laugh on me a bit already about that; and—

VIOLET. The beast! I hate Jack Tanner.

HECTOR (*magnanimously*). Oh, he's all right: he only needs the love of a good woman to ennoble him. Besides, he's proposed a motoring trip to Nice; and I'm going to take you.

VIOLET. How jolly!

HECTOR. Yes; but how are we going to manage? You see, they've warned me off going with you, so to speak. They've told me in confidence that you're married. That's just the most overwhelming confidence I've ever been honored with.

Tanner returns with Straker, who goes to his car.

TANNER. Your car is a great success, Mr. Malone. Your engineer is showing it off to Mr. Ramsden.

HECTOR (*eagerly—forgetting himself*). Let's come, Vi.

VIOLET (*coldly, warning him with her eyes*). I beg your pardon, Mr. Malone, I did not quite catch—

HECTOR (*recollecting himself*). I ask to be allowed the pleasure of shewing you my little American steam car, Miss Robinson.

VIOLET. I shall be very pleased. (*They go off together down the avenue.*)

TANNER. About this trip, Straker.

STRAKER (*preoccupied with the car*). Yes?

TANNER. Miss Whitefield is supposed to be coming with me.

STRAKER. So I gather.

TANNER. Mr. Robinson is to be one of the party.

STRAKER. Yes.

TANNER. Well, if you can manage so as to be a good deal occupied with me, and leave Mr. Robinson a good deal occupied with Miss Whitefield, he will be deeply grateful to you.

STRAKER (*looking round at him*). Evidently.

TANNER. "Evidently"! Your grandfather would have simply winked.

STRAKER. My grandfather would have touched his 'at.

TANNER. And I should have given your good nice respectful grandfather a sovereign.

STRAKER. Five shillins, more likely. (*He leaves the car and approaches Tanner.*) What about the lady's views?

TANNER. She is just as willing to be left to Mr. Robinson as Mr. Robinson is to be left to her. (*Straker looks at his principal with cool scepticism; then turns to the car whistling his favorite air.*) Stop that aggravating noise. What do you mean by it? (*Straker calmly resumes the melody and finishes it. Tanner politely hears it out before he again addresses Straker, this time with elaborate seriousness.*) Enry: I have ever been a warm advocate of the spread of music among the masses; but I object to your obliging the company whenever Miss Whitefield's name is mentioned. You did it this morning, too.

STRAKER (*obstinately*). It's not a bit o' use. Mr. Robinson may as well give it up first as last.

TANNER. Why?

STRAKER. Garn! You know why. Course it's not my business; but you needn't start kiddin' me about it.

TANNER. I am not kidding. I don't know why.

STRAKER (*cheerfully sulky*). Oh, very well. All right. It ain't my business.

TANNER (*impressively*). I trust, Enry, that, as between employer and engineer, I shall always know how to keep my proper distance, and not intrude my private affairs on you. Even our business arrangements are subject to the approval of your Trade Union. But don't abuse your advantages. Let me remind you that Voltaire said that what was too silly to be said could be sung.

STRAKER. It wasn't Voltaire: it was Bow Mar Shay.

TANNER. I stand corrected: Beaumarchais of course. Now you seem to think that what is too delicate to be said can be whistled. Unfortunately your whistling, though melodious, is unintelligible. Come! there's nobody listening: neither my genteel relatives nor the secretary of your confounded Union. As man to man, Enry, why do you think that my friend has no chance with Miss Whitefield?

STRAKER. Cause she's arter summun else.

TANNER. Bosh! who else?

STRAKER. You.

TANNER. Me!!!

STRAKER. Mean to tell me you didn't know? Oh, come, Mr. Tanner!

TANNER (*in fierce earnest*). Are you playing the fool, or do you mean it?

STRAKER (*with a flash of temper*). I'm not playin' no fool. (*More coolly.*) Why, it's as plain as the nose on your face. If you ain't spotted that, you don't know much about these sort of things. (*Serene again.*) Ex-cuse me, you know, Mr. Tanner; but you asked me as man to man; and I told you as man to man.

TANNER (*wildly appealing to the heavens*). Then I—*I* am the bee, the spider, the marked down victim, the destined prey.

STRAKER. I dunno about the bee and the spider. But the marked down victim, that's what you are and no mistake; and a jolly good job for you, too, I should say.

TANNER (*momentously*). Henry Straker: the golden moment of your life has arrived.

STRAKER. What d'y'mean?

TANNER. That record to Biskra.

STRAKER (*eagerly*). Yes?

TANNER. Break it.

STRAKER (*rising to the height of his destiny*). D'y'mean it?

TANNER. I do.

STRAKER. When?

TANNER. Now. Is that machine ready to start?

STRAKER (*quailing*). But you can't—

TANNER (*cutting him short by getting into the car*). Off we go. First to the bank for money; then to my rooms for my kit; then to your rooms for your kit; then break the record from London to Dover or Folkestone; then across the channel and away like mad to Marseilles, Gibraltar, Genoa, any port from which we can sail to a Mahometan country where men are protected from women.

STRAKER. Garn! you're kiddin'.

TANNER (*resolutely*). Stay behind then. If you won't come I'll do it alone. (*He starts the motor.*)

STRAKER (*running after him*). Here! Mister! arf a mo! steady on! (*He scrambles in as the car plunges forward.*)

ACT III

Evening in the Sierra Nevada. Rolling slopes of brown, with olive trees instead of apple trees in the cultivated patches, and occasional prickly pears instead of gorse and bracken in the wilds. Higher up, tall stone peaks and precipices, all handsome and distinguished. No wild nature here: rather a most aristocratic mountain landscape made by a fastidious artist-creator. No vulgar profusion of vegetation: even a touch of aridity in the frequent patches of stones: Spanish magnificence and Spanish economy everywhere.

Not very far north of a spot at which the high road over one of the passes crosses a tunnel on the railway from Malaga to Granada, is one of the mountain amphitheatres of the Sierra. Looking at it from the wide end of the horse-shoe, one sees, a little to the right, in the face of the cliff, a romantic cave which is really an abandoned quarry, and towards the left a little hill, commanding a view of the road, which skirts the amphitheatre on the left, maintaining its higher level on embankments and an occasional stone arch. On the hill, watching the road, is a man who is either a Spaniard or a Scotchman. Probably a Spaniard, since he wears the dress of a Spanish goatherd and seems at home in the Sierra Nevada, but very like a Scotchman for all that. In the hollow, on the slope leading to the quarry-cave, are about a dozen men who, as they recline at their ease round a heap of smoldering white ashes of dead leaf and brushwood, have an air of being conscious of themselves as picturesque scoundrels honoring the Sierra by using it as an effective pictorial background. As a matter of artistic fact they are not picturesque; and the mountains tolerate them as lions tolerate lice. An English policeman or Poor Law Guardian would recognize them as a selected band of tramps and ablebodied paupers.

This description of them is not wholly contemptuous. Whoever has intelligently observed the tramp, or visited the ablebodied ward of a workhouse, will admit that our social failures *are not all drunkards and weaklings. Some of them are men who do not fit the class they were born into. Precisely the same qualities that make the educated gentleman an artist may make an uneducated manual laborer an ablebodied pauper. There are men who fall helplessly into the workhouse because they are good for nothing; but there are also men who are there because they are strongminded enough to disregard the social convention (obviously not a distinterested one on the part of the ratepayer) which bids a man live by heavy and badly paid drudgery when he has the alternative of walking into the workhouse, announcing himself as a destitute person, and legally compelling the Guardians to feed, clothe and house him better than he could feed, clothe and house himself without great exertion. When a man who is born a poet refuses a stool in a stockbroker's office, and starves in a garret, sponging on a poor landlady or on his friends and relatives sooner than work against his grain; or when a lady, because she is a lady, will face any extremity of parasitic dependence rather than take a situation as cook or parlormaid, we make large allowances for them. To such allowances the ablebodied pauper, and his nomadic variant the tramp, are equally entitled.*

Further, the imaginative man, if his life is to be tolerable to him, must have leisure to tell himself stories, and a position which lends itself to imaginative decoration. The ranks of unskilled labor offer no such positions. We misuse our laborers horribly; and when a man refuses to be misused, we have no right to say that he is refusing honest work. Let us be frank in this matter before we go on with our play; so that we may enjoy it without hypocrisy. If we are reasoning, farsighted people, four fifths of us would go straight to the Guardians for relief, and knock the whole social system to pieces with most beneficial reconstructive results. The reason we do not do this is because we work like bees or ants, by instinct or habit, not reasoning about the matter at all. Therefore when a man comes along who can and does reason, and who, applying the Kantian test to his conduct, can truly say to us, If everybody did as I do, the world would be compelled to reform itself industrially, and abolish slavery and squalor, which exist only because everybody does as you do, let us honor that man and seriously consider the advisability of following his example. Such a man is the able-bodied, able-minded pauper. Were he a gentleman doing his best to get a pension or a sinecure instead of sweeping a crossing, nobody would blame him for deciding that so long as the alternative lies between living mainly at the expense of the community and allowing the community to live mainly at his, it would be folly to accept what is to him personally the greater of the two evils.

We may therefore contemplate the tramps of the Sierra without prejudice, admitting cheerfully that our objects— briefly, to be gentlemen of fortune—are much the same as theirs, and the difference in our position and methods merely accidental. One or two of them, perhaps, it would be wiser to kill without malice in a friendly and frank manner; for there are bipeds, just as there are quadrupeds, who are too dangerous to be left unchained and unmuzzled; and these cannot fairly expect to have other men's lives wasted in the work of watching them. But as society has not the courage to kill them, and, when it catches them, simply wreaks on them some superstitious expiatory rites of torture and degradation, and then lets them loose with heightened qualifications for mischief, it is just as well that they are at large in the Sierra, and in the hands of a chief who looks as if he might possibly, on provocation, order them to be shot.

This chief, seated in the center of the group on a squared block of stone from the quarry, is a tall strong man, with a striking cockatoo nose, glossy black hair, pointed beard, upturned moustache, and a Mephistophelean affection which is fairly imposing, perhaps because the scenery admits of a larger swagger than Piccadilly, perhaps because of a certain sentimentality in the man which gives him that touch of grace which alone can excuse deliberate picturesqueness. His eyes and mouth are by no means rascally; he has a fine voice and a ready wit; and whether he is really the strongest man in the party or not, he looks it. He is certainly the best fed, the best dressed, and the best trained. The fact that he speaks English is not unexpected, in spite of the Spanish landscape; for with the exception of one man who might be guessed as a bullfighter ruined by drink, and one unmistakable Frenchman, they are all cockney or American; therefore, in a land of cloaks and sombreros, they mostly wear seedy overcoats, woollen mufflers, hard hemispherical hats, and dirty brown gloves. Only a very few dress after their leader, whose broad sombrero with a cock's feather in the band, and voluminous cloak

descending to his high boots, are as un-English as possible.
None of them are armed; and the ungloved ones keep their
hands in their pockets because it is their national belief that
it must be dangerously cold in the open air with the night
coming on. (It is as warm an evening as any reasonable man
could desire.)

Except the bullfighting inebriate there is only one person in
the company who looks more than, say, thirty-three. He is a
small man with reddish whiskers, weak eyes, and the anxious
look of a small tradesman in difficulties. He wears the only tall
hat visible: it shines in the sunset with the sticky glow of some
sixpenny patent hat reviver, often applied and constantly tending to produce a worse state of the original surface than the
ruin it was applied to remedy. He has a collar and cuffs of
celluloid; and his brown Chesterfield overcoat, with velvet
collar, is still presentable. He is pre-eminently the respectable
man of the party, and is certainly over forty, possibly over fifty.
He is the corner man on the leader's right, opposite three men
in scarlet ties on his left. One of these three is the Frenchman.
Of the remaining two, who are both English, one is argumentative, solemn, and obstinate; the other rowdy and mischievous.

The chief, with a magnificent fling of the end of his cloak
across his left shoulder, rises to address them. The applause
which greets him shews that he is a favorite orator.

THE CHIEF. Friends and fellow brigands. I have a proposal
to make to this meeting. We have now spent three evenings
in discussing the question Have Anarchists or Social-Democrats the most personal courage? We have gone into the principles of Anarchism and Social-Democracy at great length.
The cause of Anarchy has been ably represented by our
one Anarchist, who doesn't know what Anarchism means
(laughter)—

THE ANARCHIST (rising). A point of order, Mendoza—

MENDOZA (forcibly). No, by thunder: your last point of
order took half an hour. Besides, Anarchists don't believe in
order.

THE ANARCHIST (mild, polite but persistent: he is, in fact,
the respectable looking elderly man in the celluloid collar and
cuffs). That is a vulgar error. I can prove—

MENDOZA. Order, order.

THE OTHERS (*shouting*). Order, order. Sit down. Chair! Shut up.

The Anarchist is suppressed.

MENDOZA. On the other hand we have three Social-Democrats among us. They are not on speaking terms; and they have put before us three distinct and incompatible views of Social-Democracy.

THE THREE MEN IN SCARLET TIES. 1. Mr. Chairman, I protest. A personal explanation. 2. It's a lie. I never said so. Be fair, Mendoza. 3. Je demande la parole. C'est absolument faux. C'est faux! faux!! faux!!! Assas-s-s-s-sin!!!!!!

MENDOZA. Order, order.

THE OTHERS. Order, order, order! Chair!

The Social-Democrats are suppressed.

MENDOZA. Now, we tolerate all opinions here. But after all, comrades, the vast majority of us are neither Anarchists nor Socialists, but gentlemen and Christians.

THE MAJORITY (*shouting assent*). Hear, hear! So we are. Right.

THE ROWDY SOCIAL-DEMOCRAT (*smarting under suppression*). You ain't no Christian. You're a Sheeny, you are.

MENDOZA (*with crushing magnanimity*). My friend: *I* am an exception to all rules. It is true that I have the honor to be a Jew; and when the Zionists need a leader to reassemble our race on its historic soil of Palestine, Mendoza will not be the last to volunteer (*sympathetic applause—hear, hear, etc.*). But I am not a slave to any superstition. I have swallowed all the formulas, even that of Socialism; though, in a sense, once a Socialist, always a Socialist.

THE SOCIAL-DEMOCRATS. Hear, hear!

MENDOZA. But I am well aware that the ordinary man—even the ordinary brigand, who can scarcely be called an ordinary man (hear, hear!)—is not a philosopher. Common sense is good enough for him; and in our business affairs common sense is good enough for me. Well, what is our business here in the Sierra Nevada, chosen by the Moors as the fairest spot in Spain? Is it to discuss abstruse questions of political economy? No: it is to hold up motor cars and secure a more equitable distribution of wealth.

THE SULKY SOCIAL-DEMOCRAT. All made by labor, mind you.

MENDOZA (*urbanely*). Undoubtedly. All made by labor,

and on its way to be squandered by wealthy vagabonds in the dens of vice that disfigure the sunny shores of the Mediterranean. We intercept that wealth. We restore it to circulation among the class that produced it and that chiefly needs it—the working class. We do this at the risk of our lives and liberties, by the exercise of the virtues of courage, endurance, foresight, and abstinence—especially abstinence. I myself have eaten nothing but prickly pears and broiled rabbit for three days.

THE SULKY SOCIAL-DEMOCRAT (*stubbornly*). No more ain't we.

MENDOZA (*indignantly*). Have I taken more than my share?

THE SULKY SOCIAL-DEMOCRAT (*unmoved*). Why should you?

THE ANARCHIST. Why should he not? To each according to his needs: from each according to his means.

THE FRENCHMAN (*shaking his fist at the Anarchist*). Fumiste!

MENDOZA (*diplomatically*). I agree with both of you.

THE GENUINELY ENGLISH BRIGANDS. Hear, hear! Bravo, Mendoza!

MENDOZA. What I say is, let us treat one another as gentlemen, and strive to excel in personal courage only when we take the field.

THE ROWDY SOCIAL-DEMOCRAT (*derisively*). Shikespear.

A whistle comes from the goatherd on the hill. He springs up and points excitedly forward along the road to the north.

THE GOATHERD. Automobile! Automobile! (*He rushes down the hill and joins the rest, who all scramble to their feet.*)

MENDOZA (*in ringing tones*). To arms! Who has the gun?

THE SULKY SOCIAL-DEMOCRAT (*handing a rifle to Mendoza*). Here.

MENDOZA. Have the nails been strewn in the road?

THE ROWDY SOCIAL-DEMOCRAT. Two ahnces of em.

MENDOZA. Good! (*To the Frenchman.*) With me, Duval. If the nails fail, puncture their tires with a bullet. (*He gives the rifle to Duval, who follows him up the hill. Mendoza produces an opera glass. The others hurry across to the road and disappear to the north.*)

MENDOZA (*on the hill, using his glass*). Two only, a capitalist and his chauffeur. They look English.

DUVAL. Angliche! Aoh yess. Cochons! (*Handling the rifle.*) Faut tirer, n'est-ce-pas?

MENDOZA. No: the nails have gone home. Their tire is down: they stop.

DUVAL (*shouting to the others*). Fondez sur eux, nom de Dieu!

MENDOZA (*rebuking his excitement*). Du calme, Duval: keep your hair on. They take it quietly. Let us descend and receive them.

Mendoza descends, passing behind the fire and coming forward, whilst Tanner and Straker, in their motoring goggles, leather coats, and caps, are led in from the road by the brigands.

TANNER. Is this the gentleman you describe as your boss? Does he speak English?

THE ROWDY SOCIAL-DEMOCRAT. Course he does. Y' downt suppowz we Hinglishmen lets ahrselves be bossed by a bloomin Spenniard, do you?

MENDOZA (*with dignity*). Allow me to introduce myself: Mendoza, President of the League of the Sierra! (*Posing loftily.*) I am a brigand: I live by robbing the rich.

TANNER (*promptly*). I am a gentleman: I live by robbing the poor. Shake hands.

THE ENGLISH SOCIAL-DEMOCRATS. Hear, hear!

General laughter and good humor. Tanner and Mendoza shake hands. The Brigands drop into their former places.

STRAKER. Ere! where do I come in?

TANNER (*introducing*). My friend and chauffeur.

THE SULKY SOCIAL-DEMOCRAT (*suspiciously*). Well, which is he? friend or show-foor? It makes all the difference, you know.

MENDOZA (*explaining*). We should expect ransom for a friend. A professional chauffeur is free of the mountains. He even takes a trifling percentage of his principal's ransom if he will honor us by accepting it.

STRAKER. I see. Just to encourage me to come this way again. Well, I'll think about it.

DUVAL (*impulsively rushing across to Straker*). Mon frère! (*He embraces him rapturously and kisses him on both cheeks.*)

STRAKER (*disgusted*). Ere, git out: don't be silly. Who are you, pray?

DUVAL. Duval: Social-Democrat.

STRAKER. Oh, you're a Social-Democrat, are you?

THE ANARCHIST. He means that he has sold out to the parliamentary humbugs and the bourgeoisie. Compromise! that is his faith.

DUVAL (*furiously*). I understand what he say. He say Bourgeois. He say Compromise. Jamais de la vie! Misérable menteur—

STRAKER. See here, Captain Mendoza, ow much o this sort o thing do you put up with here? Are we avin a pleasure trip in the mountains, or are we at a Socialist meetin?

THE MAJORITY. Hear, hear! Shut up. Chuck it. Sit down, &c. &c. (*The Social-Democrats and the Anarchist are bustled into the background. Straker, after superintending this proceeding with satisfaction, places himself on Mendoza's left, Tanner being on his right.*)

MENDOZA. Can we offer you anything? Broiled rabbit and prickly pears—

TANNER. Thank you: we have dined.

MENDOZA (*to his followers*). Gentlemen: business is over for the day. Go as you please until morning.

The Brigands disperse into groups lazily. Some go into the cave. Others sit down or lie down to sleep in the open. A few produce a pack of cards and move off towards the road; for it is now starlight; and they know that motor cars have lamps which can be turned to account for lighting a card party.

STRAKER (*calling after them*). Don't none of you go fooling with that car, d'ye hear?

MENDOZA. No fear, Monsieur le Chauffeur. The first one we captured cured us of that.

STRAKER (*interested*). What did it do?

MENDOZA. It carried three brave comrades of ours, who did not know how to stop it, into Granada, and capsized them opposite the police station. Since then we never touch one without sending for the chauffeur. Shall we chat at our ease?

TANNER. By all means.

Tanner, Mendoza, and Straker sit down on the turf by the fire. Mendoza delicately waives his presidential dignity, of which the right to sit on the squared stone block is the appanage, by sitting on the ground like his guests, and using the stone only as a support for his back.

MENDOZA. It is the custom in Spain always to put off

business until to-morrow. In fact, you have arrived out of office hours. However, if you would prefer to settle the question of ransom at once, I am at your service.

TANNER. To-morrow will do for me. I am rich enough to pay anything in reason.

MENDOZA (*respectfully, much struck by this admission*). You are a remarkable man, sir. Our guests usually describe themselves as miserably poor.

TANNER. Pooh! Miserably poor people don't own motor cars.

MENDOZA. Precisely what we say to them.

TANNER. Treat us well: we shall not prove ungrateful.

STRAKER. No prickly pears and broiled rabbits, you know. Don't tell me you can't do us a bit better than that if you like.

MENDOZA. Wine, kids, milk, cheese and bread can be procured for ready money.

STRAKER (*graciously*). Now you're talking.

TANNER. Are you all Socialists here, may I ask?

MENDOZA (*repudiating this humiliating misconception*). Oh no, no, no: nothing of the kind, I assure you. We naturally have modern views as to the justice of the existing distribution of wealth: otherwise we should lose our self-respect. But nothing that you could take exception to, except two or three faddists.

TANNER. I had no intention of suggesting anything discreditable. In fact, I am a bit of a Socialist myself.

STRAKER (*drily*). Most rich men are, I notice.

MENDOZA. Quite so. It has reached us, I admit. It is in the air of the century.

STRAKER. Socialism must be looking up a bit if your chaps are taking to it.

MENDOZA. That is true, sir. A movement which is confined to philosophers and honest men can never exercise any real political influence: there are too few of them. Until a movement shews itself capable of spreading among brigands, it can never hope for a political majority.

TANNER. But are your brigands any less honest than ordinary citizens?

MENDOZA. Sir: I will be frank with you. Brigandage is abnormal. Abnormal professions attract two classes: those who are not good enough for ordinary bourgeois life and those who are too good for it. We are dregs and scum, sir: the dregs very filthy, the scum very superior.

STRAKER. Take care; some of the dregs'll hear you.

MENDOZA. It does not matter: each brigand thinks him-self scum, and likes to hear the others called dregs.

TANNER. Come! you are a wit. (*Mendoza inclines his head, flattered.*) May one ask you a blunt question?

MENDOZA. As blunt as you please.

TANNER. How does it pay a man of your talent to shepherd such a flock as this on broiled rabbit and prickly pears? I have seen men less gifted, and I'll swear less honest, supping at the Savoy on foie gras and champagne.

MENDOZA. Pooh! they have all had their turn at the broiled rabbit, just as I shall have my turn at the Savoy. Indeed, I have had a turn there already—as waiter.

TANNER. A waiter! You astonish me!

MENDOZA (*reflectively*). Yes: I, Mendoza of the Sierra was a waiter. Hence, perhaps, my cosmopolitanism. (*With sudden intensity.*) Shall I tell you the story of my life?

STRAKER (*apprehensively*). If it ain't too long, old chap—

TANNER (*interrupting him*). Tsh-sh: you are a Philistine, Henry: you have no romance in you. (*To Mendoza.*) You interest me extremely, President. Never mind Henry: he can go to sleep.

MENDOZA. The woman I loved—

STRAKER. Oh, this is a love story, is it? Right you are. Go on: I was only afraid you were going to talk about your-self.

MENDOZA. Myself! I have thrown myself away for her sake: that is why I am here. No matter: I count the world well lost for her. She had, I pledge you my word, the most mag-nificent head of hair I ever saw. She had humor; she had in-tellect; she could cook to perfection; and her highly strung temperament made her uncertain, incalculable, variable, capricious, cruel, in a word, enchanting.

STRAKER. A six shillin novel sort o woman, all but the cookin. Er name was Lady Gladys Plantagenet, wasn't it?

MENDOZA. No, sir: she was not an earl's daughter. Photog-raphy, reproduced by the half-tone process, has made me familiar with the appearance of the daughters of the English peerage; and I can honestly say that I would have sold the lot, faces, dowries, clothes, titles, and all, for a smile from this woman. Yet she was a woman of the people, a worker:

otherwise—let me reciprocate your bluntness—I should have scorned her.

TANNER. Very properly. And did she respond to your love?

MENDOZA. Should I be here if she did? She objected to marry a Jew.

TANNER. On religious grounds?

MENDOZA. No: she was a freethinker. She said that every Jew considers in his heart that English people are dirty in their habits.

TANNER (*surprised*). Dirty!

MENDOZA. It shewed her extraordinary knowledge of the world; for it is undoubtedly true. Our elaborate sanitary code makes us unduly contemptuous of the Gentile.

TANNER. Did you ever hear that, Henry?

STRAKER. I've heard my sister say so. She was cook in a Jewish family once.

MENDOZA. I could not deny it; neither could I eradicate the impression it made on her mind. I could have got round any other objection; but no woman can stand a suspicion of indelicacy as to her person. My entreaties were in vain: she always retorted that she wasn't good enough for me, and recommended me to marry an accursed barmaid named Rebecca Lazarus, whom I loathed. I talked of suicide: she offered me a packet of beetle poison to do it with. I hinted at murder: she went into hysterics; and as I am a living man I went to America so that she might sleep without dreaming that I was stealing upstairs to cut her throat. In America I went out west and fell in with a man who was wanted by the police for holding up trains. It was he who had the idea of holding up motor cars in the South of Europe: a welcome idea to a desperate and disappointed man. He gave me some valuable introductions to capitalists of the right sort. I formed a syndicate; and the present enterprise is the result. I became leader, as the Jew always becomes leader, by his brains and imagination. But with all my pride of race I would give everything I possess to be an Englishman. I am like a boy: I cut her name on the trees and her initials on the sod. When I am alone I lie down and tear my wretched hair and cry Louisa—

STRAKER (*startled*). Louisa!

MENDOZA. It is her name—Louisa—Louisa Straker—

TANNER. Straker!

STRAKER (*scrambling up on his knees most indignantly*). Look here: Louisa Straker is my sister, see? Wot do you mean by gassin about her like this? Wotshe got to do with you?

MENDOZA. A dramatic coincidence! You are Enry, her favorite brother!

STRAKER. Oo are you callin Enry? What call have you to take a liberty with my name or with hers? For two pins I'd punch your fat ed, so I would.

MENDOZA (*with grandiose calm*). If I let you do it, will you promise to brag of it afterwards to her? She will be reminded of her Mendoza: that is all I desire.

TANNER. This is genuine devotion, Henry. You should respect it.

STRAKER (*fiercely*). Funk, more likely.

MENDOZA (*springing to his feet*). Funk! Young man: I come of a famous family of fighters; and as your sister well knows, you would have as much chance against me as a perambulator against your motor car.

STRAKER (*secretly daunted, but rising from his knees with an air of reckless pugnacity*). I ain't afraid of you. With your Louisa! Louisa! Miss Straker is good enough for you, I should think.

MENDOZA. I wish you could persuade her to think so.

STRAKER (*exasperated*). Here—

TANNER (*rising quickly and interposing*). Oh come, Henry: even if you could fight the President you can't fight the whole League of the Sierra. Sit down again and be friendly. A cat may look at a king; and even a President of brigands may look at your sister. All this family pride is really very old fashioned.

STRAKER (*subdued, but grumbling*). Let him look at her. But wot does he mean by makin out that she ever looked at im? (*Reluctantly resuming his couch on the turf.*) Ear im talk, one ud think she was keepin company with him. (*He turns his back on them and composes himself to sleep.*)

MENDOZA (*to Tanner, becoming more confidential as he finds himself virtually alone with a sympathetic listener in the still starlight of the mountains; for all the rest are asleep by this time*). It was just so with her, sir. Her intellect reached forward into the twentieth century: her social prejudices and family affections reached back into the dark ages. Ah,

sir, how the words of Shakespear seem to fit every crisis in
our emotions!

> I loved Louisa: 40,000 brothers
> Could not with all their quantity of love
> Make up my sum.

And so on. I forget the rest. Call it madness if you will—
infatuation. I am an able man, a strong man: in ten years
I should have owned a first-class hotel. I met her; and—
you see!—I am a brigand, an outcast. Even Shakespear cannot do justice to what I feel for Louisa. Let me read you
some lines that I have written about her myself. However
slight their literary merit may be, they express what I feel
better than any casual words can. (*He produces a packet
of hotel bills scrawled with manuscript, and kneels at the
fire to decipher them, poking it with a stick to make it glow.*)

TANNER (*slapping him rudely on the shoulder*). Put them
in the fire, President.

MENDOZA (*startled*). Eh?

TANNER. You are sacrificing your career to a monomania.

MENDOZA. I know it.

TANNER. No you don't. No man would commit such a
crime against himself if he really knew what he was doing.
How can you look round at these august hills, look up at
this divine sky, taste this finely tempered air, and then talk
like a literary hack on a second floor in Bloomsbury?

MENDOZA (*shaking his head*). The Sierra is no better than
Bloomsbury when once the novelty has worn off. Besides,
these mountains make you dream of women—of women with
magnificent hair.

TANNER. Of Louisa, in short. They will not make me dream
of women, my friend: I am heartwhole.

MENDOZA. Do not boast until morning, sir. This is a strange
country for dreams.

TANNER. Well, we shall see. Goodnight. (*He lies down
and composes himself to sleep.*)

*Mendoza, with a sigh, follows his example; and for a few
moments there is peace in the Sierra. Then Mendoza sits up
suddenly and says pleadingly to Tanner—*

MENDOZA. Just allow me to read a few lines before you
go to sleep. I should really like your opinion of them.

Tanner (*drowsily*). Go on. I am listening.

Mendoza.   I saw thee first in Whitsun week
                  Louisa, Louisa—

Tanner (*rousing himself*). My dear President, Louisa is a
very pretty name; but it really doesn't rhyme well to Whitsun
week.

Mendoza. Of course not. Louisa is not the rhyme, but the
refrain.

Tanner (*subsiding*). Ah, the refrain. I beg your pardon.
Go on.

Mendoza. Perhaps you do not care for that one: I think
you will like this better. (*He recites, in rich soft tones, and
in slow time.*)

> Louisa, I love thee.
> I love thee, Louisa.
> Louisa, Louisa, Louisa, I love thee.
> One name and one phrase make my music, Louisa.
> Louisa, Louisa, Louisa, I love thee.
>
> Mendoza thy lover,
> Thy lover, Mendoza,
> Mendoza adoringly lives for Louisa.
> There's nothing but that in the world for Mendoza.
> Louisa, Louisa, Mendoza adores thee.

(*Affected.*) There is no merit in producing beautiful lines
upon such a name. Louisa is an exquisite name, is it not?

Tanner (*all but asleep, responds with a faint groan*).

Mendoza. O wert thou, Louisa
                  The wife of Mendoza,
                  Mendoza's Louisa, Louisa Mendoza,
                  How blest were the life of Louisa's Mendoza!
                  How painless his longing of love for Louisa!

That is real poetry—from the heart—from the heart of
hearts. Don't you think it will move her?

No answer.

(*Resignedly.*) Asleep, as usual. Doggrel to all the world:
heavenly music to me! Idiot that I am to wear my heart on
my sleeve. (*He composes himself to sleep, murmuring.*)

Louisa, I love thee; I love thee, Louisa; Louisa, Louisa, Louisa, I—

Straker snores; rolls over on his side; and relapses into sleep. Stillness settles on the Sierra; and the darkness deepens. The fire has again buried itself in white ash and ceased to glow. The peaks shew unfathomably dark against the starry firmament; but now the stars dim and vanish; and the sky seems to steal away out of the universe. Instead of the Sierra there is nothing; omnipresent nothing. No sky, no peaks, no light, no sound, no time nor space, utter void. Then somewhere the beginning of a pallor, and with it a faint throbbing buzz as of a ghostly violoncello palpitating on the same note endlessly. A couple of ghostly violins presently takes advan-

tage of this bass and therewith the pallor reveals a man in the void, an incorporeal but visible man, seated, absurdly enough, on nothing. For a moment he raises his head as the music passes him by. Then, with a heavy sigh, he droops in utter dejection; and the violins, discouraged, retrace their melody in despair and at last give it up, extinguished by wailings from uncanny wind instruments, thus:—

It is all very odd. One recognizes the Mozartian strain; and on this hint, and by the aid of certain sparkles of violet light in the pallor, the man's costume explains itself as that of a Spanish nobleman of the XV–XVI century. Don Juan, of course; but where? why? how? Besides, in the brief lifting of his face, now hidden by his hat brim, there was a curious suggestion of Tanner. A more critical, fastidious, handsome face, paler and colder, without Tanner's impetuous credulity and enthusiasm, and without a touch of his modern plutocratic vulgarity, but still a resemblance, even an identity.

The name too: Don Juan Tenorio, John Tanner. Where on earth—or elsewhere—have we got to from the XX century and the Sierra?

Another pallor in the void, this time not violet, but a disagreeable smoky yellow. With it, the whisper of a ghostly clarionet turning this tune into infinite sadness:

The yellowish pallor moves: there is an old crone wandering in the void, bent and toothless; draped, as well as one can guess, in the coarse brown frock of some religious order. She wanders and wanders in her slow hopeless way, much as a wasp flies in its rapid busy way, until she blunders against the thing she seeks: companionship. With a sob of relief the poor old creature clutches at the presence of the man and addresses him in her dry unlovely voice, which can still express pride and resolution as well as suffering.

THE OLD WOMAN. Excuse me; but I am so lonely; and this place is so awful.

DON JUAN. A new comer?

THE OLD WOMAN. Yes: I suppose I died this morning. I confessed; I had extreme unction; I was in bed with my family about me and my eyes fixed on the cross. Then it grew dark; and when the light came back it was this light by which I walk seeing nothing. I have wandered for hours in horrible loneliness.

DON JUAN (*sighing*). Ah! you have not yet lost the sense of time. One soon does, in eternity.

THE OLD WOMAN. Where are we?

DON JUAN. In hell.

THE OLD WOMAN (*proudly*). Hell! I in hell! How dare you?

DON JUAN (*unimpressed*). Why not, Señora?

THE OLD WOMAN. You do not know to whom you are speaking. I am a lady, and a faithful daughter of the Church.

DON JUAN. I do not doubt it.

THE OLD WOMAN. But how then can I be in hell? Purgatory, perhaps: I have not been perfect: who has? But hell! oh, you are lying.

DON JUAN. Hell, Señora, I assure you; hell at its best: that is, its most solitary—though perhaps you would prefer company.

THE OLD WOMAN. But I have sincerely repented; I have confessed—

DON JUAN. How much?

THE OLD WOMAN. More sins than I really committed. I loved confession.

DON JUAN. Ah, that is perhaps as bad as confessing too little. At all events, Señora, whether by oversight or intention, you are certainly damned, like myself; and there is nothing for it now but to make the best of it.

THE OLD WOMAN (indignantly). Oh! and I might have been so much wickeder! All my good deeds wasted! It is unjust.

DON JUAN. No: you were fully and clearly warned. For your bad deeds, vicarious atonement, mercy without justice. For your good deeds, justice without mercy. We have many good people here.

THE OLD WOMAN. Were you a good man?

DON JUAN. I was a murderer.

THE OLD WOMAN. A murderer! Oh, how dare they send me to herd with murderers! I was not as bad as that: I was a good woman. There is some mistake: where can I have it set right?

DON JUAN. I do not know whether mistakes can be corrected here. Probably they will not admit a mistake even if they have made one.

THE OLD WOMAN. But whom can I ask?

DON JUAN. I should ask the Devil, Señora: he understands the ways of this place, which is more than I ever could.

THE OLD WOMAN. The Devil! I speak to the Devil!

DON JUAN. In hell, Señora, the Devil is the leader of the best society.

THE OLD WOMAN. I tell you, wretch, I know I am not in hell.

DON JUAN. How do you know?

THE OLD WOMAN. Because I feel no pain.

DON JUAN. Oh, then there is no mistake: you are intentionally damned.

THE OLD WOMAN. Why do you say that?

DON JUAN. Because hell, Señora, is a place for the wicked.

The wicked are quite comfortable in it: it was made for them. You tell me you feel no pain. I conclude you are one of those for whom Hell exists.

THE OLD WOMAN. Do you feel no pain?

DON JUAN. I am not one of the wicked, Señora; therefore it bores me, bores me beyond description, beyond belief.

THE OLD WOMAN. Not one of the wicked! You said you were a murderer.

DON JUAN. Only a duel. I ran my sword through an old man who was trying to run his through me.

THE OLD WOMAN. If you were a gentleman, that was not a murder.

DON JUAN. The old man called it murder, because he was, he said, defending his daughter's honor. By this he meant that because I foolishly fell in love with her and told her so, she screamed; and he tried to assassinate me after calling me insulting names.

THE OLD WOMAN. You were like all men. Libertines and murderers all, all, all!

DON JUAN. And yet we meet here, dear lady.

THE OLD WOMAN. Listen to me. My father was slain by just such a wretch as you, in just such a duel, for just such a cause. I screamed: it was my duty. My father drew on my assailant: his honor demanded it. He fell: that was the reward of honor. I am here: in hell, you tell me: that is the reward of duty. Is there justice in heaven?

DON JUAN. No; but there is justice in hell: heaven is far above such idle human personalities. You will be welcome in hell, Señora. Hell is the home of honor, duty, justice, and the rest of the seven deadly virtues. All the wickedness on earth is done in their name: where else but in hell should they have their reward? Have I not told you that the truly damned are those who are happy in hell?

THE OLD WOMAN. And are you happy here?

DON JUAN (*springing to his feet*). No; and that is the enigma on which I ponder in darkness. Why am I here? I, who repudiated all duty, trampled honor underfoot, and laughed at justice!

THE OLD WOMAN. Oh, what do I care why you are here? Why am *I* here? I, who sacrificed all my inclinations to womanly virtue and propriety!

DON JUAN. Patience, lady: you will be perfectly happy

and at home here. As saith the poet, "Hell is a city much like Seville."

THE OLD WOMAN. Happy! here! where I am nothing! where I am nobody!

DON JUAN. Not at all: you are a lady; and wherever ladies are is hell. Do not be surprised or terrified: you will find everything here that a lady can desire, including devils who will serve you from sheer love of servitude, and magnify your importance for the sake of dignifying their service—the best of servants.

THE OLD WOMAN. My servants will be devils!

DON JUAN. Have you ever had servants who were not devils?

THE OLD WOMAN. Never: they were devils, perfect devils, all of them. But that is only a manner of speaking. I thought you meant that my servants here would be real devils.

DON JUAN. No more real devils than you will be a real lady. Nothing is real here. That is the horror of damnation.

THE OLD WOMAN. Oh, this is all madness. This is worse than fire and the worm.

DON JUAN. For you, perhaps, there are consolations. For instance: how old were you when you changed from time to eternity?

THE OLD WOMAN. Do not ask me how old I was—as if I were a thing of the past. I am 77.

DON JUAN. A ripe age, Señora. But in hell old age is not tolerated. It is too real. Here we worship Love and Beauty. Our souls being entirely damned, we cultivate our hearts. As a lady of 77, you would not have a single acquaintance in hell.

THE OLD WOMAN. How can I help my age, man?

DON JUAN. You forget that you have left your age behind you in the realm of time. You are no more 77 than you are 7 or 17 or 27.

THE OLD WOMAN. Nonsense!

DON JUAN. Consider, Señora: was not this true even when you lived on earth? When you were 70, were you really older underneath your wrinkles and your grey hairs than when you were 30?

THE OLD WOMAN. No, younger: at 30 I was a fool. But of what use is it to feel younger and look older?

DON JUAN. You see, Señora, the look was only an illusion.

Your wrinkles lied, just as the plump smooth skin of many a stupid girl of 17, with heavy spirits and decrepit ideas, lies about her age. Well, here we have no bodies: we see each other as bodies only because we learnt to think about one another under that aspect when we were alive; and we still think in that way, knowing no other. But we can appear to one another at what age we choose. You have but to will any of your old looks back, and back they will come.

THE OLD WOMAN. It cannot be true.

DON JUAN. Try.

THE OLD WOMAN. Seventeen!

DON JUAN. Stop. Before you decide, I had better tell you that these things are a matter of fashion. Occasionally we have a rage for 17; but it does not last long. Just at present the fashionable age is 40—or say 37; but there are signs of a change. If you were at all good-looking at 27, I should suggest your trying that, and setting a new fashion.

THE OLD WOMAN. I do not believe a word you are saying. However, 27 be it. (*Whisk! the old woman becomes a young one, and so handsome that in the radiance into which her dull yellow halo has suddenly lightened one might almost mistake her for Ann Whitefield.*)

DON JUAN. Doña Ana de Ulloa!

ANA. What? You know me!

DON JUAN. And you forget me!

ANA. I cannot see your face. (*He raises his hat.*) Don Juan Tenorio! Monster! You who slew my father! even here you pursue me.

DON JUAN. I protest I do not pursue you. Allow me to withdraw. (*Going.*)

ANA (*seizing his arm*). You shall not leave me alone in this dreadful place.

DON JUAN. Provided my staying be not interpreted as pursuit.

ANA (*releasing him*). You may well wonder how I can endure your presence. My dear, dear father!

DON JUAN. Would you like to see him?

ANA. My father here!!!

DON JUAN. No: he is in heaven.

ANA. I knew it. My noble father! He is looking down on us now. What must he feel to see his daughter in this place, and in conversation with his murderer!

DON JUAN. By the way, if we should meet him—

ANA. How can we meet him? He is in heaven.

DON JUAN. He condescends to look in upon us here from time to time. Heaven bores him. So let me warn you that if you meet him he will be mortally offended if you speak of me as his murderer! He maintains that he was a much better swordsman than I, and that if his foot had not slipped he would have killed me. No doubt he is right: I was not a good fencer. I never dispute the point; so we are excellent friends.

ANA. It is no dishonor to a soldier to be proud of his skill in arms.

DON JUAN. You would rather not meet him, probably.

ANA. How dare you say that?

DON JUAN. Oh, that is the usual feeling here. You may remember that on earth—though of course we never confessed it—the death of anyone we knew, even those we liked best, was always mingled with a certain satisfaction at being finally done with them.

ANA. Monster! Never, never.

DON JUAN (*placidly*). I see you recognize the feeling. Yes: a funeral was always a festivity in black, especially the funeral of a relative. At all events, family ties are rarely kept up here. Your father is quite accustomed to this: he will not expect any devotion from you.

ANA. Wretch: I wore mourning for him all my life.

DON JUAN. Yes: it became you. But a life of mourning is one thing: an eternity of it quite another. Besides, here you are as dead as he. Can anything be more ridiculous than one dead person mourning for another? Do not look shocked, my dear Ana; and do not be alarmed: there is plenty of humbug in hell (indeed there is hardly anything else); but the humbug of death and age and change is dropped because here we are all dead and all eternal. You will pick up our ways soon.

ANA. And will all the men call me their dear Ana?

DON JUAN. No. That was a slip of the tongue. I beg your pardon.

ANA (*almost tenderly*). Juan: did you really love me when you behaved so disgracefully to me?

DON JUAN (*impatiently*). Oh, I beg you not to begin talking about love. Here they talk of nothing else but love—its

beauty, its holiness, its spirituality, its devil knows what!—
excuse me; but it does so bore me. They don't know what
they're talking about. I do. They think they have achieved the
perfection of love because they have no bodies. Sheer imaginative debauchery! Faugh!

ANA. Has even death failed to refine your soul, Juan? Has
the terrible judgment of which my father's statue was the
minister taught you no reverence?

DON JUAN. How is that very flattering statue, by the way?
Does it still come to supper with naughty people and cast
them into this bottomless pit?

ANA. It has been a great expense to me. The boys in the
monastery school would not let it alone: the mischievous ones
broke it; and the studious ones wrote their names on it. Three
new noses in two years, and fingers without end. I had to
leave it to its fate at last; and now I fear it is shockingly
mutilated. My poor father!

DON JUAN. Hush! Listen! (*Two great chords rolling on
syncopated waves of sound break forth: D minor and its
dominant: a sound of dreadful joy to all musicians.*) Ha!
Mozart's statue music. It is your father. You had better disappear until I prepare him. (*She vanishes.*)

*From the void comes a living statue of white marble, de-
signed to represent a majestic old man. But he waives his
majesty with infinite grace; walks with a feather-like step;
and makes every wrinkle in his war worn visage brim over
with holiday joyousness. To his sculptor he owes a perfectly
trained figure, which he carries erect and trim; and the ends
of his moustache curl up, elastic as watchsprings, giving him
an air which, but for its Spanish dignity, would be called
jaunty. He is on the pleasantest terms with Don Juan. His
voice, save for a much more distinguished intonation, is so
like the voice of Roebuck Ramsden that it calls attention to
the fact that they are not unlike one another in spite of their
very different fashions of shaving.*

DON JUAN. Ah, here you are, my friend. Why don't you
learn to sing the splendid music Mozart has written for you?

THE STATUE. Unluckily he has written it for a bass voice.
Mine is a counter tenor. Well: have you repented yet?

DON JUAN. I have too much consideration for you to repent, Don Gonzalo. If I did, you would have no excuse for
coming from Heaven to argue with me.

THE STATUE. True. Remain obdurate, my boy. I wish I had killed you, as I should have done but for an accident. Then I should have come here; and you would have had a statue and a reputation for piety to live up to. Any news?

DON JUAN. Yes: your daughter is dead.

THE STATUE (*puzzled*). My daughter? (*Recollecting.*) Oh! the one you were taken with. Let me see: what was her name?

DON JUAN. Ana.

THE STATUE. To be sure: Ana. A goodlooking girl, if I recollect aright. Have you warned Whatshisname—her husband?

DON JUAN. My friend Ottavio? No: I have not seen him since Ana arrived.

Ana comes indignantly to light.

ANA. What does this mean? Ottavio here and your friend! And you, father, have forgotten my name. You are indeed turned to stone.

THE STATUE. My dear: I am so much more admired in marble than I ever was in my own person that I have retained the shape the sculptor gave me. He was one of the first men of his day: you must acknowledge that.

ANA. Father! Vanity! personal vanity! from you!

THE STATUE. Ah, you outlived that weakness, my daughter: you must be nearly 80 by this time. I was cut off (by an accident) in my 64th year, and am considerably your junior in consequence. Besides, my child, in this place, what our libertine friend here would call the farce of parental wisdom is dropped. Regard me, I beg, as a fellow creature, not as a father.

ANA. You speak as this villain speaks.

THE STATUE. Juan is a sound thinker, Ana. A bad fencer, but a sound thinker.

ANA (*horror creeping upon her*). I begin to understand. These are devils, mocking me. I had better pray.

THE STATUE (*consoling her*). No, no, no, my child: do not pray. If you do, you will throw away the main advantage of this place. Written over the gate here are the words "Leave every hope behind, ye who enter." Only think what a relief that is! For what is hope? A form of moral responsibility. Here there is no hope, and consequently no duty, no work, nothing to be gained by praying, nothing to be lost by doing what you like. Hell, in short, is a place where you have nothing to do but amuse yourself. (*Don Juan sighs deeply.*) You sigh, friend Juan; but if you dwelt in heaven, as I do, you would realize your advantages.

DON JUAN. You are in good spirits to-day, Commander. You are positively brilliant. What is the matter?

THE STATUE. I have come to a momentous decision, my boy. But first, where is our friend the Devil? I must consult him in the matter. And Ana would like to make his acquaintance, no doubt.

ANA. You are preparing some torment for me.

DON JUAN. All that is superstition, Ana. Reassure yourself. Remember: the devil is not so black as he is painted.

THE STATUE. Let us give him a call.

At the wave of the statue's hand the great chords roll out again; but this time Mozart's music gets grotesquely adulterated with Gounod's. A scarlet halo begins to glow; and into it the Devil rises, very Mephistophelean, and not at all unlike Mendoza, though not so interesting. He looks older; is getting prematurely bald; and, in spite of an effusion of good-nature and friendliness, is peevish and sensitive when his advances are not reciprocated. He does not inspire much confidence in his powers of hard work or endurance, and is, on the whole, a disagreeably self-indulgent looking person; but he is clever and plausible, though perceptibly less well bred than the two other men, and enormously less vital than the woman.

THE DEVIL (*heartily*). Have I the pleasure of again receiving a visit from the illustrious Commander of Calatrava? (*Coldly.*) Don Juan, your servant. (*Politely.*) And a strange lady? My respects, Señora.

ANA. Are you—

THE DEVIL (*bowing*). Lucifer, at your service.

ANA. I shall go mad.

THE DEVIL (*gallantly*). Ah, Señora, do not be anxious. You come to us from earth, full of the prejudices and terrors of that priest-ridden place. You have heard me ill spoken of; and yet, believe me, I have hosts of friends there.

ANA. Yes: you reign in their hearts.

THE DEVIL (*shaking his head*). You flatter me, Señora; but you are mistaken. It is true that the world cannot get on without me; but it never gives me credit for that: in its heart it mistrusts and hates me. Its sympathies are all with misery, with poverty, with starvation of the body and of the heart. I call on it to sympathize with joy, with love, with happiness, with beauty—

DON JUAN (*nauseated*). Excuse me: I am going. You know I cannot stand this.

THE DEVIL (*angrily*). Yes: I know that you are no friend of mine.

THE STATUE. What harm is he doing you, Juan? It seems to me that he was talking excellent sense when you interrupted him.

THE DEVIL (*warmly shaking the statue's hand*). Thank you, my friend: thank you. You have always understood me: he has always disparaged and avoided me.

DON JUAN. I have treated you with perfect courtesy.

THE DEVIL. Courtesy; What is courtesy? I care nothing for mere courtesy. Give me warmth of heart, true sincerity, the bond of sympathy with love and joy—

DON JUAN. You are making me ill.

THE DEVIL. There! (*Appealing to the statue.*) You hear, sir! Oh, by what irony of fate was this cold selfish egotist sent to my kingdom, and you taken to the icy mansions of the sky!

THE STATUE. I can't complain. I was a hypocrite; and it served me right to be sent to heaven.

THE DEVIL. Why, sir, do you not join us, and leave a sphere for which your temperament is too sympathetic, your heart too warm, your capacity for enjoyment too generous?

THE STATUE. I have this day resolved to do so. In future, excellent Son of the Morning, I am yours. I have left Heaven for ever.

THE DEVIL (*again grasping his hand*). Ah, what an honor for me! What a triumph for our cause! Thank you, thank you. And now, my friend—I may call you so at last—could you not persuade him to take the place you have left vacant above?

THE STATUE (*shaking his head*). I cannot conscientiously recommend anybody with whom I am on friendly terms to deliberately make himself dull and uncomfortable.

THE DEVIL. Of course not; but are you sure he would be uncomfortable? Of course you know best: you brought him here originally; and we had the greatest hopes of him. His sentiments were in the best taste of our best people. You remember how he sang? (*He begins to sing in a nasal operatic baritone, tremulous from an eternity of misuse in the French manner.*)

> Vivan le femmine!
> Viva il buon vino!

THE STATUE (*taking up the tune an octave higher in his counter tenor*).

> Sostegno e gloria
> D'umanità.

THE DEVIL. Precisely. Well, he never sings for us now.

DON JUAN. Do you complain of that? Hell is full of musical amateurs: music is the brandy of the damned. May not one lost soul be permitted to abstain?

THE DEVIL. You dare blaspheme against the sublimest of the arts!

DON JUAN (*with cold disgust*). You talk like a hysterical woman fawning on a fiddler.

THE DEVIL. I am not angry. I merely pity you. You have no soul; and you are unconscious of all that you lose. Now you, Señor Commander, are a born musician. How well you sing! Mozart would be delighted if he were still here; but he moped and went to heaven. Curious how these clever men, whom you would have supposed born to be popular here, have turned out social failures, like Don Juan!

DON JUAN. I am really very sorry to be a social failure.

THE DEVIL. Not that we don't admire your intellect, you know. We do. But I look at the matter from your own point of view. You don't get on with us. The place doesn't suit you. The truth is, you have—I won't say no heart; for we know that beneath all your affected cynicism you have a warm one—

DON JUAN (*shrinking*). Don't, please don't.

THE DEVIL (*nettled*). Well, you've no capacity for enjoyment. Will that satisfy you?

DON JUAN. It is a somewhat less insufferable form of cant than the other. But if you'll allow me, I'll take refuge, as usual, in solitude.

THE DEVIL. Why not take refuge in Heaven? That's the proper place for you. (*To Ana.*) Come, Señora! could you not persuade him for his own good to try change of air?

ANA. But can he go to Heaven if he wants to?

THE DEVIL. What's to prevent him?

ANA. Can anybody—can *I* go to Heaven if I want to?

THE DEVIL (*rather contemptuously*). Certainly, if your taste lies that way.

ANA. But why doesn't everybody go to Heaven, then?

THE STATUE (*chuckling*). *I* can tell you that, my dear. It's because heaven is the most angelically dull place in all creation: that's why.

THE DEVIL. His excellency the Commander puts it with military bluntness; but the strain of living in Heaven is intolerable. There is a notion that I was turned out of it; but as a matter of fact nothing could have induced me to stay there. I simply left it and organized this place.

THE STATUE. I don't wonder at it. Nobody could stand an eternity of heaven.

THE DEVIL. Oh, it suits some people. Let us be just, Commander: it is a question of temperament. I don't admire the heavenly temperament: I don't understand it: I don't know that I particularly want to understand it; but it takes all sorts to make a universe. There is no accounting for tastes: there are people who like it. I think Don Juan would like it.

DON JUAN. But—pardon my frankness—could you really go back there if you desired to; or are the grapes sour?

THE DEVIL. Back there! I often go back there. Have you never read the book of Job? Have you any canonical authority for assuming that there is any barrier between our circle and the other one?

ANA. But surely there is a great gulf fixed.

THE DEVIL. Dear lady: a parable must not be taken literally. The gulf is the difference between the angelic and the diabolic temperament. What more impassable gulf could you have? Think of what you have seen on earth. There is no physical gulf between the philosopher's class room and the bull ring; but the bull fighters do not come to the class room for all that. Have you ever been in the country where I have the largest following—England? There they have great racecourses, and also concert rooms where they play the classical compositions of his Excellency's friend Mozart. Those who go to the racecourses can stay away from them and go to the classical concerts instead if they like: there is no law against it; for Englishmen never will be slaves: they are free to do whatever the Government and public opinion allow them to do. And the classical concert is admitted to be a higher, more cultivated, poetic, intellectual, ennobling place than the racecourse. But do the lovers of racing desert their sport and flock to the concert room? Not they. They would suffer there all the weariness the Commander has suffered in heaven. There is the great gulf of the parable between the two places. A mere physical gulf they could bridge; or at least I could bridge it for them (the earth is full of Devil's Bridges); but the gulf of dislike is impassable and eternal. And that is the only gulf that separates my friends here from those who are invidiously called the blest.

ANA. I shall go to heaven at once.

THE STATUE. My child: one word of warning first. Let me complete my friend Lucifer's similitude of the classical concert. At every one of those concerts in England you will find rows of weary people who are there, not because they really like classical music, but because they think they ought to like it. Well, there is the same thing in heaven. A number of people sit there in glory, not because they are happy, but because they think they owe it to their position to be in heaven. They are almost all English.

THE DEVIL. Yes: the Southerners give it up and join me just as you have done. But the English really do not seem to know when they are thoroughly miserable. An Englishman thinks he is moral when he is only uncomfortable.

THE STATUE. In short, my daughter, if you go to Heaven without being naturally qualified for it, you will not enjoy yourself there.

ANA. And who dares say that I am not naturally qualified for it? The most distinguished princes of the Church have never questioned it. I owe it to myself to leave this place at once.

THE DEVIL (*offended*). As you please, Señora. I should have expected better taste from you.

ANA. Father: I shall expect you to come with me. You cannot stay here. What will people say?

THE STATUE. People! Why, the best people are here—

princes of the church and all. So few go to Heaven, and so many come here, that the blest, once called a heavenly host, are a continually dwindling minority. The saints, the fathers, the elect of long ago are the cranks, the faddists, the outsiders of to-day.

THE DEVIL. It is true. From the beginning of my career I knew that I should win in the long run by sheer weight of public opinion, in spite of the long campaign of misrepresentation and calumny against me. At bottom the universe is a constitutional one; and with such a majority as mine I cannot be kept permanently out of office.

DON JUAN. I think, Ana, you had better stay here.

ANA (*jealously*). You do not want me to go with you.

DON JUAN. Surely you do not want to enter Heaven in the company of a reprobate like me.

ANA. All souls are equally precious. You repent, do you not?

DON JUAN. My dear Ana, you are silly. Do you suppose heaven is like earth, where people persuade themselves that what is done can be undone by repentance; that what is spoken can be unspoken by withdrawing it; that what is true can be annihilated by a general agreement to give it the lie? No: heaven is the home of the masters of reality: that is why I am going thither.

ANA. Thank you: I am going to heaven for happiness. I have had quite enough of reality on earth.

DON JUAN. Then you must stay here; for hell is the home of the unreal and of the seekers for happiness. It is the only refuge from heaven, which is, as I tell you, the home of the masters of reality, and from earth, which is the home of the slaves of reality. The earth is a nursery in which men and women play at being heros and heroines, saints and sinners; but they are dragged down from their fool's paradise by their bodies: hunger and cold and thirst, age and decay and disease, death above all, make them slaves of reality: thrice a day meals must be eaten and digested: thrice a century a new generation must be engendered: ages of faith, of romance, and of science are all driven at last to have but one prayer "Make me a healthy animal." But here you escape this tyranny of the flesh; for here you are not an animal at all: you are a ghost, an appearance, an illusion, a convention, deathless, ageless: in a word, bodiless. There are no social

questions here, no political questions, no religious questions,
best of all, perhaps, no sanitary questions. Here you call your
appearance beauty, your emotions love, your sentiments heroism, your aspirations virtue, just as you did on earth; but
here there are no hard facts to contradict you, no ironic
contrast of your needs with your pretensions, no human
comedy, nothing but a perpetual romance, a universal melodrama. As our German friend put it in his poem, "the poeti-
cally nonsensical here is good sense; and the Eternal Feminine
draws us ever upward and on"—without getting us a step
farther. And yet you want to leave this paradise!

ANA. But if Hell be so beautiful as this, how glorious must
heaven be!

*The Devil, the Statue, and Don Juan all begin to speak at
once in violent protest; then stop, abashed.*

DON JUAN. I beg your pardon.

THE DEVIL. Not at all. I interrupted you.

THE STATUE. You were going to say something.

DON JUAN. After you, gentlemen.

THE DEVIL (*to Don Juan*). You have been so eloquent on
the advantages of my dominions that I leave you to do equal
justice to the drawbacks of the alternative establishment.

DON JUAN. In Heaven, as I picture it, dear lady, you live
and work instead of playing and pretending. You face things
as they are; you escape nothing but glamor; and your steadfastness and your peril are your glory. If the play still goes
on here and on earth, and all the world is a stage, Heaven
is at least behind the scenes. But Heaven cannot be described
by metaphor. Thither I shall go presently, because there I
hope to escape at last from lies and from the tedious, vulgar
pursuit of happiness, to spend my eons in contemplation—

THE STATUE. Ugh!

DON JUAN. Señor Commander: I do not blame your disgust: a picture gallery is a dull place for a blind man. But
even as you enjoy the contemplation of such romantic mirages
as beauty and pleasure; so would I enjoy the contemplation
of that which interests me above all things: namely, Life:
the force that ever strives to attain greater power of con-
templating itself. What made this brain of mine, do you
think? Not the need to move my limbs; for a rat with half my
brains moves as well as I. Not merely the need to do, but

the need to know what I do, lest in my blind efforts to live I should be slaying myself.

THE STATUE. You would have slain yourself in your blind efforts to fence but for my foot slipping, my friend.

DON JUAN. Audacious ribald: your laughter will finish in hideous boredom before morning.

THE STATUE. Ha ha! Do you remember how I frightened you when I said something like that to you from my pedestal in Seville? It sounds rather flat without my trombones.

DON JUAN. They tell me it generally sounds flat with them, Commander.

ANA. Oh, do not interrupt with these frivolities, father. Is there nothing in Heaven but contemplation, Juan?

DON JUAN. In the Heaven I seek, no other joy. But there is the work of helping Life in its struggle upward. Think of how it wastes and scatters itself, how it raises up obstacles to itself and destroys itself in its ignorance and blindness. It needs a brain, this irresistible force, lest in its ignorance it should resist itself. What a piece of work is man! says the poet. Yes: but what a blunderer! Here is the highest miracle of organization yet attained by life, the most intensely alive thing that exists, the most conscious of all the organisms; and yet, how wretched are his brains! Stupidity made sordid and cruel by the realities learnt from toil and poverty: Imagination resolved to starve sooner than face these realities, piling up illusions to hide them, and calling itself cleverness, genius! And each accusing the other of its own defect: Stupidity accusing Imagination of folly, and Imagination accusing Stupidity of ignorance: whereas, alas! Stupidity has all the knowledge, and Imagination all the intelligence.

THE DEVIL. And a pretty kettle of fish they make of it between them. Did I not say, when I was arranging that affair of Faust's, that all Man's reason has done for him is to make him beastlier than any beast. One splendid body is worth the brains of a hundred dyspeptic, flatulent philosophers.

DON JUAN. You forget that brainless magnificence of body has been tried. Things immeasurably greater than man in every respect but brain have existed and perished. The megatherium, the icthyosaurus have paced the earth with seven-league steps and hidden the day with cloud vast wings. Where are they now? Fossils in museums, and so few and imperfect at that, that a knuckle bone or a tooth of one of them is prized beyond the lives of a thousand soldiers. These things lived and wanted to live; but for lack of brains they did not know how to carry out their purpose, and so destroyed themselves.

THE DEVIL. And is Man any the less destroying himself for all this boasted brain of his? Have you walked up and down upon the earth lately? I have; and I have examined Man's wonderful inventions. And I tell you that in the arts of life man invents nothing; but in the arts of death he outdoes Nature herself, and produces by chemistry and machinery all the slaughter of plague, pestilence and famine. The peasant I tempt to-day eats and drinks what was eaten and drunk by the peasants of ten thousand years ago; and the house he lives in has not altered as much in a thousand centuries as the fashion of a lady's bonnet in a score of weeks. But when he goes out to slay, he carries a marvel of mechanism that lets loose at the touch of his finger all the hidden molecular energies, and leaves the javelin, the arrow, the blowpipe of his fathers far behind. In the arts of peace Man is a bungler. I have seen his cotton factories and the like, with machinery that a greedy dog could have invented if it had wanted money instead of food. I know his clumsy typewriters and bungling locomotives and tedious bicycles: they are toys compared to the Maxim gun, the submarine torpedo boat. There is nothing in Man's industrial machinery but his greed and sloth: his heart is in his weapons. This marvellous force of Life of which you boast is a force of Death: Man measures his strength by his destructiveness. What is his religion? An excuse for hating me. What is his law? An excuse for hanging you. What is his morality? Gentility! an excuse for consuming without producing. What is his art? An excuse for gloating over pictures of slaughter. What are his politics? Either the worship of a despot because a despot can kill, or parliamentary cockfighting. I spent an evening lately in a certain celebrated legislature, and heard the pot lecturing the kettle for its blackness, and ministers answering questions. When I left I chalked up on the door the old nursery saying "Ask no questions and you will be told no lies." I bought a sixpenny family magazine, and found it full of pictures of young men shooting and stabbing one another. I saw a man die: he was a London bricklayer's laborer with seven children. He left seventeen

pounds club money; and his wife spent it all on his funeral
and went into the workhouse with the children next day. She
would not have spent sevenpence on her children's schooling:
the law had to force her to let them be taught gratuitously;
but on death she spent all she had. Their imagination glows,
their energies rise up at the idea of death, these people: they
love it; and the more horrible it is the more they enjoy it. Hell
is a place far above their comprehension: they derive their
notion of it from two of the greatest fools that ever lived, an
Italian and an Englishman. The Italian described it as a place
of mud, frost, filth, fire, and venomous serpents: all torture.
This ass, when he was not lying about me, was maundering
about some woman whom he saw once in the street. The
Englishman described me as being expelled from Heaven
by cannons and gunpowder; and to this day every Briton
believes that the whole of his silly story is in the Bible.
What else he says I do not know; for it is all in a long
poem which neither I nor anyone else ever succeeded in
wading through. It is the same in everything. The highest
form of literature is the tragedy, a play in which everybody
is murdered at the end. In the old chronicles you read of
earthquakes and pestilences, and are told that these shewed
the power and majesty of God and the littleness of Man.
Nowadays the chronicles describe battles. In a battle two
bodies of men shoot at one another with bullets and explosive shells until one body runs away, when the others
chase the fugitives on horseback and cut them to pieces as
they fly. And this, the chronicle concludes, shews the
greatness and majesty of empires, and the littleness of
the vanquished. Over such battles the people run about the
streets yelling with delight, and egg their Governments on
to spend hundreds of millions of money in the slaughter,
whilst the strongest Ministers dare not spend an extra penny
in the pound against the poverty and pestilence through
which they themselves daily walk. I could give you a thousand
instances; but they all come to the same thing: the power that
governs the earth is not the power of Life but of Death; and
the inner need that has nerved Life to the effort of organizing
itself into the human being is not the need for higher life but
for a more efficient engine of destruction. The plague, the
famine, the earthquake, the tempest were too spasmodic in
their action; the tiger and crocodile were too easily satiated

and not cruel enough: something more constantly, more ruthlessly, more ingeniously destructive was needed; and that something was Man, the inventor of the rack, the stake, the gallows, and the electrocutor; of the sword and gun; above all, of justice, duty, patriotism and all the other isms by which even those who are clever enough to be humanely disposed are persuaded to become the most destructive of all the destroyers.

DON JUAN. Pshaw! all this is old. Your weak side, my diabolic friend, is that you have always been a gull: you take Man at his own valuation. Nothing would flatter him more than your opinion of him. He loves to think of himself as bold and bad. He is neither one nor the other: he is only a coward. Call him tyrant, murderer, pirate, bully; and he will adore you, and swagger about with the consciousness of having the blood of the old sea kings in his veins. Call him liar and thief; and he will only take an action against you for libel. But call him coward; and he will go mad with rage: he will face death to outface that stinging truth. Man gives every reason for his conduct save one, every excuse for his crimes save one, every plea for his safety save one; and that one is his cowardice. Yet all his civilization is founded on his cowardice, on his abject tameness, which he calls his respectability. There are limits to what a mule or an ass will stand; but Man will suffer himself to be degraded until his vileness becomes so loathsome to his oppressors that they themselves are forced to reform it.

THE DEVIL. Precisely. And these are the creatures in whom you discover what you call a Life Force!

DON JUAN. Yes; for now comes the most surprising part of the whole business.

THE STATUE. What's that?

DON JUAN. Why, that you can make any of these cowards brave by simply putting an idea into his head.

THE STATUE. Stuff! As an old soldier I admit the cowardice: it's as universal as sea sickness, and matters just as little. But that about putting an idea into a man's head is stuff and nonsense. In a battle all you need to make you fight is a little hot blood and the knowledge that it's more dangerous to lose than to win.

DON JUAN. That is perhaps why battles are so useless. But men never really overcome fear until they imagine they are

fighting to further a universal purpose—fighting for an idea,
as they call it. Why was the Crusader braver than the pirate?
Because he fought, not for himself, but for the Cross. What
force was it that met him with a valor as reckless as his own?
The force of men who fought, not for themselves, but for
Islam. They took Spain from us, though we were fighting for
our very hearths and homes; but when we, too, fought for that
mighty idea, a Catholic Church, we swept them back to Africa.

THE DEVIL (*ironically*). What! you a Catholic, Señor Don
Juan. A devotee! My congratulations.

THE STATUE (*seriously*). Come, come! as a soldier, I can
listen to nothing against the Church.

DON JUAN. Have no fear, Commander: this idea of a
Catholic Church will survive Islam, will survive the Cross,
will survive even that vulgar pageant of incompetent schoolboyish gladiators which you call the Army.

THE STATUE. Juan: you will force me to call you to account
for this.

DON JUAN. Useless: I cannot fence. Every idea for which
Man will die will be a Catholic idea. When the Spaniard
learns at last that he is no better than the Saracen, and his
prophet no better than Mahomet, he will arise, more Catholic
than ever, and die on a barricade across the filthy slum he
starves in, for universal liberty and equality.

THE STATUE. Bosh!

DON JUAN. What you call bosh is the only thing men dare
die for. Later on, Liberty will not be Catholic enough: men
will die for human perfection, to which they will sacrifice all
their liberty gladly.

THE DEVIL. Ay: they will never be at a loss for an excuse
for killing one another.

DON JUAN. What of that? It is not death that matters, but
the fear of death. It is not killing and dying that degrades us,
but base living, and accepting the wages and profits of
degradation. Better ten dead men than one live slave or his
master. Men shall yet rise up, father against son and brother
against brother, and kill one another for the great Catholic
idea of abolishing slavery.

THE DEVIL. Yes, when the Liberty and Equality of which
you prate shall have made free white Christians cheaper in
the labor market than black heathen slaves sold by auction at
the block.

DON JUAN. Never fear! the white laborer shall have his turn too. But I am not now defending the illusory forms the great ideas take. I am giving you examples of the fact that this creature Man, who in his own selfish affairs is a coward to the backbone, will fight for an idea like a hero. He may be abject as a citizen; but he is dangerous as a fanatic. He can only be enslaved whilst he is spiritually weak enough to listen to reason. I tell you, gentlemen, if you can shew a man a piece of what he now calls God's work to do, and what he will later on call by many new names, you can make him entirely reckless of the consequences to himself personally.

ANA. Yes: he shirks all his responsibilities, and leaves his wife to grapple with them.

THE STATUE. Well said, daughter. Do not let him talk you out of your common sense.

THE DEVIL. Alas! Señor Commander, now that we have got on to the subject of Woman, he will talk more than ever. However, I confess it is for me the one supremely interesting subject.

DON JUAN. To a woman, Señora, man's duties and responsibilities begin and end with the task of getting bread for her children. To her, Man is only a means to the end of getting children and rearing them.

ANA. Is that your idea of a woman's mind? I call it cynical and disgusting materialism.

DON JUAN. Pardon me, Ana: I said nothing about a woman's whole mind. I spoke of her view of Man as a separate sex. It is no more cynical than her view of herself as above all things a Mother. Sexually, Woman is Nature's contrivance for perpetuating its highest achievement. Sexually, Man is Woman's contrivance for fulfilling Nature's behest in the most economical way. She knows by instinct that far back in the evolutional process she invented him, differentiated him, created him in order to produce something better than the single-sexed process can produce. Whilst he fulfils the purpose for which she made him, he is welcome to his dreams, his follies, his ideals, his heroisms, provided that the keystone of them all is the worship of woman, of motherhood, of the family, of the hearth. But how rash and dangerous it was to invent a separate creature whose sole function was her own impregnation! For mark what has happened. First, Man has multiplied on her hands until there are as many men as women; so that she has been unable to employ for her purposes more than a fraction of the immense energy she has left at his disposal by saving him the exhausting labor of gestation. This superfluous energy has gone to his brain and to his muscle. He has become too strong to be controlled by her bodily, and too imaginative and mentally vigorous to be content with mere self-reproduction. He has created civilization without consulting her, taking her domestic labor for granted as the foundation of it.

ANA. That is true, at all events.

THE DEVIL. Yes; and this civilization! what is it, after all?

DON JUAN. After all, an excellent peg to hang your cynical commonplaces on; but before all, it is an attempt on Man's part to make himself something more than the mere instrument of Woman's purpose. So far, the result of Life's continual effort not only to maintain itself, but to achieve higher and higher organization and completer self-consciousness, is only, at best, a doubtful campaign between its forces and those of Death and Degeneration. The battles in this campaign are mere blunders, mostly won, like actual military battles, in spite of the commanders.

THE STATUE. That is a dig at me. No matter: go on, go on.

DON JUAN. It is a dig at a much higher power than you, Commander. Still, you must have noticed in your profession that even a stupid general can win battles when the enemy's general is a little stupider.

THE STATUE (very seriously). Most true, Juan, most true. Some donkeys have amazing luck.

DON JUAN. Well, the Life Force is stupid; but it is not so stupid as the forces of Death and Degeneration. Besides, these are in its pay all the time. And so Life wins, after a fashion. What mere copiousness of fecundity can supply and mere greed preserve, we possess. The survival of whatever form of civilization can produce the best rifle and the best fed riflemen is assured.

THE DEVIL. Exactly! the survival, not of the most effective means of Life but of the most effective means of Death. You always come back to my point, in spite of your wrigglings and evasions and sophistries, not to mention the intolerable length of your speeches.

DON JUAN. Oh come! who began making long speeches? However, if I overtax your intellect, you can leave us and seek the society of love and beauty and the rest of your favorite boredoms.

THE DEVIL (*much offended*). This is not fair, Don Juan, and not civil. I am also on the intellectual plane. Nobody can appreciate it more than I do. I am arguing fairly with you, and, I think, utterly refuting you. Let us go on for another hour if you like.

DON JUAN. Good: let us.

THE STATUE. Not that I see any prospect of your coming to any point in particular, Juan. Still, since in this place, instead of merely killing time we have to kill eternity, go ahead by all means.

DON JUAN (*somewhat impatiently*). My point, you marble-headed old masterpiece, is only a step ahead of you. Are we agreed that Life is a force which has made innumerable experiments in organizing itself; that the mammoth and the man, the mouse and the megatherium, the flies and the fleas and the Fathers of the Church, are all more or less successful attempts to build up that raw force into higher and higher individuals, the ideal individual being omnipotent, omniscient, infallible, and withal completely, unilludedly self-conscious: in short, a god?

THE DEVIL. I agree, for the sake of argument.

THE STATUE. I agree, for the sake of avoiding argument.

ANA. I most emphatically disagree as regards the Fathers of the Church; and I must beg you not to drag them into the argument.

DON JUAN. I did so purely for the sake of alliteration, Ana; and I shall make no further allusion to them. And now, since we are, with that exception, agreed so far, will you not agree with me further that Life has not measured the success of its attempts at godhead by the beauty or bodily perfection of the result, since in both these respects the birds, as our friend Aristophanes long ago pointed out, are so extraordinarily superior, with their power of flight and their lovely plumage, and, may I add, the touching poetry of their loves and nestings, that it is inconceivable that Life, having once produced them, should, if love and beauty were her object, start off on another line and labor at the clumsy elephant and the hideous ape, whose grandchildren we are?

ANA. Aristophanes was a heathen; and you, Juan, I am afraid, are very little better.

THE DEVIL. You conclude, then, that Life was driving at clumsiness and ugliness?

DON JUAN. No, perverse devil that you are, a thousand times no. Life was driving at brains—at its darling object: an organ by which it can attain not only self-consciousness but self-understanding.

THE STATUE. This is metaphysics, Juan. Why the devil should—(*To The Devil.*) I beg your pardon.

THE DEVIL. Pray don't mention it. I have always regarded the use of my name to secure additional emphasis as a high compliment to me. It is quite at your service, Commander.

THE STATUE. Thank you: that's very good of you. Even in heaven, I never quite got out of my old military habits of speech. What I was going to ask Juan was why Life should bother itself about getting a brain. Why should it want to understand itself? Why not be content to enjoy itself?

DON JUAN. Without a brain, Commander, you would enjoy yourself without knowing it, and so lose all the fun.

THE STATUE. True, most true. But I am quite content with brain enough to know that I'm enjoying myself. I don't want to understand why. In fact, I'd rather not. My experience is that one's pleasures don't bear thinking about.

DON JUAN. That is why intellect is so unpopular. But to Life, the force behind the Man, intellect is a necessity, because without it he blunders into death. Just as Life, after ages of struggle, evolved that wonderful bodily organ the eye, so that the living organism could see where it was going and what was coming to help or threaten it, and thus avoid a thousand dangers that formerly slew it, so it is evolving today a mind's eye that shall see, not the physical world, but the purpose of Life, and thereby enable the individual to work for that purpose instead of thwarting and baffling it by setting up shortsighted personal aims as at present. Even as it is, only one sort of man has ever been happy, has ever been universally respected among all the conflicts of interests and illusions.

THE STATUE. You mean the military man.

DON JUAN. Commander: I do not mean the military man. When the military man approaches, the world locks up its spoons and packs off its womankind. No: I sing, not arms and the hero, but the philosophic man: he who seeks in contemplation to discover the inner will of the world, in invention to discover the means of fulfilling that will, and in action to do that will by the so-discovered means. Of all other sorts of men I declare myself tired. They are tedious failures. When I was on earth, professors of all sorts prowled round me feeling for an unhealthy spot in me on which they could fasten. The doctors of medicine bade me consider what I must do to save my body, and offered me quack cures for imaginary diseases. I replied that I was not a hypochondriac; so they called me Ignoramus and went their way. The doctors of divinity bade me consider what I must do to save my soul; but I was not a spiritual hypochondriac any more than a bodily one, and would not trouble myself about that either; so they called me Atheist and went their way. After them came the politician, who said there was only one purpose in Nature, and that was to get him into parliament. I told him I did not care whether he got into parliament or not; so he called me Mugwump and went his way. Then came the romantic man, the Artist, with his love songs and his paintings and his poems; and with him I had great delight for many years, and some profit; for I cultivated my senses for his sake; and his songs taught me to hear better, his paintings to see better, and his poems to feel more deeply. But he led me at last into the worship of Woman.

ANA. Juan!

DON JUAN. Yes: I came to believe that in her voice was all the music of the song, in her face all the beauty of the painting, and in her soul all the emotion of the poem.

ANA. And you were disappointed, I suppose. Well, was it her fault that you attributed all these perfections to her?

DON JUAN. Yes, partly. For with a wonderful instinctive cunning, she kept silent and allowed me to glorify her; to mistake my own visions, thoughts, and feelings for hers. Now my friend the romantic man was often too poor or too timid to approach those women who were beautiful or refined enough to seem to realize his ideal; and so he went to his grave believing in his dream. But I was more favored by nature and circumstance. I was of noble birth and rich; and when my person did not please, my conversation flattered, though I generally found myself fortunate in both.

THE STATUE. Coxcomb!

DON JUAN. Yes; but even my coxcombry pleased. Well, I

found that when I had touched a woman's imagination, she would allow me to persuade myself that she loved me; but when my suit was granted she never said "I am happy: my love is satisfied": she always said, first, "At last, the barriers are down," and second, "When will you come again?"

ANA. That is exactly what men say.

DON JUAN. I protest I never said it. But all women say it. Well, these two speeches always alarmed me; for the first meant that the lady's impulse had been solely to throw down my fortifications and gain my citadel; and the second openly announced that henceforth she regarded me as her property, and counted my time as already wholly at her disposal.

THE DEVIL. That is where your want of heart came in.

THE STATUE (*shaking his head*). You shouldn't repeat what a woman says, Juan.

ANA (*severely*). It should be sacred to you.

THE STATUE. Still, they certainly do always say it. I never minded the barriers; but there was always a slight shock about the other, unless one was very hard hit indeed.

DON JUAN. Then the lady, who had been happy and idle enough before, became anxious, preoccupied with me, always intriguing, conspiring, pursuing, watching, waiting, bent wholly on making sure of her prey—I being the prey, you understand. Now this was not what I had bargained for. It may have been very proper and very natural; but it was not music, painting, poetry and joy incarnated in a beautiful woman. I ran away from it. I ran away from it very often: in fact I became famous for running away from it.

ANA. Infamous, you mean.

DON JUAN. I did not run away from you. Do you blame me for running away from the others?

ANA. Nonsense, man. You are talking to a woman of 77 now. If you had had the chance, you would have run away from me too—if I had let you. You would not have found it so easy with me as with some of the others. If men will not be faithful to their home and their duties, they must be made to be. I daresay you all want to marry lovely incarnations of music and painting and poetry. Well, you can't have them, because they don't exist. If flesh and blood is not good enough for you you must go without: that's all. Women have to put up with flesh-and-blood husbands—and little enough of that too, sometimes; and you will have to put up with flesh-and-blood wives. (*The Devil looks dubious. The Statue makes a wry face.*) I see you don't like that, any of you; but it's true, for all that; so if you don't like it you can lump it.

Don Juan. My dear lady, you have put my whole case against romance into a few sentences. That is just why I turned my back on the romantic man with the artist nature, as he called his infatuation. I thanked him for teaching me to use my eyes and ears; but I told him that his beauty worshipping and happiness hunting and woman idealizing was not worth a dump as a philosophy of life; so he called me Philistine and went his way.

Ana. It seems that Woman taught you something, too, with all her defects.

Don Juan. She did more: she interpreted all the other teaching for me. Ah, my friends, when the barriers were down for the first time, what an astounding illumination! I had been prepared for infatuation, for intoxication, for all the illusions of love's young dream; and lo! never was my perception clearer, nor my criticism more ruthless. The most jealous rival of my mistress never saw every blemish in her more keenly than I. I was not duped: I took her without chloroform.

Ana. But you did take her.

Don Juan. That was the revelation. Up to that moment I had never lost the sense of being my own master; never consciously taken a single step until my reason had examined and approved it. I had come to believe that I was a purely rational creature: a thinker! I said, with the foolish philosopher, "I think; therefore I am." It was Woman who taught me to say "I am; therefore I think." And also "I would think more; therefore I must be more."

The Statue. This is extremely abstract and metaphysical, Juan. If you would stick to the concrete, and put your discoveries in the form of entertaining anecdotes about your adventures with women, your conversation would be easier to follow.

Don Juan. Bah! what need I add? Do you not understand that when I stood face to face with Woman, every fibre in my clear critical brain warned me to spare her and save myself. My morals said No. My conscience said No. My chivalry and pity for her said No. My prudent regard for myself said No. My ear, practised on a thousand songs and symphonies; my eye, exercised on a thousand paintings; tore her voice, her

features, her color to shreds. I caught all those tell-tale re-
semblances to her father and mother by which I knew what
she would be like in thirty years time. I noted the gleam of
gold from a dead tooth in the laughing mouth: I made curious
observations of the strange odors of the chemistry of the
nerves. The visions of my romantic reveries, in which I had
trod the plains of heaven with a deathless, ageless creature of
coral and ivory, deserted me in that supreme hour. I remembered them and desperately strove to recover their illusion;
but they now seemed the emptiest of inventions: my judgment
was not to be corrupted: my brain still said No on every issue.
And whilst I was in the act of framing my excuse to the lady,
Life seized me and threw me into her arms as a sailor throws
a scrap of fish into the mouth of a seabird.

THE STATUE. You might as well have gone without thinking
such a lot about it, Juan. You are like all the clever men: you
have more brains than is good for you.

THE DEVIL. And were you not the happier for the experience, Señor Don Juan?

DON JUAN. The happier, no: the wiser, yes. That moment
introduced me for the first time to myself, and, through myself,
to the world. I saw then how useless it is to attempt to impose
conditions on the irresistible force of Life; to preach prudence,
careful selection, virtue, honor, chastity—

ANA. Don Juan: a word against chastity is an insult to me.

DON JUAN. I say nothing against your chastity, Señora,
since it took the form of a husband and twelve children. What
more could you have done had you been the most abandoned
of women?

ANA. I could have had twelve husbands and no children:
that's what I could have done, Juan. And let me tell you
that that would have made all the difference to the earth
which I replenished.

THE STATUE. Bravo Ana! Juan: you are floored, quelled,
annihilated.

DON JUAN. No; for though that difference is the true
essential difference—Doña Ana has, I admit, gone straight
to the real point—yet it is not a difference of love or chastity,
or even constancy; for twelve children by twelve different husbands would have replenished the earth perhaps more
effectively. Suppose my friend Ottavio had died when you
were thirty, you would never have remained a widow: you

were too beautiful. Suppose the successor of Ottavio had died when you were forty, you would still have been irresistible; and a woman who marries twice marries three times if she becomes free to do so. Twelve lawful children borne by one highly respectable lady to three different fathers is not impossible nor condemned by public opinion. That such a lady may be more law abiding than the poor girl whom we used to spurn into the gutter for bearing one unlawful infant is no doubt true; but dare you say she is less self-indulgent?

ANA. She is less virtuous: that is enough for me.

DON JUAN. In that case, what is virtue but the Trade Unionism of the married? Let us face the facts, dear Ana. The Life Force respects marriage only because marriage is a contrivance of its own to secure the greatest number of children and the closest care of them. For honor, chastity and all the rest of your moral figments it cares not a rap. Marriage is the most licentious of human institutions—

ANA. Juan!

THE STATUE (*protesting*). Really!—

DON JUAN (*determinedly*). I say the most licentious of human institutions: that is the secret of its popularity. And a woman seeking a husband is the most unscrupulous of all the beasts of prey. The confusion of marriage with morality has done more to destroy the conscience of the human race than any other single error. Come, Ana! do not look shocked: you know better than any of us that marriage is a mantrap baited with simulated accomplishments and delusive idealizations. When your sainted mother, by dint of scoldings and punishments, forced you to learn how to play half a dozen pieces on the spinet—which she hated as much as you did—had she any other purpose than to delude your suitors into the belief that your husband would have in his home an angel who would fill it with melody, or at least play him to sleep after dinner? You married my friend Ottavio: well, did you ever open the spinet from the hour when the Church united him to you?

ANA. You are a fool, Juan. A young married woman has something else to do than sit at the spinet without any support for her back; so she gets out of the habit of playing.

DON JUAN. Not if she loves music. No: believe me, she only throws away the bait when the bird is in the net.

ANA (*bitterly*). And men, I suppose, never throw off the

mask when their bird is in the net. The husband never becomes negligent, selfish, brutal—oh never!

DON JUAN. What do these recriminations prove, Ana? Only that the hero is as gross an imposture as the heroine.

ANA. It is all nonsense: most marriages are perfectly comfortable.

DON JUAN. "Perfectly" is a strong expression, Ana. What you mean is that sensible people make the best of one another. Send me to the galleys and chain me to the felon whose number happens to be next before mine; and I must accept the inevitable and make the best of the companionship. Many such companionships, they tell me, are touchingly affectionate; and most are at least tolerably friendly. But that does not make a chain a desirable ornament nor the galleys an abode of bliss. Those who talk most about the blessings of marriage and the constancy of its vows are the very people who declare that if the chain were broken and the prisoners left free to choose, the whole social fabric would fly asunder. You cannot have the argument both ways. If the prisoner is happy, why lock him in? If he is not, why pretend that he is?

ANA. At all events, let me take an old woman's privilege again, and tell you flatly that marriage peoples the world and debauchery does not.

DON JUAN. How if a time come when this shall cease to be true? Do you not know that where there is a will there is a way—that whatever Man really wishes to do he will finally discover a means of doing? Well, you have done your best, you virtuous ladies, and others of your way of thinking, to bend Man's mind wholly towards honorable love as the highest good, and to understand by honorable love romance and beauty and happiness in the possession of beautiful, refined, delicate, affectionate women. You have taught women to value their own youth, health, shapeliness, and refinement above all things. Well, what place have squalling babies and household cares in this exquisite paradise of the senses and emotions? Is it not the inevitable end of it all that the human will shall say to the human brain: Invent me a means by which I can have love, beauty, romance, emotion, passion without their wretched penalties, their expenses, their worries, their trials, their illnesses and agonies and risks of death, their retinue of servants and nurses and doctors and schoolmasters

THE DEVIL. All this, Señor Don Juan, is realized here in my realm.

DON JUAN. Yes, at the cost of death. Man will not take it at that price: he demands the romantic delights of your hell whilst he is still on earth. Well, the means will be found: the brain will not fail when the will is in earnest. The day is coming when great nations will find their numbers dwindling from census to census; when the six roomed villa will rise in price above the family mansion: when the viciously reckless poor and the stupidly pious rich will delay the extinction of the race only by degrading it; whilst the boldly prudent, the thriftily selfish and ambitious, the imaginative and poetic, the lovers of money and solid comfort, the worshippers of success, of art, and of love, will all oppose to the Force of Life the device of sterility.

THE STATUE. That is all very eloquent, my young friend; but if you had lived to Ana's age, or even to mine, you would have learned that the people who get rid of the fear of poverty and children and all the other family troubles, and devote themselves to having a good time of it, only leave their minds free for the fear of old age and ugliness and impotence and death. The childless laborer is more tormented by his wife's idleness and her constant demands for amusement and distraction than he could be by twenty children; and his wife is more wretched than he. I have had my share of vanity; for as a young man I was admired by women; and as a statue I am praised by art critics. But I confess that had I found nothing to do in the world but wallow in these delights I should have cut my throat. When I married Ana's mother—or perhaps, to be strictly correct, I should rather say when I at last gave in and allowed Ana's mother to marry me—I knew that I was planting thorns in my pillow, and that marriage for me, a swaggering young officer thitherto unvanquished, meant defeat and capture.

ANA (*scandalized*). Father!

THE STATUE. I am sorry to shock you, my love; but since Juan has stripped every rag of decency from the discussion I may as well tell the frozen truth.

ANA. Hmf! I suppose I was one of the thorns.

THE STATUE. By no means: you were often a rose. You see, your mother had most of the trouble you gave.

DON JUAN. Then may I ask, Commander, why you have

left Heaven to come here and wallow, as you express it, in
sentimental beatitudes which you confess would once have
driven you to cut your throat?

THE STATUE (*struck by this*). Egad, that's true.

THE DEVIL (*alarmed*). What! You are going back from
your word! (*To Don Juan.*) And all your philosophizing has
been nothing but a mask for proselytizing! (*To the Statue.*)
Have you forgotten already the hideous dulness from which
I am offering you a refuge here? (*To Don Juan.*) And does
your demonstration of the approaching sterilization and extinction of mankind lead to anything better than making the
most of those pleasures of art and love which you yourself
admit refined you, elevated you, developed you?

DON JUAN. I never demonstrated the extinction of mankind.
Life cannot will its own extinction either in its blind
amorphous state or in any of the forms into which it has organized itself. I had not finished when His Excellency interrupted me.

THE STATUE. I begin to doubt whether you ever will finish,
my friend. You are extremely fond of hearing yourself talk.

DON JUAN. True; but since you have endured so much, you
may as well endure to the end. Long before this sterilization
which I described becomes more than a clearly foreseen
possibility, the reaction will begin. The great central purpose
of breeding the race, ay, breeding it to heights now deemed
superhuman: that purpose which is now hidden in a mephitic
cloud of love and romance and prudery and fastidiousness,
will break through into clear sunlight as a purpose no longer
to be confused with the gratification of personal fancies, the
impossible realization of boys' and girls' dreams of bliss, or
the need of older people for companionship or money. The
plain-spoken marriage services of the vernacular Churches
will no longer be abbreviated and half suppressed as indelicate. The sober decency, earnestness and authority of their
declaration of the real purpose of marriage will be honored
and accepted, whilst their romantic vowings and pledgings
and until-death-do-us-partings and the like will be expunged
as unbearable frivolities. Do my sex the justice to admit,
Señora, that we have always recognized that the sex relation
is not a personal or friendly relation at all.

ANA. Not a personal or friendly relation! What relation is
more personal? more sacred? more holy?

DON JUAN. Sacred and holy, if you like, Ana, but not personally friendly. Your relation to God is sacred and holy: dare you call it personally friendly? In the sex relation the universal creative energy, of which the parties are both the helpless agents, over-rides and sweeps away all personal considerations and dispenses with all personal relations. The pair may be utter strangers to one another, speaking different languages, differing in race and color, in age and disposition, with no bond between them but a possibility of that fecundity for the sake of which the Life Force throws them into one another's arms at the exchange of a glance. Do we not recognize this by allowing marriages to be made by parents without consulting the woman? Have you not often expressed your disgust at the immorality of the English nation, in which women and men of noble birth become acquainted and court each other like peasants? And how much does even the peasant know of his bride or she of him before he engages himself? Why, you would not make a man your lawyer or your family doctor on so slight an acquaintance as you would fall in love with and marry him!

ANA. Yes, Juan: we know the libertine's philosophy. Always ignore the consequences to the woman.

DON JUAN. The consequences, yes: they justify her fierce grip of the man. But surely you do not call that attachment a sentimental one. As well call the policeman's attachment to his prisoner a love relation.

ANA. You see you have to confess that marriage is necessary, though, according to you, love is the slightest of all the relations.

DON JUAN. How do you know that it is not the greatest of all the relations? far too great to be a personal matter. Could your father have served his country if he had refused to kill any enemy of Spain unless he personally hated him? Can a woman serve her country if she refuses to marry any man she does not personally love? You know it is not so: the woman of noble birth marries as the man of noble birth fights, on political and family grounds, not on personal ones.

THE STATUE (*impressed*). A very clever point that, Juan: I must think it over. You are really full of ideas. How did you come to think of this one?

DON JUAN. I learnt it by experience. When I was on earth, and made those proposals to ladies which, though universally condemned, have made me so interesting a hero of legend, I was not infrequently met in some such way as this. The lady would say that she would countenance my advances, provided they were honorable. On inquiring what that proviso meant, I found that it meant that I proposed to get possession of her property if she had any, or to undertake her support for life if she had not; that I desired her continual companionship, counsel and conversation to the end of my days, and would bind myself under penalties to be always enraptured by them; and, above all, that I would turn my back on all other women for ever for her sake. I did not object to these conditions because they were exorbitant and inhuman: it was their extraordinary irrelevance that prostrated me. I invariably replied with perfect frankness that I had never dreamt of any of these things; that unless the lady's character and intellect were equal or superior to my own, her conversation must degrade and her counsel mislead me; that her constant companionship might, for all I knew, become intolerably tedious to me; that I could not answer for my feelings for a week in advance, much less to the end of my life; that to cut me off from all natural and unconstrained relations with the rest of my fellow creatures would narrow and warp me if I submitted to it, and, if not, would bring me under the curse of clandestinity; that, finally, my proposals to her were wholly unconnected with any of these matters, and were the outcome of a perfectly simple impulse of my manhood towards her womanhood.

ANA. You mean that it was an immoral impulse.

DON JUAN. Nature, my dear lady, is what you call immoral. I blush for it; but I cannot help it. Nature is a pander, Time a wrecker, and Death a murderer. I have always preferred to stand up to those facts and build institutions on their recognition. You prefer to propitiate the three devils by proclaiming their chastity, their thrift, and their loving kindness; and to base your institutions on these flatteries. Is it any wonder that the institutions do not work smoothly?

THE STATUE. What used the ladies to say, Juan?

DON JUAN. Oh come! Confidence for confidence. First tell me what you used to say to the ladies.

THE STATUE. I! Oh, I swore that I would be faithful to the death; that I should die if they refused me; that no woman could ever be to me what she was—

ANA. She! Who?

THE STATUE. Whoever it happened to be at the time, my dear. I had certain things I always said. One of them was that even when I was eighty, one white hair of the woman I loved would make me tremble more than the thickest gold tress from the most beautiful young head. Another was that I could not bear the thought of anyone else being the mother of my children.

DON JUAN (*revolted*). You old rascal!

THE STATUE (*stoutly*). Not a bit; for I really believed it with all my soul at the moment. I had a heart: not like you. And it was this sincerity that made me successful.

DON JUAN. Sincerity! To be fool enough to believe a ramping, stamping, thumping lie: that is what you call sincerity! To be so greedy for a woman that you deceive yourself in your eagerness to deceive her: sincerity, you call it!

THE STATUE. Oh, damn your sophistries! I was a man in love, not a lawyer. And the women loved me for it, bless them!

DON JUAN. They made you think so. What will you say when I tell you that though I played the lawyer so callously, they made me think so too? I also had my moments of infatuation in which I gushed nonsense and believed it. Sometimes the desire to give pleasure by saying beautiful things so rose in me on the flood of emotion that I said them recklessly. At other times I argued against myself with a devilish coldness that drew tears. But I found it just as hard to escape in the one case as in the others. When the lady's instinct was set on me, there was nothing for it but lifelong servitude or flight.

ANA. You dare boast, before me and my father, that every woman found you irresistible.

DON JUAN. Am I boasting? It seems to me that I cut the most pitiable of figures. Besides, I said "when the lady's instinct was set on me." It was not always so; and then, heavens! what transports of virtuous indignation! what overwhelming defiance to the dastardly seducer! what scenes of Imogen and Iachimo!

ANA. I made no scenes. I simply called my father.

DON JUAN. And he came, sword in hand, to vindicate outraged honor and morality by murdering me.

THE STATUE. Murdering! What do you mean? Did I kill you or did you kill me?

DON JUAN. Which of us was the better fencer?

THE STATUE. I was.

DON JUAN. Of course you were. And yet you, the hero of those scandalous adventures you have just been relating to us, you had the effrontery to pose as the avenger of outraged morality and condemn me to death! You would have slain me but for an accident.

THE STATUE. I was expected to, Juan. That is how things were arranged on earth. I was not a social reformer; and I always did what it was customary for a gentleman to do.

DON JUAN. That may account for your attacking me, but not for the revolting hypocrisy of your subsequent proceedings as a statue.

THE STATUE. That all came of my going to Heaven.

THE DEVIL. I still fail to see, Señor Don Juan, that these episodes in your earthly career and in that of the Señor Commander in any way discredit my view of life. Here, I repeat, you have all that you sought without anything that you shrank from.

DON JUAN. On the contrary, here I have everything that disappointed me without anything that I have not already tried and found wanting. I tell you that as long as I can conceive something better than myself I cannot be easy unless I am striving to bring it into existence or clearing the way for it. That is the law of my life. That is the working within me of Life's incessant aspiration to higher organization, wider, deeper, intenser self-consciousness, and clearer self-understanding. It was the supremacy of this purpose that reduced love for me to the mere pleasure of a moment, art for me to the mere schooling of my faculties, religion for me to a mere excuse for laziness, since it had set up a God who looked at the world and saw that it was good, against the instinct in me that looked through my eyes at the world and saw that it could be improved. I tell you that in the pursuit of my own pleasure, my own health, my own fortune, I have never known happiness. It was not love for Woman that delivered me into her hands: it was fatigue, exhaustion. When I was a child, and bruised my head against a stone, I ran to the nearest woman and cried away my pain against her apron. When I grew up, and bruised my soul against the brutalities and stupidities with which I had to strive, I did again just what I had done as a child. I have enjoyed, too, my rests, my recuperations, my breathing times, my very prostrations after strife; but rather would I be dragged through all the circles of the foolish Italian's Inferno than through the pleasures of Europe. That is what has made this place of eternal pleasures so deadly to me. It is the absence of this instinct in you that makes you that strange monster called a Devil. It is the success with which you have diverted the attention of men from their real purpose, which in one degree or another is the same as mine, to yours, that has earned you the name of The Tempter. It is the fact that they are doing your will, or rather drifting with your want of will, instead of doing their own, that makes them the uncomfortable, false, restless, artificial, petulant, wretched creatures they are.

THE DEVIL (*mortified*). Señor Don Juan: you are uncivil to my friends.

DON JUAN. Pooh! why should I be civil to them or to you? In this Palace of Lies a truth or two will not hurt you. Your friends are all the dullest dogs I know. They are not beautiful: they are only decorated. They are not clean: they are only shaved and starched. They are not dignified: they are only fashionably dressed. They are not educated: they are only college passmen. They are not religious: they are only pewrenters. They are not moral: they are only conventional. They are not virtuous: they are only cowardly. They are not even vicious: they are only "frail." They are not artistic: they are only lascivious. They are not prosperous: they are only rich. They are not loyal, they are only servile; not dutiful, only sheepish; not public spirited, only patriotic; not courageous, only quarrelsome; not determined, only obstinate; not masterful, only domineering; not self-controlled, only obtuse; not self-respecting, only vain; not kind, only sentimental; not social, only gregarious; not considerate, only polite; not intelligent, only opinionated; not progressive, only factious; not imaginative, only superstitious; not just, only vindictive; not generous, only propitiatory; not disciplined, only cowed; and not truthful at all—liars every one of them, to the very backbone of their souls.

THE STATUE. Your flow of words is simply amazing, Juan. How I wish I could have talked like that to my soldiers.

THE DEVIL. It is mere talk, though. It has all been said

before; but what change has it ever made? What notice has the world ever taken of it?

DON JUAN. Yes, it is mere talk. But why is it mere talk? Because, my friend, beauty, purity, respectability, religion, morality, art, patriotism, bravery and the rest are nothing but words which I or anyone else can turn inside out like a glove. Were they realities, you would have to plead guilty to my indictment; but fortunately for your self-respect, my diabolical friend, they are not realities. As you say, they are mere words, useful for duping barbarians into adopting civilization, or the civilized poor into submitting to be robbed and enslaved. That is the family secret of the governing caste; and if we who are of that caste aimed at more Life for the world instead of at more power and luxury for our miserable selves, that secret would make us great. Now, since I, being a nobleman, am in the secret too, think how tedious to me must be your unending cant about all these moralistic figments, and how squalidly disastrous your sacrifice of your lives to them! If you even believed in your moral game enough to play it fairly, it would be interesting to watch; but you don't: you cheat at every trick; and if your opponent outcheats you, you upset the table and try to murder him.

THE DEVIL. On earth there may be some truth in this, because the people are uneducated and cannot appreciate my religion of love and beauty; but here—

DON JUAN. Oh yes: I know. Here there is nothing but love and beauty. Ugh! it is like sitting for all eternity at the first act of a fashionable play, before the complications begin. Never in my worst moments of superstitious terror on earth did I dream that Hell was so horrible. I live, like a hairdresser, in the continental contemplation of beauty, toying with silken tresses. I breathe an atmosphere of sweetness, like a confectioner's shopboy. Commander: are there any beautiful women in Heaven?

THE STATUE. None. Absolutely none. All dowdies. Not two pennorth of jewellery among a dozen of them. They might be men of fifty.

DON JUAN. I am impatient to get there. Is the word beauty ever mentioned; and are there any artistic people?

THE STATUE. I give you my word they won't admire a fine statue even when it walks past them.

Don Juan. I go.

The Devil. Don Juan: shall I be frank with you?

Don Juan. Were you not so before?

The Devil. As far as I went, yes. But I will now go further, and confess to you that men get tired of everything, of heaven no less than of hell; and that all history is nothing but a record of the oscillations of the world between these two extremes. An epoch is but a swing of the pendulum; and each generation thinks the world is progressing because it is always moving. But when you are as old as I am; when you have a thousand times wearied of heaven, like myself and the Commander, and a thousand times wearied of hell, as you are wearied now, you will no longer imagine that every swing from heaven to hell is an emancipation, every swing from hell to heaven an evolution. Where you now see reform, progress, fulfilment of upward tendency, continual ascent by Man on the stepping stones of his dead selves to higher things, you will see nothing but an infinite comedy of illusion. You will discover the profound truth of the saying of my friend Koheleth, that there is nothing new under the sun. Vanitas vanitatum—

Don Juan (*out of all patience*). By Heaven, this is worse than your cant about love and beauty. Clever dolt that you are, is a man no better than a worm, or a dog than a wolf, because he gets tired of everything? Shall he give up eating because he destroys his appetite in the act of gratifying it? Is a field idle when it is fallow? Can the Commander expend his hellish energy here without accumulating heavenly energy for his next term of blessedness? Granted that the great Life Force has hit on the device of the clockmaker's pendulum, and uses the earth for its bob; that the history of each oscillation, which seems so novel to us the actors, is but the history of the last oscillation repeated; nay more, that in the unthinkable infinitude of time the sun throws off the earth and catches it again a thousand times as a circus rider throws up a ball, and that the total of all our epochs is but the moment between the toss and the catch, has the colossal mechanism no purpose?

The Devil. None, my friend. You think, because you have a purpose, Nature must have one. You might as well expect it to have fingers and toes because you have them.

Don Juan. But I should not have them if they served no

purpose. And I, my friend, am as much a part of Nature as my own finger is a part of me. If my finger is the organ by which I grasp the sword and the mandoline, my brain is the organ by which Nature strives to understand itself. My dog's brain serves only my dog's purposes; but my brain labors at a knowledge which does nothing for me personally but make my body bitter to me and my decay and death a calamity. Were I not possessed with a purpose beyond my own I had better be a ploughman than a philosopher; for the ploughman lives as long as the philosopher, eats more, sleeps better, and rejoices in the wife of his bosom with less misgiving. This is because the philosopher is in the grip of the Life Force. This Life Force says to him "I have done a thousand wonderful things unconsciously by merely willing to live and following the line of least resistance: now I want to know myself and my destination, and choose my path; so I have made a special brain—a philosopher's brain—to grasp this knowledge for me as the husbandman's hand grasps the plough for me. And this" says the Life Force to the philosopher "must thou strive to do for me until thou diest, when I will make another brain and another philosopher to carry on the work."

THE DEVIL. What is the use of knowing?

DON JUAN. Why, to be able to choose the line of greatest advantage instead of yielding in the direction of the least resistance. Does a ship sail to its destination no better than a log drifts nowhither? The philosopher is Nature's pilot. And there you have our difference: to be in hell is to drift: to be in heaven is to steer.

THE DEVIL. On the rocks, most likely.

DON JUAN. Pooh! which ship goes oftenest on the rocks or to the bottom—the drifting ship or the ship with a pilot on board?

THE DEVIL. Well, well, go your way, Señor Don Juan. I prefer to be my own master and not the tool of any blundering universal force. I know that beauty is good to look at; that music is good to hear; that love is good to feel; and that they are all good to think about and talk about. I know that to be well exercised in these sensations, emotions, and studies is to be a refined and cultivated being. Whatever they may say of me in churches on earth, I know that it is universally admitted in good society that the Prince of Darkness is a gentleman; and that is enough for me. As to your Life Force, which you think irresistible, it is the most resisting thing in the world for a person of any character. But if you are naturally vulgar and credulous, as all reformers are, it will thrust you first into religion, where you will sprinkle water on babies to save their souls from me; then it will drive you from religion into science, where you will snatch the babies from the water sprinkling and inoculate them with disease to save them from catching it accidentally; then you will take to politics, where you will become the cat's-paw of corrupt functionaries and the henchman of ambitious humbugs; and the end will be despair and decrepitude, broken nerve and shattered hopes, vain regrets for that worst and silliest of wastes and sacrifices, the waste and sacrifice of the power of enjoyment: in a word, the punishment of the fool who pursues the better before he has secured the good.

Don Juan. But at least I shall not be bored. The service of the Life Force has that advantage, at all events. So fare you well, Señor Satan.

The Devil (*amiably*). Fare you well, Don Juan. I shall often think of our interesting chats about things in general. I wish you every happiness: Heaven, as I said before, suits some people. But if you should change your mind, do not forget that the gates are always open here to the repentant prodigal. If you feel at any time that warmth of heart, sincere unforced affection, innocent enjoyment, and warm, breathing, palpitating reality—

Don Juan. Why not say flesh and blood at once, though we have left those two greasy commonplaces behind us?

The Devil (*angrily*). You throw my friendly farewell back in my teeth, then, Don Juan?

Don Juan. By no means. But though there is much to be learnt from a cynical devil, I really cannot stand a sentimental one. Señor Commander: you know the way to the frontier of hell and heaven. Be good enough to direct me.

The Statue. Oh, the frontier is only the difference between two ways of looking at things. Any road will take you across it if you really want to get there.

Don Juan. Good. (*Saluting Doña Ana.*) Señora: your servant.

Ana. But I am going with you.

DON JUAN. I can find my own way to heaven, Ana; but I cannot find yours. (*He vanishes.*)

ANA. How annoying!

THE STATUE (*calling after him*). Bon voyage, Juan! (*He wafts a final blast of his great rolling chords after him as a parting salute. A faint echo of the first ghostly melody comes back in acknowledgment.*) Ah; there he goes. (*Puffing a long breath out through his lips.*) Whew! How he does talk! They'll never stand it in heaven.

THE DEVIL (*gloomily*). His going is a political defeat. I cannot keep these Life Worshippers: they all go. This is the greatest loss I have had since that Dutch painter went—a fellow who would paint a hag of 70 with as much enjoyment as a Venus of 20.

THE STATUE. I remember: he came to heaven. Rembrandt.

THE DEVIL. Ay, Rembrandt. There is something unnatural about these fellows. Do not listen to their gospel, Señor Commander: it is dangerous. Beware of the pursuit of the Superhuman: it leads to an indiscriminate contempt for the Human. To a man, horses and dogs and cats are mere species, outside the moral world. Well, to the Superman, men and women are a mere species too, also outside the moral world. This Don Juan was kind to women and courteous to men as your daughter here was kind to her pet cats and dogs; but such kindness is a denial of the exclusively human character of the soul.

THE STATUE. And who the deuce is the Superman?

THE DEVIL. Oh, the latest fashion among the Life Force fanatics. Did you not meet in Heaven, among the new arrivals, that German Polish madman—what was his name? Nietzsche?

THE STATUE. Never heard of him.

THE DEVIL. Well, he came here first, before he recovered his wits. I had some hopes of him; but he was a confirmed Life Force worshipper. It was he who raked up the Superman, who is as old as Prometheus; and the 20th century will run after this newest of the old crazes when it gets tired of the world, the flesh, and your humble servant.

THE STATUE. Superman is a good cry; and a good cry is half the battle. I should like to see this Nietzsche.

THE DEVIL. Unfortunately he met Wagner here, and had a quarrel with him.

THE STATUE. Quite right, too. Mozart for me!

THE DEVIL. Oh, it was not about music. Wagner once drifted into Life Force worship, and invented a Superman called Siegfried. But he came to his senses afterwards. So when they met here, Nietzsche denounced him as a renegade; and Wagner wrote a pamphlet to prove that Nietzsche was a Jew; and it ended in Nietzsche's going to heaven in a huff. And a good riddance too. And now, my friend, let us hasten to my palace and celebrate your arrival with a grand musical service.

THE STATUE. With pleasure: you're most kind.

THE DEVIL. This way, Commander. We go down the old trap (*he places himself on the grave trap*).

THE STATUE. Good. (*Reflectively.*) All the same, the Superman is a fine conception. There is something statuesque about it. (*He places himself on the grave trap beside The Devil. It begins to descend slowly. Red glow from the abyss.*) Ah, this reminds me of old times.

THE DEVIL. And me also.

ANA. Stop! (*The trap stops.*)

THE DEVIL. You, Señora, cannot come this way. You will have an apotheosis. But you will be at the palace before us.

ANA. That is not what I stopped you for. Tell me: where can I find the Superman?

THE DEVIL. He is not yet created, Señora.

THE STATUE. And never will be, probably. Let us proceed: the red fire will make me sneeze. (*They descend.*)

ANA. Not yet created! Then my work is not yet done. (*Crossing herself devoutly.*) I believe in the Life to Come. (*Crying to the universe.*) A father—a father for the Superman!

She vanishes into the void; and again there is nothing: all existence seems suspended infinitely. Then, vaguely, there is a live human voice crying somewhere. One sees, with a shock, a mountain peak shewing faintly against a lighter background. The sky has returned from afar; and we suddenly remember where we were. The cry becomes distinct and urgent: it says Automobile, Automobile. *The complete reality comes back with a rush: in a moment it is full morning in the Sierra; and the brigands are scrambling to their feet and making for the road as the goatherd runs down from the hill, warning them of the approach of another motor. Tanner and Mendoza rise*

amazedly and stare at one another with scattered wits. Straker
sits up to yawn for a moment before he gets on his feet, mak-
ing it a point of honor not to show any undue interest in the
excitement of the bandits. Mendoza gives a quick look to see
that his followers are attending to the alarm; then exchanges
a private word with Tanner.

MENDOZA. Did you dream?

TANNER. Damnably. Did you?

MENDOZA. Yes. I forget what. You were in it.

TANNER. So were you. Amazing!

MENDOZA. I warned you. (*A shot is heard from the road.*)
Dolts! they will play with that gun. (*The brigands come*
running back scared.) Who fired that shot? (*to Duval*)
was it you?

DUVAL (*breathless*). I have not shoot. Dey shoot first.

ANARCHIST. I told you to begin by abolishing the State.
Now we are all lost.

THE ROWDY SOCIAL-DEMOCRAT (*stampeding across the*
amphitheatre). Run, everybody.

MENDOZA (*collaring him; throwing him on his back; and*
drawing a knife). I stab the man who stirs. (*He blocks the*
way. The stampede is checked.) What has happened?

THE SULKY SOCIAL-DEMOCRAT. A motor—

THE ANARCHIST. Three men—

DUVAL. Deux femmes—

MENDOZA. Three men and two women! Why have you
not brought them here? Are you afraid of them?

THE ROWDY ONE (*getting up*). Thy've a hescort. Ow,
de-ooh lut's ook it, Mendowza.

THE SULKY ONE. Two armored cars full o' soldiers at the
'ed o' the valley.

ANARCHIST. The shot was fired in the air. It was a signal.

Straker whistles his favorite air, which falls on the ears
of the brigands like a funeral march.

TANNER. It is not an escort, but an expedition to capture
you. We were advised to wait for it; but I was in a hurry.

THE ROWDY ONE (*in an agony of apprehension*). And Ow
my good Lord, 'ere we are, wytin' for 'em! Lut's tike to the
mahntns.

MENDOZA. Idiot, what do you know about the mountains?
Are you a Spaniard? You would be given up by the firs'

shepherd you met. Besides, we are already within range of their rifles.

THE ROWDY ONE. Bat—

MENDOZA. Silence. Leave this to me. (*To Tanner.*) Comrade: you will not betray us.

STRAKER. Oo are you callin' comrade?

MENDOZA. Last night the advantage was with me. The robber of the poor was at the mercy of the robber of the rich. You offered your hand: I took it.

TANNER. I bring no charge against you, comrade. We have spent a pleasant evening with you: that is all.

STRAKER. I gev my and to nobody, see?

MENDOZA (*turning on him impressively*). Young man, if I am tried, I shall plead guilty, and explain what drove me from England, home and duty. Do you wish to have the respectable name of Straker dragged through the mud of a Spanish criminal court? The police will search me. They will find Louisa's portrait. It will be published in the illustrated papers. You blench. It will be your doing, remember.

STRAKER (*with baffled rage*). I don't care about the court. It's 'avin' our name mixed up with yours that I object to, you blackmailin' swine, you.

MENDOZA. Language unworthy of Louisa's brother! But no matter: you are muzzled: that is enough for us. (*He turns to face his own men, who back uneasily across the amphitheatre towards the cave to take refuge behind him, as a fresh party, muffled for motoring, comes from the road in riotous spirits. Ann, who makes straight for Tanner, comes first; then Violet, helped over the rough ground by Hector holding her right hand and Ramsden her left. Mendoza goes to his presidential block and seats himself calmly with his rank and file grouped behind him, and his Staff, consisting of Duval and the Anarchist on his right and the two Social-Democrats on his left, supporting him in flank.*

ANN. It's Jack!

TANNER. Caught!

HECTOR. Why, certainly it is. I said it was you Tanner. We've just been stopped by a puncture: the road is full of nails.

VIOLET. What are you doing here with all these men?

ANN. Why did you leave us without a word of warning?

HECTOR. I want that bunch of roses, Miss Whitefield. (*To Tanner.*) When we found you were gone, Miss Whitefield bet me a bunch of roses my car would not overtake yours before you reached Monte Carlo.

TANNER. But this is not the road to Monte Carlo.

HECTOR. No matter. Miss Whitefield tracked you at every stopping place: she is a regular Sherlock Holmes.

TANNER. The Life Force! I am lost.

OCTAVIUS (*bounding gaily down from the road into the amphitheatre, and coming between Tanner and Straker*). I am so glad you are safe, old chap. We were afraid you had been captured by brigands.

RAMSDEN (*who has been staring at Mendoza*). I seem to remember the face of your friend here. (*Mendoza rises politely and advances with a smile between Ann and Ramsden.*)

HECTOR. Why, so do I.

OCTAVIUS. I know you perfectly well, sir; but I can't think where I have met you.

MENDOZA (*to Violet*). Do you remember me, madam?

VIOLET. Oh, quite well; but I am so stupid about names.

MENDOZA. It was at the Savoy Hotel. (*To Hector.*) You, sir, used to come with this lady (*Violet*) to lunch. (*To Octavius.*) You, sir, often brought this lady (*Ann*) and her mother to dinner on your way to the Lyceum Theatre. (*To Ramsden.*) You, sir, used to come to supper, with (*dropping his voice to a confidential but perfectly audible whisper*) several different ladies.

RAMSDEN (*angrily*). Well, what is that to you, pray?

OCTAVIUS. Why, Violet, I thought you hardly knew one another before this trip, you and Malone!

VIOLET (*vexed*). I suppose this person was the manager.

MENDOZA. The waiter, madam. I have a grateful recollection of you all. I gathered from the bountiful way in which you treated me that you all enjoyed your visits very much.

VIOLET. What impertinence! (*She turns her back on him, and goes up the hill with Hector.*)

RAMSDEN. That will do, my friend. You do not expect these ladies to treat you as an acquaintance, I suppose, because you have waited on them at table.

MENDOZA. Pardon me: it was you who claimed my acquaintance. The ladies followed your example. However, this display of the unfortunate manners of your class closes the incident. For the future, you will please address me with the respect due to a stranger and fellow traveller. (*He turns haughtily away and resumes his presidential seat.*)

TANNER. There! I have found one man on my journey capable of reasonable conversation; and you all instinctively insult him. Even the New Man is as bad as any of you. Enry: you have behaved just like a miserable gentleman.

STRAKER. Gentleman! Not me.

RAMSDEN. Really, Tanner, this tone—

ANN. Don't mind him, Granny: you ought to know him by this time. (*She takes his arms and coaxes him away to the hill to join Violet and Hector. Octavius follows her, doglike.*)

VIOLET (*calling from the hill*). Here are the soldiers. They are getting out of their motors.

DUVAL (*panicstricken*). Oh, nom de Dieu!

THE ANARCHIST. Fools: the State is about to crush you because you spread it at the prompting of the political hangers-on of the bourgeoisie.

THE SULKY SOCIAL-DEMOCRAT (*argumentative to the last*). On the contrary, only by capturing the State machine—

THE ANARCHIST. It is going to capture you.

THE ROWDY SOCIAL-DEMOCRAT (*his anguish culminating*). Ow, chack it. Wot are we 'ere for? Wot are we wytin' for?

MENDOZA (*between his teeth*). Go on. Talk politics, you idiots: nothing sounds more respectable. Keep it up, I tell you.

The soldiers line the road, commanding the amphitheatre with their rifles. The brigands, struggling with an overwhelming impulse to hide behind one another, look as unconcerned as they can. Mendoza rises superbly, with undaunted front. The officer in command steps down from the road into the amphitheatre; looks hard at the brigands; and then inquiringly at Tanner.

THE OFFICER. Who are these men, Señor Ingles?

TANNER. My escort.

Mendoza, with a Mephisophelean smile, bows profoundly. An irrepressible grin runs from face to face among the brigands. They touch their hats, except the Anarchist, who defies the State with folded arms.

ACT IV

The garden of a villa in Granada. Whoever wishes to know what it is like must go to Granada and see. One may prosaically specify a group of hills dotted with villas, the Alhambra on the top of one of the hills, and a considerable town in the valley, approached by dusty white roads in which the children, no matter what they are doing or thinking about, automatically whine for halfpence and reach out little clutching brown palms for them; but there is nothing in this description except the Alhambra, the begging, and the color of the roads, that does not fit Surrey as well as Spain. The difference is that the Surrey hills are comparatively small and ugly, and should properly be called the Surrey Protuberances; but these Spanish hills are of mountain stock: the amenity which conceals their size does not compromise their dignity.

This particular garden is on a hill opposite the Alhambra; and the villa is as expensive and pretentious as a villa must be if it is to be let furnished by the week to opulent American and English visitors. If we stand on the lawn at the foot of the garden and look uphill, our horizon is the stone balustrade of a flagged platform on the edge of infinite space at the top of the hill. Between us and this platform is a flower garden with a circular basin and fountain in the centre, surrounded by geometrical flower beds, gravel paths, and clipped yew trees in the genteelest order. The garden is higher than our lawn; so we reach it by a few steps in the middle of its embankment. The platform is higher again than the garden, from which we mount a couple more steps to look over the balustrade at a fine view of the town up the valley and of the hills that stretch away beyond it to where, in the remotest distance, they become mountains. On our left is the villa, accessible by steps from the left hand corner of the garden. Returning from the platform through the garden and down again to the lawn (a movement which leaves the villa behind us on our right) we find evidence of literary interests on the part of the tenants

411

*in the fact that there is no tennis net nor set of croquet hoops,
but, on our left, a little iron garden table with books on it,
mostly yellow-backed, and a chair beside it. A chair on the
right has also a couple of open books upon it. There are no
newspapers, a circumstance which, with the absence of
games, might lead an intelligent spectator to the most far
reaching conclusions as to the sort of people who live in the
villa. Such speculations are checked, however, on this delight-
fully fine afternoon, by the appearance at a little gate in a
paling on our left, of Henry Straker in his professional costume. He opens the gate for an elderly gentleman, and follows
him on to the lawn.*

*This elderly gentleman defies the Spanish sun in a black
frock coat, tall silk hat, trousers in which narrow stripes of
dark grey and lilac blend into a highly respectable color, and a
black necktie tied into a bow over spotless linen. Probably
therefore a man whose social position needs constant and
scrupulous affirmation without regard to climate: one who
would dress thus for the middle of the Sahara or the top of
Mont Blanc. And since he has not the stamp of the class which
accepts as its life-mission the advertizing and maintenance of
first rate tailoring and millinery, he looks vulgar in his finery,
though in a working dress of any kind he would look dignified
enough. He is a bullet cheeked man with a red complexion,
stubbly hair, smallish eyes, a hard mouth that folds down at
the corners, and a dogged chin. The looseness of skin that
comes with age has attacked his throat and the laps of his
cheeks; but he is still hard as an apple above the mouth; so
that the upper half of his face looks younger than the lower.
He has the self-confidence of one who has made money, and
something of the truculence of one who has made it in a
brutalizing struggle, his civility having under it a perceptible
menace that he has other methods in reserve if necessary.
Withal, a man to be rather pitied when he is not to be feared;
for there is something pathetic about him at times, as if the
huge commercial machine which has worked him into his
frock coat had allowed him very little of his own way and left
his affections hungry and baffled. At the first word that falls
from him it is clear that he is an Irishman whose native intonation has clung to him through many changes of place and
rank. One can only guess that the original material of his
speech was perhaps the surly Kerry brogue; but the degrada-*

tion of speech that occurs in London, Glasgow, Dublin and big cities generally has been at work on it so long that nobody but an arrant cockney would dream of calling it a brogue now; for its music is almost gone, though its surliness is still perceptible. Straker, as a very obvious cockney, inspires him with implacable contempt, as a stupid Englishman who cannot even speak his own language properly. Straker, on the other hand, regards the old gentleman's accent as a joke thoughtfully provided by Providence expressly for the amusement of the British race, and treats him normally with the indulgence due to an inferior and unlucky species, but occasionally with indignant alarm when the old gentleman shews signs of intending his Irish nonsense to be taken seriously.

STRAKER. I'll go tell the young lady. She said you'd prefer to stay here. (*He turns to go up through the garden to the villa.*)

MALONE (*who has been looking round him with lively curiosity*). The young lady? That's Miss Violet, eh?

STRAKER (*stopping on the steps with sudden suspicion*). Well, you know, don't you?

MALONE. Do I?

STRAKER (*his temper rising*). Well, do you or don't you?

MALONE. What business is that of yours?

Straker, now highly indignant, comes back from the steps and confronts the visitor.

STRAKER. I'll tell you what business it is of mine. Miss Robinson—

MALONE (*interrupting*). Oh, her name is Robinson, is it? Thank you.

STRAKER. Why, you don't know even her name?

MALONE. Yes I do, now that you've told me.

STRAKER (*after a moment of stupefaction at the old man's readiness in repartee*). Look here: what do you mean by gittin' into my car and lettin' me bring you here if you're not the person I took that note to?

MALONE. Who else did you take it to, pray?

STRAKER. I took it to Mr. Ector Malone, at Miss Robinson's request, see? Miss Robinson is not my principal: I took it to oblige her. I know Mr. Malone; and he ain't you, not by a long chalk. At the hotel they told me that your name is Ector Malone—

MALONE. Hector Malone.

STRAKER (*with calm superiority*). Hector in your own country: that's what comes o' livin' in provincial places like Ireland and America. Over here you're Ector: if you 'avn't noticed it before you soon will.

The growing strain of the conversation is here relieved by Violet, who has sallied from the villa and through the garden to the steps, which she now descends, coming very opportunely between Malone and Straker.

VIOLET (*to Straker*). Did you take my message?

STRAKER. Yes, miss. I took it to the hotel and sent it up, expecting to see young Mr. Malone. Then out walks this gent, and says it's all right and he'll come with me. So as the hotel people said he was Mr. Ector Malone, I fetched him. And now he goes back on what he said. But if he isn't the gentleman you meant, say the word: it's easy enough to fetch him back again.

MALONE. I should esteem it a great favor if I might have a short conversation with you, madam. I am Hector's father, as this bright Britisher would have guessed in the course of another hour or so.

STRAKER (*coolly defiant*). No, not in another year or so. When we've 'ad you as long to polish up as we've 'ad 'im, perhaps you'll begin to look a little bit up to 'is mark. At present you fall a long way short. You've got too many aitches, for one thing. (*To Violet, amiably.*) All right, Miss: you want to talk to him: I shan't intrude. (*He nods affably to Malone and goes out through the little gate in the paling.*)

VIOLET (*very civilly*). I am so sorry, Mr. Malone, if that man has been rude to you. But what can we do? He is our chauffeur.

MALONE. Your hwat?

VIOLET. The driver of our automobile. He can drive a motor car at seventy miles an hour, and mend it when it breaks down. We are dependent on our motor cars; and our motor cars are dependent on him; so of course we are dependent on him.

MALONE. I've noticed, madam, that every thousand dollars an Englishman gets seems to add one to the number of people he's dependent on. However, you needn't apologize for your man: I made him talk on purpose. By doing so I learnt that you're staying here in Grannida with a party of English, including my son Hector.

VIOLET (*conversationally*). Yes. We intended to go to Nice; but we had to follow a rather eccentric member of our party who started first and came here. Won't you sit down? (*She clears the nearest chair of the two books on it.*)

MALONE (*impressed by this attention*). Thank you. (*He sits down, examining her curiously as she goes to the iron table to put down the books. When she turns to him again, he says.*) Miss Robinson, I believe?

VIOLET (*sitting down*). Yes.

MALONE (*taking a letter from his pocket*). Your note to Hector runs as follows (*Violet is unable to repress a start. He pauses quietly to take out and put on his spectacles, which have gold rims*): "Dearest: they have all gone to the Alhambra for the afternoon. I have shammed headache and have the garden all to myself. Jump into Jack's motor: Straker will rattle you here in a jiffy. Quick, quick, quick. Your loving Violet." (*He looks at her; but by this time she has recovered herself, and meets his spectacles with perfect composure. He continues slowly.*) Now I don't know on what terms young people associate in English society; but in America that note would be considered to imply a very considerable degree of affectionate intimacy between the parties.

VIOLET. Yes: I know your son very well, Mr. Malone. Have you any objection?

MALONE (*somewhat taken aback*). No, no objection exactly. Provided it is understood that my son is altogether dependent on me, and that I have to be consulted in any important step he may propose to take.

VIOLET. I am sure you would not be unreasonable with him, Mr. Malone.

MALONE. I hope not, Miss Robinson; but at your age you might think many things unreasonable that don't seem so to me.

VIOLET (*with a little shrug*). Oh well, I suppose there's no use our playing at cross purposes, Mr. Malone. Hector wants to marry me.

MALONE. I inferred from your note that he might. Well, Miss Robinson, he is his own master; but if he marries you he shall not have a rap from me. (*He takes off his spectacles and pockets them with the note.*)

VIOLET (*with some severity*). That is not very complimentary to me, Mr. Malone.

MALONE. I say nothing against you, Miss Robinson: I daresay you are an amiable and excellent young lady. But I have other views for Hector.

VIOLET. Hector may not have other views for himself, Mr. Malone.

MALONE. Possibly not. Then he does without me: that's all. I daresay you are prepared for that. When a young lady writes to a young man to come to her quick, quick, quick, money seems nothing and love seems everything.

VIOLET (*sharply*). I beg your pardon, Mr. Malone: I do not think anything so foolish. Hector must have money.

MALONE (*staggered*). Oh, very well, very well. No doubt he can work for it.

VIOLET. What is the use of having money if you have to work for it? (*She rises impatiently.*) It's all nonsense, Mr. Malone: you must enable your son to keep up his position. It is his right.

MALONE (*grimly*). I should not advise you to marry him on the strength of that right, Miss Robinson.

Violet, who has almost lost her temper, controls herself with an effort; unclenches her fingers; and resumes her seat with studied tranquillity and reasonableness.

VIOLET. What objection have you to me, pray? My social position is as good as Hector's, to say the least. He admits it.

MALONE (*shrewdly*). You tell him so from time to time, eh? Hector's social position in England, Miss Robinson, is just what I choose to buy for him. I have made him a fair offer. Let him pick out the most historic house, castle or abbey that England contains. The day that he tells me he wants it for a wife worthy of its traditions, I buy it for him, and give him the means of keeping it up.

VIOLET. What do you mean by a wife worthy of its traditions? Cannot any well bred woman keep such a house for him?

MALONE. No: she must be born to it.

VIOLET. Hector was not born to it, was he?

MALONE. His grandmother was a barefooted Irish girl that nursed me by a turf fire. Let him marry another such, and I will not stint her marriage portion. Let him raise himself socially with my money or raise somebody else; so long as there is a social profit somewhere, I'll regard my expenditure as justified. But there must be a profit for someone. A marriage with you would leave things just where they are.

VIOLET. Many of my relations would object very much to my marrying the grandson of a common woman, Mr. Malone. That may be prejudice; but so is your desire to have him marry a title prejudice.

MALONE (*rising, and approaching her with a scrutiny in which there is a good deal of reluctant respect*). You seem a pretty straightforward downright sort of a young woman.

VIOLET. I do not see why I should be made miserably poor because I cannot make profits for you. Why do you want to make Hector unhappy?

MALONE. He will get over it all right enough. Men thrive better on disappointments in love than on disappointments in money. I daresay you think that sordid; but I know what I'm talking about. My father died of starvation in Ireland in the black '47. Maybe you've heard of it.

VIOLET. The Famine?

MALONE (*with smoldering passion*). No, the starvation. When a country is full of food, and exporting it, there can be no famine. My father was starved dead; and I was starved out to America in my mother's arms. English rule drove me and mine out of Ireland. Well, you can keep Ireland. I and my like are coming back to buy England; and we'll buy the best of it. I want no middle-class properties and no middle-class women for Hector. That's straightforward, isn't it, like yourself?

VIOLET (*icily pitying his sentimentality*). Really, Mr. Malone, I am astonished to hear a man of your age and good sense talking in that romantic way. Do you suppose English noblemen will sell their places to you for the asking?

MALONE. I have the refusal of two of the oldest family mansions in England. One historic owner can't afford to keep all the rooms dusted: the other can't afford the death duties. What do you say now?

VIOLET. Of course it is very scandalous; but surely you know that the Government will sooner or later put a stop to all these Socialistic attacks on property.

MALONE (*grinning*). D'y' think they'll be able to get that done before I buy the house—or rather the abbey? They're both abbeys.

VIOLET (*putting that aside rather impatiently*). Oh, well, let us talk sense, Mr. Malone. You must feel that we haven't been talking sense so far.

MALONE. I can't say I do. I mean all I say.

VIOLET. Then you don't know Hector as I do. He is romantic and faddy—he gets it from you, I fancy—and he wants a certain sort of wife to take care of him. Not a faddy sort of person, you know.

MALONE. Somebody like you, perhaps?

VIOLET (*quietly*). Well, yes. But you cannot very well ask me to undertake this with absolutely no means of keeping up his position.

MALONE (*alarmed*). Stop a bit, stop a bit. Where are we getting to? I'm not aware that I'm asking you to undertake anything.

VIOLET. Of course, Mr. Malone, you can make it very difficult for me to speak to you if you choose to misunderstand me.

MALONE (*half bewildered*). I don't wish to take any unfair advantage; but we seem to have got off the straight track somehow.

Straker, with the air of a man who has been making haste, opens the little gate, and admits Hector, who, snorting with indignation, comes upon the lawn, and is making for his father when Violet, greatly dismayed, springs up and intercepts him. Straker does not wait; at least he does not remain visibly within earshot.

VIOLET. Oh, how unlucky! Now please, Hector, say nothing. Go away until I have finished speaking to your father.

HECTOR (*inexorably*). No, Violet: I mean to have this thing out, right away. (*He puts her aside; passes her by; and faces his father, whose cheeks darken as his Irish blood begins to simmer.*) Dad: you've not played this hand straight.

MALONE. Hwat d'y'mean?

HECTOR. You've opened a letter addressed to me. You've impersonated me and stolen a march on this lady. That's dishonorable.

MALONE (*threateningly*). Now you take care what you're saying, Hector. Take care, I tell you.

HECTOR. I have taken care. I am taking care. I'm taking care of my honor and my position in English society.

MALONE (*hotly*). Your position has been got by my money: do you know that?

HECTOR. Well, you've just spoiled it all by opening that letter. A letter from an English lady, not addressed to you —a confidential letter! a delicate letter! a private letter! opened by my father! That's a sort of thing a man can't struggle against in England. The sooner we go back together the better. (*He appeals mutely to the heavens to witness the shame and anguish of two outcasts.*)

VIOLET (*snubbing him with an instinctive dislike for scene making*). Don't be unreasonable, Hector. It was quite natural of Mr. Malone to open my letter: his name was on the envelope.

MALONE. There! You've no common sense, Hector. I thank you, Miss Robinson.

HECTOR. I thank you, too. It's very kind of you. My father knows no better.

MALONE (*furiously clenching his fists*). Hector—

HECTOR (*with undaunted moral force*). Oh, it's no use hectoring me. A private letter's a private letter, dad: you can't get over that.

MALONE (*raising his voice*). I won't be talked back to by you, d'y'hear?

VIOLET. Ssh! please, please. Here they all come.

Father and son, checked, glare mutely at one another as Tanner comes in through the little gate with Ramsden, followed by Octavius and Ann.

VIOLET. Back already!

TANNER. The Alhambra is not open this afternoon.

VIOLET. What a sell!

Tanner passes on, and presently finds himself between Hector and a strange elder, both apparently on the verge of personal combat. He looks from one to the other for an explanation. They sulkily avoid his eye, and nurse their wrath in silence.

RAMSDEN. Is it wise for you to be out in the sunshine with such a headache, Violet?

TANNER. Have you recovered too, Malone?

VIOLET. Oh, I forgot. We have not all met before. Mr. Malone: won't you introduce your father?

HECTOR (*with Roman firmness*). No I will not. He is no father of mine.

MALONE (*very angry*). You disown your dad before your English friends, do you?

VIOLET. Oh please don't make a scene.

Ann and Octavius, lingering near the gate, exchange an astonished glance, and discreetly withdraw up the steps to the garden, where they can enjoy the disturbance without intruding. On their way to the steps Ann sends a little grimace of mute sympathy to Violet, who is standing with her back to the little table, looking on in helpless annoyance as her husband soars to higher and higher moral eminences without the least regard to the old man's millions.

HECTOR. I'm very sorry, Miss Robinson; but I'm contending for a principle. I am a son, and, I hope, a dutiful one; but before everything I'm a Man!!! And when dad treats my private letters as his own, and takes it on himself to say that I shan't marry you if I am happy and fortunate enough to gain your consent, then I just snap my fingers and go my own way.

TANNER. Marry Violet!

RAMSDEN. Are you in your senses?

TANNER. Do you forget what we told you?

HECTOR (*recklessly*). I don't care what you told me.

RAMSDEN (*scandalized*). Tut tut, sir! Monstrous! (*He flings away towards the gate, his elbows quivering with indignation.*)

TANNER. Another madman! These men in love should be locked up. (*He gives Hector up as hopeless, and turns away towards the garden; but Malone, taking offence in a new direction, follows him and compels him, by the aggressiveness of his tone, to stop.*)

MALONE. I don't understand this. Is Hector not good enough for this lady, pray?

TANNER. My dear sir, the lady is married already. Hector knows it; and yet he persists in his infatuation. Take him home and lock him up.

MALONE (*bitterly*). So this is the high-born social tone I've spoilt be me ignorant, uncultivated behavior! Makin love to a married woman! (*He comes angrily between Hector and Violet, and almost bawls into Hector's left ear.*) You've picked up that habit of the British aristocracy, have you?

HECTOR. That's all right. Don't you trouble yourself about that. I'll answer for the morality of what I'm doing.

TANNER (*coming forward to Hector's right hand with flash-*

ing eyes). Well said, Malone! You also see that mere marriage laws are not morality! I agree with you; but unfortunately Violet does not.

MALONE. I take leave to doubt that, sir. (*Turning on Violet.*) Let me tell you, Mrs. Robinson, or whatever your right name is, you had no right to send that letter to my son when you were the wife of another man.

HECTOR (*outraged*). This is the last straw. Dad: you have insulted my wife.

MALONE. Your wife!

TANNER. You the missing husband! Another moral impostor! (*He smites his brow, and collapses into Malone's chair.*)

MALONE. You've married without my consent!

RAMSDEN. You have deliberately humbugged us, sir!

HECTOR. Here: I have had just about enough of being badgered. Violet and I are married: that's the long and the short of it. Now what have you got to say—any of you?

MALONE. I know what I've got to say. She's married a beggar.

HECTOR. No; she's married a Worker. (*His American pronunciation imparts an overwhelming intensity to this simple and unpopular word.*) I start to earn my own living this very afternoon.

MALONE (*sneering angrily*). Yes: you're very plucky now, because you got your remittance from me yesterday or this morning, I reckon. Wait till it's spent. You won't be so full of cheek then.

HECTOR (*producing a letter from his pocketbook*). Here it is (*thrusting it on his father*). Now you just take your remittance and yourself out of my life. I'm done with remittances; and I'm done with you. I don't sell the privilege of insulting my wife for a thousand dollars.

MALONE (*deeply wounded and full of concern*). Hector: you don't know what poverty is.

HECTOR (*fervidly*). Well, I want to know what it is. I want to be a Man. Violet: you come along with me, to your own home: I'll see you through.

OCTAVIUS (*jumping down from the garden to the lawn and running to Hector's left hand*). I hope you'll shake hands with me before you go, Hector. I admire and respect you more than I can say. (*He is affected almost to tears as they shake hands.*)

VIOLET (*also almost in tears, but of vexation*). Oh don't be an idiot, Tavy. Hector's about as fit to become a workman as you are.

TANNER (*rising from his chair on the other side of Hector*). Never fear: there's no question of his becoming a navvy, Mrs. Malone. (*To Hector.*) There's really no difficulty about capital to start with. Treat me as a friend: draw on me.

OCTAVIUS (*impulsively*). Or on me.

MALONE (*with fierce jealousy*). Who wants your durty money? Who should he draw on but his own father? (*Tanner and Octavius recoil, Octavius rather hurt, Tanner consoled by the solution of the money difficulty. Violet looks up hopefully.*) Hector: don't be rash, my boy. I'm sorry for what I said: I never meant to insult Violet: I take it all back. She's just the wife you want: there!

HECTOR (*patting him on the shoulder*). Well, that's all right, dad. Say no more: we're friends again. Only, I take no money from anybody.

MALONE (*pleading abjectly*). Don't be hard on me, Hector. I'd rather you quarreled and took the money than made friends and starved. You don't know what the world is: I do.

HECTOR. No, no, NO. That's fixed: that's not going to change. (*He passes his father inexorably by, and goes to Violet.*) Come, Mrs. Malone: you've got to move to the hotel with me, and take your proper place before the world.

VIOLET. But I must go in, dear, and tell Davis to pack. Won't you go on and make them give you a room overlooking the garden for me? I'll join you in half an hour.

HECTOR. Very well. You'll dine with us, Dad, won't you?

MALONE (*eager to conciliate him*). Yes, yes.

HECTOR. See you all later. (*He waves his hand to Ann, who has now been joined by Tanner, Octavius, and Ramsden in the garden, and goes out through the little gate, leaving his father and Violet together on the lawn.*)

MALONE. You'll try to bring him to his senses, Violet: I know you will.

VIOLET. I had no idea he could be so headstrong. If he goes on like that, what can I do?

MALONE. Don't be discurridged: domestic pressure may be slow; but it's sure. You'll wear him down. Promise me you will.

VIOLET. I will do my best. Of course I think it's the greatest nonsense deliberately making us poor like that.

MALONE. Of course it is.

VIOLET (*after a moment's reflection*). You had better give me the remittance. He will want it for his hotel bill. I'll see whether I can induce him to accept it. Not now, of course, but presently.

MALONE (*eagerly*). Yes, yes, yes: that's just the thing. (*He hands her the thousand dollar bill, and adds cunningly.*) Y'understand that this is only a bachelor allowance.

VIOLET (*coolly*). Oh, quite. (*She takes it.*) Thank you. By the way, Mr. Malone, those two houses you mentioned —the abbeys.

MALONE. Yes?

VIOLET. Don't take one of them until I've seen it. One never knows what may be wrong with these places.

MALONE. I won't. I'll do nothing without consulting you, never fear.

VIOLET (*politely, but without a ray of gratitude*). Thanks: that will be much the best way. (*She goes calmly back to the villa, escorted obsequiously by Malone to the upper end of the garden.*)

TANNER (*drawing Ramsden's attention to Malone's cringing attitude as he takes leave of Violet*). And that poor devil is a billionaire! one of the master spirits of the age! Led in a string like a pug dog by the first girl who takes the trouble to despise him. I wonder will it ever come to that with me. (*He comes down to the lawn.*)

RAMSDEN (*following him*). The sooner the better for you.

MALONE (*slapping his hands as he returns through the garden*). That'll be a grand woman for Hector. I wouldn't exchange her for ten duchesses. (*He descends to the lawn and comes between Tanner and Ramsden.*)

RAMSDEN (*very civil to the billionaire*). It's an unexpected pleasure to find you in this corner of the world, Mr. Malone. Have you come to buy up the Alhambra?

MALONE. Well, I don't say I mightn't. I think I could do better with it than the Spanish government. But that's not what I came about. To tell you the truth, about a month ago I overheard a deal between two men over a bundle of shares. They differed about the price: they were young and greedy, and didn't know that if the shares were worth what was bid for them they must be worth what was asked, the margin being too small to be of any account, you see. To amuse meself, I cut in and bought the shares. Well, to this day I haven't found out what the business is. The office is in this town; and the name is Mendoza, Limited. Now whether Mendoza's a mine, or a steamboat line, or a bank, or a patent article—

TANNER. He's a man. I know him: his principles are thoroughly commercial. Let us take you round the town in our motor, Mr. Malone, and call on him on the way.

MALONE. If you'll be so kind, yes. And may I ask who—

TANNER. Mr. Roebuck Ramsden, a very old friend of your daughter-in-law.

MALONE. Happy to meet you, Mr. Ramsden.

RAMSDEN. Thank you. Mr. Tanner is also one of our circle.

MALONE. Glad to know you also, Mr. Tanner.

TANNER. Thanks. (*Malone and Ramsden go out very amicably through the little gate. Tanner calls to Octavius, who is wandering in the garden with Ann.*) Tavy! (*Tavy comes to the steps, Tanner whispers loudly to him.*) Violet has married a financier of brigands. (*Tanner hurries away to overtake Malone and Ramsden. Ann strolls to the steps with an idle impulse to torment Octavius.*)

ANN. Won't you go with them, Tavy?

OCTAVIUS (*tears suddenly flushing his eyes*). You cut me to the heart, Ann, by wanting me to go. (*He comes down on the lawn to hide his face from her. She follows him caressingly.*)

ANN. Poor Ricky Ticky Tavy! Poor heart!

OCTAVIUS. It belongs to you, Ann. Forgive me: I must speak of it. I love you. You know I love you.

ANN. What's the good, Tavy? You know that my mother is determined that I shall marry Jack.

OCTAVIUS (*amazed*). Jack!

ANN. It seems absurd, doesn't it?

OCTAVIUS (*with growing resentment*). Do you mean to say that Jack has been playing with me all this time? That he has been urging me not to marry you because he intends to marry you himself?

ANN (*alarmed*). No no; you mustn't lead him to believe that I said that: I don't for a moment think that Jack knows his own mind. But it's clear from my father's will that he wished me to marry Jack. And my mother is set on it.

OCTAVIUS. But you are not bound to sacrifice yourself always to the wishes of your parents.

ANN. My father loved me. My mother loves me. Surely their wishes are a better guide than my own selfishness.

OCTAVIUS. Oh, I know how unselfish you are, Ann. But believe me—though I know I am speaking in my own interest —there is another side to this question. Is it fair to Jack to marry him if you do not love him? Is it fair to destroy my happiness as well as your own if you can bring yourself to love me?

ANN (*looking at him with a faint impulse of pity*). Tavy, my dear, you are a nice creature—a good boy.

OCTAVIUS (*humiliated*). Is that all?

ANN (*mischievously in spite of her pity*). That's a great deal, I assure you. You would always worship the ground I trod on, wouldn't you?

OCTAVIUS. I do. It sounds ridiculous; but it's no exaggeration. I do; and I always shall.

ANN. Always is a long word, Tavy. You see, I shall have to live up always to your idea of my divinity; and I don't think I could do that if we were married. But if I marry Jack, you'll never be disillusioned—at least not until I grow too old.

OCTAVIUS. I too shall grow old, Ann. And when I am eighty, one white hair of the woman I love will make me tremble more than the thickest gold tress from the most beautiful young head.

ANN (*quite touched*). Oh, that's poetry, Tavy, real poetry. It gives me that strange sudden sense of an echo from a former existence which always seems to me such a striking proof that we have immortal souls.

OCTAVIUS. Do you believe that it is true?

ANN. Tavy: if it is to come true, you must lose me as well as love me.

OCTAVIUS. Oh! (*He hastily sits down at the little table and covers his face with his hands.*)

ANN (*with conviction*). Tavy: I wouldn't for worlds destroy your illusions. I can neither take you nor let you go. I can see exactly what will suit you. You must be a sentimental old bachelor for my sake.

OCTAVIUS (*desperately*). Ann: I'll kill myself.

ANN. Oh no you won't: that wouldn't be kind. You won't have a bad time. You will be very nice to women; and you will go a good deal to the opera. A broken heart is a very pleasant complaint for a man in London if he has a comfortable income.

OCTAVIUS (*considerably cooled, but believing that he is only recovering his self-control*). I know you mean to be kind, Ann. Jack has persuaded you that cynicism is a good tonic for me. (*He rises with quiet dignity.*)

ANN (*studying him slyly*). You see, I'm disillusionizing you already. That's what I dread.

OCTAVIUS. You do not dread disillusionizing Jack.

ANN (*her face lighting up with mischievous ecstasy—whispering*). I can't: he has no illusions about me. I shall surprise Jack the other way. Getting over an unfavorable impression is ever so much easier than living up to an ideal. Oh, I shall enrapture Jack sometimes!

OCTAVIUS (*resuming the calm phase of despair, and beginning to enjoy his broken heart and delicate attitude without knowing it*). I don't doubt that. You will enrapture him always. And he—the fool!—thinks you would make him wretched.

ANN. Yes: that's the difficulty, so far.

OCTAVIUS (*heroically*). Shall *I* tell him that you love him?

ANN (*quickly*). Oh no: he'd run away again.

OCTAVIUS (*shocked*). Ann: would you marry an unwilling man?

ANN. What a queer creature you are, Tavy! There's no such thing as a willing man when you really go for him. (*She laughs naughtily.*) I'm shocking you, I suppose. But you know you are really getting a sort of satisfaction already in being out of danger yourself.

OCTAVIUS (*startled*). Satisfaction! (*Reproachfully.*) You say that to me!

ANN. Well, if it were really agony, would you ask for more of it?

OCTAVIUS. Have I asked for more of it?

ANN. You have offered to tell Jack that I love him. That's self-sacrifice, I suppose; but there must be some satisfaction in it. Perhaps it's because you're a poet. You are like the bird that presses its breast against the sharp thorn to make itself sing.

OCTAVIUS. It's quite simple. I love you; and I want you to

be happy. You don't love me; so I can't make you happy myself; but I can help another man to do it.

ANN. Yes: it seems quite simple. But I doubt if we ever know why we do things. The only really simple thing is to go straight for what you want and grab it. I suppose I don't love you, Tavy; but sometimes I feel as if I should like to make a man of you somehow. You are very foolish about women.

OCTAVIUS (*almost coldly*). I am content to be what I am in that respect.

ANN. Then you must keep away from them, and only dream about them. I wouldn't marry you for worlds, Tavy.

OCTAVIUS. I have no hope, Ann: I accept my ill luck. But I don't think you quite know how much it hurts.

ANN. You are so softhearted! It's queer that you should be so different from Violet. Violet's as hard as nails.

OCTAVIUS. Oh no. I am sure Violet is thoroughly womanly at heart.

ANN (*with some impatience*). Why do you say that? Is it unwomanly to be thoughtful and businesslike and sensible? Do you want Violet to be an idiot—or something worse, like me?

OCTAVIUS. Something worse—like you! What do you mean, Ann?

ANN. Oh well, I don't mean that, of course. But I have a great respect for Violet. She gets her own way always.

OCTAVIUS (*sighing*). So do you.

ANN. Yes; but somehow she gets it without coaxing—without having to make people sentimental about her.

OCTAVIUS (*with brotherly callousness*). Nobody could get very sentimental about Violet, I think, pretty as she is.

ANN. Oh yes they could, if she made them.

OCTAVIUS. But surely no really nice woman would deliberately practise on men's instincts in that way.

ANN (*throwing up her hands*). Oh Tavy, Tavy, Ricky Ticky Tavy, heaven help the woman who marries you!

OCTAVIUS (*his passion reviving at the name*). Oh why, why, why do you say that? Don't torment me. I don't understand.

ANN. Suppose she were to tell fibs, and lay snares for men?

OCTAVIUS. Do you think *I* could marry such a woman—I, who have known and loved you?

ANN. Hm! Well, at all events, she wouldn't let you if she

were wise. So that's settled. And now I can't talk any more. Say you forgive me, and that the subject is closed.

OCTAVIUS. I have nothing to forgive; and the subject is closed. And if the wound is open, at least you shall never see it bleed.

ANN. Poetic to the last, Tavy. Goodbye, dear. (*She pats his cheek; has an impulse to kiss him and then another impulse of distaste which prevents her; finally runs away through the garden and into the villa.*)

Octavius again takes refuge at the table, bowing his head on his arms and sobbing softly. Mrs. Whitefield, who has been pottering round the Granada shops, and has a net full of little parcels in her hand, comes in through the gate and sees him.

MRS. WHITEFIELD (*running to him and lifting his head*). What's the matter, Tavy? Are you ill?

OCTAVIUS. No, nothing, nothing.

MRS. WHITEFIELD (*still holding his head, anxiously*). But you're crying. Is it about Violet's marriage?

OCTAVIUS. No, no. Who told you about Violet?

MRS. WHITEFIELD (*restoring the head to its owner*). I met Roebuck and that awful old Irishman. Are you sure you're not ill? What's the matter?

OCTAVIUS (*affectionately*). It's nothing—only a man's broken heart. Doesn't that sound ridiculous?

MRS. WHITEFIELD. But what is it all about? Has Ann been doing anything to you?

OCTAVIUS. It's not Ann's fault. And don't think for a moment that I blame you.

MRS. WHITEFIELD (*startled*). For what?

OCTAVIUS (*pressing her hand consolingly*). For nothing. I said I didn't blame you.

MRS. WHITEFIELD. But I haven't done anything. What's the matter?

OCTAVIUS (*smiling sadly*). Can't you guess? I daresay you are right to prefer Jack to me as a husband for Ann; but I love Ann; and it hurts rather. (*He rises and moves away from her towards the middle of the lawn.*)

MRS. WHITEFIELD (*following him hastily*). Does Ann say that I want her to marry Jack?

OCTAVIUS. Yes: she has told me.

MRS. WHITEFIELD (*thoughtfully*). Then I'm very sorry for

you, Tavy. It's only her way of saying she wants to marry Jack. Little she cares what I say or what I want!

OCTAVIUS. But she would not say it unless she believed it. Surely you don't suspect Ann of—of deceit!!

MRS. WHITEFIELD. Well, never mind, Tavy. I don't know which is best for a young man: to know too little, like you, or too much, like Jack.

Tanner returns.

TANNER. Well, I've disposed of old Malone. I've introduced him to Mendoza, Limited; and left the two brigands together to talk it out. Hullo, Tavy! anything wrong?

OCTAVIUS. I must go wash my face, I see. (*To Mrs. Whitefield.*) Tell him what you wish. (*To Tanner.*) You may take it from me, Jack, that Ann approves of it.

TANNER (*puzzled by his manner*). Approves of what?

OCTAVIUS. Of what Mrs. Whitefield wishes. (*He goes his way with sad dignity to the villa.*)

TANNER (*to Mrs. Whitefield*). This is very mysterious. What is it you wish? It shall be done, whatever it is.

MRS. WHITEFIELD (*with snivelling gratitude*). Thank you, Jack. (*She sits down. Tanner brings the other chair from the table and sits close to her with his elbows on his knees, giving her his whole attention.*) I don't know why it is that other people's children are so nice to me, and that my own have so little consideration for me. It's no wonder I don't seem able to care for Ann and Rhoda as I do for you and Tavy and Violet. It's a very queer world. It used to be so straightforward and simple; and now nobody seems to think and feel as they ought. Nothing has been right since that speech that Professor Tyndall made at Belfast.

TANNER. Yes: life is more complicated than we used to think. But what am I to do for you?

MRS. WHITEFIELD. That's just what I want to tell you. Of course you'll marry Ann whether I like it or not—

TANNER (*starting*). It seems to me that I shall presently be married to Ann whether I like it myself or not.

MRS. WHITEFIELD (*peacefully*). Oh, very likely you will: you know what she is when she has set her mind on anything. But don't put it on me: that's all I ask. Tavy has just let out that she's been saying that I am making her marry you; and the poor boy is breaking his heart about it; for he is in love with her himself, though what he sees in her so wonderful, goodness knows: *I* don't. It's no use telling Tavy that Ann puts things into people's heads by telling them that I want them when the thought of them never crossed my mind. It only sets Tavy against me. But you know better than that. So if you marry her, don't put the blame on me.

TANNER (*emphatically*). I havn't the slightest intention of marrying her.

MRS. WHITEFIELD (*slyly*). She'd suit you better than Tavy. She'd meet her match in you, Jack. I'd like to see her meet her match.

TANNER. No man is a match for a woman, except with a poker and a pair of hobnailed boots. Not always even then. Anyhow, *I* can't take the poker to her. I should be a mere slave.

MRS. WHITEFIELD. No: she's afraid of you. At all events, you would tell her the truth about herself. She wouldn't be able to slip out of it as she does with me.

TANNER. Everybody would call me a brute if I told Ann the truth about herself in terms of her own moral code. To begin with, Ann says things that are not strictly true.

MRS. WHITEFIELD. I'm glad somebody sees she is not an angel.

TANNER. In short—to put it as a husband would put it when exasperated to the point of speaking out—she is a liar. And since she has plunged Tavy head over ears in love with her without any intention of marrying him, she is a coquette, according to the standard definition of a coquette as a woman who rouses passions she has no intention of gratifying. And as she has now reduced you to the point of being willing to sacrifice me at the altar for the mere satisfaction of getting me to call her a liar to her face, I may conclude that she is a bully as well. She can't bully men as she bullies women; so she habitually and unscrupulously uses her personal fascination to make men give her whatever she wants. That makes her almost something for which I know no polite name.

MRS. WHITEFIELD (*in mild expostulation*). Well, you can't expect perfection, Jack.

TANNER. I don't. But what annoys me is that Ann does. I know perfectly well that all this about her being a liar and a bully and a coquette and so forth is a trumped-up moral indictment which might be brought against anybody.

We all lie; we all bully as much as we dare; we all bid for admiration without the least intention of earning it; we all get as much rent as we can out of our powers of fascination. If Ann would admit this I shouldn't quarrel with her. But she won't. If she has children she'll take advantage of their telling lies to amuse herself by whacking them. If another woman makes eyes at me, she'll refuse to know a coquette. She will do just what she likes herself whilst insisting on everybody else doing what the conventional code prescribes. In short, I can stand everything except her confounded hypocrisy. That's what beats me.

MRS. WHITEFIELD (*carried away by the relief of hearing her own opinion so eloquently expressed*). Oh, she is a hypocrite. She is: she is. Isn't she?

TANNER. Then why do you want to marry me to her?

MRS. WHITEFIELD (*querulously*). There now! put it on me, of course. I never thought of it until Tavy told me she said I did. But, you know, I'm very fond of Tavy: he's a sort of son to me; and I don't want him to be trampled on and made wretched.

TANNER. Whereas I don't matter, I suppose.

MRS. WHITEFIELD. Oh, you are different, somehow: you are able to take care of yourself. You'd serve her out. And anyhow, she must marry somebody.

TANNER. Aha! there speaks the life instinct. You detest her; but you feel that you must get her married.

MRS. WHITEFIELD (*rising, shocked*). Do you mean that I detest my own daughter! Surely you don't believe me to be so wicked and unnatural as that, merely because I see her faults.

TANNER (*cynically*). You love her, then?

MRS. WHITEFIELD. Why, of course I do. What queer things you say, Jack! We can't help loving our own blood relations.

TANNER. Well, perhaps it saves unpleasantness to say so. But for my part, I suspect that the tables of consanguinity have a natural basis in a natural repugnance. (*He rises.*)

MRS. WHITEFIELD. You shouldn't say things like that, Jack. I hope you won't tell Ann that I have been speaking to you. I only wanted to set myself right with you and Tavy. I couldn't sit mumchance and have everything put on me.

TANNER (*politely*). Quite so.

MRS. WHITEFIELD (*dissatisfied*). And now I've only made matters worse. Tavy's angry with me because I don't worship Ann. And when it's been put into my head that Ann ought to marry you, what can I say except that it would serve her right?

TANNER. Thank you.

MRS. WHITEFIELD. Now don't be silly and twist what I say into something I don't mean. I ought to have fair play—

Ann comes from the villa, followed presently by Violet, who is dressed for driving.

ANN (*coming to her mother's right hand with threatening suavity*). Well, mamma darling, you seem to be having a delightful chat with Jack. We can hear you all over the place.

MRS. WHITEFIELD (*appalled*). Have you overheard—

TANNER. Never fear: Ann is only—well, we were discussing that habit of hers just now. She hasn't heard a word.

MRS. WHITEFIELD (*stoutly*). I don't care whether she has or not: I have a right to say what I please.

VIOLET (*arriving on the lawn and coming between Mrs. Whitefield and Tanner*). I've come to say goodbye. I'm off for my honeymoon.

MRS. WHITEFIELD (*crying*). Oh don't say that, Violet. And no wedding, no breakfast, no clothes, nor anything.

VIOLET (*petting her*). It won't be for long.

MRS. WHITEFIELD. Don't let him take you to America. Promise me that you won't.

VIOLET (*very decidedly.*) I should think not, indeed. Don't cry, dear: I'm only going to the hotel.

MRS. WHITEFIELD. But going in that dress, with your luggage, makes one realize— (*She chokes, and then breaks out again.*) How I wish you were my daughter, Violet!

VIOLET (*soothing her*). There, there: so I am. Ann will be jealous.

MRS. WHITEFIELD. Ann doesn't care a bit for me.

ANN. Fie, mother! Come, now: you mustn't cry any more: you know Violet doesn't like it (*Mrs. Whitefield dries her eyes, and subsides*).

VIOLET. Goodbye, Jack.

TANNER. Goodbye, Violet.

VIOLET. The sooner you get married too, the better. You will be much less misunderstood.

TANNER (*restively*). I quite expect to get married in the course of the afternoon. You all seem to have set your minds on it.

VIOLET. You might do worse. (*To Mrs. Whitefield: putting her arm round her.*) Let me take you to the hotel with me: the drive will do you good. Come in and get a wrap. (*She takes her towards the villa.*)

MRS. WHITEFIELD (*as they go up through the garden*). I don't know what I shall do when you are gone, with no one but Ann in the house; and she always occupied with the men! It's not to be expected that your husband will care to be bothered with an old woman like me. Oh, you needn't tell me: politeness is all very well; but I know what people think—(*She talks herself and Violet out of sight and hearing.*)

Ann, musing on Violet's opportune advice, approaches Tanner; examines him humorously for a moment from toe to top; and finally delivers her opinion.

ANN. Violet is quite right. You ought to get married.

TANNER (*explosively*). Ann: I will not marry you. Do you hear? I won't, won't, won't, won't, WON'T marry you.

ANN (*placidly*). Well, nobody axd you, sir she said, sir she said, sir she said. So that's settled.

TANNER. Yes, nobody has asked me; but everybody treats the thing as settled. It's in the air. When we meet, the others go away on absurd pretexts to leave us alone together. Ramsden no longer scowls at me: his eye beams, as if he were already giving you away to me in church. Tavy refers me to your mother and gives me his blessing. Straker openly treats you as his future employer: it was he who first told me of it.

ANN. Was that why you ran away?

TANNER. Yes, only tó be stopped by a lovesick brigand and run down like a truant schoolboy.

ANN. Well, if you don't want to be married, you needn't be. (*She turns away from him and sits down, much at her ease.*)

TANNER (*following her*). Does any man want to be hanged? Yet men let themselves be hanged without a struggle for life, though they could at least give the chaplain a black eye. We do the world's will, not our own. I have a frightful feeling that I shall let myself be married beeause it is the world's will that you should have a husband.

ANN. I daresay I shall, someday.

TANNER. But why me—me of all men? Marriage is to me apostasy, profanation of the sanctuary of my soul, violation of my manhood, sale of my birthright, shameful surrender, ignominious capitulation, acceptance of defeat. I shall decay like a thing that has served its purpose and is done with; I shall change from a man with a future to a man with a past; I shall see in the greasy eyes of all the other husbands their relief at the arrival of a new prisoner to share their ignominy. The young men will scorn me as one who has sold out: to the young women I, who have always been an enigma and a possibility, shall be merely somebody else's property—and damaged goods at that: a second-hand man at best.

ANN. Well, your wife can put on a cap and make herself ugly to keep you in countenance, like my grandmother.

TANNER. So that she may make her triumph more insolent by publicly throwing away the bait the moment the trap snaps on the victim!

ANN. After all, though, what difference would it make? Beauty is all very well at first sight; but who ever looks at it when it has been in the house three days? I thought our pictures very lovely when papa bought them; but I haven't looked at them for years. You never bother about my looks: you are too well used to me. I might be the umbrella stand.

TANNER. You lie, you vampire: you lie.

ANN. Flatterer. Why are you trying to fascinate me, Jack, if you don't want to marry me?

TANNER. The Life Force. I am in the grip of the Life Force.

ANN. I don't understand in the least: it sounds like the Life Guards.

TANNER. Why don't you marry Tavy? He is willing. Can you not be satisfied unless your prey struggles?

ANN (*turning to him as if to let him into a secret*). Tavy will never marry. Havn't you noticed that that sort of man never marries?

TANNER. What! a man who idolizes women! who sees nothing in nature but romantic scenery for love duets! Tavy, the chivalrous, the faithful, the tenderhearted and true! Tavy never marry! Why, he was born to be swept up by the first pair of blue eyes he meets in the street.

ANN. Yes, I know. All the same, Jack, men like that always live in comfortable bachelor lodgings with broken hearts, and are adored by their landladies, and never get married. Men like you always get married.

TANNER (*smiting his brow*). How frightfully, horribly true! It has been staring me in the face all my life; and I never saw it before.

ANN. Oh, it's the same with women. The poetic temperament's a very nice temperament, very amiable, very harmless and poetic, I daresay; but it's an old maid's temperament.

TANNER. Barren. The Life Force passes it by.

ANN. If that's what you mean by the Life Force, yes.

TANNER. You don't care for Tavy?

ANN (*looking round carefully to make sure that Tavy is not within earshot*). No.

TANNER. And you do care for me?

ANN (*rising quietly and shaking her finger at him*). Now, Jack! Behave yourself.

TANNER. Infamous, abandoned woman! Devil!

ANN. Boa-constrictor! Elephant!

TANNER. Hypocrite!

ANN (*softly*). I must be, for my future husband's sake.

TANNER. For mine! (*Correcting himself savagely.*) I mean for his.

ANN (*ignoring the correction*). Yes, for yours. You had better marry what you call a hypocrite, Jack. Women who are not hypocrites go about in rational dress and are insulted and get into all sorts of hot water. And then their husbands get dragged in too, and live in continual dread of fresh complications. Wouldn't you prefer a wife you could depend on?

TANNER. No, a thousand times no: hot water is the revolutionist's element. You clean men as you clean milkpails, by scalding them.

ANN. Cold water has its uses too. It's healthy.

TANNER (*despairingly*). Oh, you are witty: at the supreme moment the Life Force endows you with every quality. Well, I too can be a hypocrite. Your father's will appointed me your guardian, not your suitor. I shall be faithful to my trust.

ANN (*in low siren tones*). He asked me who would I have as my guardian before he made that will. I chose you!

TANNER. The will is yours then! The trap was laid from the beginning.

ANN (*concentrating all her magic*). From the beginning— from our childhood—for both of us—by the Life Force.

TANNER. I will not marry you. I will not marry you.

ANN. Oh, you will, you will.

TANNER. I tell you, no, no, no.

ANN. I tell you, yes, yes, yes.

TANNER. No.

ANN (*coaxing—imploring—almost exhausted*). Yes. Before it is too late for repentance. Yes.

TANNER (*struck by the echo from the past*). When did all this happen to me before? Are we two dreaming?

ANN (*suddenly losing her courage, with an anguish that she does not conceal*). No. We are awake; and you have said no: that is all.

TANNER (*brutally*). Well?

ANN. Well, I made a mistake: you do not love me.

TANNER (*seizing her in his arms*). It is false: I love you. The Life Force enchants me: I have the whole world in my arms when I clasp you. But I am fighting for my freedom, for my honor, for my self, one and indivisible.

ANN. Your happiness will be worth them all.

TANNER. You would sell freedom and honor and self for happiness?

ANN. It will not be all happiness for me. Perhaps death.

TANNER (*groaning*). Oh, that clutch holds and hurts. What have you grasped in me? Is there a father's heart as well as a mother's?

ANN. Take care, Jack: if anyone comes while we are like this, you will have to marry me.

TANNER. If we two stood now on the edge of a precipice, I would hold you tight and jump.

ANN (*panting, failing more and more under the strain*). Jack: let me go. I have dared so frightfully—it is lasting longer than I thought. Let me go: I can't bear it.

TANNER. Nor I. Let it kill us.

ANN. Yes: I don't care. I am at the end of my forces. I don't care. I think I am going to faint.

At this moment Violet and Octavius come from the villa

with Mrs. Whitefield, who is wrapped up for driving. Simul-
taneously Malone and Ramsden, followed by Mendoza and
Straker, come in through the little gate in the paling. Tanner
shamefacedly releases Ann, who raises her hand giddily to her
forehead.

MALONE. Take care. Something's the matter with the lady.

RAMSDEN. What does this mean?

VIOLET (*running between Ann and Tanner*). Are you ill?

ANN (*reeling, with a supreme effort*). I have promised to
marry Jack. (*She swoons. Violet kneels by her and chafes her
hand. Tanner runs round to her other hand, and tries to lift
her head. Octavius goes to Violet's assistance, but does not
know what to do. Mrs. Whitefield hurries back into the villa.
Octavius, Malone and Ramsden run to Ann and crowd round
her, stooping to assist. Straker coolly comes to Ann's feet, and
Mendoza to her head, both upright and self-possessed.*)

STRAKER. Now then, ladies and gentlemen: she don't want
a crowd round her: she wants air—all the air she can git.
If you please, gents—(*Malone and Ramsden allow him to
drive them gently past Ann and up the lawn towards the
garden, where Octavius, who has already become conscious
of his uselessness, joins them. Straker, following them up,
pauses for a moment to instruct Tanner.*) Don't lift er ed,
Mr. Tanner: let it go flat so's the blood can run back into it.

MENDOZA. He is right, Mr. Tanner. Trust to the air of the
Sierra. (*He withdraws delicately to the garden steps.*)

TANNER (*rising*). I yield to your superior knowledge of
physiology, Henry. (*He withdraws to the corner of the lawn;
and Octavius immediately hurries down to him.*)

TAVY (*aside to Tanner, grasping his hand*). Jack: be very
happy.

TANNER (*aside to Tavy*). I never asked her. It is a trap for
me. (*He goes up the lawn towards the garden. Octavius remains petrified.*)

MENDOZA (*intercepting Mrs. Whitefield, who comes from
the villa with a glass of brandy*). What is this, madam? (*He
takes it from her.*)

MRS. WHITEFIELD. A little brandy.

MENDOZA. The worst thing you could give her. Allow me.
(*He swallows it.*) Trust to the air of the Sierra, madam.

For a moment the men all forget Ann and stare at Mendoza.

ANN (*in Violet's ear, clutching her round the neck*). Violet: did Jack say anything when I fainted?

VIOLET. No.

ANN. Ah! (*With a sigh of intense relief she relapses.*)

MRS. WHITEFIELD. Oh, she's fainted again.

They are about to rush back to her; but Mendoza stops them with a warning gesture.

ANN (*supine*). No I haven't. I'm quite happy.

TANNER (*suddenly walking determinedly to her, and snatching her hand from Violet to feel her pulse*). Why, her pulse is positively bounding. Come, get up. What nonsense! Up with you. (*He gets her up summarily.*)

ANN. Yes: I feel strong enough now. But you very nearly killed me, Jack, for all that.

MALONE. A rough wooer, eh? They're the best sort, Miss Whitefield. I congratulate Mr. Tanner; and I hope to meet you and him as frequent guests at the Abbey.

ANN. Thank you. (*She gets past Malone to Octavius.*) Ricky Ticky Tavy: congratulate me. (*Aside to him.*) I want to make you cry for the last time.

TAVY (*steadfastly*). No more tears. I am happy in your happiness. And I believe in you in spite of everything.

RAMSDEN (*coming between Malone and Tanner*). You are a happy man, Jack Tanner. I envy you.

MENDOZA (*advancing between Violet and Tanner*). Sir: there are two tragedies in life. One is not to get your heart's desire. The other is to get it. Mine and yours, sir.

TANNER. Mr. Mendoza: I have no heart's desires. Ramsden: it is very easy for you to call me a happy man: you are only a spectator. I am one of the principals; and I know better. Ann: stop tempting Tavy, and come back to me.

ANN (*complying*). You are absurd, Jack. (*She takes his proffered arm.*)

TANNER (*continuing*). I solemnly say that I am not a happy man. Ann looks happy; but she is only triumphant, successful, victorious. That is not happiness, but the price for which the strong sell their happiness. What we have both done this afternoon is to renounce happiness, renounce freedom, renounce tranquillity, above all, renounce the romantic possibilities of an unknown future, for the cares of a household and a family. I beg that no man may seize the occasion to get half drunk and utter imbecile speeches and coarse pleasantries at my expense. We propose to furnish our own house according to our own taste; and I hereby give notice that the seven or eight travelling clocks, the four or five dressing cases, the salad bowls, the carvers and fish slices, the copy of Tennyson in extra morocco, and all the other articles you are preparing to heap upon us, will be instantly sold, and the proceeds devoted to circulating free copies of the Revolutionist's Handbook. The wedding will take place three days after our return to England, by special license, at the office of the district superintendent registrar, in the presence of my solicitor and his clerk, who, like his clients, will be in ordinary walking dress—

VIOLET (*with intense conviction*). You are a brute, Jack.

ANN (*looking at him with fond pride and caressing his arm*). Never mind her, dear. Go on talking.

TANNER. Talking!

Universal laughter.

The Revolutionist's Handbook

"No one can contemplate the present condition of the masses of the people without desiring something like a revolution for the better." *Sir Robert Giffen*. Essays in Finance, vol. ii. p. 393.

FOREWORD

A revolutionist is one who desires to discard the existing social order and try another.

The constitution of England is revolutionary. To a Russian or Anglo-Indian bureaucrat, a general election is as much a revolution as a referendum or plebiscite in which the people fight instead of voting. The French Revolution overthrew one set of rulers and substituted another with different interests and different views. That is what a general election enables the people to do in England every seven years if they choose. Revolution is therefore a national institution in England; and its advocacy by an Englishman needs no apology.

Every man is a revolutionist concerning the thing he understands. For example, every person who has mastered a profession is a sceptic concerning it, and consequently a revolutionist.

Every genuinely religious person is a heretic and therefore a revolutionist.

All who achieve real distinction in life begin as revolutionists. The most distinguished persons become more revolutionary as they grow older, though they are commonly supposed to become more conservative owing to their loss of faith in conventional methods of reform.

Any person under the age of thirty, who, having any knowledge of the existing social order, is not a revolutionist, is an inferior.

AND YET

Revolutions have never lightened the burden of tyranny: they have only shifted it to another shoulder.

JOHN TANNER

THE REVOLUTIONIST'S
HANDBOOK

I

On Good Breeding

If there were no God, said the eighteenth-century Deist, it would be necessary to invent Him. Now this XVIII-century god was *deus ex machina,* the god who helped those who could not help themselves, the god of the lazy and incapable. The nineteenth century decided that there is indeed no such god; and now Man must take in hand all the work that he used to shirk with an idle prayer. He must, in effect, change himself into the political Providence which he formerly conceived as god; and such change is not only possible, but the only sort of change that is real. The mere transfigurations of institutions, as from military and priestly dominance to commercial and scientific dominance, from commercial dominance to proletarian democracy, from slavery to serfdom, from serfdom to capitalism, from monarchy to republicanism, from polytheism to monotheism, from monotheism to atheism, from atheism to pantheistic humanitarianism, from general illiteracy to general literacy, from romance to realism, from realism to mysticism, from metaphysics to physics, are all but changes from Tweedledum to Tweedledee: *"plus ça change, plus c'est la méme chose."* But the changes from the crab apple to the pippin, from the wolf and fox to the house dog, from the charger of Henry V to the brewer's draught horse and the race-horse, are real; for here Man has played the god, subduing Nature to his intention, and ennobling or debasing Life for a set purpose. And what can be done with a wolf can be done with a man. If such monsters as the tramp and the gentleman can appear as mere by-products of Man's individual greed and folly, what might we not hope for as a main product of his universal aspiration?

This is no new conclusion. The despair of institutions, and

the inexorable "ye must be born again," with Mrs. Poyser's stipulation, "and born different," recurs in every generation. The cry for the Superman did not begin with Nietzsche, nor will it end with his vogue. But it has always been silenced by the same question: what kind of person is this Superman to be? You do not ask for a super-apple, but for an eatable apple; nor for a superhorse, but for a horse of greater draught or velocity. Neither is it of any use to ask for a Superman: you must furnish a specification of the sort of man you want. Unfortunately you do not know what sort of man you want. Some sort of goodlooking philosopher-athlete, with a handsome healthy woman for his mate, perhaps.

Vague as this is, it is a great advance on the popular demand for a perfect gentleman and a perfect lady. And, after all, no market demand in the world takes the form of exact technical specification of the article required. Excellent poultry and potatoes are produced to satisfy the demand of housewives who do not know the technical differences between a tuber and a chicken. They will tell you that the proof of the pudding is in the eating; and they are right. The proof of the Superman will be in the living; and we shall find out how to produce him by the old method of trial and error, and not by waiting for a completely convincing prescription of his ingredients.

Certain common and obvious mistakes may be ruled out from the beginning. For example, we agree that we want superior mind; but we need not fall into the football club folly of counting on this as a product of superior body. Yet if we recoil so far as to conclude that superior mind consists in being the dupe of our ethical classifications of virtues and vices, in short, of conventional morality, we shall fall out of the fryingpan of the football club into the fire of the Sunday School. If we must choose between a race of athletes and a race of "good" men, let us have the athletes: better Samson and Milo than Calvin and Robespierre. But neither alternative is worth changing for: Samson is no more a Superman than Calvin. What then are we to do?

II

Property and Marriage

Let us hurry over the obstacles set up by property and marriage. Revolutionists make too much of them. No doubt it is easy to demonstrate that property will destroy society unless society destroys it. No doubt, also, property has hitherto held its own and destroyed all the empires. But that was because the superficial objection to it (that it distributes social wealth and the social labor burden in a grotesquely inequitable manner) did not threaten the existence of the race, but only the individual happiness of its units, and finally the maintenance of some irrelevant political form or other, such as a nation, an empire, or the like. Now as happiness never matters to Nature, as she neither recognizes flags and frontiers nor cares a straw whether the economic system adopted by a society is feudal, capitalistic or collectivist, provided it keeps the race afoot (the hive and the anthill being as acceptable to her as Utopia), the demonstrations of Socialists, though irrefutable, will never make any serious impression on property. The knell of that overrated institution will not sound until it is felt to conflict with some more vital matter than mere personal inequities in industrial economy. No such conflict was perceived whilst society had not yet grown beyond national communities too small and simple to disastrously overtax Man's limited political capacity. But we have now reached the stage of international organization. Man's political capacity and magnanimity are clearly beaten by the vastness and complexity of the problems forced on him. And it is at this anxious moment that he finds, when he looks upward for a mightier mind to help him, that the heavens are empty. He will presently see that his discarded formula that Man is the Temple of the Holy Ghost happens to be precisely true, and that it is only through his own brain and hand that this Holy Ghost, formerly the most nebulous

447

person in the Trinity, and now become its sole survivor as it has always been its real Unity, can help him in any way. And so, if the Superman is to come, he must be born of Woman by Man's intentional and well-considered contrivance. Conviction of this will smash everything that opposes it. Even Property and Marriage, which laugh at the laborer's petty complaint that he is defrauded of "surplus value," and at the domestic miseries of the slaves of the wedding ring, will themselves be laughed aside as the lightest of trifles if they cross this conception when it becomes a fully realized vital purpose of the race.

That they must cross it becomes obvious the moment we acknowledge the futility of breeding men for special qualities as we breed cocks for game, greyhounds for speed, or sheep for mutton. What is really important in Man is the part of him that we do not yet understand. Of much of it we are not even conscious, just as we are not normally conscious of keeping up our circulation by our heart-pump, though if we neglect it we die. We are therefore driven to the conclusion that when we have carried selection as far as we can by rejecting from the list of eligible parents all persons who are uninteresting, unpromising, or blemished without any set-off, we shall still have to trust to the guidance of fancy (*alias* Voice of Nature), both in the breeders and the parents, for that superiority in the unconscious self which will be the true characteristic of the Superman.

At this point we perceive the importance of giving fancy the widest possible field. To cut humanity up into small cliques, and effectively limit the selection of the individual to his own clique, is to postpone the Superman for eons, if not for ever. Not only should every person be nourished and trained as a possible parent, but there also should be no possibility of such an obstacle to natural selection as the objection of a countess to a navvy or of a duke to a charwoman. Equality is essential to good breeding; and equality, as all economists know, is incompatible with property.

Besides, equality is an essential condition of bad breeding also; and bad breeding is indispensable to the weeding out of the human race. When the conception of heredity took hold of the scientific imagination in the middle of last century, its devotees announced that it was a crime to marry the lunatic to the lunatic or the consumptive to the con-

sumptive. But pray are we to try to correct our diseased
stocks by infecting our healthy stocks with them? Clearly
the attraction which disease has for diseased people is beneficial to the race. If two really unhealthy people get married, they will, as likely as not, have a great number of children who will all die before they reach maturity. This is a
far more satisfactory arrangement than the tragedy of a
union between a healthy and an unhealthy person. Though
more costly than sterilization of the unhealthy, it has the
enormous advantage that in the event of our notions of health
and unhealth being erroneous (which to some extent they
most certainly are), the error will be corrected by experience
instead of confirmed by evasion.

One fact must be faced resolutely, in spite of the shrieks
of the romantic. There is no evidence that the best citizens
are the offspring of congenial marriages, or that a conflict
of temperament is not a highly important part of what breeders call crossing. On the contrary, it is quite sufficiently prob-
able that good results may be obtained from parents who
would be extremely unsuitable companions and partners, to
make it certain that the experiment of mating them will
sooner or later be tried purposely almost as often as it is
now tried accidentally. But mating such couples must clearly
not involve marrying them. In conjugation two comple-
mentary persons may supply one another's deficiencies: in
the domestic partnership of marriage they only feel them
and suffer from them. Thus the son of a robust, cheerful,
eupeptic British country squire, with the tastes and range of
his class, and of a clever, imaginative, intellectual, highly
civilized Jewess, might be very superior to both his parents;
but it is not likely that the Jewess would find the squire
an interesting companion, or his habits, his friends, his place
and mode of life congenial to her. Therefore marriage, whilst
it is made an indispensable condition of mating, will delay the
advent of the Superman as effectually as Property, and will
be modified by the impulse towards him just as effectually.

The practical abrogation of Property and Marriage as they
exist at present will occur without being much noticed. To
the mass of men, the intelligent abolition of property would
mean nothing except an increase in the quantity of food,
clothing, housing and comfort at their personal disposal, as
well as a greater control over their time and circumstances.

Very few persons now make any distinction between virtually complete property and property held on such highly developed public conditions as to place its income on the same footing as that of a propertyless clergyman, officer, or civil servant. A landed proprietor may still drive men and women off his land, demolish their dwellings, and replace them with sheep or deer; and in the unregulated trades the private trader may still sponge on the regulated trades and sacrifice the life and health of the nation as lawlessly as the Manchester cotton manufacturers did at the beginning of last century. But though the Factory Code on the one hand, and Trade Union organization on the other, have, within the lifetime of men still living, converted the old unrestricted property of the cotton manufacturer in his mill and the cotton spinner in his labor into a mere permission to trade or work on stringent public or collective conditions, imposed in the interest of the general welfare without any regard for individual hard cases, people in Lancashire still speak of their "property" in the old terms, meaning nothing more by it than the things a thief can be punished for stealing. The total abolition of property, and the conversion of every citizen into a salaried functionary in the public service, would leave much more than 99 per cent of the nation quite unconscious of any greater change than now takes place when the son of a shipowner goes into the navy. They would still call their watches and umbrellas and back gardens their property.

Marriage also will persist as a name attached to a general custom long after the custom itself will have altered. For example, modern English marriage, as modified by divorce and by Married Women's Property Acts, differs more from early XIX-century marriage than Byron's marriage did from Shakespear's. At the present moment marriage in England differs not only from marriage in France, but also from marriage in Scotland. Marriage as modified by the divorce laws in South Dakota would be called mere promiscuity in Clapham. Yet the Americans, far from taking a profligate and cynical view of marriage, do homage to its ideals with a seriousness that seems old fashioned in Clapham. Neither in England nor America would a proposal to abolish marriage be tolerated for a moment; and yet nothing is more certain than that in both countries the progressive modification of the marriage contract will be continued until it is no more onerous nor irrevocable than any ordinary commercial deed of partnership. Were even this dispensed with, people would still call themselves husbands and wives; describe their companionships as marriages; and be for the most part unconscious that they were any less married than Henry VIII. For though a glance at the legal conditions of marriage in different Christian countries shews that marriage varies legally from frontier to frontier, domesticity varies so little that most people believe their own marriage laws to be universal. Consequently here again, as in the case of Property, the absolute confidence of the public in the stability of the institution's name, makes it all the easier to alter its substance.

However, it cannot be denied that one of the changes in public opinion demanded by the need for the Superman is a very unexpected one. It is nothing less than the dissolution of the present necessary association of marriage with conjugation, which most unmarried people regard as the very diagnostic of marriage. They are wrong, of course: it would be quite as near the truth to say that conjugation is the one purely accidental and incidental condition of marriage. Conjugation is essential to nothing but the propagation of the race; and the moment that paramount need is provided for otherwise than by marriage, conjugation, from Nature's creative point of view, ceases to be essential in marriage. But marriage does not thereupon cease to be so economical, convenient, and comfortable, that the Superman might safely bribe the matrimonomaniacs by offering to revive all the old inhuman stringency and irrevocability of marriage, to abolish divorce, to confirm the horrible bond which still chains decent people to drunkards, criminals and wasters, provided only the complete extrication of conjugation from it were conceded to him. For if people could form domestic companionships on no easier terms than these, they would still marry. The Roman Catholic, forbidden by his Church to avail himself of the divorce laws, marries as freely as the South Dakotan Presbyterians who can change partners with a facility that scandalizes the old world; and were his Church to dare a further step towards Christianity and enjoin celibacy on its laity as well as on its clergy, marriages would still be contracted for the sake of domesticity by perfectly obedient sons and daughters of the Church. One need not further pursue these hypotheses: they are only suggested here to help the reader to analyze marriage into its two functions of regulating conjugation and supplying a form of domesticity. These two functions are quite separable; and domesticity is the only one of the two which is essential to the existence of marriage, because conjugation without domesticity is not marriage at all, whereas domesticity without conjugation is still marriage: in fact it is necessarily the actual condition of all fertile marriages during a great part of their duration, and of some marriages during the whole of it.

Taking it, then, that Property and Marriage, by destroying Equality and thus hampering sexual selection with irrelevant conditions, are hostile to the evolution of the Superman, it is easy to understand why the only generally known modern experiment in breeding the human race took place in a community which discarded both institutions.

III

The Perfectionist Experiment at Oneida Creek

In 1848 the Oneida Community was founded in America to carry out a resolution arrived at by a handful of Perfectionist Communists "that we will devote ourselves exclusively to the establishment of the Kingdom of God." Though the American nation declared that this sort of thing was not to be tolerated in a Christian country, the Oneida Community held its own for over thirty years, during which period it seems to have produced healthier children and done and suffered less evil than any Joint Stock Company on record. It was, however, a highly selected community; for a genuine communist (roughly definable as an intensely proud person who proposes to enrich the common fund instead of to sponge on it) is superior to an ordinary joint stock capitalist precisely as an ordinary joint stock capitalist is superior to a pirate. Further, the Perfectionists were mightily shepherded by their chief Noyes, one of those chance attempts at the Superman which occur from time to time in spite of the interference of Man's blundering institutions. The existence of Noyes simplified the breeding problem for the Communists, the question as to what sort of man they should strive to breed being settled at once by the obvious desirability of breeding another Noyes.

But an experiment conducted by a handful of people, who, after thirty years of immunity from the unintentional child slaughter that goes on by ignorant parents in private homes, numbered only 300, could do very little except prove that the Communists, under the guidance of a Superman "devoted exclusively to the establishment of the Kingdom of God," and caring no more for property and marriage than a Camberwell minister cares for Hindoo Caste or Suttee, might make a much better job of their lives than ordinary folk under the harrow of both these institutions. Yet their

Superman himself admitted that this apparent success was
only part of the abnormal phenomenon of his own occurrence;
for when he came to the end of his powers through age, he
himself guided and organized the voluntary relapse of the
communists into marriage, capitalism, and customary private
life, thus admitting that the real social solution was not what
a casual Superman could persuade a picked company to do
for him, but what a whole community of Supermen would
do spontaneously. If Noyes had had to organize, not a few
dozen Perfectionists, but the whole United States, America
would have beaten him as completely as England beat Oliver
Cromwell, France Napoleon, or Rome Julius Cæsar. Cromwell learnt by bitter experience that God himself cannot
raise a people above its own level, and that even though you
stir a nation to sacrifice all its appetites to its conscience, the
result will still depend wholly on what sort of conscience the
nation has got. Napoleon seems to have ended by regarding
mankind as a troublesome pack of hounds only worth keeping for the sport of hunting with them. Cæsar's capacity for
fighting without hatred or resentment was defeated by the
determination of his soldiers to kill their enemies in the
field instead of taking them prisoners to be spared by Cæsar;
and his civil supremacy was purchased by colossal bribery
of the citizens of Rome. What great rulers cannot do, codes
and religions cannot do. Man reads his own nature into every
ordinance: if you devise a superhuman commandment so
cunningly that it cannot be misinterpreted in terms of his
will, he will denounce it as seditious blasphemy, or else disregard it as either crazy or totally unintelligible. Parliaments
and synods may tinker as much as they please with their
codes and creeds as circumstances alter the balance of classes
and their interests; and, as a result of the tinkering, there
may be an occasional illusion of moral evolution, as when the
victory of the commercial caste over the military caste leads
to the substitution of social boycotting and pecuniary dam-
ages for duelling. At certain moments there may even be a
considerable material advance, as when the conquest of political power by the working class produces a better distribution of wealth through the simple action of the selfishness of
the new masters; but all this is mere readjustment and re-
formation: until the heart and mind of the people is changed
the very greatest man will no more dare to govern on the

assumption that all are as great as he than a drover dare leave his flock to find its way through the streets as he himself would. Until there is an England in which every man is a Cromwell, a France in which every man is a Napoleon, a Rome in which every man is a Cæsar, a Germany in which every man is a Luther plus a Goethe, the world will be no more improved by its heroes than a Brixton villa is improved by the pyramid of Cheops. The production of such nations is the only real change possible to us.

IV

Man's Objection to His Own Improvement

But would such a change be tolerated if Man must rise above himself to desire it? It would, through his misconception of its nature. Man does desire an ideal Superman with such energy as he can spare from his nutrition, and has in every age magnified the best living substitute for it he can find. His least incompetent general is set up as an Alexander; his king is the first gentleman in the world; his Pope is a saint. He is never without an array of human idols who are all nothing but sham Supermen. That the real Superman will snap his superfingers at all Man's present trumpery ideals of right, duty, honor, justice, religion, even decency, and accept moral obligations beyond present human endurance, is a thing that contemporary Man does not foresee: in fact he does not notice it when our casual Supermen do it in his very face. He actually does it himself every day without knowing it. He will therefore make no objection to the production of a race of what he calls Great Men or Heroes, because he will imagine them, not as true Supermen, but as himself endowed with infinite brains, infinite courage, and infinite money.

The most troublesome opposition will arise from the general fear of mankind that any interference with our conjugal customs will be interference with our pleasure and our romance. This fear, by putting on airs of offended morality, has always intimidated people who have not measured its essential weakness; but it will prevail with those degenerates only in whom the instinct of fertility has faded into a mere itching for pleasure. The modern devices for combining pleasure with sterility, now universally known and accessible, enable these persons to weed themselves out of the race, a process already vigorously at work; and the consequent survival of the intelligently fertile means the survival of the partizans of the Superman; for what is proposed is nothing but the replacement of the old unintelligent, inevitable, almost unconscious fertility by an intelligently controlled, conscious fertility, and the elimination of the mere voluptuary from the evolutionary process.[1] Even if this selective agency had not been invented, the purpose of the race would still shatter the opposition of individual instincts. Not only do the bees and the ants satisfy their reproductive and parental instincts vicariously; but marriage itself successfully imposes celibacy on millions of unmarried normal men and women. In short, the individual instinct in this matter, overwhelming as it is thoughtlessly supposed to be, is really a finally negligible one.

---

[1] The part played in evolution by the voluptuary will be the same as that already played by the glutton. The glutton, as the man with the strongest motive for nourishing himself, will always take more pains than his fellows to get food. When food is so difficult to get that only great exertions can secure a sufficient supply of it, the glutton's appetite develops his cunning and enterprise to the utmost; and he becomes not only the best fed but also the ablest man in the community. But in more hospitable climates, or where the social organization of the food supply makes it easy for a man to overeat, then the glutton eats himself out of health and finally out of existence. All other voluptuaries prosper and perish in the same way; and this is why the survival of the fittest means finally the survival of the self-controlled, because they alone can adapt themselves to the perpetual shifting of conditions produced by industrial progress.

V

The Political Need for the Superman

The need for the Superman is, in its most imperative aspect, a political one. We have been driven to Proletarian Democracy by the failure of all the alternative systems; for these depended on the existence of Supermen acting as despots or oligarchs; and not only were these Supermen not always or even often forthcoming at the right moment and in an eligible social position, but when they were forthcoming they could not, except for a short time and by morally suicidal coercive methods, impose superhumanity on those whom they governed; so, by mere force of "human nature," government by consent of the governed has supplanted the old plan of governing the citizen as a public-schoolboy is governed.

Now, we have yet to see the man who, having any practical experience of Proletarian Democracy, has any belief in its capacity for solving great political problems, or even for doing ordinary parochial work intelligently and economically. Only under despotisms and oligarchies has the Radical faith in "universal suffrage" as a political panacea arisen. It withers the moment it is exposed to practical trial, because Democracy cannot rise above the level of the human material of which its voters are made. Switzerland seems happy in comparison with Russia; but if Russia were as small as Switzerland, and had her social problems simplified in the same way by impregnable natural fortifications and a population educated by the same variety and intimacy of international intercourse, there might be little to choose between them. At all events Australia and Canada, which are virtually protected democratic republics, and France and the United States, which are avowedly independent democratic republics, are neither healthy, wealthy nor wise; and they would be worse instead of better if their popular ministers were not experts in the art of dodging popular enthusiasms and duping popular ignorance. The politician who once had to learn how to flatter Kings has now to learn how to fascinate, amuse, coax, humbug, frighten or otherwise strike the fancy of the electorate; and though in advanced modern States, where the artizan is better educated than the King, it takes a much bigger man to be a successful demagogue than to be a successful courtier, yet he who holds popular convictions with prodigious energy is the man for the mob, whilst the frailer sceptic who is cautiously feeling his way towards the next century has no chance unless he happens by accident to have the specific artistic talent of the mountebank as well, in which case it is as a mountebank that he catches votes, and not as a meliorist. Consequently the demagogue, though he professes (and fails) to readjust matters in the interests of the majority of the electors, yet stereotypes mediocrity, organizes intolerance, disparages exhibitions of uncommon qualities, and glorifies conspicuous exhibitions of common ones. He manages a small job well: he muddles rhetorically through a large one. When a great political movement takes place, it is not consciously led nor organized: the unconscious self in mankind breaks its way through the problem as an elephant breaks through a jungle; and the politicians make speeches about whatever happens in the process, which, with the best intentions, they do all in their power to prevent. Finally, when social aggregation arrives at a point demanding international organization before the demagogues and electorates have learnt how to manage even a country parish properly much less internationalize Constantinople, the whole political business goes to smash; and presently we have Ruins of Empires, New Zealanders sitting on a broken arch of London Bridge, and so forth.

To that recurrent catastrophe we shall certainly come again unless we can have a Democracy of Supermen; and the production of such a Democracy is the only change that is now hopeful enough to nerve us to the effort that Revolution demands.

VI

Prudery Explained

Why the bees should pamper their mothers whilst we pamper only our operatic prima donnas is a question worth reflecting on. Our notion of treating a mother is, not to increase her supply of food, but to cut it off by forbidding her to work in a factory for a month after her confinement. Everything that can make birth a misfortune to the parents as well as a danger to the mother is conscientiously done. When a great French writer, Emile Zola, alarmed at the sterilization of his nation, wrote an eloquent and powerful book to restore the prestige of parentage, it was at once assumed in England that a work of this character, with such a title as Fecundity, was too abominable to be translated, and that any attempt to deal with the relations of the sexes from any other than the voluptuary or romantic point of view must be sternly put down. Now if this assumption were really founded on public opinion, it would indicate an attitude of disgust and resentment towards the Life Force that could only arise in a diseased and moribund community in which Ibsen's Hedda Gabler would be the typical woman. But it has no vital foundation at all. The prudery of the newspapers is, like the prudery of the dinner table, a mere difficulty of education and language. We are not taught to think decently on these subjects, and consequently we have no language for them except indecent language. We therefore have to declare them unfit for public discussion, because the only terms in which we can conduct the discussions are unfit for public use. Physiologists, who have a technical vocabulary at their disposal, find no difficulty; and masters of language who think decently can write popular stories like Zola's Fecundity or Tolstoy's Resurrection without giving the smallest offence to readers who can also think decently. But the ordinary modern journalist, who has never discussed such matters except in ribaldry, cannot write a simple comment on a divorce case without a conscious shamefulness or a furtive facetiousness that makes it impossible to read the comment aloud in company. All this ribaldry and prudery (the two are the same) does not mean that people do not feel decently on the subject: on the contrary, it is just the depth and seriousness of our feeling that makes its desecration by vile language and coarse humor intolerable; so that at last we cannot bear to have it spoken of at all because only one in a thousand can speak of it without wounding our self-respect, especially the self-respect of women. Add to the horrors of popular language the horrors of popular poverty. In crowded populations poverty destroys the possibility of cleanliness; and in the absence of cleanliness many of the natural conditions of life become offensive and noxious, with the result that at last the association of uncleanliness with these natural conditions becomes so overpowering that among civilized people (that is, people massed in the labyrinths of slums we call cities), half their bodily life becomes a guilty secret, unmentionable except to the doctor in emergencies; and Hedda Gabler shoots herself because maternity is so unladylike. In short, popular prudery is only a mere incident of popular squalor: the subjects which it taboos remain the most interesting and earnest of subjects in spite of it.

VII

Progress an Illusion

Unfortunately the earnest people get drawn off the track
of evolution by the illusion of progress. Any Socialist can
convince us easily that the difference between Man as he is
and Man as he might become, without further evolution,
under millennial conditions of nutrition, environment, and
training, is enormous. He can shew that inequality and
iniquitous distribution of wealth and allotment of labor have
arisen through an unscientific economic system, and that Man,
faulty as he is, no more intended to establish any such ordered
disorder than a moth intends to be burnt when it flies into a
candle flame. He can shew that the difference between the
grace and strength of the acrobat and the bent back of the
rheumatic field laborer is a difference produced by conditions, not by nature. He can shew that many of the most
detestable human vices are not radical, but are mere re-
actions of our institutions on our very virtues. The Anarchist,
the Fabian, the Salvationist, the Vegetarian, the doctor, the
lawyer, the parson, the professor of ethics, the gymnast, the
soldier, the sportsman, the inventor, the political program-
maker, all have some prescription for bettering us; and almost
all their remedies are physically possible and aimed at admitted evils. To them the limit of progress is, at worst, the
completion of all the suggested reforms and the levelling up
of all men to the point attained already by the most highly
nourished and cultivated in mind and body.

Here, then, as it seems to them, is an enormous field for
the energy of the reformer. Here are many noble goals attainable by many of those paths up the Hill Difficulty along which
great spirits love to aspire. Unhappily, the hill will never be
climbed by Man as we know him. It need not be denied that
if we all struggled bravely to the end of the reformer's paths
we should improve the world prodigiously. But there is no

more hope in that If than in the equally plausible assurance that if the sky falls we shall all catch larks. We are not going to tread those paths: we have not sufficient energy. We do not desire the end enough: indeed in most cases we do not effectively desire it at all. Ask any man would he like to be a better man; and he will say yes, most piously. Ask him would he like to have a million of money; and he will say yes, most sincerely. But the pious citizen who would like to be a better man goes on behaving just as he did before. And the tramp who would like the million does not take the trouble to earn ten shillings: multitudes of men and women, all eager to accept a legacy of a million, live and die without having ever possessed five pounds at one time, although beggars have died in rags on mattresses stuffed with gold which they accummulated because they desired it enough to nerve them to get it and keep it. The economists who discovered that demand created supply soon had to limit the proposition to "effective demand," which turned out, in the final analysis, to mean nothing more than supply itself; and this holds good in politics, morals, and all other departments as well: the actual supply is the measure of the effective demand; and the mere aspirations and professions produce nothing. No community has ever yet passed beyond the initial phases in which its pugnacity and fanaticism enabled it to found a nation, and its cupidity to establish and develop a commercial civilization. Even these stages have never been attained by public spirit, but always by intolerant wilfulness and brute force. Take the Reform Bill of 1832 as an example of a conflict between two sections of educated Englishmen concerning a political measure which was as obviously necessary and inevitable as any political measure has ever been or is ever likely to be. It was not passed until the gentlemen of Birmingham had made arrangements to cut the throats of the gentlemen of St. James's parish in due military form. It would not have been passed to this day if there had been no force behind it except the logic and public conscience of the Utilitarians. A despotic ruler with as much sense as Queen Elizabeth would have done better than the mob of grown-up Eton boys who governed us then by privilege, and who, since the introduction of practically Manhood Suffrage in 1884, now govern us at the request of proletarian Democracy.

At the present time we have, instead of the Utilitarians, the

Fabian Society, with its peaceful, constitutional, moral, economical policy of Socialism, which needs nothing for its bloodless and benevolent realization except that the English people shall understand it and approve of it. But why are the Fabians well spoken of in circles where thirty years ago the word Socialist was understood as equivalent to cut-throat and incendiary? Not because the English have the smallest intention of studying or adopting the Fabian policy, but because they believe that the Fabians, by eliminating the element of intimidation from the Socialist agitation, have drawn the teeth of insurgent poverty and saved the existing order from the only method of attack it really fears. Of course, if the nation adopted the Fabian policy, it would be carried out by brute force exactly as our present property system is. It would become the law; and those who resisted it would be fined, sold up, knocked on the head by policemen, thrown into prison, and in the last resort "executed" just as they are when they break the present law. But as our proprietary class has no fear of that conversion taking place, whereas it does fear sporadic cut-throats and gunpowder plots, and strives with all its might to hide the fact that there is no moral difference whatever between the methods by which it enforces its proprietary rights and the method by which the dynamitard asserts his conception of natural human rights, the Fabian Society is patted on the back just as the Christian Social Union is, whilst the Socialist who says bluntly that a Social revolution can be made only as all other revolutions have been made, by the people who want it killing, coercing and intimidating the people who don't want it, is denounced as a misleader of the people, and imprisoned with hard labor to shew him how much sincerity there is in the objection of his captors to physical force.

Are we then to repudiate Fabian methods, and return to those of the barricader, or adopt those of the dynamitard and the assassin? On the contrary, we are to recognize that both are fundamentally futile. It seems easy for the dynamitard to say "Have you not just admitted that nothing is ever conceded except to physical force? Did not Gladstone admit that the Irish Church was disestablished, not by the spirit of Liberalism, but by the explosion which wrecked Clerkenwell prison?" Well, we need not foolishly and timidly deny it. Let it be fully granted. Let us grant, further, that all this lies in the nature of things; that the most ardent Socialist, if he owns property, can by no means do otherwise than Conservative proprietors until property is forcibly abolished by the whole nation; nay, that ballots and parliamentary divisions, in spite of their vain ceremony of discussion, differ from battles only as the bloodless surrender of an outnumbered force in the field differs from Waterloo or Trafalgar. I make a present of all these admissions to the Fenian who collects money from thoughtless Irishmen in America to blow up Dublin Castle; to the detective who persuades foolish young workmen to order bombs from the nearest ironmonger and then delivers them up to penal servitude; to our military and naval commanders who believe, not in preaching, but in an ultimatum backed by plenty of lyddite; and, generally, to all whom it may concern. But of what use is it to substitute the will of reckless and bloodyminded Progressives for cautious and humane ones? Is England any the better for the wreck of Clerkenwell prison, or Ireland for the disestablishment of the Irish Church? Is there the smallest reason to suppose that the nation which sheepishly let Charles and Laud and Strafford coerce it, gained anything because it afterwards, still more sheepishly, let a few strongminded Puritans, inflamed by the masterpieces of Jewish revolutionary literature, cut off the heads of the three? Suppose the Gunpowder plot had succeeded, and a Fawkes dynasty were at present on the throne, would it have made any difference to the present state of the nation? The guillotine was used in France up to the limit of human endurance, both on Girondins and Jacobins. Fouquier Tinville followed Marie Antoinette to the scaffold; and Marie Antoinette might have asked the crowd, just as pointedly as Fouquier did, whether their bread would be any cheaper when her head was off. And what came of it all? The Imperial France of the Rougon Macquart family, and the Republican France of the Panama scandal and the Dreyfus case. Was the difference worth the guillotining of all those unlucky ladies and gentlemen, useless and mischievous as many of them were? Would any sane man guillotine a mouse to bring about such a result? Turn to Republican America. America has no Star Chamber, and no feudal barons. But it has Trusts; and it has millionaires whose factories, fenced in by live electric wires and defended by Pinkerton retainers with magazine rifles, would have made a Radical of Reginald

Front de Boeuf. Would Washington or Franklin have lifted a finger in the cause of American Independence if they had foreseen its reality?

No: what Cæsar, Cromwell and Napoleon could not do with all the physical force and moral prestige of the State in their mighty hands, cannot be done by enthusiastic criminals and lunatics. Even the Jews, who, from Moses to Marx and Lassalle, have inspired all the revolutions, have had to confess that, after all, the dog will return to his vomit and the sow that was washed to her wallowing in the mire; and we may as well make up our minds that Man will return to his idols and his cupidities, in spite of all "movements" and all revolutions, until his nature is changed. Until then, his early successes in building commercial civilizations (and such civilizations, Good Heavens!) are but preliminaries to the inevitable later stage, now threatening us, in which the passions which built the civilization become fatal instead of productive, just as the same qualities which make the lion king in the forest ensure his destruction when he enters a city. Nothing can save society then except the clear head and the wide purpose: war and competition, potent instruments of selection and evolution in one epoch, become ruinous instruments of degeneration in the next. In the breeding of animals and plants, varieties which have arisen by selection through many generations relapse precipitously into the wild type in a generation or two when selection ceases; and in the same way a civilization in which lusty pugnacity and greed have ceased to act as selective agents and have begun to obstruct and destroy, rushes downwards and backwards with a suddenness that enables an observer to see with consternation the upward steps of many centuries retraced in a single lifetime. This has often occurred even within the period covered by history; and in every instance the turning point has been reached long before the attainment, or even the general advocacy on paper, of the levelling-up of the mass to the highest point attainable by the best nourished and cultivated normal individuals.

We must therefore frankly give up the notion that Man as he exists is capable of net progress. There will always be an illusion of progress, because wherever we are conscious of an evil we remedy it, and therefore always seem to ourselves to be progressing, forgetting that most of the evils

we see are the effects, finally become acute, of long-un-
noticed retrogressions; that our compromising remedies seldom
fully recover the lost ground; above all, that on the lines along
which we are degenerating, good has become evil in our eyes,
and is being undone in the name of progress precisely as evil
is undone and replaced by good on the lines along which we
are evolving. This is indeed the Illusion of Illusions; for it
gives us infallible and appalling assurance that if our political
ruin is to come, it will be effected by ardent reformers and
supported by enthusiastic patriots as a series of necessary
steps in our progress. Let the Reformer, the Progressive, the
Meliorist then reconsider himself and his eternal ifs and ans
which never become pots and pans. Whilst Man remains what
he is, there can be no progress beyond the point already
attained and fallen headlong from at every attempt at civilization; and since even that point is but a pinnacle to which a
few people cling in giddy terror above an abyss of squalor,
mere progress should no longer charm us.

VIII

The Conceit of Civilization

After all, the progress illusion is not so very subtle. We begin by reading the satires of our fathers' contemporaries; and we conclude (usually quite ignorantly) that the abuses exposed by them are things of the past. We see also that reforms of crying evils are frequently produced by the sectional shifting of political power from oppressors to oppressed. The poor man is given a vote by the Liberals in the hope that he will cast it for his emancipators. The hope is not fulfilled; but the lifelong imprisonment of penniless men for debt ceases; Factory Acts are passed to mitigate sweating; schooling is made free and compulsory; sanitary by-laws are multiplied; public steps are taken to house the masses decently; the bare-footed get boots; rags become rare; and bathrooms and pianos, smart tweeds and starched collars, reach numbers of people who once, as "the unsoaped," played the Jew's harp or the accordion in moleskins and belchers. Some of these changes are gains: some of them are losses. Some of them are not changes at all: all of them are merely the changes that money makes. Still, they produce an illusion of bustling progress; and the reading class infers from them that the abuses of the early Victorian period no longer exist except as amusing pages in the novels of Dickens. But the moment we look for a reform due to character and not to money, to statesmanship and not to interest or mutiny, we are disillusioned. For example, we remembered the maladministration and incompetence revealed by the Crimean War as part of a bygone state of things until the South African War shewed that the nation and the War Office, like those poor Bourbons who have been so impudently blamed for a universal characteristic, had learnt nothing and forgotten nothing. We had hardly recovered from the fruitless irritation of this discovery when it transpired that the officers' mess of our

468

most select regiment included a flogging club presided over by the senior subaltern. The disclosure provoked some disgust at the details of this schoolboyish debauchery, but no surprise at the apparent absence of any conception of manly honor and virtue, of personal courage and self-respect, in the front rank of our chivalry. In civil affairs we had assumed that the sycophancy and idolatry which encouraged Charles I to undervalue the Puritan revolt of the XVII century had been long outgrown; but it has needed nothing but favorable circumstances to revive, with added abjectness to compensate for its lost piety. We have relapsed into disputes about transubstantiation at the very moment when the discovery of the wide prevalence of theophagy as a tribal custom has deprived us of the last excuse for believing that our official religious rites differ in essentials from those of barbarians. The Christian doctrine of the uselessness of punishment and the wickedness of revenge has not, in spite of its simple common sense, found a single convert among the nations: Christianity means nothing to the masses but a sensational public execution which is made an excuse for other executions. In its name we take ten years of a thief's life minute by minute in the slow misery and degradation of modern reformed imprisonment with as little remorse as Laud and his Star Chamber clipped the ears of Bastwick and Burton. We dug up and mutilated the remains of the Mahdi the other day exactly as we dug up and mutilated the remains of Cromwell two centuries ago. We have demanded the decapitation of the Chinese Boxer princes as any Tartar would have done; and our military and naval expeditions to kill, burn, and destroy tribes and villages for knocking an Englishman on the head are so common a part of our Imperial routine that the last dozen of them has not elicited as much sympathy as can be counted on by any lady criminal. The judicial use of torture to extort confession is supposed to be a relic of darker ages; but whilst these pages are being written an English judge has sentenced a forger to twenty years penal servitude with an open declaration that the sentence will be carried out in full unless he confesses where he has hidden the notes he forged. And no comment whatever is made either on this or on a telegram from the seat of war in Somaliland mentioning that certain information has been given by a prisoner of war "under punishment." Even if these reports were false, the fact that they are accepted without protest as indicating a natural and proper course of public conduct shows that we are still as ready to resort to torture as Bacon was. As to vindictive cruelty, an incident in the South African War, when the relatives and friends of a prisoner were forced to witness his execution, betrayed a baseness of temper and character which hardly leaves us the right to plume ourselves on our superiority to Edward III at the surrender of Calais. And the democratic American officer indulges in torture in the Philippines just as the aristocratic English officer did in South Africa. The incidents of the white invasion of Africa in search of ivory, gold, diamonds and sport, have proved that the modern European is the same beast of prey that formerly marched to the conquest of new worlds under Alexander, Antony, and Pizarro. Parliaments and vestries are just what they were when Cromwell suppressed them and Dickens ridiculed them. The democratic politician remains exactly as Plato described him; the physician is still the credulous impostor and petulant scientific coxcomb whom Molière ridiculed; the schoolmaster remains at best a pedantic child farmer and at worst a flagellomaniac; arbitrations are more dreaded by honest men than lawsuits; the philanthropist is still a parasite on misery as the doctor is on disease; the miracles of priestcraft are none the less fraudulent and mischievous because they are now called scientific experiments and conducted by professors; witchcraft, in the modern form of patent medicines and prophylactic inoculations, is rampant; the landowner who is no longer powerful enough to set the mantrap of Rhampsinitis improves on it by barbed wire; the modern gentleman who is too lazy to daub his face with vermilion as a symbol of bravery employs a laundress to daub his shirt with starch as a symbol of cleanliness; we shake our heads at the dirt of the middle ages in cities made grimy with soot and foul and disgusting with shameless tobacco smoking; holy water, in its latest form of disinfectant fluid, is more widely used and believed in than ever; public health authorities deliberately go through incantations with burning sulphur (which they know to be useless) because the people believe in it as devoutly as the Italian peasant believes in the liquefaction of the blood of St. Januarius; and straightforward public lying has reached gigantic developments, there being nothing to choose in this respect between the pickpocket at the police station and the minister on the treasury bench, the editor in the newspaper office, the city magnate advertising bicycle tires that do not side-slip, the clergyman subscribing the thirty-nine articles, and the vivisector who pledges his knightly honor that no animal operated on in the physiological laboratory suffers the slightest pain. Hypocrisy is at its worst; for we not only persecute bigotedly but sincerely in the name of the cure-mongering witchcraft we do believe in, but also callously and hypocritically in the name of the Evangelical creed that our rulers privately smile at as the Italian patricians of the fifth century smiled at Jupiter and Venus. Sport is, as it has always been, murderous excitement: the impulse to slaughter is universal; and museums are set up throughout the country to encourage little children and elderly gentlemen to make collections of corpses preserved in alcohol, and to steal birds' eggs and keep them as the red Indian used to keep scalps. Coercion with the lash is as natural to an Englishman as it was to Solomon spoiling Rehoboam; indeed, the comparison is unfair to the Jews in view of the facts that the Mosaic law forbade more than forty lashes in the name of humanity, and that floggings of a thousand lashes were inflicted on English soldiers in the XVIII and XIX centuries, and would be inflicted still but for the change in the balance of political power between the military caste and the commercial classes and the proletariat. In spite of that change, flogging is still an institution in the public school, in the military prison, on the training ship, and in that school of littleness called the home. The lascivious clamor of the flagellomaniac for more of it, constant as the clamor for more insolence, more war, and lower rates, is tolerated and even gratified because, having no moral ends in view, we have sense enough to see that nothing but brute coercion can impose our selfish will on others. Cowardice is universal: patriotism, public opinion, parental duty, discipline, religion, morality, are only fine names for intimidation; and cruelty, gluttony, and credulity keep cowardice in countenance. We cut the throat of a calf and hang it up by the heels to bleed to death so that our veal cutlet may be white; we nail geese to a board and cram them with food because we like the taste of liver disease; we tear birds to pieces to decorate our women's hats; we mutilate domestic animals for no reason at all except to follow an instinctively cruel fashion; and we connive at the most abominable tortures in the hope of discovering some magical cure for our own diseases by them.

Now please observe that these are not exceptional developments of our admitted vices, deplored and prayed against by all good men. Not a word has been said here of the excesses of our Neros, of whom we have the full usual percentage. With the exception of the few military examples, which are mentioned mainly to shew that the education and standing of a gentleman, reinforced by the strongest conventions of honor, *esprit de corps*, publicity and responsibility, afford no better guarantees of conduct than the passions of a mob, the illustrations given above are commonplaces taken from the daily practices of our best citizens, vehemently defended in our newspapers and in our pulpits. The very humanitarians who abhor them are stirred to murder by them: the dagger of Brutus and Ravaillac is still active in the hands of Caserio and Luccheni; and the pistol has come to its aid in the hands of Guiteau and Czolgosz. Our remedies are still limited to endurance or assassination; and the assassin is still judicially assassinated on the principle that two blacks make a white. The only novelty is in our methods: through the discovery of dynamite the overloaded musket of Hamilton of Bothwellhaugh has been superseded by the bomb; but Ravachol's heart burns just as Hamilton's did. The world will not bear thinking of those who know what it is, even with the largest discount for the restraints of poverty on the poor and cowardice on the rich.

All that can be said for us is that people must and do live and let live up to a certain point. Even the horse, with his docked tail and bitted jaw, finds his slavery mitigated by the fact that a total disregard of his need for food and rest would put his master to the expense of buying a new horse every second day; for you cannot work a horse to death and then pick up another one for nothing, as you can a laborer. But this natural check on inconsiderate selfishness is itself checked, partly by our shortsightedness, and partly by deliberate calculation; so that beside the man who, to his own loss, will shorten his horse's life in mere stinginess, we have the tramway company which discovers actuarially that though a horse may live from 24 to 40 years, yet it pays better to work him to death in 4 and then replace him by a fresh victim. And human slavery, which has reached its worst recorded point within our own time in the form of free wage labor, has encountered the same personal and commercial limits to both its aggravation and its mitigation. Now that the freedom of wage labor has produced a scarcity of it, as in South Africa, the leading English newspaper and the leading English weekly review have openly and without apology demanded a return to compulsory labor: that is, to the methods by which, as we believe, the Egyptians built the pyramids. We know now that the crusade against chattel slavery in the XIX century succeeded solely because chattel slavery was neither the most effective nor the least humane method of labor exploitation; and the world is now feeling its way towards a still more effective system which shall abolish the freedom of the worker without again making his exploiter responsible for him as a chattel.

Still, there is always some mitigation: there is the fear of revolt; and there are the effects of kindliness and affection. Let it be repeated therefore that no indictment is here laid against the world on the score of what its criminals and monsters do. The fires of Smithfield and of the Inquisition were lighted by earnestly pious people, who were kind and good as kindness and goodness go. And when a Negro is dipped in kerosene and set on fire in America at the present time, he is not a good man lynched by ruffians: he is a criminal lynched by crowds of respectable, charitable, virtuously indignant, high-minded citizens, who, though they act outside the law, are at least more merciful than the American legislators and judges who not so long ago condemned men to solitary confinement for periods, not of five months, as our own practice is, but of five years and more. The things that our moral monsters do may be left out of account with St. Bartholomew massacres and other momentary outbursts of social disorder. Judge us by the admitted and respected practice of our most reputable circles; and, if you know the facts and are strong enough to look them in the face, you must admit that unless we are replaced by a more highly evolved animal—in short, by the Superman—the world must remain a den of dangerous animals among whom our few accidental supermen, our Shakespears, Goethes, Shelleys and their like, must live as precariously as lion tamers do, taking the humor of their situation, and the dignity of their superiority, as a set-off to the horror of the one and the loneliness of the other.

IX

The Verdict of History

It may be said that though the wild beast breaks out in
Man and casts him back momentarily into barbarism under
the excitement of war and crime, yet his normal life is higher
than the normal life of his forefathers. This view is very
acceptable to Englishmen, who always lean sincerely to
virtue's side as long as it costs them nothing either in money
or in thought. They feel deeply the injustice of foreigners,
who allow them no credit for this conditional highmindedness.
But there is no reason to suppose that our ancestors were less
capable of it than we are. To all such claims for the existence
of a progressive moral evolution operating visibly from
grandfather to grandson, there is the conclusive reply that a
thousand years of such evolution would have produced
enormous social changes, of which the historical evidence
would be overwhelming. But not Macaulay himself, the most
confident of Whig meliorists, can produce any such evidence
that will bear cross-examination. Compare our conduct and
our codes with those mentioned contemporarily in such
ancient scriptures and classics as have come down to us, and
you will find no jot of ground for the belief that any moral
progress whatever has been made in historic time, in spite
of all the romantic attempts of historians to reconstruct the
past on that assumption. Within that time it has happened to
nations as to private families and individuals that they have
flourished and decayed, repented and hardened their hearts,
submitted and protested, acted and reacted, oscillated between natural and artificial sanitation (the oldest house in
the world, unearthed the other day in Crete, has quite modern
sanitary arrangements), and rung a thousand changes on the
different scales of income and pressure of population, firmly
believing all the time that mankind was advancing by leaps
and bounds because men were constantly busy. And the

mere chapter of accidents has left a small accumulation of
chance discoveries, such as the wheel, the arch, the safety
pin, gunpowder, the magnet, the Voltaic pile and so forth:
things which, unlike the gospels and philosophic treatises of
the ages, can be usefully understood and applied by common
men; so that steam locomotion is possible without a nation of
Stephensons, although national Christianity is impossible
without a nation of Christs. But does any man seriously believe that the *chauffeur* who drives a motor car from Paris
to Berlin is a more highly evolved man than the charioteer of
Achilles, or that a modern Prime Minister is a more enlightened ruler than Cæsar because he rides a tricycle, writes
his dispatches by the electric light, and instructs his stockbroker through the telephone?

Enough, then, of this goose-cackle about Progress: Man,
as he is, never will nor can add a cubit to his stature by
any of its quackeries, political, scientific, educational, religious, or artistic. What is likely to happen when this conviction gets into the minds of the men whose present faith
in these illusions is the cement of our social system, can be
imagined only by those who know how suddenly a civilization
which has long ceased to think (or in the old phrase, to
watch and pray) can fall to pieces when the vulgar belief
in its hypocrisies and impostures can no longer hold out
against its failures and scandals. When religious and ethical
formulæ become so obsolete that no man of strong mind can
believe them, they have also reached the point at which no
man of high character will profess them; and from that moment until they are formally disestablished, they stand at the
door of every profession and every public office to keep out
every able man who is not a sophist or a liar. A nation
which revises its parish councils once in three years, but will
not revise its articles of religion once in three hundred, even
when those articles avowedly began as a political compromise
dictated by Mr. Facing-Both-Ways, is a nation that needs
remaking.

Our only hope, then, is in evolution. We must replace the
Man by the Superman. It is frightful for the citizen, as the
years pass him, to see his own contemporaries so exactly
reproduced by the younger generation, that his companions
of thirty years ago have their counterparts in every city
crowd; so that he has to check himself repeatedly in the

act of saluting as an old friend some young man to whom he is only an elderly stranger. All hope of advance dies in his bosom as he watches them: he knows that they will do just what their fathers did, and that the few voices which will still, as always before, exhort them to do something else and be something better, might as well spare their breath to cool their porridge (if they can get any). Men like Ruskin and Carlyle will preach to Smith and Brown for the sake of preaching, just as St. Francis preached to the birds and St. Anthony to the fishes. But Smith and Brown, like the fishes and birds, remain as they are; and poets who plan Utopias and prove that nothing is necessary for their realization but that Man should will them, perceive at last, like Richard Wagner, that the fact to be faced is that Man does not effectively will them. And he never will until he becomes Superman.

And so we arrive at the end of the Socialist's dream of "the socialization of the means of production and exchange," of the Positivist's dream of moralizing the capitalist, and of the ethical professor's, legislator's, educator's dream of putting commandments and codes and lessons and examination marks on a man as harness is put on a horse, ermine on a judge, pipeclay on a soldier, or a wig on an actor, and pretending that his nature has been changed. The only fundamental and possible Socialism is the socialization of the selective breeding of Man: in other terms, of human evolution. We must eliminate the Yahoo, or his vote will wreck the commonwealth.

X

The Method

As to the method, what can be said as yet except that where there is a will, there is a way? If there be no will, we are lost. That is a possibility for our crazy little empire, if not for the universe; and as such possibilities are not to be entertained without despair, we must, whilst we survive, proceed on the assumption that we have still energy enough to not only will to live, but to will to live better. That may mean that we must establish a State Department of Evolution, with a seat in the Cabinet for its chief, and a revenue to defray the cost of direct State experiments and provide inducements to private persons to achieve successful results. It may mean a private society or a chartered company for the improvement of human live stock. But for the present it is far more likely to mean a blatant repudiation of such proposals as indecent and immoral, with, nevertheless, a general secret pushing of the human will in the repudiated direction; so that all sorts of institutions and public authorities will under some pretext or other feel their way furtively towards the Superman. Mr. Graham Wallas has already ventured to suggest, as Chairman of the School Management Committee of the London School Board, that the accepted policy of the Sterilization of the Schoolmistress, however administratively convenient, is open to criticism from the national stock-breeding point of view; and this is as good an example as any of the way in which the drift towards the Superman may operate in spite of all our hypocrisies. One thing at least is clear to begin with. If a woman can, by careful selection of a father, and nourishment of herself, produce a citizen with efficient senses, sound organs and a good digestion, she should clearly be secured a sufficient reward for that natural service to make her willing to undertake and repeat it. Whether she be financed in the undertaking by herself, or by the father, or by a speculative capitalist, or by a new department of, say, the Royal Dublin Society, or (as a present) by the War Office maintaining her "on the strength" and authorizing a particular soldier to marry her, or by a local authority under a by-law directing that women may under certain circumstances have a year's leave of absence on full salary, or by the central government, does not matter provided the result be satisfactory.

It is a melancholy fact that as the vast majority of women and their husbands have, under existing circumstances, not enough nourishment, no capital, no credit, and no knowledge of science or business, they would, if the State would pay for birth as it now pays for death, be exploited by joint stock companies for dividends, just as they are in ordinary industries. Even a joint stock human stud farm (piously disguised as a reformed Foundling Hospital or something of that sort) might well, under proper inspection and regulation, produce better results than our present reliance on promiscuous marriage. It may be objected that when an ordinary contractor produces stores for sale to the Government, and the Government rejects them as not up to the required standard, the condemned goods are either sold for what they will fetch or else scrapped: that is, treated as waste material; whereas if the goods consisted of human beings, all that could be done would be to let them loose or send them to the nearest workhouse. But there is nothing new in private enterprise throwing its human refuse on the cheap labor market and the workhouse; and the refuse of the new industry would presumably be better bred than the staple product of ordinary poverty. In our present happy-go-lucky industrial disorder, all the human products, successful or not, would have to be thrown on the labor market; but the unsuccessful ones would not entitle the company to a bounty and so would be a dead loss to it. The practical commercial difficulty would be the uncertainty and the cost in time and money of the first experiments. Purely commercial capital would not touch such heroic operations during the experimental stage; and in any case the strength of mind needed for so momentous a new departure could not be fairly expected from the Stock Exchange. It will have to be handled by statesmen with character enough to tell our democracy and plutocracy that statecraft does not consist in flattering their

follies or applying their suburban standards of propriety to
the affairs of four continents. The matter must be taken up
either by the State or by some organization strong enough
to impose respect upon the State.

The novelty of any such experiment, however, is only in
the scale of it. In one conspicuous case, that of royalty, the
State does already select the parents on purely political
grounds; and in the peerage, though the heir to a dukedom
is legally free to marry a dairymaid, yet the social pressure
on him to confine his choice to politically and socially eligible
mates is so overwhelming that he is really no more free to
marry the dairymaid than George IV was to marry Mrs.
Fitzherbert; and such a marriage could only occur as a result of extraordinary strength of character on the part of the
duke. Let those who think the whole conception of intelligent
breeding absurd and scandalous ask themselves why George
IV was not allowed to choose his own wife whilst any tinker
could marry whom he pleased? Simply because it did not
matter a rap politically whom the tinker married, whereas
it mattered very much whom the king married. The way in
which all considerations of the king's personal rights, of the
claims of the heart, of the sanctity of the marriage oath, and
of romantic morality crumpled up before this political need
shews how negligible all these apparently irresistible prejudices are when they come into conflict with the demand for
quality in our rulers. We learn the same lesson from the
case of the soldier, whose marriage, when it is permitted at
all, is despotically controlled with a view solely to military
efficiency.

Well, nowadays it is not the King that rules, but the
tinker. Dynastic wars are no longer feared, dynastic alli-
ances no longer valued. Marriages in royal families are becoming rapidly less political, and more popular, domestic
and romantic. If all the kings in Europe were made as free
to-morrow as King Cophetua, nobody but their aunts and
chamberlains would feel a moment's anxiety as to the consequences. On the other hand a sense of the social importance
of the tinker's marriage has been steadily growing. We have
made a public matter of his wife's health in the month after
her confinement. We have taken the minds of his children
out of his hands and put them into those of our State schoolmaster. We shall presently make their bodily nourishment

independent of him. But they are still riff-raff; and to hand the country over to riff-raff is national suicide, since riff-raff can neither govern nor will let anyone else govern except the highest bidder of bread and circuses. There is no public enthusiast alive of twenty years practical democratic experience who believes in the political adequacy of the electorate or of the bodies it elects. The overthrow of the aristocrat has created the necessity for the Superman.

Englishmen hate Liberty and Equality too much to understand them. But every Englishman loves and desires a pedigree. And in that he is right. King Demos must be bred like all other Kings; and with Must there is no arguing. It is idle for an individual writer to carry so great a matter further in a pamphlet. A conference on the subject is the next step needed. It will be attended by men and women who, no longer believing that they can live for ever, are seeking for some immortal work into which they can build the best of themselves before their refuse is thrown into that arch dust destructor, the cremation furnace.

MAXIMS FOR REVOLUTIONISTS

The Golden Rule

Do not do unto others as you would that they should do unto you. Their tastes may not be the same.

Never resist temptation: prove all things: hold fast that which is good.

Do not love your neighbor as yourself. If you are on good terms with yourself it is an impertinence: if on bad, an injury.

The golden rule is that there are no golden rules.

Idolatry

The art of government is the organization of idolatry.

The bureaucracy consists of functionaries; the aristocracy, of idols; the democracy, of idolaters.

The populace cannot understand the bureaucracy: it can only worship the national idols.

The savage bows down to idols of wood and stone: the civilized man to idols of flesh and blood.

A limited monarchy is a device for combining the inertia of a wooden idol with the credibility of a flesh and blood one.

When the wooden idol does not answer the peasant's prayer, he beats it: when the flesh and blood idol does not satisfy the civilized man, he cuts its head off.

He who slays a king and he who dies for him are alike idolaters.

Royalty

Kings are not born: they are made by artificial hallucination. When the process is interrupted by adversity at a critical age, as in the case of Charles II, the subject becomes sane and never completely recovers his kingliness.

The Court is the servant's hall of the sovereign.

Vulgarity in a king flatters the majority of the nation.

The flunkeyism propagated by the throne is the price we pay for its political convenience.

DEMOCRACY

If the lesser mind could measure the greater as a foot-rule can measure a pyramid, there would be finality in universal suffrage. As it is, the political problem remains unsolved.

Democracy substitutes election by the incompetent many for appointment by the corrupt few.

Democratic republics can no more dispense with national idols than monarchies with public functionaries.

Government presents only one problem: the discovery of a trustworthy anthropometric method.

IMPERIALISM

Excess of insularity makes a Briton an Imperialist.

Excess of local self-assertion makes a colonist an Imperialist.

A colonial Imperialist is one who raises colonial troops, equips a colonial squadron, claims a Federal Parliament sending its measures to the Throne instead of to the Colonial Office, and, being finally brought by this means into insoluble conflict with the insular British Imperialist, "cuts the painter" and breaks up the Empire.

LIBERTY AND EQUALITY

He who confuses political liberty with freedom and political equality with similarity has never thought for five minutes about either.

Nothing can be unconditioned: consequently nothing can be free.

Liberty means responsibility. That is why most men dread it.

The duke inquires contemptuously whether his game-keeper is the equal of the Astronomer Royal; but he insists that they shall both be hanged equally if they murder him.

The notion that the colonel need be a better man than the private is as confused as the notion that the keystone need be stronger than the coping stone.

Where equality is undisputed, so also is subordination.

Equality is fundamental in every department of social organization.

The relation of superior to inferior excludes good manners.

EDUCATION

When a man teaches something he does not know to somebody else who has no aptitude for it, and gives him a certificate of proficiency, the latter has completed the education of a gentleman.

A fool's brain digests philosophy into folly, science into superstition, and art into pedantry. Hence University education.

The best brought-up children are those who have seen their parents as they are. Hypocrisy is not the parent's first duty.

The vilest abortionist is he who attempts to mold a child's character.

At the University every great treatise is postponed until its author attains impartial judgment and perfect knowledge. If a horse could wait as long for its shoes and would pay for them in advance, our blacksmiths would all be college dons.

He who can, does. He who cannot, teaches.

A learned man is an idler who kills time with study. Beware of his false knowledge: it is more dangerous than ignorance.

Activity is the only road to knowledge.

Every fool believes what his teachers tell him, and calls his credulity science or morality as confidently as his father called it divine revelation.

No man fully capable of his own language ever masters another.

No man can be a pure specialist without being in the strict sense an idiot.

Do not give your children moral and religious instruction unless you are quite sure they will not take it too seriously. Better be the mother of Henri Quatre and Nell Gwynne than of Robespierre and Queen Mary Tudor.

MARRIAGE

Marriage is popular because it combines the maximum of temptation with the maximum of opportunity.

Marriage is the only legal contract which abrogates as between the parties all the laws that safeguard the particular relation to which it refers.

The essential function of marriage is the continuance of the race, as stated in the Book of Common Prayer.

The accidental function of marriage is the gratification of the amoristic sentiment of mankind.

The artificial sterilization of marriage makes it possible for marriage to fulfil its accidental function whilst neglecting its essential one.

The most revolutionary invention of the XIX century was the artificial sterilization of marriage.

Any marriage system which condemns a majority of the population to celibacy will be violently wrecked on the pretext that it outrages morality.

Polygamy, when tried under modern democratic conditions, as by the Mormons, is wrecked by the revolt of the mass of inferior men who are condemned to celibacy by it; for the maternal instinct leads a woman to prefer a tenth share in a first-rate man to the exclusive possession of a third-rate one. Polyandry has not been tried under these conditions.

The minimum of national celibacy (ascertained by dividing the number of males in the community by the number of females, and taking the quotient as the number of wives or husbands permitted to each person) is secured in England (where the quotient is 1) by the institution of monogamy.

The modern sentimental term for the national minimum of celibacy is Purity.

Marriage, or any other form of promiscuous amoristic monogamy, is fatal to large States because it puts its ban on the deliberate breeding of man as a political animal.

CRIME AND PUNISHMENT

All scoundrelism is summed up in the phrase "Que Messieurs les Assassins commencent!"

The man who has graduated from the flogging block at

Eton to the bench from which he sentences the garotter to be flogged is the same social product as the garotter who has been kicked by his father and cuffed by his mother until he has grown strong enough to throttle and rob the rich citizen whose money he desires.

Imprisonment is as irrevocable as death.

Criminals do not die by the hands of the law. They die by the hands of other men.

The assassin Czolgosz made President McKinley a hero by assassinating him. The United States of America made Czolgosz a hero by the same process.

Assassination on the scaffold is the worst form of assassination, because there it is invested with the approval of society.

It is the deed that teaches, not the name we give it. Murder and capital punishment are not opposites that cancel one another, but similars that breed their kind.

Crime is only the retail department of what, in wholesale, we call penal law.

When a man wants to murder a tiger he calls it sport: when the tiger wants to murder him he calls it ferocity. The distinction between Crime and Justice is no greater.

Whilst we have prisons it matters little which of us occupy the cells.

The most anxious man in a prison is the governor.

It is not necessary to replace a guillotined criminal: it is necessary to replace a guillotined social system.

TITLES

Titles distinguish the mediocre, embarrass the superior, and are disgraced by the inferior.

Great men refuse titles because they are jealous of them.

HONOR

There are no perfectly honorable men; but every true man has one main point of honor and a few minor ones.

You cannot believe in honor until you have achieved it. Better keep yourself clean and bright: you are the window through which you must see the world.

Your word can never be as good as your bond, because your memory can never be as trustworthy as your honor.

PROPERTY

Property, said Proudhon, is theft. This is the only perfect truism that has been uttered on the subject.

SERVANTS

When domestic servants are treated as human beings it is not worth while to keep them.

The relation of master and servant is advantageous only to masters who do not scruple to abuse their authority, and to servants who do not scruple to abuse their trust.

The perfect servant, when his master makes humane advances to him, feels that his existence is threatened, and hastens to change his place.

Masters and servants are both tyrannical; but the masters are the more dependent of the two.

A man enjoys what he uses, not what his servants use.

Man is the only animal which esteems itself rich in proportion to the number and voracity of its parasites.

Ladies and gentlemen are permitted to have friends in the kennel, but not in the kitchen.

Domestic servants, by making spoiled children of their masters, are forced to intimidate them in order to be able to live with them.

In a slave state, the slaves rule: in Mayfair, the tradesman rules.

How to Beat Children

If you strike a child, take care that you strike it in anger, even at the risk of maiming it for life. A blow in cold blood neither can nor should be forgiven.

If you beat children for pleasure, avow your object frankly, and play the game according to the rules, as a foxhunter does; and you will do comparatively little harm. No foxhunter is such a cad as to pretend that he hunts the fox to teach it not to steal chickens, or that he suffers more acutely than the fox at the death. Remember that even in childbeating there is the sportsman's way and the cad's way.

RELIGION

Beware of the man whose god is in the skies.

What a man believes may be ascertained, not from his creed, but from the assumptions on which he habitually acts.

VIRTUES AND VICES

No specific virtue or vice in a man implies the existence of any other specific virtue or vice in him, however closely the imagination may associate them.

Virtue consists, not in abstaining from vice, but in not desiring it.

Self-denial is not a virtue: it is only the effect of prudence on rascality.

Obedience simulates subordination as fear of the police simulates honesty.

Disobedience, the rarest and most courageous of the virtues, is seldom distinguished from neglect, the laziest and commonest of the vices.

Vice is waste of life. Poverty, obedience and celibacy are the canonical vices.

Economy is the art of making the most of life.

The love of economy is the root of all virtue.

FAIRPLAY

The love of fairplay is a spectator's virtue, not a principal's.

GREATNESS

Greatness is only one of the sensations of littleness.

In heaven an angel is nobody in particular.

Greatness is the secular name for Divinity: both mean simply what lies beyond us.

If a great man could make us understand him, we should hang him.

We admit that when the divinity we worshipped made itself visible and comprehensible we crucified it.

To a mathematician the eleventh means only a single unit:

to the bushman who cannot count further than his ten fingers it is an incalculable myriad.

The difference between the shallowest routineer and the deepest thinker appears, to the latter, trifling; to the former, infinite.

In a stupid nation the man of genius becomes a god: everybody worships him and nobody does his will.

BEAUTY AND HAPPINESS, ART AND RICHES

Happiness and Beauty are by-products.

Folly is the direct pursuit of Happiness and Beauty.

Riches and Art are spurious receipts for the production of Happiness and Beauty.

He who desires a lifetime of happiness with a beautiful woman desires to enjoy the taste of wine by keeping his mouth always full of it.

The most intolerable pain is produced by prolonging the keenest pleasure.

The man with toothache thinks everyone happy whose teeth are sound. The poverty stricken man makes the same mistake about the rich man.

The more a man possesses over and above what he uses, the more careworn he becomes.

The tyranny that forbids you to make the road with pick and shovel is worse than that which prevents you from lolling along it in a carriage and pair.

In an ugly and unhappy world the richest man can purchase nothing but ugliness and unhappiness.

In his efforts to escape from ugliness and unhappiness the rich man intensifies both. Every new yard of West End creates a new acre of East End.

The XIX century was the Age of Faith in Fine Art. The results are before us.

THE PERFECT GENTLEMAN

The fatal reservation of the gentleman is that he sacrifices everything to his honor except his gentility.

A gentleman of our days is one who has money enough to do what every fool would do if he could afford it: that is, consume without producing.

The true diagnostic of modern gentility is parasitism.

No elaboration of physical or moral accomplishment can atone for the sin of parasitism.

A modern gentleman is necessarily the enemy of his country. Even in war he does not fight to defend it, but to prevent his power of preying on it from passing to a foreigner. Such combatants are patriots in the same sense as two dogs fighting for a bone are lovers of animals.

The North American Indian was a type of the sportsman warrior gentleman. The Periclean Athenian was a type of the intellectually and artistically cultivated gentleman. Both were political failures. The modern gentleman, without the hardihood of the one or the culture of the other, has the appetite of both put together. He will not succeed where they failed.

He who believes in education, criminal law, and sport, needs only property to make him a perfect modern gentleman.

MODERATION

Moderation is never applauded for its own sake.

A moderately honest man with a moderately faithful wife, moderate drinkers both, in a moderately healthy house: that is the true middle class unit.

THE UNCONSCIOUS SELF

The unconscious self is the real genius. Your breathing goes wrong the moment your conscious self meddles with it.

Except during the nine months before he draws his first breath, no man manages his affairs as well as a tree does.

REASON

The reasonable man adapts himself to the world: the unreasonable one persists in trying to adapt the world to himself. Therefore all progress depends on the unreasonable man.

The man who listens to Reason is lost: Reason enslaves all whose minds are not strong enough to master her.

DECENCY

Decency is Indecency's Conspiracy of Silence.

EXPERIENCE

Men are wise in proportion, not to their experience, but to their capacity for experience.

If we could learn from mere experience, the stones of London would be wiser than its wisest men.

TIME'S REVENGES

Those whom we called brutes had their revenge when Darwin shewed us that they were our cousins.

The thieves had their revenge when Marx convicted the bourgeoisie of theft.

GOOD INTENTIONS

Hell is paved with good intentions, not with bad ones.
All men mean well.

NATURAL RIGHTS

The Master of Arts, by proving that no man has any natural rights, compels himself to take his own for granted.

The right to live is abused whenever it is not constantly challenged.

FAUTE DE MIEUX

In my childhood I demurred to the description of a certain young lady as "the pretty Miss So and So." My aunt rebuked me by saying "Remember always that the least homely sister is the family beauty."

No age or condition is without its heroes. The least incapable general in a nation is its Cæsar, the least imbecile statesman its Solon, the least confused thinker its Socrates, the least commonplace poet its Shakespear.

CHARITY

Charity is the most mischievous sort of pruriency.

Those who minister to poverty and disease are accomplices in the two worst of all the crimes.

He who gives money he has not earned is generous with other people's labor.

Every genuinely benevolent person loathes almsgiving and mendicity.

FAME

Life levels all men: death reveals the eminent.

DISCIPLINE

Mutiny Acts are needed only by officers who command without authority. Divine right needs no whip.

WOMEN IN THE HOME

Home is the girl's prison and the woman's workhouse.

CIVILIZATION

Civilization is a disease produced by the practice of building societies with rotten material.

Those who admire modern civilization usually identify it with the steam engine and the electric telegraph.

Those who understand the steam engine and the electric telegraph spend their lives in trying to replace them with something better.

The imagination cannot conceive a viler criminal than he who should build London like the present one, nor a greater benefactor than he who should destroy it.

GAMBLING

The most popular method of distributing wealth is the method of the roulette table.

The roulette table pays nobody except him who keeps it. Nevertheless a passion for gaming is common, though a passion for keeping roulette tables is unknown.

Gambling promises the poor what Property performs for the rich: that is why the bishops dare not denounce it fundamentally.

THE SOCIAL QUESTION

Do not waste your time on Social Questions. What is the matter with the poor is Poverty: what is the matter with the Rich is Uselessness.

STRAY SAYINGS

We are told that when Jehovah created the world he saw that it was good. What would he say now?

The conversion of a savage to Christianity is the conversion of Christianity to savagery.

No man dares say so much of what he thinks as to appear to himself an extremist.

Mens sana in corpore sano is a foolish saying. The sound body is a product of the sound mind.

Decadence can find agents only when it wears the mask of progress.

In moments of progress the noble succeed, because things are going their way: in moments of decadence the base succeed for the same reason: hence the world is never without the exhilaration of contemporary success.

The reformer for whom the world is not good enough finds himself shoulder to shoulder with him that is not good enough for the world.

Every man over forty is a scoundrel.

Youth, which is forgiven everything, forgives itself nothing: age, which forgives itself everything, is forgiven nothing.

When we learn to sing that Britons never will be masters we shall make an end of slavery.

Do not mistake your objection to defeat for an objection to fighting, your objection to being a slave for an objection to slavery, your objection to not being as rich as your neighbor for an objection to poverty. The cowardly, the insubordinate, and the envious share your objections.

Take care to get what you like or you will be forced to like what you get. Where there is no ventilation fresh air is declared unwholesome. Where there is no religion hypocrisy becomes good taste. Where there is no knowledge ignorance calls itself science.

If the wicked flourish and the fittest survive, Nature must be the God of rascals.

If history repeats itself, and the unexpected always happens, how incapable must Man be of learning from experience!

Compassion is the fellow-feeling of the unsound.

Those who understand evil pardon it: those who resent it destroy it.

Acquired notions of propriety are stronger than natural instincts. It is easier to recruit for monasteries and convents than to induce an Arab woman to uncover her mouth in public, or a British officer to walk through Bond Street in a golfing cap on an afternoon in May.

It is dangerous to be sincere unless you are also stupid.

The Chinese tame fowls by clipping their wings, and women by deforming their feet. A petticoat round the ankles serves equally well.

Political Economy and Social Economy are amusing intellectual games; but Vital Economy is the Philosopher's Stone.

When a heretic wishes to avoid martyrdom he speaks of "Orthodoxy, True and False" and demonstrates that the True is his heresy.

Beware of the man who does not return your blow: he neither forgives you nor allows you to forgive yourself.

If you injure your neighbor, better not do it by halves.

Sentimentality is the error of supposing that quarter can be given or taken in moral conflicts.

Two starving men cannot be twice as hungry as one; but two rascals can be ten times as vicious as one.

Make your cross your crutch; but when you see another man do it, beware of him.

SELF-SACRIFICE

Self-sacrifice enables us to sacrifice other people without blushing.

If you begin by sacrificing yourself to those you love, you will end by hating those to whom you have sacrificed yourself.